MARK TWAIN was born Samuel Langhorne Clemens in Florida, Missouri, in 1835, and died at Redding, Connecticut, in 1910. In his person and in his pursuits he was a man of extraordinary contrasts. Although he left school at twelve when his father died, he was eventually awarded honorary degrees from Yale University, the University of Missouri, and Oxford University. His career encompassed such varied occupations as printer, Mississippi riverboat pilot, journalist, travel writer, and publisher. He made fortunes from his writing but toward the end of his life he had to resort to lecture tours to pay his debts. He was hot-tempered, profane, and sentimental—and also pessimistic, cynical, and tortured by self-doubt. His nostalgia for the past helped produce some of his best books. He lives in American letters as a great artist, the writer whom William Dean Howells called "the Lincoln of our literature."

MARK TWAIN

THE INNOCENTS ABROAD
or
THE NEW PILGRIMS PROGRESS

BEING SOME ACCOUNT OF THE STEAMSHIP
QUAKER CITY'S PLEASURE EXCURSION TO EU-
ROPE AND THE HOLY LAND; WITH DESCRIP-
TIONS OF COUNTRIES, NATIONS, INCIDENTS
AND ADVENTURES, AS THEY APPEARED TO THE
AUTHOR.

WITH AN AFTERWORD BY **LESLIE A. FIEDLER**

A SIGNET CLASSIC

PUBLISHED BY
THE NEW AMERICAN LIBRARY, NEW YORK AND TORONTO
THE NEW ENGLISH LIBRARY LIMITED, LONDON

Afterword Copyright © 1966 by Leslie A. Fiedler

A hardcover edition of the text is published by
Harper & Row, Publishers, Inc.

Third Printing

SIGNET CLASSICS

are published *in the United States* by The New American Library, Inc.,
1301 Avenue of the Americas, New York, New York 10019
in Canada by The New American Library of Canada Limited,
295 King Street East, Toronto 2, Ontario
in the United Kingdom by The New English Library Limited,
Barnard's Inn, Holborn, London, E. C. 1, England

First Printing, February, 1966

Printed in the United States of America

TO
MY MOST PATIENT READER
AND
MOST CHARITABLE CRITIC,

My Aged Mother,

THIS VOLUME IS AFFECTIONATELY
INSCRIBED

CONTENTS

CONTENTS   xiii

PREFACE

THIS book is a record of a pleasure trip. If it were a record of a solemn scientific expedition, it would have about it that gravity, that profundity, and that impressive incomprehensibility which are so proper to works of that kind, and withal so attractive. Yet notwithstanding it is only a record of a picnic, it has a purpose, which is to suggest to the reader how *he* would be likely to see Europe and the East if he looked at them with his own eyes instead of the eyes of those who traveled in those countries before him. I make small pretense of showing anyone how he *ought* to look at objects of interest beyond the sea—other books do that, and therefore, even if I were competent to do it, there is no need.

I offer no apologies for any departures from the usual style of travel writing that may be charged against me—for I think I have seen with impartial eyes, and I am sure I have written at least honestly, whether wisely or not.

In this volume I have used portions of letters which I wrote for the *Daily Alta California,* of San Francisco, the proprietors of that journal having waived their rights and given me the necessary permission. I have also inserted portions of several letters written for the New York *Tribune* and the New York *Herald.*

THE AUTHOR

SAN FRANCISCO, 1869

1

For months the great pleasure excursion to Europe and the Holy Land was chatted about in the newspapers everywhere in America and discussed at countless firesides. It was a novelty in the way of excursions—its like had not been thought of before—and it compelled that interest which attractive novelties always command. It was to be a picnic on a gigantic scale. The participants in it, instead of freighting an ungainly steam ferryboat with youth and beauty and pies and doughnuts, and paddling up some obscure creek to disembark upon a grassy lawn and wear themselves out with a long summer day's laborious frolicking under the impression that it was fun, were to sail away in a great steamship with flags flying and cannon pealing, and take a royal holiday beyond the broad ocean in many a strange clime and in many a land renowned in history! They were to sail for months over the breezy Atlantic and the sunny Mediterranean; they were to scamper about the decks by day, filling the ship with shouts and laughter, or read novels and poetry in the shade of the smokestacks, or watch for the jellyfish and the nautilus over the side, and the shark, the whale, and other strange monsters of the deep; and at night they were to dance in the open air, on the upper deck, in the midst of a ballroom that stretched from horizon to horizon, and was domed by the bending heavens and lighted by no meaner lamps than the stars and the magnificent moon—dance, and promenade, and smoke, and sing, and make love, and search the skies for constellations that never associate with the "Big Dipper" they were so tired of; and they were to see the ships of twenty navies—the customs and costumes of twenty curious peoples —the great cities of half a world—they were to hobnob with nobility and hold friendly converse with kings and princes,

17

grand moguls, and the anointed lords of mighty empires!

It was a brave conception; it was the offspring of a most ingenious brain. It was well advertised, but it hardly needed it: the bold originality, the extraordinary character, the seductive nature, and the vastness of the enterprise provoked comment everywhere and advertised it in every household in the land. Who could read the program of the excursion without longing to make one of the party? I will insert it here. It is almost as good as a map. As a text for this book, nothing could be better:

BROOKLYN, *February* 1*st*, 1867

The undersigned will make an excursion as above during the coming season, and begs to submit to you the following program:

A first-class steamer, to be under his own command, and capable of accommodating at least one hundred and fifty cabin passengers, will be selected, in which will be taken a select company, numbering not more than three-fourths of the ship's capacity. There is good reason to believe that this company can be easily made up in this immediate vicinity, of mutual friends and acquaintances.

The steamer will be provided with every necessary comfort, including library and musical instruments.

An experienced physician will be on board.

Leaving New York about June 1st, a middle and pleasant route will be taken across the Atlantic, and passing through the group of Azores, St. Michael will be reached in about ten days. A day or two will be spent here, enjoying the fruit and wild scenery of these islands, and the voyage continued, and Gibraltar reached in three or four days.

A day or two will be spent here in looking over the wonderful subterraneous fortifications, permission to visit these galleries being readily obtained.

From Gibraltar, running along the coasts of Spain and France, Marseilles will be reached in three days. Here ample time will be given not only to look over the city, which was founded six hundred years before the Christian era, and its artificial port, the finest of the kind in the Mediterranean, but to visit Paris during the Great Exhibition; and the beautiful city of Lyons, lying intermediate, from the heights of which, on a clear day, Mont Blanc and the Alps can be distinctly seen. Passengers who may wish to extend the time at Paris can do so, and, passing down through Switzerland, rejoin the steamer at Genoa.

From Marseilles to Genoa is a run of one night. The excursionists will have an opportunity to look over this, the "magnificent city of palaces," and visit the birthplace of Columbus, twelve miles off, over a beautiful road built by Napoleon I. From this point, excursions may be made to Milan, Lakes Como and Maggiore, or to Milan, Verona (famous for its extraordinary fortifications), Padua, and Venice. Or, if passengers desire to visit Parma (famous for Correggio's frescoes) and Bologna, they can by rail go on to Florence, and rejoin the steamer at Leghorn, thus spending about three weeks amid the cities most famous for art in Italy.

From Genoa the run to Leghorn will be made along the coast in one night, and time appropriated to this point in which to visit Florence, its palaces and galleries; Pisa, its cathedral and "Leaning Tower," and Lucca and its baths, and Roman amphitheater; Florence, the most remote, being distant by rail about sixty miles.

From Leghorn to Naples (calling at Civita Vecchia to land any who may prefer to go to Rome from that point), the distance will be made in about thirty-six hours; the route will lay along the coast of Italy, close by Caprera, Elba, and Corsica. Arrangements have been made to take on board at Leghorn a pilot for Caprera, and, if practicable, a call will be made there to visit the home of Garibaldi.

Rome [by rail], Herculaneum, Pompeii, Vesuvius, Vergil's tomb, and possibly the ruins of Paestum can be visited, as well as the beautiful surroundings of Naples and its charming bay.

The next point of interest will be Palermo, the most beautiful city of Sicily, which will be reached in one night from Naples. A day will be spent here, and leaving in the evening, the course will be taken towards Athens.

Skirting along the north coast of Sicily, passing through the group of Aeolian Isles, in sight of Stromboli and Vulcania, both active volcanoes, through the Straits of Messina, with "Scylla" on the one hand and "Charybdis" on the other, along the east coast of Sicily, and in sight of Mount Etna, along the south coast of Italy, the west and south coast of Greece, in sight of ancient Crete, up Athens Gulf, and into the Piraeus, Athens will be reached in two and a half or three days. After tarrying here awhile, the Bay of Salamis will be crossed, and a day given to Corinth, whence the voyage will be continued to Constantinople, passing on the way through the Grecian Archipelago, the Dardanelles, the Sea of Marmora, and the mouth of the Golden Horn, and arriving in about forty-eight hours from Athens.

After leaving Constantinople, the way will be taken out through the beautiful Bosphorus, across the Black Sea to Sebastopol and Balaklava, a run of about twenty-four hours. Here it is proposed to remain two days, visiting the harbors, fortifications, and battlefields of the Crimea; thence back through the Bosphorus, touching at Constantinople to take in any who may have preferred to remain there; down through the Sea of Marmora and the Dardanelles, along the coasts of ancient Troy and Lydia in Asia, to Smyrna, which will be reached in two or two and a half days from Constantinople. A sufficient stay will be made here to give opportunity of visiting Ephesus, fifty miles distant by rail.

From Smyrna towards the Holy Land the course will lay through the Grecian Archipelago, close by the Isle of Patmos, along the coast of Asia, ancient Pamphylia, and the Isle of Cyprus. Beirut will be reached in three days. At Beirut time will be given to visit Damascus; after which the steamer will proceed to Joppa.

From Joppa, Jerusalem, the River Jordan, the Sea of Tiberias, Nazareth, Bethany, Bethlehem, and other points of interest in the Holy Land can be visited, and here those who may have preferred to make the journey from Beirut *through* the country, passing through Damascus, Galilee, Capernaum, Samaria, and by the River Jordan and Sea of Tiberias, can rejoin the steamer.

Leaving Joppa, the next point of interest to visit will be Alexandria, which will be reached in twenty-four hours. The ruins of Caesar's Palace, Pompey's Pillar, Cleopatra's Needle, the Catacombs, and ruins of ancient Alexandria will be found worth the visit. The journey to Cairo, one hundred and thirty miles by rail, can be made in a few hours, and from which can be visited the site of ancient Memphis, Joseph's Granaries, and the Pyramids.

From Alexandria the route will be taken homeward, calling at Malta, Cagliari (in Sardinia), and Palma (in Majorca), all magnificent harbors, with charming scenery, and abounding in fruits.

A day or two will be spent at each place, and leaving Parma in the evening, Valencia in Spain will be reached the next morning. A few days will be spent in this, the finest city of Spain.

From Valencia, the homeward course will be continued, skirting along the coast of Spain. Alicant, Carthagena, Palos, and Malaga will be passed but a mile or two distant, and Gibraltar reached in about twenty-four hours.

A stay of one day will be made here, and the voyage continued to Madeira, which will be reached in about three days. Captain Marryatt writes: "I do not know a spot on the globe which so much astonishes and delights upon first arrival as Madeira." A stay of one or two days will be made here, which, if time permits, may be extended, and passing on through the islands, and probably in sight of the Peak of Teneriffe, a southern track will be taken, and the Atlantic crossed within the latitudes of the northeast trade winds, where mild and pleasant weather, and a smooth sea, can always be expected.

A call will be made at Bermuda, which lies directly in this

route homeward, and will be reached in about ten days from Madeira, and after spending a short time with our friends the Bermudians, the final departure will be made for home, which will be reached in about three days.

Already, applications have been received from parties in Europe wishing to join the Excursion there.

The ship will at all times be a home, where the excursionists, if sick, will be surrounded by kind friends, and have all possible comfort and sympathy.

Should contagious sickness exist in any of the ports named in the program, such ports will be passed, and others of interest substituted.

The price of passage is fixed at $1,250, currency, for each adult passenger. Choice of rooms and of seats at the tables apportioned in the order in which passages are engaged, and no passage considered engaged until ten percent of the passage money is deposited with the treasurer.

Passengers can remain on board of the steamer, at all ports, if they desire, without additional expense, and all boating at the expense of the ship.

All passages must be paid for when taken, in order that the most perfect arrangements be made for starting at the appointed time.

Applications for passage must be approved by the committee before tickets are issued, and can be made to the undersigned.

Articles of interest or curiosity, procured by the passengers during the voyage, may be brought home in the steamer free of charge.

Five dollars per day, in gold, it is believed, will be a fair calculation to make for *all* traveling expenses onshore and at the various points where passengers may wish to leave the steamer for days at a time.

The trip can be extended, and the route changed, by *unanimous* vote of the passengers.

CHAS. C. DUNCAN,
117 WALL STREET, NEW YORK

R. R. G******, Treasurer

COMMITTEE ON APPLICATIONS

J. T. H*****, ESQ.   R. R. G*****, ESQ.   C. C. Duncan

COMMITTEE ON SELECTING STEAMER

CAPT. W. W. S****, *Surveyor for Board of Underwriters*
C. W. C******, *Consulting Engineer for U.S. and Canada*
J. T. H*****, ESQ.
C. C. DUNCAN

P. S.—The very beautiful and substantial side-wheel steamship *Quaker City* has been chartered for the occasion, and will leave New York June 8th. Letters have been issued by the government commending the party to courtesies abroad.

What was there lacking about that program to make it perfectly irresistible? Nothing that any finite mind could discover. Paris, England, Scotland, Switzerland, Italy—Garibaldi! The Grecian Archipelago! Vesuvius! Constantinople! Smyrna! The Holy Land! Egypt and "our friends the Bermudians"! People in Europe desiring to join the excursion—contagious sickness to be avoided—boating at the expense of the ship—physician on board—the circuit of the globe to be made if the passengers unanimously desired it—the company to be rigidly selected by a pitiless "Committee on Applications" —the vessel to be as rigidly selected by as pitiless a "Committee on Selecting Steamer." Human nature could not withstand these bewildering temptations. I hurried to the treasurer's office and deposited my ten percent. I rejoiced to know that a few vacant staterooms were still left. I *did* avoid a critical personal examination into my character by that boweless committee, but I referred to all the people of high standing I could think of in the community who would be least likely to know anything about me.

Shortly a supplementary program was issued which set forth that the *Plymouth Collection of Hymns* would be used on board the ship. I then paid the balance of my passage money.

I was provided with a receipt and duly and officially accepted as an excursionist. There was happiness in that, but it was tame compared to the novelty of being "select."

This supplementary program also instructed the excursionists to provide themselves with light musical instruments for amusement in the ship, with saddles for Syrian travel, green spectacles and umbrellas, veils for Egypt, and substantial clothing to use in rough pilgrimizing in the Holy Land. Furthermore, it was suggested that although the ship's library would afford a fair amount of reading matter, it would still be well if each passenger would provide himself with a few guidebooks, a Bible, and some standard works of travel. A list was appended, which consisted chiefly of books relating to the Holy Land, since the Holy Land was part of the excursion and seemed to be its main feature.

Reverend Henry Ward Beecher was to have accompanied the expedition, but urgent duties obliged him to give up the idea. There were other passengers who could have been spared better and would have been spared more willingly. Lieutenant General Sherman was to have been of the party also, but the Indian war compelled his presence on the plains. A popular actress had entered her name on the ship's books, but something interfered and *she* couldn't go. The "Drummer Boy of the Potomac" deserted, and lo, we had never a celebrity left!

However, we were to have a "battery of guns" from the Navy Department (as per advertisement) to be used in answering royal salutes; and the document furnished by the Secretary of the Navy, which was to make "General Sherman and party" welcome guests in the courts and camps of the old world, was still left to us, though both document and battery, I think, were shorn of somewhat of their original august proportions. However, had not we the seductive program still, with its Paris, its Constantinople, Smyrna, Jerusalem, Jericho, and "our friends the Bermudians"? What did we care?

2

Occasionally, during the following month, I dropped in at 117 Wall Street to inquire how the repairing and refurnishing of the vessel was coming on, how additions to the passenger list were averaging, how many people the committee were decreeing not "select" every day and banishing in sorrow and tribulation. I was glad to know that we were to have a little printing press on board and issue a daily newspaper of our own. I was glad to learn that our piano, our parlor organ, and our melodeon were to be the best instruments of the kind that could be had in the market. I was proud to observe that among our excursionists were three ministers of the gospel, eight doctors, sixteen or eighteen ladies, several military and naval chieftains with sounding titles, an ample crop of "Professors" of various kinds, and a gentleman who had "COMMISSIONER OF THE UNITED STATES OF AMERICA TO EUROPE, ASIA, AND

AFRICA" thundering after his name in one awful blast! I had carefully prepared myself to take rather a back seat in that ship because of the uncommonly select material that would alone be permitted to pass through the camel's eye of that committee on credentials; I had schooled myself to expect an imposing array of military and naval heroes and to have to set that back seat still further back in consequence of it maybe; but I state frankly that I was all unprepared for *this* crusher.

I fell under that titular avalanche a torn and blighted thing. I said that if that potentate *must* go over in our ship, why, I supposed he must—but that to my thinking, when the United States considered it necessary to send a dignitary of that tonnage across the ocean, it would be in better taste, and safer, to take him apart and cart him over in sections in several ships.

Ah, if I had only known then that he was only a common mortal, and that his mission had nothing more overpowering about it than the collecting of seeds and uncommon yams and extraordinary cabbages and peculiar bullfrogs for that poor, useless, innocent, mildewed old fossil the Smithsonian Institute, I would have felt *so* much relieved.

During that memorable month I basked in the happiness of being for once in my life drifting with the tide of a great popular movement. Everybody was going to Europe—I, too, was going to Europe. Everybody was going to the famous Paris Exposition—I, too, was going to the Paris Exposition. The steamship lines were carrying Americans out of the various ports of the country at the rate of four or five thousand a week in the aggregate. If I met a dozen individuals during that month who were not going to Europe shortly, I have no distinct remembrance of it now. I walked about the city a good deal with a young Mr. Blucher, who was booked for the excursion. He was confiding, good-natured, unsophisticated, companionable; but he was not a man to set the river on fire. He had the most extraordinary notions about this European exodus and came at last to consider the whole nation as packing up for emigration to France. We stepped into a store on Broadway one day, where he bought a handkerchief, and when the man could not make change, Mr. B. said:

"Never mind, I'll hand it to you in Paris."

"But I am not going to Paris."

"How is—what did I understand you to say?"

"I said I am not going to Paris."

"Not going to *Paris!* Not g— well, then, where in the nation *are* you going to?"

"Nowhere at all."

"Not anywhere whatsoever? Not any place on earth but this?"

"Not any place at all but just this—stay here all summer."

My comrade took his purchase and walked out of the store without a word—walked out with an injured look upon his countenance. Up the street apiece he broke silence and said impressively: "It was a lie—that is my opinion of it!"

In the fullness of time the ship was ready to receive her passengers. I was introduced to the young gentleman who was to be my roommate, and found him to be intelligent, cheerful of spirit, unselfish, full of generous impulses, patient, considerate, and wonderfully good-natured. Not any passenger that sailed in the *Quaker City* will withhold his endorsement of what I have just said. We selected a stateroom forward of the wheel, on the starboard side, "below decks." It had two berths in it, a dismal deadlight, a sink with a washbowl in it, and a long, sumptuously cushioned locker, which was to do service as a sofa—partly—and partly as a hiding place for our things. Notwithstanding all this furniture, there was still room to turn around in, but not to swing a cat in, at least with entire security to the cat. However, the room was large, for a ship's stateroom, and was in every way satisfactory.

The vessel was appointed to sail on a certain Saturday early in June.

A little after noon on that distinguished Saturday I reached the ship and went on board. All was bustle and confusion. [I have seen that remark before somewhere.] The pier was crowded with carriages and men; passengers were arriving and hurrying on board; the vessel's decks were encumbered with trunks and valises; groups of excursionists, arrayed in unattractive traveling costumes, were moping about in a drizzling rain and looking as droopy and woebegone as so many molting chickens. The gallant flag was up, but it was under the spell, too, and hung limp and disheartened by the mast. Altogether, it was the bluest, bluest spectacle! It was a pleasure excursion—there was no gainsaying that, because the program said so—it was so nominated in the bond—but it surely hadn't the general aspect of one.

Finally, above the banging, and rumbling, and shouting, and

hissing of steam rang the order to "cast off!"—a sudden rush to the gangways—a scampering ashore of visitors—a revolution of the wheels, and we were off—the picnic was begun! Two very mild cheers went up from the dripping crowd on the pier; we answered them gently from the slippery decks; the flag made an effort to wave, and failed; the "battery of guns" spake not—the ammunition was out.

We steamed down to the foot of the harbor and came to anchor. It was still raining. And not only raining, but storming. "Outside" we could see, ourselves, that there was a tremendous sea on. We must lie still, in the calm harbor, till the storm should abate. Our passengers hailed from fifteen states; only a few of them had ever been to sea before; manifestly it would not do to pit them against a full-blown tempest until they had got their sea legs on. Toward evening the two steam tugs that had accompanied us with a rollicking champagne party of young New Yorkers on board who wished to bid farewell to one of our number in due and ancient form departed, and we were alone on the deep. On deep five fathoms, and anchored fast to the bottom. And out in the solemn rain at that. This was pleasuring with a vengeance.

It was an appropriate relief when the gong sounded for prayer meeting. The first Saturday night of any other pleasure excursion might have been devoted to whist and dancing; but I submit it to the unprejudiced mind if it would have been in good taste for *us* to engage in such frivolities, considering what we had gone through and the frame of mind we were in. We would have shone at a wake, but not at anything more festive.

However, there is always a cheering influence about the sea; and in my berth that night, rocked by the measured swell of the waves and lulled by the murmur of the distant surf, I soon passed tranquilly out of all consciousness of the dreary experiences of the day and damaging premonitions of the future.

3

All day Sunday at anchor. The storm had gone down a great deal, but the sea had not. It was still piling its frothy hills high in air "outside," as we could plainly see with the glasses. We could not properly begin a pleasure excursion on Sunday; we could not offer untried stomachs to so pitiless a sea as that. We must lie still till Monday. And we did. But we had repetitions of church and prayer meetings; and so, of course, we were just as eligibly situated as we could have been anywhere.

I was up early that Sabbath morning and was early to breakfast. I felt a perfectly natural desire to have a good, long, unprejudiced look at the passengers at a time when they should be free from self-consciousness—which is at breakfast, when such a moment occurs in the lives of human beings at all.

I was greatly surprised to see so many elderly people—I might almost say, so many venerable people. A glance at the long lines of heads was apt to make one think it was *all* gray. But it was not. There was a tolerably fair sprinkling of young folks, and another fair sprinkling of gentlemen and ladies who were noncommittal as to age, being neither actually old or absolutely young.

The next morning we weighed anchor and went to sea. It was a great happiness to get away after this dragging, dispiriting delay. I thought there never was such gladness in the air before, such brightness in the sun, such beauty in the sea. I was satisfied with the picnic then and with all its belongings. All my malicious instincts were dead within me; and as America faded out of sight, I think a spirit of charity rose up in their place that was as boundless, for the time being, as the broad ocean that was heaving its billows about us. I wished to express my feelings—I wished to lift up my voice and sing; but I did not know anything to sing, and so I was obliged to give up the idea. It was no loss to the ship, though, perhaps.

It was breezy and pleasant, but the sea was still very rough. One could not promenade without risking his neck; at one moment the bowsprit was taking a deadly aim at the sun in mid-heaven, and at the next it was trying to harpoon a shark in the bottom of the ocean. What a weird sensation it is to feel the stern of a ship sinking swiftly from under you and see the bow climbing high away among the clouds! One's safest course that day was to clasp a railing and hang on; walking was too precarious a pastime.

By some happy fortune I was not seasick. That was a thing to be proud of. I had not always escaped before. If there is one thing in the world that will make a man peculiarly and insufferably self-conceited, it is to have his stomach behave itself, the first day at sea, when nearly all his comrades are seasick. Soon a venerable fossil, shawled to the chin and bandaged like a mummy, appeared at the door of the after deck-house, and the next lurch of the ship shot him into my arms. I said:

"Good-morning, sir. It is a fine day."

He put his hand on his stomach and said, "*Oh*, my!" and then staggered away and fell over the coop of a skylight.

Presently another old gentleman was projected from the same door with great violence. I said:

"Calm yourself, sir—there is no hurry. It is a fine day, sir."

He, also, put his hand on his stomach and said "*Oh*, my!" and reeled away.

In a little while another veteran was discharged abruptly from the same door, clawing at the air for a saving support. I said:

"Good morning, sir. It is a fine day for pleasuring. You were about to say—"

"*Oh*, my!"

I thought so. I anticipated *him*, anyhow. I stayed there and was bombarded with old gentlemen for an hour, perhaps; and all I got out of any of them was "*Oh*, my!"

I went away then in a thoughtful mood. I said, this is a good pleasure excursion. I like it. The passengers are not garrulous, but still they are sociable. I like those old people, but somehow they all seem to have the "Oh, my" rather bad.

I knew what was the matter with them. They were seasick. And I was glad of it. We all like to see people seasick when we are not, ourselves. Playing whist by the cabin lamps when it is storming outside is pleasant; walking the quarterdeck in the moonlight is pleasant; smoking in the breezy foretop is pleasant when one is not afraid to go up there; but these are all feeble and commonplace compared with the joy of seeing people suffering the miseries of seasickness.

I picked up a good deal of information during the afternoon. At one time I was climbing up the quarterdeck when the vessel's stern was in the sky; I was smoking a cigar and feeling passably comfortable. Somebody ejaculated:

"Come, now, *that* won't answer. Read the sign up there— No SMOKING ABAFT THE WHEEL!"

It was Captain Duncan, chief of the expedition. I went forward, of course. I saw a long spyglass lying on a desk in one of the upper-deck staterooms back of the pilothouse and reached after it—there was a ship in the distance.

"Ah, ah—hands off! Come out of that!"

I came out of that. I said to a deck sweep—but in a low voice:

"Who is that overgrown pirate with the whiskers and the discordant voice?"

"It's Captain Bursley—executive officer—sailing master."

I loitered about awhile, and then, for want of something better to do, fell to carving a railing with my knife. Somebody said, in an insinuating, admonitory voice:

"Now, *say*—my friend—don't you know any better than to be whittling the ship all to pieces that way? *You* ought to know better than that."

I went back and found the deck sweep.

"Who is that smooth-faced, animated outrage yonder in the fine clothes?"

"That's Captain L****, the owner of the ship—he's one of the main bosses."

In the course of time I brought up on the starboard side of the pilot-house and found a sextant lying on a bench. Now, I said, they "take the sun" through this thing; I should think I might see that vessel through it. I had hardly got it to my eye when someone touched me on the shoulder and said deprecatingly:

"I'll have to get you to give that to me, sir. If there's anything you'd like to know about taking the sun, I'd as soon tell you as not—but I don't like to trust anybody with that instrument. If you want any figuring done— Aye, aye, sir!"

He was gone to answer a call from the other side. I sought the deck sweep.

"Who is that spider-legged gorilla yonder with the sanctimonious countenance?"

"It's Captain Jones, sir—the chief mate."

"Well. This goes clear away ahead of anything I ever heard of before. Do you—now I ask you as a man and a brother —*do* you think I could venture to throw a rock here in any given direction without hitting a captain of this ship?"

"Well, sir, I don't know—I think likely you'd fetch the captain of the watch maybe, because he's a-standing right yonder in the way."

I went below—meditating and a little downhearted. I thought, if five cooks can spoil a broth, what may not five captains do with a pleasure excursion?

4

We plowed along bravely for a week or more, and without any conflict of jurisdiction among the captains worth mentioning. The passengers soon learned to accommodate themselves to their new circumstances, and life in the ship became nearly as systematically monotonous as the routine of a barrack. I do not mean that it was dull, for it was not entirely so by any means—but there was a good deal of sameness about it. As is always the fashion at sea, the passengers shortly began to pick up sailor terms—a sign that they were beginning to feel at home. Half-past six was no longer half-past six to these pilgrims from New England, the South, and the Mississippi Valley, it was "seven bells"; eight, twelve, and four o'clock were "eight bells"; the captain did not take the longitude at nine o'clock, but at "two bells." They spoke glibly of the "after cabin," the "forrard cabin," " port and starboard" and the "fo'castle."

At seven bells the first gong rang; at eight there was breakfast, for such as were not too seasick to eat it. After that all the well people walked arm in arm up and down the long promenade deck, enjoying the fine summer mornings, and the seasick ones crawled out and propped themselves up in the lee of the paddle boxes and ate their dismal tea and toast, and looked wretched. From eleven o'clock until luncheon, and from luncheon until dinner at six in the evening, the employments and amusements were various. Some reading was done, and much smoking and sewing, though not by the same parties; there were the monsters of the deep to be looked after and wondered at; strange ships had to be scrutinized through opera glasses, and sage decisions arrived at concerning them; and more than that, everybody took a personal interest in seeing that the flag was run up and politely dipped three times in response to the salutes of those strangers; in the smoking room there were always parties of gentlemen playing euchre, draughts, and dominoes, especially dominoes, that delightfully harmless game; and down on the main deck, "forrard"—forrard of the chicken coops and the cattle—we had what was called "horse billiards." Horse billiards is a fine game. It affords good, active exercise, hilarity, and consuming excitement. It is a mixture of "hopscotch" and shuffleboard played with a crutch. A large hopscotch diagram is marked out on the deck with chalk, and each compartment numbered. You stand off three or four steps, with some broad wooden disks before you on the deck, and these you send forward with a vigorous thrust of a long crutch. If a disk stops on a chalk line, it does not count anything. If it stops in division No. 7, it counts 7; in 5, it counts 5, and so on. The game is 100, and four can play at a time. That game would be very simple played on a stationary floor, but with us, to play it well required science. We had to allow for the reeling of the ship to the right or the left. Very often one made calculations for a heel to the right and the ship did not go that way. The consequence was that that disk missed the whole hopscotch plan a yard or two, and then there was humiliation on one side and laughter on the other.

When it rained the passengers had to stay in the house, of course—or at least the cabins—and amuse themselves with games, reading, looking out of the windows at the very familiar billows, and talking gossip.

By seven o'clock in the evening, dinner was about over; an hour's promenade on the upper deck followed; then the gong sounded and a large majority of the party repaired to the

after cabin (upper), a handsome saloon fifty or sixty feet
long, for prayers. The unregenerated called this saloon the
"Synagogue." The devotions consisted only of two hymns from
the *Plymouth Collection* and a short prayer, and seldom
occupied more than fifteen minutes. The hymns were accompanied by parlor-organ music when the sea was smooth enough
to allow a performer to sit at the instrument without being
lashed to his chair.

After prayers the Synagogue shortly took the semblance of
a writing school. The like of that picture was never seen in
a ship before. Behind the long dining tables on either side of
the saloon, and scattered from one end to the other of the latter, some twenty or thirty gentlemen and ladies sat them
down under the swaying lamps and for two or three hours
wrote diligently in their journals. Alas that journals so volu-
minously begun should come to so lame and impotent a conclusion as most of them did! I doubt if there is a single pilgrim of all that host but can show a hundred fair pages of
journal concerning the first twenty days' voyaging in the
Quaker City, and I am morally certain that not ten of the party
can show twenty pages of journal for the succeeding twenty
thousand miles of voyaging! At certain periods it becomes
the dearest ambition of a man to keep a faithful record of
his performances in a book; and he dashes at this work with
an enthusiasm that imposes on him the notion that keeping a
journal is the veriest pastime in the world, and the pleasantest.
But if he only lives twenty-one days, he will find out that only
those rare natures that are made up of pluck, endurance, devotion to duty for duty's sake, and invincible determination
may hope to venture upon so tremendous an enterprise as the
keeping of a journal and not sustain a shameful defeat.

One of our favorite youths, Jack, a splendid young fellow
with a head full of good sense, and a pair of legs that were a
wonder to look upon in the way of length and straightness
and slimness, used to report progress every morning in the
most glowing and spirited way, and say:

"Oh, I'm coming along bully!" (He was a little given to
slang in his happier moods.) "I wrote ten pages in my journal
last night—and you know I wrote nine the night before and
twelve the night before that. Why, it's only fun!"

"What do you find to put in it, Jack?"

"Oh, everything. Latitude and longitude, noon every day;
and how many miles we made last twenty-four hours; and all

the domino games I beat and horse billiards; and whales and sharks and porpoises; and the text of the sermon Sundays (because that'll tell at home, you know); and the ships we saluted and what nation they were; and which way the wind was, and whether there was a heavy sea, and what sail we carried, though we don't ever carry *any*, principally, going against a head wind always—wonder what is the reason of that?—and how many lies Moult has told—oh, everything! I've got everything down. My father told me to keep that journal. Father wouldn't take a thousand dollars for it when I get it done."

"No, Jack; it will be worth more than a thousand dollars—when you get it done."

"Do you? No, but do you think it will, though?"

"Yes, it will be worth at least as much as a thousand dollars—when you get it done. Maybe more."

"Well, I about half think so, myself. It ain't no slouch of a journal."

But it shortly became a most lamentable "slouch of a journal." One night in Paris, after a hard day's toil in sightseeing, I said:

"Now I'll go and stroll around the cafés awhile, Jack, and give you a chance to write up your journal, old fellow."

His countenance lost its fire. He said:

"Well, no, you needn't mind. I think I won't run that journal anymore. It is awful tedious. Do you know—I reckon I'm as much as four thousand pages behindhand. I haven't got any France in it at all. First I thought I'd leave France out and start fresh. But that wouldn't do, *would* it? The governor would say, 'Hello, here—didn't see anything in France?' *That* cat wouldn't fight, you know. First I thought I'd copy France out of the guidebook, like old Badger in the forrard cabin, who's writing a book, but there's more than three hundred pages of it. Oh, *I* don't think a journal's any use—do you? They're only a bother, *ain't* they?"

"Yes, a journal that is incomplete isn't of much use, but a journal properly kept is worth a thousand dollars—when you've got it done."

"A thousand!—well, I should think so. *I* wouldn't finish it for a million."

His experience was only the experience of the majority of that industrious night school in the cabin. If you wish to inflict a heartless and malignant punishment upon a young person, pledge him to keep a journal a year.

A good many expedients were resorted to to keep the excursionists amused and satisfied. A club was formed, of all the passengers, which met in the writing school after prayers and read aloud about the countries we were approaching and discussed the information so obtained.

Several times the photographer of the expedition brought out his transparent pictures and gave us a handsome magic-lantern exhibition. His views were nearly all of foreign scenes, but there were one or two home pictures among them. He advertised that he would "open his performance in the after cabin at 'two bells' (nine P.M.) and show the passengers where they shall eventually arrive"—which was all very well, but by a funny accident the first picture that flamed out upon the canvas was a view of Greenwood Cemetery!

On several starlight nights we danced on the upper deck, under the awnings, and made something of a ballroom display of brilliancy by hanging a number of ship's lanterns to the stanchions. Our music consisted of the well-mixed strains of a melodeon which was a little asthmatic and apt to catch its breath where it ought to come out strong, a clarinet which was a little unreliable on the high keys and rather melancholy on the low ones, and a disreputable accordion that had a leak somewhere and breathed louder than it squawked—a more elegant term does not occur to me just now. However, the dancing was infinitely worse than the music. When the ship rolled to starboard the whole platoon of dancers came charging down to starboard with it, and brought up in mass at the rail; and when it rolled to port they went floundering down to port with the same unanimity of sentiment. Waltzers spun around precariously for a matter of fifteen seconds and then went scurrying down to the rail as if they meant to go overboard. The Virginia reel, as performed on board the *Quaker City,* had more genuine reel about it than any reel I ever saw before, and was as full of interest to the spectator as it was full of desperate chances and hairbreadth escapes to the participant. We gave up dancing, finally.

We celebrated a lady's birthday anniversary with toasts, speeches, a poem, and so forth. We also had a mock trial. No ship ever went to sea that hadn't a mock trial on board. The purser was accused of stealing an overcoat from stateroom No. 10. A judge was appointed; also clerks, a crier of the court, constables, sheriffs; counsel for the State and for the defendant; witnesses were subpoenaed, and a jury empaneled after much challenging. The witnesses were stupid and unreliable and contradictory, as witnesses always are. The counsel were eloquent, argumentative, and vindictively abusive of each other, as was characteristic and proper. The case was at last submitted and duly finished by the judge with an absurd decision and a ridiculous sentence.

The acting of charades was tried on several evenings by the young gentlemen and ladies, in the cabins, and proved the most distinguished success of all the amusement experiments.

An attempt was made to organize a debating club, but it was a failure. There was no oratorical talent in the ship.

We all enjoyed ourselves—I think I can safely say that, but it was in a rather quiet way. We very, very seldom played the piano; we played the flute and the clarinet together, and made good music, too, what there was of it, but we always played the same old tune; it was a very pretty tune—how well I remember it—I wonder when I shall ever get rid of it. We never played either the melodeon or the organ except at devotions —but I am too fast: young Albert *did* know part of a tune— something about "O Something-or-Other How Sweet It Is to Know That He's His What's-His-Name" (I do not remember the exact title of it, but it was very plaintive and full of sentiment); Albert played that pretty much all the time until we contracted with him to restrain himself. But nobody ever sang by moonlight on the upper deck, and the congregational singing at church and prayers was not of a superior order of architecture. I put up with it as long as I could and then joined in and tried to improve it, but this encouraged young George to join in too, and that made a failure of it; because George's voice was just "turning," and when he was singing a dismal sort of bass it was apt to fly off the handle and startle everybody with a most discordant cackle on the upper notes. George didn't know the tunes, either, which was also a drawback to his performances. I said:

"Come, now, George, *don't* improvise. It looks too egotistical. It will provoke remark. Just stick to 'Coronation,' like the others. It is a good tune—*you* can't improve it any, just offhand, in this way."

"Why, I'm not trying to improve it— and I *am* singing like the others—just as it is in the notes."

And he honestly thought he was, too; and so he had no one

to blame but himself when his voice caught on the center occasionally and gave him the lockjaw.

There were those among the unregenerated who attributed the unceasing head winds to our distressing choir music. There were those who said openly that it was taking chances enough to have such ghastly music going on, even when it was at its best; and that to exaggerate the crime by letting George help was simply flying in the face of Providence. These said that the choir would keep up their lacerating attempts at melody until they would bring down a storm some day that would sink the ship.

There were even grumblers at the prayers. The executive officer said the pilgrims had no charity:

"There they are, down there every night at eight bells, praying for fair winds—when they know as well as I do that this is the only ship going east this time of the year, but there's a thousand coming west—what's a fair wind for us is a *head* wind to them—the Almighty's blowing a fair wind for a thousand vessels, and this tribe wants him to turn it clear around so as to accommodate *one*—and she a steamship at that! It ain't good sense, it ain't good reason, it ain't good Christianity, it ain't common human charity. Avast with such nonsense!"

5

Taking it "by and large," as the sailors say, we had a pleasant ten days' run from New York to the Azores islands—not a fast run, for the distance is only twenty-four hundred miles, but a right pleasant one in the main. True, we had head winds *all* the time, and several stormy experiences which sent fifty percent of the passengers to bed sick and made the ship look dismal and deserted—stormy experiences that all will remember who weathered them on the tumbling deck and caught the vast sheets of spray that every now and then sprang high in air from the weather bow and swept the ship like a thundershower; but for the most part we had balmy summer weather and nights that were even finer than the days. We had the phenomenon of a full moon located just in the same spot in the heavens at the same hour every night. The reason of this singular conduct on the part of the moon did not occur to us at first, but it did afterward when we reflected that we were gaining about twenty minutes every day because we were going east so fast—we gained just about enough every day to keep along with the moon. It was becoming an old moon to the friends we had left behind us, but to us Joshuas it stood still in the same place and remained always the same.

Young Mr. Blucher, who is from the Far West and is on his first voyage, was a good deal worried by the constantly changing "ship time." He was proud of his new watch at first and used to drag it out promptly when eight bells struck at noon, but he came to look after a while as if he were losing confidence in it. Seven days out from New York he came on deck and said with great decision:

"This thing's a swindle!"

"What's a swindle?"

"Why, this watch. I bought her out in Illinois—gave $150 for her—and I thought she was good. And, by George, she *is* good onshore, but somehow she don't keep up her lick here on the water—gets seasick maybe. She skips; she runs along regular enough till half-past eleven, and then, all of a sudden, she lets down. I've set that old regulator up faster and faster, till I've shoved it clear around, but it don't do any good; she just distances every watch in the ship, and clatters along in a way that's astonishing till it is noon, but them eight bells always gets in about ten minutes ahead of her anyway. I don't know what to do with her now. She's doing all she can—she's going her best gait, but it won't save her. Now, don't you know, there ain't a watch in the ship that's making better time than she is, but what does it signify? When you hear them eight bells you'll find her just about ten minutes short of her score sure."

The ship was gaining a full hour every three days, and this fellow was trying to make his watch go fast enough to keep up to her. But, as he had said, he had pushed the regulator up as far as it would go, and the watch was "on its best gait," and so nothing was left him but to fold his hands and see the ship beat the race. We sent him to the captain, and he explained to him the mystery of "ship time" and set his troubled mind at rest. This young man asked a great many questions about seasickness before we left, and wanted to know what its characteristics were and how he was to tell when he had it. He found out.

We saw the usual sharks, blackfish, porpoises, etc., of course, and by and by large schools of Portuguese men-of-war were added to the regular list of sea wonders. Some of them were white and some of a brilliant carmine color. The nautilus is nothing but a transparent web of jelly that spreads itself to catch the wind, and has fleshy-looking strings a foot or two long dangling from it to keep it steady in the water. It is an accomplished sailor and has good sailor judgment. It reefs its sail when a storm threatens or the wind blows pretty hard, and furls it entirely and goes down when a gale blows. Ordinarily it keeps its sail wet and in good sailing order by turning over and dipping it in the water for a moment. Seamen say the nautilus is only found in these waters between the thirty-fifth and forty-fifth parallels of latitude.

At three o'clock on the morning of the twenty-first of June, we were awakened and notified that the Azores islands were in sight. I said I did not take any interest in islands at three o'clock in the morning. But another persecutor came, and then another and another, and finally believing that the general enthusiasm would permit no one to slumber in peace, I got up and went sleepily on deck. It was five and a half o'clock now, and a raw, blustering morning. The passengers were huddled about the smokestacks and fortified behind ventilators, and all were wrapped in wintry costumes and looking sleepy and unhappy in the pitiless gale and the drenching spray.

The island in sight was Flores. It seemed only a mountain of mud standing up out of the dull mists of the sea. But as we bore down upon it the sun came out and made it a beautiful picture—a mass of green farms and meadows that swelled up to a height of fifteen hundred feet and mingled its upper outlines with the clouds. It was ribbed with sharp, steep ridges and cloven with narrow canyons, and here and there on the heights, rocky upheavals shaped themselves into mimic battlements and castles; and out of rifted clouds came broad shafts of sunlight that painted summit and slope and glen with bands of fire and left belts of somber shade between. It was the aurora borealis of the frozen pole exiled to a summer land!

We skirted around two-thirds of the island, four miles from shore, and all the opera glasses in the ship were called into requisition to settle disputes as to whether mossy spots on the uplands were groves of trees or groves of weeds, or whether the white villages down by the sea were really villages or only the clustering tombstones of cemeteries. Finally we stood to sea and bore away for San Miguel, and Flores shortly became a dome of mud again and sank down among the mists and disappeared. But to many a seasick passenger it was good to see the green hills again, and all were more cheerful after this episode than anybody could have expected them to be, considering how sinfully early they had gotten up.

But we had to change our purpose about San Miguel, for a storm came up about noon that so tossed and pitched the vessel that common sense dictated a run for shelter. Therefore we steered for the nearest island of the group—Fayal (the people there pronounce it Fy-all, and put the accent on the first syllable). We anchored in the open roadstead of Horta, half a mile from the shore. The town has eight thousand to ten thousand inhabitants. Its snow-white houses nestle cosily in a sea of fresh green vegetation, and no village could look prettier or more attractive. It sits in the lap of an amphitheater of hills which are three hundred to seven hundred feet high, and carefully cultivated clear to their summits—not a foot of soil left idle. Every farm and every acre is cut up into little square enclosures by stone walls, whose duty it is to protect the growing products from the destructive gales that blow there. These hundreds of green squares, marked by their black lava walls, make the hills look like vast checkerboards.

The islands belong to Portugal, and everything in Fayal has Portuguese characteristics about it. But more of that anon. A swarm of swarthy, noisy, lying, shoulder-shrugging, gesticulating Portuguese boatmen, with brass rings in their ears and fraud in their hearts, climbed the ship's sides, and various parties of us contracted with them to take us ashore at so much a head, silver coin of any country. We landed under the walls of a little fort, armed with batteries of twelve- and thirty-two-pounders, which Horta considered a most formidable institution, but if we were ever to get after it with one of our turreted monitors, they would have to move it out in the country if they wanted it where they could go and find it again when they needed it. The group on the pier was a rusty one—men and women, and boys and girls, all ragged and barefoot, uncombed and unclean, and by instinct, education, and profession beggars. They trooped after us, and never more while we tarried in Fayal did we get rid of them. We walked up the middle of the principal street, and these vermin surrounded us on all sides and glared upon us; and every moment excited couples shot ahead of the procession to get a good look back, just as village boys do when they accompany the elephant on his advertising trip from street to street. It was very flattering to me to be part of the material for such a sensation. Here and there in the doorways we saw women with fashionable Portuguese hoods on. This hood is of thick blue cloth, attached to a cloak of the same stuff, and is a marvel of ugliness. It stands up high and spreads far abroad, and is unfathomably deep. It fits like a circus tent, and a woman's head is hidden away in it like the man's who prompts the singers from his tin shed in the stage of an opera. There is no particle of trimming about this monstrous capote, as they call it—it is just a plain, ugly dead-blue mass of sail, and a woman can't go within eight points of the wind with one of them on; she has to go before the wind or not at all. The general style of the capote is the same in all the islands, and will remain so for the next ten thousand years, but each island shapes its capotes just enough differently from the others to enable an observer to tell at a glance what particular island a lady hails from.

The Portuguese pennies, or reis (pronounced rays), are prodigious. It takes one thousand reis to make a dollar, and all financial estimates are made in reis. We did not know this until after we had found it out through Blucher. Blucher said he was so happy and so grateful to be on solid land once more that he wanted to give a feast—said he had heard it was a cheap land, and he was bound to have a grand banquet. He invited nine of us, and we ate an excellent dinner at the principal hotel. In the midst of the jollity produced by good cigars, good wine, and passable anecdotes, the landlord presented his bill. Blucher glanced at it and his countenance fell. He took another look to assure himself that his senses had not deceived him and then read the items aloud, in a faltering voice, while the roses in his cheeks turned to ashes:

" 'Ten dinners, at 600 reis, 6,000 reis!' Ruin and desolation!

" 'Twenty-five cigars, at 100 reis, 2,500 reis!' Oh, my sainted mother!

" 'Eleven bottles of wine, at 1,200 reis, 13,200 reis!' Be with us all!

" 'TOTAL, TWENTY-ONE THOUSAND SEVEN HUNDRED REIS!' The suffering Moses! There ain't money enough in the ship to pay that bill! Go—leave me to my misery, boys, I am a ruined community."

I think it was the blankest-looking party I ever saw. Nobody could say a word. It was as if every soul had been stricken dumb. Wine glasses descended slowly to the table, their contents untasted. Cigars dropped unnoticed from nerveless fingers. Each man sought his neighbor's eye, but found in it no ray of hope, no encouragement. At last the fearful silence was broken. The shadow of a desperate resolve settled upon Blucher's countenance like a cloud, and he rose up and said:

"Landlord, this is a low, mean swindle, and I'll never, never stand it. Here's a hundred and fifty dollars, sir, and it's all you'll get—I'll swim in blood before I'll pay a cent more."

Our spirits rose and the landlord's fell—at least we thought so; he was confused, at any rate, notwithstanding he had not understood a word that had been said. He glanced from the little pile of gold pieces to Blucher several times and then went out. He must have visited an American, for when he returned, he brought back his bill translated into a language that a Christian could understand—thus:

10 dinners, 6,000 reis, or.................	$6.00
25 cigars, 2,500 reis, or...................	2.50
11 bottles wine, 13,200 reis, or............	13.20
Total 21,700 reis, or.................	$21.70

Happiness reigned once more in Blucher's dinner party. More refreshments were ordered.

6

I think the Azores must be very little known in America. Out of our whole ship's company there was not a solitary individual who knew anything whatever about them. Some of the party, well read concerning most other lands, had no other information about the Azores than that they were a group of nine or ten small islands far out in the Atlantic, something more than halfway between New York and Gibraltar. That was all. These considerations move me to put in a paragraph of dry facts just here.

The community is eminently Portuguese—that is to say, it is slow, poor, shiftless, sleepy, and lazy. There is a civil governor, appointed by the King of Portugal, and also a military governor, who can assume supreme control and suspend the civil government at his pleasure. The islands contain a population of about 200,000, almost entirely Portuguese. Everything is staid and settled, for the country was one hundred years old when Columbus discovered America. The principal crop is corn, and they raise it and grind it just as their great-great-great-grandfathers did. They plow with a board slightly shod with iron; their trifling little harrows are drawn by men and women; small windmills grind the corn, ten bushels a day, and there is one assistant superintendent to feed the mill and a general superintendent to stand by and keep him from going to sleep. When the wind changes they hitch on some donkeys and actually turn the whole upper half of the mill around until the sails are in proper position, instead of fixing the concern so that the sails could be moved instead of the mill. Oxen tread the wheat from the ear, after the fashion prevalent in the time of Methuselah. There is not a wheelbarrow in the land—they carry everything on their heads, or on donkeys, or in a wicker-bodied cart, whose wheels are solid blocks of wood and whose axles turn with the wheel. There is not a modern plow in the islands or a threshing machine. All attempts to introduce them have failed. The good Catholic Portuguese crossed himself and prayed God to shield him from all blasphemous desire to know more than his father did before him. The climate is mild; they never have snow or ice, and I saw no chimneys in the town. The donkeys and the men, women, and children of a family all eat and sleep in the same room, and are unclean, are ravaged by vermin, and are truly happy. The people lie, and cheat the stranger, and are desperately ignorant, and have hardly any reverence for their dead. The latter trait shows how little better they are than the donkeys they eat and sleep with. The only well-dressed Portuguese in the camp are the half a dozen well-to-do families, the Jesuit priests, and the soldiers of the little garrison. The wages of a laborer are twenty to twenty-four cents a day, and those of a good mechanic about twice as much. They count it in reis at a thousand to the dollar, and this makes them rich and contented. Fine grapes used to grow in the islands, and an excellent wine was made and exported. But a disease killed all the vines fifteen years ago, and since that time no wine has been made. The islands being wholly of volcanic origin, the soil is necessarily very rich. Nearly every foot of ground is under cultivation, and two or three crops a year of each article are produced, but nothing is exported save a few oranges—chiefly to England. Nobody comes here, and nobody goes away. News is a thing unknown in Fayal. A thirst for it is a passion equally unknown. A Portuguese of average intelligence inquired if our civil war was over. Because, he said, somebody had told him it was—or at least it ran in his mind that somebody had told him something like that! And when a passenger gave an officer of the garrison copies of the *Tribune,* the *Herald,* and *Times,* he was surprised to find later news in them from Lisbon than he had just received by the little monthly steamer. He was told that it came by cable. He said he knew they had tried to lay a cable ten years ago, but it had been in his mind somehow that they hadn't succeeded!

It is in communities like this that Jesuit humbuggery flourishes. We visited a Jesuit cathedral nearly two hundred years old and found in it a piece of the veritable cross upon which our Saviour was crucified. It was polished and hard, and in as excellent a state of preservation as if the dread tragedy on Calvary had occurred yesterday instead of eighteen centuries ago. But these confiding people believe in that piece of wood unhesitatingly.

In a chapel of the cathedral is an altar with facings of solid silver—at least they call it so, and I think myself it would go a couple of hundred to the ton (to speak after the fashion of the silver miners)—and before it is kept forever burning a small lamp. A devout lady who died, left money and contracted for unlimited masses for the repose of her soul, and also stipulated that this lamp should be kept lighted always, day and night. She did all this before she died, you understand. It is a very small lamp and a very dim one, and it could not work her much damage, I think, if it went out altogether.

The great altar of the cathedral and also three or four minor ones are a perfect mass of gilt gimcracks and gingerbread. And they have a swarm of rusty, dusty, battered apostles standing around the filagree work, some on one leg and some with one eye out but a gamey look in the other, and some with two or three fingers gone, and some with not enough nose left to blow—all of them crippled and discouraged, and fitter subjects for the hospital than the cathedral.

The walls of the chancel are of porcelain, all pictured over with figures of almost life size, very elegantly wrought and dressed in the fanciful costumes of two centuries ago. The design was a history of something or somebody, but none of us were learned enough to read the story. The old father, reposing under a stone close by, dated 1686, might have told us if he could have risen. But he didn't.

As we came down through the town we encountered a squad of little donkeys ready saddled for use. The saddles were peculiar, to say the least. They consisted of a sort of sawbuck with a small mattress on it, and this furniture covered about half the donkey. There were no stirrups, but really such supports were not needed—to use such a saddle was the next thing to riding a dinner table—there was ample support clear out to one's knee joints. A pack of ragged Portuguese muleteers crowded around us, offering their beasts at half a dollar an hour—more rascality to the stranger, for the market price is sixteen cents. Half a dozen of us mounted the ungainly affairs and submitted to the indignity of making a ridiculous spectacle of ourselves through the principal streets of a town of 10,000 inhabitants.

We started. It was not a trot, a gallop, or a canter, but a

stampede, and made up of all possible or conceivable gaits. No spurs were necessary. There was a muleteer to every donkey and a dozen volunteers beside, and they banged the donkeys with their goad sticks, and pricked them with their spikes, and shouted something that sounded like *"Sekki-yah!"* and kept up a din and a racket that was worse than Bedlam itself. These rascals were all on foot, but no matter, they were always up to time—they can outrun and outlast a donkey. Altogether, ours was a lively and a picturesque procession, and drew crowded audiences to the balconies wherever we went.

Blucher could do nothing at all with his donkey. The beast scampered zigzag across the road and the others ran into him; he scraped Blucher against carts and the corners of houses; the road was fenced in with high stone walls, and the donkey gave him a polishing first on one side and then on the other, but never once took the middle; he finally came to the house he was born in and darted into the parlor, scraping Blucher off at the doorway. After remounting, Blucher said to the muleteer, "Now, that's enough, you know; you go slow hereafter." But the fellow knew no English and did not understand, so he simply said, *"Sekki-yah!"* and the donkey was off again like a shot. He turned a corner suddenly, and Blucher went over his head. And, to speak truly, every mule stumbled over the two, and the whole cavalcade was piled up in a heap. No harm done. A fall from one of those donkeys is of little more consequence than rolling off a sofa. The donkeys all stood still after the catastrophe and waited for their dismembered saddles to be patched up and put on by the noisy muleteers. Blucher was pretty angry and wanted to swear, but every time he opened his mouth his animal did so also and let off a series of brays that drowned all other sounds.

It was fun, scurrying around the breezy hills and through the beautiful canyons. There was that rare thing, novelty, about it; it was a fresh, new, exhilarating sensation, this donkey riding, and worth a hundred worn and threadbare home pleasures.

The roads were a wonder, and well they might be. Here was an island with only a handful of people in it—25,000— and yet such fine roads do not exist in the United States outside of Central Park. Everywhere you go, in any direction, you find either a hard, smooth, level thoroughfare, just sprinkled with black lava sand, and bordered with little gutters neatly paved with small smooth pebbles, or compactly paved ones like Broadway. They talk much of the Russ pavement in New York, and call it a new invention—yet here they have been using it in this remote little isle of the sea for two hundred years! Every street in Horta is handsomely paved with the heavy Russ blocks, and the surface is neat and true as a floor—not marred by holes like Broadway. And every road is fenced in by tall, solid lava walls, which will last a thousand years in this land where frost is unknown. They are very thick, and are often plastered and whitewashed and capped with projecting slabs of cut stone. Trees from gardens above hang their swaying tendrils down, and contrast their bright green with the whitewash or the black lava of the walls and make them beautiful. The trees and vines stretch across these narrow roadways sometimes and so shut out the sun that you seem to be riding through a tunnel. The pavements, the roads, and the bridges are all government work.

The bridges are of a single span—a single arch—of cut stone, without a support, and paved on top with flags of lava and ornamental pebblework. Everywhere are walls, walls, walls, and all of them tasteful and handsome—and eternally substantial; and everywhere are those marvelous pavements, so neat, so smooth, and so indestructible. And if ever roads and streets and the outsides of houses were perfectly free from any sign or semblance of dirt, or dust, or mud, or uncleanliness of any kind, it is Horta, it is Fayal. The lower classes of the people, in their persons and their domiciles, are not clean—but there it stops—the town and the island are miracles of cleanliness.

We arrived home again finally, after a ten-mile excursion, and the irrepressible muleteers scampered at our heels through the main street, goading the donkeys, shouting the everlasting *"Sekki-yah,"* and singing "John Brown's Body" in ruinous English.

When we were dismounted and it came to settling, the shouting and jawing and swearing and quarreling among the muleteers and with us was nearly deafening. One fellow would demand a dollar an hour for the use of his donkey; another claimed half a dollar for pricking him up, another a quarter for helping in that service, and about fourteen guides presented bills for showing us the way through the town and its environs; and every vagrant of them was more vociferous, and more vehement and more frantic in gesture than his neighbor. We paid one guide and paid for one muleteer to each donkey.

The mountains on some of the islands are very high. We sailed along the shore of the island of Pico, under a stately green pyramid that rose up with one unbroken sweep from our very feet to an altitude of 7,613 feet, and thrust its summit above the white clouds like an island adrift in a fog!

We got plenty of fresh oranges, lemons, figs, apricots, etc., in these Azores, of course. But I will desist. I am not here to write Patent Office reports.

We are on our way to Gibraltar, and shall reach there five or six days out from the Azores.

7

A week of buffeting a tempestuous and relentless sea; a week of seasickness and deserted cabins; of lonely quarterdecks drenched with spray—spray so ambitious that it even coated the smokestacks thick with a white crust of salt to their very tops; a week of shivering in the shelter of the lifeboats and deckhouses by day and blowing suffocating "clouds" and boisterously performing at dominoes in the smoking room at night.

And the last night of the seven was the stormiest of all. There was no thunder, no noise but the pounding bows of the ship, the keen whistling of the gale through the cordage, and the rush of the seething waters. But the vessel climbed aloft as if she would climb to heaven—then paused an instant that seemed a century and plunged headlong down again, as from a precipice. The sheeted sprays drenched the decks like rain. The blackness of darkness was everywhere. At long intervals a flash of lightning clove it with a quivering line of fire that revealed a heaving world of water where was nothing before, kindled the dusky cordage to glittering silver, and lit up the faces of the men with a ghastly luster!

Fear drove many on deck that were used to avoiding the

night winds and the spray. Some thought the vessel could not
live through the night, and it seemed less dreadful to stand
out in the midst of the wild tempest and *see* the peril that
threatened than to be shut up in the sepulchral cabins, under
the dim lamps, and imagine the horrors that were abroad
on the ocean. And once out—once where they could see the
ship struggling in the strong grasp of the storm—once where
they could hear the shriek of the winds and face the driving
spray and look out upon the majestic picture the lightnings
disclosed, they were prisoners to a fierce fascination they
could not resist, and so remained. It was a wild night—and
a very, very long one.

Everybody was sent scampering to the deck at seven
o'clock this lovely morning of the thirtieth of June with the
glad news that land was in sight! It was a rare thing and a
joyful, to see *all* the ship's family abroad once more,
albeit the happiness that sat upon every countenance could
only partly conceal the ravages which that long siege of
storms had wrought there. But dull eyes soon sparkled with
pleasure, pallid cheeks flushed again, and frames weakened
by sickness gathered new life from the quickening influences of the bright, fresh morning. Yea, and from a still
more potent influence: the worn castaways were to see the
blessed land again!—and to see it was to bring back that
motherland that was in all their thoughts.

Within the hour we were fairly within the Straits of Gibraltar, the tall yellow-splotched hills of Africa on our right,
with their bases veiled in a blue haze and their summits
swathed in clouds—the same being according to Scripture,
which says that "clouds and darkness are over the land."
The words were spoken of this particular portion of Africa,
I believe. On our left were the granite-ribbed domes of old
Spain. The strait is only thirteen miles wide in its narrowest
part.

At short intervals along the Spanish shore were quaint-
looking old stone towers—Moorish, we thought—but learned
better afterwards. In former times the Morocco rascals used
to coast along the Spanish Main in their boats till a safe
opportunity seemed to present itself, and then dart in and
capture a Spanish village and carry off all the pretty women
they could find. It was a pleasant business, and was very popular. The Spaniards built these watchtowers on the hills to

enable them to keep a sharper lookout on the Moroccan speculators.

The picture on the other hand was very beautiful to eyes weary of the changeless sea, and by and by the ship's company grew wonderfully cheerful. But while we stood admiring the cloud-capped peaks and the lowlands robed in misty gloom a finer picture burst upon us and chained every eye like a magnet—a stately ship, with canvas piled on canvas till she was one towering mass of bellying sail! She came speeding over the sea like a great bird. Africa and Spain were forgotten. All homage was for the beautiful stranger. While everybody gazed she swept superbly by and flung the Stars and Stripes to the breeze! Quicker than thought, hats and handkerchiefs flashed in the air, and a cheer went up! She was beautiful before—she was radiant now. Many a one on our decks knew then for the first time how tame a sight his country's flag is at home compared to what it is in a foreign land. To see it is to see a vision of home itself and all its idols, and feel a thrill that would stir a very river of sluggish blood!

We were approaching the famed Pillars of Hercules, and already the African one, "Ape's Hill," a grand old mountain with summit streaked with granite ledges, was in sight. The other, the great Rock of Gibraltar, was yet to come. The ancients considered the Pillars of Hercules the head of navigation and the end of the world. The information the ancients didn't have was very voluminous. Even the prophets wrote book after book and epistle after epistle, yet never once hinted at the existence of a great continent on our side of the water; yet they must have known it was there, I should think.

In a few moments a lonely and enormous mass of rock, standing seemingly in the center of the wide strait and apparently washed on all sides by the sea, swung magnificently into view, and we needed no tedious traveled parrot to tell us it was Gibraltar. There could not be two rocks like that in one kingdom.

The Rock of Gibraltar is about a mile and a half long, I should say, by 1,400 to 1,500 feet high, and a quarter of a mile wide at its base. One side and one end of it come about as straight up out of the sea as the side of a house, the other end is irregular and the other side is a steep slant which an army would find very difficult to climb. At the foot of this slant is the walled town of Gibraltar—or rather the town occupies part of the slant. Everywhere—on hillside, in the precipice, by the sea, on the heights—everywhere you choose to look, Gibraltar is clad with masonry and bristling with guns. It makes a striking and lively picture from whatsoever point you contemplate it. It is pushed out into the sea on the end of a flat, narrow strip of land, and is suggestive of a "gob" of mud on the end of a shingle. A few hundred yards of this flat ground at its base belongs to the English, and then, extending across the strip from the Atlantic to the Mediterranean, a distance of a quarter of a mile, comes the "Neutral Ground," a space two or three hundred yards wide, which is free to both parties.

"Are you going through Spain to Paris?" That question was bandied about the ship day and night from Fayal to Gibraltar, and I thought I never could get so tired of hearing any one combination of words again or more tired of answering, "I don't know." At the last moment six or seven had sufficient decision of character to make up their minds to go, and did go, and I felt a sense of relief at once—it was forever too late now and I could make up my mind at my leisure not to go. I must have a prodigious quantity of mind; it takes me as much as a week sometimes to make it up.

But behold how annoyances repeat themselves. We had no sooner gotten rid of the Spain distress than the Gibraltar guides started another—a tiresome repetition of a legend that had nothing very astonishing about it, even in the first place: "That high hill yonder is called the Queen's Chair; it is because one of the queens of Spain placed her chair there when the French and Spanish troops were besieging Gibraltar, and said she would never move from the spot till the English flag was lowered from the fortresses. If the English hadn't been gallant enough to lower the flag for a few hours one day, she'd have had to break her oath or die up there."

We rode on asses and mules up the steep, narrow streets and entered the subterranean galleries the English have blasted out in the rock. These galleries are like spacious railway tunnels, and at short intervals in them great guns frown out upon sea and town through portholes five or six hundred feet above the ocean. There is a mile or so of this subterranean work, and it must have cost a vast deal of money and labor. The gallery guns command the peninsula and the harbors of both oceans, but they might as well not be there, I should think, for an army could hardly climb the perpendicular wall of the rock anyhow. Those lofty portholes afford superb views of the sea, though. At one place, where a jutting crag was hollowed out into a great chamber whose furniture was huge cannon and whose windows were portholes, a glimpse was caught of a hill not far away, and a soldier said:

"That high hill yonder is called the Queen's Chair; it is because a queen of Spain placed her chair there once when the French and Spanish troops were besieging Gibraltar, and said she would never move from the spot till the English flag was lowered from the fortresses. If the English hadn't been gallant enough to lower the flag for a few hours one day, she'd have had to break her oath or die up there."

On the topmost pinnacle of Gibraltar we halted a good while, and no doubt the mules were tired. They had a right to be. The military road was good, but rather steep, and there was a good deal of it. The view from the narrow ledge was magnificent; from it vessels seeming like the tiniest little toy boats were turned into noble ships by the telescopes, and other vessels that were fifty miles away and even sixty, they said, and invisible to the naked eye, could be clearly distinguished through those same telescopes. Below, on one side, we looked down upon an endless mass of batteries and on the other straight down to the sea.

While I was resting ever so comfortably on a rampart, and cooling my baking head in the delicious breeze, an officious guide belonging to another party came up and said:

"Señor, that high hill yonder is called the Queen's Chair—"

"Sir, I am a helpless orphan in a foreign land. Have pity on me. Don't—now *don't* inflict that most in-FERNAL old legend on me anymore today!"

There—I had used strong language after promising I would never do so again; but the provocation was more than human nature could bear. If you had been bored so, when you had the noble panorama of Spain and Africa and the blue Mediterranean spread abroad at your feet, and wanted to gaze and enjoy and surfeit yourself in its beauty in silence, you might have even burst into stronger language than I did.

Gibraltar has stood several protracted sieges, one of them of nearly four years' duration (it failed), and the English only captured it by stratagem. The wonder is that anybody should ever dream of trying so impossible a project as the taking it by assault—and yet it has been tried more than once.

The Moors held the place twelve hundred years ago, and a

staunch old castle of theirs of that date still frowns from the middle of the town, with moss-grown battlements and sides well scarred by shots fired in battles and sieges that are forgotten now. A secret chamber in the rock behind it was discovered some time ago, which contained a sword of exquisite workmanship, and some quaint old armor of a fashion that antiquaries are not acquainted with, though it is supposed to be Roman. Roman armor and Roman relics of various kinds have been found in a cave in the sea extremity of Gibraltar; history says Rome held this part of the country about the Christian era, and these things seem to confirm the statement.

In that cave also are found human bones, crusted with a very thick, stony coating, and wise men have ventured to say that those men not only lived before the flood, but as much as ten thousand years before it. It may be true—it looks reasonable enough—but as long as those parties can't vote anymore, the matter can be of no great public interest. In this cave likewise are found skeletons and fossils of animals that exist in every part of Africa, yet within memory and tradition have never existed in any portion of Spain save this lone peak of Gibraltar! So the theory is that the channel between Gibraltar and Africa was once dry land, and that the low, neutral neck between Gibraltar and the Spanish hills behind it was once ocean, and of course that these African animals, being over at Gibraltar (after rock, perhaps—there is plenty there), got closed out when the great change occurred. The hills in Africa, across the channel, are full of apes, and there are now and always have been apes on the rock of Gibraltar—but not elsewhere in Spain! The subject is an interesting one.

There is an English garrison at Gibraltar of 6,000 or 7,000 men, and so uniforms of flaming red are plenty; and red and blue, and undress costumes of snowy white, and also the queer uniform of the bare-kneed Highlander; and one sees soft-eyed Spanish girls from San Roque, and veiled Moorish beauties (I suppose they are beauties) from Tarifa, and turbaned, sashed, and trousered Moorish merchants from Fez, and long-robed, bare-legged, ragged Muhammadan vagabonds from Tetuán and Tangier, some brown, some yellow and some as black as virgin ink—and Jews from all around, in gaberdine, skullcap, and slippers, just as they are in pictures and theaters, and just as they were three thousand years ago, no doubt. You can easily understand that a tribe (somehow our pilgrims suggest that expression, because they march in a straggling procession through these foreign places with such an Indian-like air of complacency and independence about them) like ours, made up from fifteen or sixteen states of the Union, found enough to stare at in this shifting panorama of fashion today.

Speaking of our pilgrims reminds me that we have one or two people among us who are sometimes an annoyance. However, I do not count the Oracle in that list. I will explain that the Oracle is an innocent old ass who eats for four and looks wiser than the whole Academy of France would have any right to look, and never uses a one-syllable word when he can think of a longer one, and never by any possible chance knows the meaning of any long word he uses or ever gets it in the right place; yet he will serenely venture an opinion on the most abstruse subject and back it up complacently with quotations from authors who never existed, and finally when cornered will slide to the other side of the question, say he has been there all the time, and come back at you with your own spoken arguments, only with the big words all tangled, and play them in your very teeth as original with himself. He reads a chapter in the guidebooks, mixes the facts all up, with his bad memory, and then goes off to inflict the whole mess on somebody as wisdom which has been festering in his brain for years and which he gathered in college from erudite authors who are dead now and out of print. This morning at breakfast he pointed out of the window and said:

"Do you see that there hill out there on that African coast? It's one of them Pillows of Herkewls, I should say—and there's the ultimate one alongside of it."

"The ultimate one—that is a good word—but the pillars are not both on the same side of the strait." (I saw he had been deceived by a carelessly written sentence in the guidebook.)

"Well, it ain't for you to say, nor for me. Some authors states it that way, and some states it different. Old Gibbons don't say nothing about it—just shirks it complete—Gibbons always done that when he got stuck—but there is Rolampton, what does *he* say? Why, he says that they was both on the same side, and Trinculian, and Sobaster, and Syraccus, and Langomarganbl——"

"Oh, that will do—that's enough. If you have got your

hand in for inventing authors and testimony, I have nothing more to say—let them *be* on the same side."

We don't mind the Oracle. We rather like him. We can tolerate the Oracle very easily, but we have a poet and a good-natured enterprising idiot on board, and they *do* distress the company. The one gives copies of his verses to consuls, commanders, hotel keepers, Arabs, Dutch—to anybody, in fact, who will submit to a grievous infliction most kindly meant. His poetry is all very well on shipboard, notwithstanding when he wrote an "Ode to the Ocean in a Storm" in one half hour, and an "Apostrophe to the Rooster in the Waist of the Ship" in the next, the transition was considered to be rather abrupt; but when he sends an invoice of rhymes to the Governor of Fayal and another to the commander in chief and other dignitaries in Gibraltar with the compliments of the Laureate of the Ship, it is not popular with the passengers.

The other personage I have mentioned is young and green, and not bright, not learned, and not wise. He will be, though, someday if he recollects the answers to all his questions. He is known about the ship as the "Interrogation Point," and this by constant use has become shortened to "Interrogation." He has distinguished himself twice already. In Fayal they pointed out a hill and told him it was 800 feet high and 1,100 feet long. And they told him there was a tunnel 2,000 feet long and 1,000 feet high running through the hill, from end to end. He believed it. He repeated it to everybody, discussed it, and read it from his notes. Finally, he took a useful hint from this remark, which a thoughtful old pilgrim made:

"Well, yes, it *is* a little remarkable—singular tunnel altogether—stands up out of the top of the hill about two hundred feet, and one end of it sticks out of the hill about nine hundred!"

Here in Gibraltar he corners these educated British officers and badgers them with braggadocio about America and the wonders she can perform. He told one of them a couple of our gunboats could come here and knock Gibraltar into the Mediterranean Sea!

At this present moment half a dozen of us are taking a private pleasure excursion of our own devising. We form rather more than half the list of white passengers on board a small steamer bound for the venerable Moorish town of Tangier, Africa. Nothing could be more absolutely certain than that we are enjoying ourselves. One can not do otherwise who speeds over these sparkling waters and breathes the soft atmosphere of this sunny land. Care cannot assail us here. We are out of its jurisdiction.

We even steamed recklessly by the frowning fortress of Malabat (a stronghold of the Emperor of Morocco) without a twinge of fear. The whole garrison turned out under arms and assumed a threatening attitude—yet still we did not fear. The entire garrison marched and counter-marched within the rampart, in full view—yet notwithstanding even this, we never flinched.

I suppose we really do not know what fear is. I inquired the name of the garrison of the fortress of Malabat, and they said it was Mehemet Ali Ben Sancom. I said it would be a good idea to get some more garrisons to help him; but they said no, he had nothing to do but hold the place, and he was competent to do that, had done it two years already. That was evidence which one could not well refute. There is nothing like reputation.

Every now and then my glove purchase in Gibraltar last night intrudes itself upon me. Dan and the ship's surgeon and I had been up to the great square, listening to the music of the fine military bands and contemplating English and Spanish female loveliness and fashion, and at nine o'clock were on our way to the theater, when we met the General, the Judge, the Commodore, the Colonel, and the Commissioner of the United States of America to Europe, Asia, and Africa, who had been to the Club House to register their several titles and impoverish the bill of fare; and they told us to go over to the little variety store near the Hall of Justice and buy some kid gloves. They said they were elegant and very moderate in price. It seemed a stylish thing to go to the theater in kid gloves, and we acted upon the hint. A very handsome young lady in the store offered me a pair of blue gloves. I did not want blue, but she said they would look very pretty on a hand like mine. The remark touched me tenderly. I glanced furtively at my hand, and somehow it did seem rather a comely member. I tried a glove on my left and blushed a little. Manifestly the size was too small for me. But I felt gratified when she said:

"Oh, it is just right!" Yet I knew it was no such thing.

I tugged at it diligently, but it was discouraging work. She said:

"Ah! I see *you* are accustomed to wearing kid gloves—but some gentlemen are *so* awkward about putting them on."

It was the last compliment I had expected. I only understand putting on the buckskin article perfectly. I made another effort and tore the glove from the base of the thumb into the palm of the hand—and tried to hide the rent. She kept up her compliments, and I kept up my determination to deserve them or die:

"Ah, you have had experience! [A rip down the back of the hand.] They are just right for you—your hand is very small—if they tear you need not pay for them. [A rent across the middle.] I can always tell when a gentleman understands putting on kid gloves. There is a grace about it that only comes with long practice." The whole afterguard of the glove "fetched away," as the sailors say, the fabric parted across the knuckles, and nothing was left but a melancholy ruin.

I was too much flattered to make an exposure and throw the merchandise on the angel's hands. I was hot, vexed, confused, but still happy; but I hated the other boys for taking such an absorbing interest in the proceedings. I wished they were in Jericho. I felt exquisitely mean when I said cheerfully:

"This one does very well; it fits elegantly. I like a glove that fits. No, never mind, ma'am, never mind; I'll put the other on in the street. It is warm here."

It *was* warm. It was the warmest place I ever was in. I paid the bill, and as I passed out with a fascinating bow I thought I detected a light in the woman's eye that was gently ironical; and when I looked back from the street, and she was laughing all to herself about something or other, I said to myself with withering sarcasm, "Oh, certainly; *you* know how to put on kid gloves, don't you? A self-complacent ass, ready to be flattered out of your senses by every petticoat that chooses to take the trouble to do it!"

The silence of the boys annoyed me. Finally Dan said musingly:

"Some gentlemen don't know how to put on kid gloves at all, but some do."

And the doctor said (to the moon, I thought):

"But it is always easy to tell when a gentleman is used to putting on kid gloves."

Dan soliloquized after a pause:

"Ah, yes; there is a grace about it that only comes with long, very long practice."

"Yes, indeed, I've noticed that when a man hauls on a kid glove like he was dragging a cat out of an ash hole by the tail, *he* understands putting on kid gloves; *he's* had ex——"

"Boys, enough of a thing's enough! You think you are very smart, I suppose, but I don't. And if you go and tell any of those old gossips in the ship about this thing, I'll never forgive you for it; that's all."

They let me alone then for the time being. We always let each other alone in time to prevent ill feeling from spoiling a joke. But they had bought gloves, too, as I did. We threw all the purchases away together this morning. They were coarse, unsubstantial, freckled all over with broad yellow splotches, and could neither stand wear nor public exhibition. We had entertained an angel unawares, but we did not take her in. She did that for us.

Tangier! A tribe of stalwart Moors are wading into the sea to carry us ashore on their backs from the small boats.

8

This is royal! Let those who went up through Spain make the best of it—these dominions of the Emperor of Morocco suit our little party well enough. We have had enough of Spain at Gibraltar for the present. Tangier is the spot we have been longing for all the time. Elsewhere we have found foreign-looking things and foreign-looking people, but always with things and people intermixed that we were familiar with before, and so the novelty of the situation lost a deal of its force. We wanted something thoroughly and uncompromisingly foreign—foreign from top to bottom—foreign from center to circumference—foreign inside and outside and all

around—nothing anywhere about it to dilute its foreign-ness
—nothing to remind us of any other people or any other
land under the sun. And lo! In Tangier we have found it.
Here is not the slightest thing that ever we have seen save
in pictures—and we always mistrusted the pictures before.
We cannot anymore. The pictures used to seem exaggerations
—they seemed too weird and fanciful for reality. But behold, they were not wild enough—they were not fanciful
enough—they have not told half the story. Tangier is a
foreign land if ever there was one, and the true spirit of it
can never be found in any book save *The Arabian Nights*.
Here are no white men visible, yet swarms of humanity are
all about us. Here is a packed and jammed city enclosed in
a massive stone wall which is more than a thousand years
old. All the houses nearly are one- and two-story, made
of thick walls of stone, plastered outside, square as a dry-
goods box, flat as a floor on top, no cornices, whitewashed all
over—a crowded city of snowy tombs! And the doors are
arched with the peculiar arch we see in Moorish pictures;
the floors are laid in varicolored diamond flags; in tessellated,
many-colored porcelain squares wrought in the furnaces of
Fez; in red tiles and broad bricks that time cannot wear;
there is no furniture in the rooms (of Jewish dwellings) save
divans—what there is in Moorish ones no man may know;
within their sacred walls no Christian dog can enter. And
the streets are oriental—some of them three feet wide, some
six, but only two that are over a dozen; a man can blockade
the most of them by extending his body across them. Isn't
it an oriental picture?

There are stalwart Bedouins of the desert here, and stately
Moors proud of a history that goes back to the night of
time; and Jews whose fathers fled hither centuries upon centuries ago; and swarthy Riffians from the mountains—born
cutthroats—and original, genuine Negroes as black as Moses;
and howling dervishes and a hundred breeds of Arabs—all
sorts and descriptions of people that are foreign and curious
to look upon.

And their dresses are strange beyond all description. Here
is a bronzed Moor in a prodigious white turban, curiously
embroidered jacket, gold and crimson sash, of many folds,
wrapped round and round his waist, trousers that only come
a little below his knee and yet have twenty yards of stuff in
them, ornamented scimitar, bare shins, stockingless feet,

yellow slippers, and gun of preposterous length—a mere soldier!—I thought he was the Emperor at least. And here are aged Moors with flowing white beards and long white robes with vast cowls; and Bedouins with long, cowled, striped cloaks; and Negroes and Riffians with heads clean-shaven except a kinky scalp lock back of the ear or, rather, upon the aftercorner of the skull; and all sorts of barbarians in all sorts of weird costumes, and all more or less ragged. And here are Moorish women who are enveloped from head to foot in coarse white robes, and whose sex can only be determined by the fact that they only leave one eye visible and never look at men of their own race, or are looked at by them in public. Here are five thousand Jews in blue gaberdines, sashes about their waists, slippers upon their feet, little skullcaps upon the backs of their heads, hair combed down on the forehead, and cut straight across the middle of it from side to side—the selfsame fashion their Tangier ancestors have worn for I don't know how many bewildering centuries. Their feet and ankles are bare. Their noses are all hooked, and hooked alike. They all resemble each other so much that one could almost believe they were of one family. Their women are plump and pretty, and do smile upon a Christian in a way which is in the last degree comforting.

What a funny old town it is! It seems like profanation to laugh and jest and bandy the frivolous chat of our day amid its hoary relics. Only the stately phraseology and the measured speech of the sons of the Prophet are suited to a venerable antiquity like this. Here is a crumbling wall that was old when Columbus discovered America; was old when Peter the Hermit roused the knightly men of the Middle Ages to arm for the first Crusade; was old when Charlemagne and his paladins beleaguered enchanted castles and battled with giants and genii in the fabled days of the olden time; was old when Christ and his disciples walked the earth; stood where it stands today when the lips of Memnon were vocal and men bought and sold in the streets of ancient Thebes!

The Phoenicians, the Carthagenians, the English, Moors, Romans, all have battled for Tangier—all have won it and lost it. Here is a ragged, oriental-looking Negro from some desert place in interior Africa, filling his goatskin with water from a stained and battered fountain built by the Romans twelve hundred years ago. Yonder is a ruined arch of a bridge built by Julius Caesar nineteen hundred years ago. Men who had seen the infant Saviour in the Virgin's arms have stood upon it, maybe.

Near it are the ruins of a dockyard where Caesar repaired his ships and loaded them with grain when he invaded Britain, fifty years before the Christian era.

Here, under the quiet stars, these old streets seem thronged with the phantoms of forgotten ages. My eyes are resting upon a spot where stood a monument which was seen and described by Roman historians less than two thousand years ago, whereon was inscribed:

WE ARE THE CANAANITES. WE ARE THEY THAT HAVE BEEN DRIVEN OUT OF THE LAND OF CANAAN BY THE JEWISH ROBBER, JOSHUA.

Joshua drove them out, and they came here. Not many leagues from here is a tribe of Jews whose ancestors fled thither after an unsuccessful revolt against King David, and these their descendants are still under a ban and keep to themselves.

Tangier has been mentioned in history for three thousand years. And it was a town, though a queer one, when Hercules, clad in his lion skin, landed here, four thousand years ago. In these streets he met Anitus, the king of the country, and brained him with his club, which was the fashion among gentlemen in those days. The people of Tangier (called Tingis then) lived in the rudest possible huts and dressed in skins and carried clubs, and were as savage as the wild beasts they were constantly obliged to war with. But they were a gentlemanly race and did no work. They lived on the natural products of the land. Their king's country residence was at the famous Garden of Hesperides, seventy miles down the coast from here. The garden, with its golden apples (oranges), is gone now—no vestige of it remains. Antiquarians concede that such a personage as Hercules did exist in ancient times and agree that he was an enterprising and energetic man, but decline to believe him a good, bona-fide god, because that would be unconstitutional.

Down here at Cape Spartel is the celebrated cave of Hercules, where that hero took refuge when he was vanquished and driven out of the Tangier country. It is full of inscriptions in the dead languages, which fact makes me think Hercules could not have traveled much, else he would not have kept a journal.

Five days' journey from here—say two hundred miles—are the ruins of an ancient city, of whose history there is neither record nor tradition. And yet its arches, its columns, and its statues proclaim it to have been built by an enlightened race.

The general size of a store in Tangier is about that of an ordinary shower bath in a civilized land. The Muhammadan merchant, tinman, shoemaker, or vendor of trifles sits cross-legged on the floor and reaches after any article you may want to buy. You can rent a whole block of these pigeon-holes for fifty dollars a month. The market people crowd the marketplace with their baskets of figs, dates, melons, apricots, etc., and among them file trains of laden asses, not much larger, if any, than a Newfoundland dog. The scene is lively, is picturesque, and smells like a police court. The Jewish money-changers have their dens close at hand, and all day long are counting bronze coins and transferring them from one bushel basket to another. They don't coin much money nowadays, I think. I saw none but what was dated four or five hundred years back, and was badly worn and battered. These coins are not very valuable. Jack went out to get a napoleon changed, so as to have money suited to the general cheapness of things, and came back and said he had "swamped the bank, had bought eleven quarts of coin, and the head of the firm had gone on the street to negotiate for the balance of the change." I bought nearly half a pint of their money for a shilling myself. I am not proud on account of having so much money, though. I care nothing for wealth.

The Moors have some small silver coins and also some silver slugs worth a dollar each. The latter are exceedingly scarce—so much so that when poor ragged Arabs see one they beg to be allowed to kiss it.

They have also a small gold coin worth two dollars. And that reminds me of something. When Morocco is in a state of war, Arab couriers carry letters through the country and charge a liberal postage. Every now and then they fall into the hands of marauding bands and get robbed. Therefore, warned by experience, as soon as they have collected two dollars' worth of money they exchange it for one of those little gold pieces, and when robbers come upon them, swallow it. The stratagem was good while it was unsuspected, but after that the marauders simply gave the sagacious United States mail an emetic and sat down to wait.

The Emperor of Morocco is a soulless despot, and the great officers under him are despots on a smaller scale. There is no regular system of taxation, but when the Emperor or the Bashaw want money, they levy on some rich man, and he has to furnish the cash or go to prison. Therefore, few men in Morocco dare to be rich. It is too dangerous a luxury. Vanity occasionally leads a man to display wealth, but sooner or later the Emperor trumps up a charge against him—any sort of one will do—and confiscates his property. Of course, there are many rich men in the empire, but their money is buried, and they dress in rags and counterfeit poverty. Every now and then the Emperor imprisons a man who is suspected of the crime of being rich, and makes things so uncomfortable for him that he is forced to discover where he has hidden his money.

Moors and Jews sometimes place themselves under the protection of the foreign consuls, and then they can flout their riches in the Emperor's face with impunity.

9

About the first adventure we had yesterday afternoon, after landing here, came near finishing that heedless Blucher. We had just mounted some mules and asses and started out under the guardianship of the stately, the princely, the magnificent Hadji Muhammad Lamarty (may his tribe increase!) when we came upon a fine Moorish mosque, with tall tower, rich with checkerwork of many-colored porcelain, and every part and portion of the edifice adorned with the quaint architecture of the Alhambra, and Blucher started to ride into the open doorway. A startling "Hi-hi!" from our camp followers and a loud "Halt!" from an English gentleman in the party checked the adventurer, and then we were in-

formed that so dire a profanation is it for a Christian dog
to set foot upon the sacred threshold of a Moorish mosque
that no amount of purification can ever make it fit for the
faithful to pray in again. Had Blucher succeeded in entering
the place, he would no doubt have been chased through the
town and stoned; and the time has been, and not many
years ago, either, when a Christian would have been most
ruthlessly slaughtered if captured in a mosque. We caught
a glimpse of the handsome tessellated pavements within and
of the devotees performing their ablutions at the fountains,
but even that we took that glimpse was a thing not relished
by the Moorish bystanders.

Some years ago the clock in the tower of the mosque got
out of order. The Moors of Tangier have so degenerated that
it has been long since there was an artificer among them
capable of curing so delicate a patient as a debilitated clock.
The great men of the city met in solemn conclave to consider how the difficulty was to be met. They discussed the
matter thoroughly but arrived at no solution. Finally, a
patriarch arose and said:

"Oh, children of the Prophet, it is known unto you that a
Portuguee dog of a Christian clock mender pollutes the city
of Tangier with his presence. Ye know, also, that when
mosques are builded, asses bear the stones and the cement,
and cross the sacred threshold. Now, therefore, send the
Christian dog on all fours, and barefoot, into the holy place
to mend the clock, and let him go as an ass!"

And in that way it was done. Therefore, if Blucher ever
sees the inside of a mosque, he will have to cast aside his
humanity and go in his natural character. We visited the
jail and found Moorish prisoners making mats and baskets.
(This thing of utilizing crime savors of civilization.) Murder
is punished with death. A short time ago three murderers
were taken beyond the city walls and shot. Moorish guns are
not good, and neither are Moorish marksmen. In this instance they set up the poor criminals at long range, like so
many targets, and practiced on them—kept them hopping
about and dodging bullets for half an hour before they
managed to drive the center.

When a man steals cattle, they cut off his right hand and
left leg and nail them up in the marketplace as a warning to
everybody. Their surgery is not artistic. They slice around
the bone a little, then break off the limb. Sometimes the

patient gets well; but, as a general thing, he don't. However, the Moorish heart is stout. The Moors were always brave. These criminals undergo the fearful operation without a wince, without a tremor of any kind, without a groan! No amount of suffering can bring down the pride of a Moor or make him shame his dignity with a cry.

Here, marriage is contracted by the parents of the parties to it. There are no valentines, no stolen interviews, no riding out, no courting in dim parlors, no lovers' quarrels and reconciliations—no nothing that is proper to approaching matrimony. The young man takes the girl his father selects for him, marries her, and after that she is unveiled, and he sees her for the first time. If after due acquaintance she suits him, he retains her; but if he suspects her purity, he bundles her back to her father; if he finds her diseased, the same; or if, after just and reasonable time is allowed her, she neglects to bear children, back she goes to the home of her childhood.

Muhammadans here who can afford it keep a good many wives on hand. They are called wives, though I believe the Koran only allows four genuine wives—the rest are concubines. The Emperor of Morocco don't know how many wives he has, but thinks he has five hundred. However, that is near enough—a dozen or so, one way or the other, don't matter.

Even the Jews in the interior have a plurality of wives.

I have caught a glimpse of the faces of several Moorish women (for they are only human, and will expose their faces for the admiration of a Christian dog when no male Moor is by), and I am full of veneration for the wisdom that leads them to cover up such atrocious ugliness.

They carry their children at their backs, in a sack, like other savages the world over.

Many of the Negroes are held in slavery by the Moors. But the moment a female slave becomes her master's concubine her bonds are broken, and as soon as a male slave can read the first chapter of the Koran (which contains the creed) he can no longer be held in bondage.

They have three Sundays a week in Tangier. The Muhammadans' comes on Friday, the Jews' on Saturday, and that of the Christian Consuls on Sunday. The Jews are the most radical. The Moor goes to his mosque about noon on his Sabbath, as on any other day, removes his shoes at the door, performs his ablutions, makes his salaams, pressing his fore-head to the pavement time and again, says his prayers, and goes back to his work.

But the Jew shuts up shop; will not touch copper or bronze money at all; soils his fingers with nothing meaner than silver and gold; attends the synagogue devoutly; will not cook or have anything to do with fire; and religiously re-frains from embarking in any enterprise.

The Moor who has made a pilgrimage to Mecca is entitled to high distinction. Men call him Hadji, and he is thence-forward a great personage. Hundreds of Moors come to Tangier every year and embark for Mecca. They go part of the way in English steamers, and the ten or twelve dol-lars they pay for passage is about all the trip costs. They take with them a quantity of food, and when the commissary department fails they "skirmish," as Jack terms it in his sin-ful, slangy way. From the time they leave till they get home again, they never wash, either on land or sea. They are usually gone from five to seven months, and as they do not change their clothes during all that time, they are totally unfit for the drawing room when they get back.

Many of them have to rake and scrape a long time to gather together the ten dollars their steamer passage costs, and when one of them gets back he is a bankrupt forever after. Few Moors can ever build up their fortunes again in one short lifetime after so reckless an outlay. In order to con-fine the dignity of Hadji to gentlemen of patrician blood and possessions, the Emperor decreed that no man should make the pilgrimage save bloated aristocrats who were worth a hundred dollars in specie. But behold how iniquity can circumvent the law! For a consideration, the Jewish money-changer lends the pilgrim one hundred dollars long enough for him to swear himself through, and then receives it back before the ship sails out of the harbor!

Spain is the only nation the Moors fear. The reason is that Spain sends her heaviest ships of war and her loudest guns to astonish these Muslims, while America and other nations send only a little contemptible tub of a gunboat occa-sionally. The Moors, like other savages, learn by what they see, not what they hear or read. We have great fleets in the Mediterranean, but they seldom touch at African ports. The Moors have a small opinion of England, France, and America, and put their representatives to a deal of red-tape circumlocution before they grant them their common rights, let alone a favor. But the moment the Spanish minister makes a demand, it is acceded to at once, whether it be just or not.

Spain chastised the Moors five or six years ago, about a disputed piece of property opposite Gibraltar, and captured the city of Tetuán. She compromised on an augmentation of her territory, twenty million dollars' indemnity in money, and peace. And then she gave up the city. But she never gave it up until the Spanish soldiers had eaten up all the cats. They would not compromise as long as the cats held out. Spaniards are very fond of cats. On the contrary, the Moors reverence cats as something sacred. So the Spaniards touched them on a tender point that time. Their unfeline conduct in eating up all the Tetuán cats aroused a hatred toward them in the breasts of the Moors, to which even the driving them out of Spain was tame and passionless. Moors and Spaniards are foes forever now. France had a minister here once who embittered the nation against him in the most innocent way. He killed a couple of battalions of cats (Tangier is full of them) and made a parlor carpet out of their hides. He made his carpet in circles—first a circle of old gray tomcats, with their tails all pointing toward the center; then a circle of yellow cats; next a circle of black cats and a circle of white ones; then a circle of all sorts of cats; and, finally, a centerpiece of assorted kittens. It was very beautiful, but the Moors curse his memory to this day.

When we went to call on our American Consul General today I noticed that all possible games for parlor amusement seemed to be represented on his center tables. I thought that hinted at lonesomeness. The idea was correct. His is the only American family in Tangier. There are many foreign consuls in this place, but much visiting is not indulged in. Tangier is clear out of the world, and what is the use of visiting when people have nothing on earth to talk about? There is none. So each consul's family stays at home chiefly and amuses itself as best it can. Tangier is full of interest for one day, but after that it is a weary prison. The Consul General has been here five years, and has got enough of it to do him for a century, and is going home shortly. His family seize upon their letters and papers when the mail arrives, read them over and over again for two days or three, talk them over and over again for two or three more till they wear them out, and after that for days together they eat and drink and sleep, and ride out over the same old road, and see the same old tiresome things that even decades of centuries have scarcely changed, and say never a single word! They have literally nothing whatever to talk about. The arrival of an American man-of-war is a godsend to them. "O Solitude, where are the charms which sages have seen in thy face?" It is the completest exile that I can conceive of. I would seriously recommend to the government of the United States that when a man commits a crime so heinous that the law provides no adequate punishment for it, they make him Consul General to Tangier.

I am glad to have seen Tangier—the second-oldest town in the world. But I am ready to bid it good-bye, I believe.

We shall go hence to Gibraltar this evening or in the morning, and doubtless the *Quaker City* will sail from that port within the next forty-eight hours.

10

We passed the Fourth of July on board the *Quaker City*, in midocean. It was in all respects a characteristic Mediterranean day—faultlessly beautiful. A cloudless sky; a refreshing summer wind; a radiant sunshine that glinted cheerily from dancing wavelets instead of crested mountains of water; a sea beneath us that was so wonderfully blue, so richly, brilliantly blue, that it overcame the dullest sensibilities with the spell of its fascination.

They even have fine sunsets on the Mediterranean—a thing that is certainly rare in most quarters of the globe. The evening we sailed away from Gibraltar, that hard-featured rock was swimming in a creamy mist so rich, so soft, so enchantingly vague and dreamy, that even the Oracle, that serene, that inspired, that overpowering humbug, scorned the dinner gong and tarried to worship!

He said: "Well, that's gorgis, ain't it! They don't have none of them things in our parts, *do* they? I consider that them effects is on account of the superior refragability, as you may say, of the sun's diramic combination with the lymphatic forces of the perihelion of Jubiter. What should you think?"

"Oh, *go* to bed!" Dan said that and went away.

"Oh, yes, it's all very well to say go to bed when a man makes an argument which another man can't answer. Dan don't never stand any chance in an argument with me. And he knows it, too. What should you say, Jack?"

"Now, Doctor, don't you come bothering around me with that dictionary bosh. I don't do you any harm, do I? Then you let *me* alone."

"He's gone, too. Well, them fellows have all tackled the old Oracle, as they say, but the old man's most too many for 'em. Maybe the Poet Lariat ain't satisfied with them deductions?"

The poet replied with a barbarous rhyme and went below.

" 'Pears that *he* can't qualify, neither. Well, I didn't expect nothing out of *him*. I never see one of them poets yet that knowed anything. He'll go down now and grind out about four reams of the awfullest slush about that old rock and give it to a consul, or a pilot, or a nigger, or anybody he comes across first which he can impose on. Pity but somebody'd take that poor old lunatic and dig all that poetry rubbage out of him. Why can't a man put his intellect onto things that's some value? Gibbons, and Hippocratus, and Sarcophagus, and all them old ancient philosophers was down on poets——"

"Doctor," I said, "you are going to invent authorities now and I'll leave you, too. I always enjoy your conversation, notwithstanding the luxuriance of your syllables, when the philosophy you offer rests on your own responsibility; but when you begin to soar—when you begin to support it with the evidence of authorities who are the creations of your own fancy—I lose confidence."

That was the way to flatter the doctor. He considered it a sort of acknowledgment on my part of a fear to argue with him. He was always persecuting the passengers with abstruse propositions framed in language that no man could understand, and they endured the exquisite torture a minute or two and then abandoned the field. A triumph like this over half a dozen antagonists was sufficient for one day; from that time forward he would patrol the decks beaming blandly upon all comers, and so tranquilly, blissfully happy!

But I digress. The thunder of our two brave cannon announced the Fourth of July, at daylight, to all who were awake. But many of us got our information at a later hour, from the almanac. All the flags were sent aloft except half a dozen that were needed to decorate portions of the ship below, and in a short time the vessel assumed a holiday appearance. During the morning, meetings were held and all manner of committees set to work on the celebration ceremonies. In the afternoon the ship's company assembled aft, on deck, under the awnings; the flute, the asthmatic melodeon, and the consumptive clarinet crippled "The Star-Spangled Banner," the choir chased it to cover, and George came in with a peculiarly lacerating screech on the final note and slaughtered it. Nobody mourned.

We carried out the corpse on three cheers (that joke was not intentional and I do not endorse it), and then the President, throned behind a cable locker with a national flag spread over it, announced the "Reader," who rose up and read that same old Declaration of Independence which we have all listened to so often without paying any attention to what it said; and after that the President piped the Orator of the Day to quarters and he made that same old speech about our national greatness which we so religiously believe and so fervently applaud. Now came the choir into court again, with the complaining instruments, and assaulted "Hail Columbia"; and when victory hung wavering in the scale, George returned with his dreadful wild-goose stop turned on and the choir won, of course. A minister pronounced the benediction, and the patriotic little gathering disbanded. The Fourth of July was safe, as far as the Mediterranean was concerned.

At dinner in the evening, a well-written original poem was recited with spirit by one of the ship's captains, and thirteen regular toasts were washed down with several baskets of champagne. The speeches were bad—execrable almost without exception. In fact, without *any* exception but one. Captain Duncan made a good speech; he made the only good speech of the evening. He said:

"Ladies and gentlemen: May we all live to a green old age and be prosperous and happy. Steward, bring up another basket of champagne."

It was regarded as a very able effort.

The festivities, so to speak, closed with another of those miraculous balls on the promenade deck. We were not used to dancing on an even keel, though, and it was only a questionable success. But take it all together, it was a bright, cheerful, pleasant Fourth.

Toward nightfall the next evening, we steamed into the great artificial harbor of this noble city of Marseilles, and saw the dying sunlight gild its clustering spires and ramparts, and flood its leagues of environing verdure with a mellow radiance that touched with an added charm the white villas that flecked the landscape far and near. [Copyright secured according to law.]

There were no stages out, and we could not get on the pier from the ship. It was annoying. We were full of enthusiasm—we wanted to see France! Just at nightfall our party of three contracted with a waterman for the privilege of using his boat as a bridge—its stern was at our companion ladder and its bow touched the pier. We got in and the fellow backed out into the harbor. I told him in French that all we wanted was to walk over his thwarts and step ashore, and asked him what he went away out there for. He said he could not understand me. I repeated. Still he could not understand. He appeared to be very ignorant of French. The doctor tried him, but he could not understand the doctor. I asked this boatman to explain his conduct, which he did; and then I couldn't understand *him*. Dan said:

"Oh, go to the pier, you old fool—that's where we want to go!"

We reasoned calmly with Dan that it was useless to speak to this foreigner in English—that he had better let us conduct this business in the French language and not let the stranger see how uncultivated he was.

"Well, go on, go on," he said, "don't mind me. I don't wish to interfere. Only, if you go on telling him in your kind of French, he never will find out where we want to go to. That is what I think about it."

We rebuked him severely for this remark and said we never knew an ignorant person yet but was prejudiced. The Frenchman spoke again, and the doctor said:

"There now, Dan, he says he is going to *allez* to the *douain*. Means he is going to the hotel. Oh, certainly—*we* don't know the French language."

This was a crusher, as Jack would say. It silenced further

criticism from the disaffected member. We coasted past the sharp bows of a navy of great steamships and stopped at last at a government building on a stone pier. It was easy to remember then that the *douain* was the customhouse and not the hotel. We did not mention it, however. With winning French politeness the officers merely opened and closed our satchels, declined to examine our passports, and sent us on our way. We stopped at the first café we came to and entered. An old woman seated us at a table and waited for orders. The doctor said:

"*Avez-vous du vin?*"

The dame looked perplexed. The doctor said again, with elaborate distinctness of articulation:

"*Avez-vous du—vin!*"

The dame looked more perplexed than before. I said:

"Doctor, there is a flaw in your pronunciation somewhere. Let me try her. *Madame, avez-vous du vin?* It isn't any use, Doctor—take the witness."

"*Madame, avez-vous du vin—ou fromage—pain*—pickled pigs' feet—*beurre—des œufs—du bœuf*—horseradish, sauerkraut, hog and hominy—anything, *anything* in the world that can stay a Christian stomach!"

She said:

"Bless you, why didn't you speak English before? I don't know anything about your plagued French!"

The humiliating taunts of the disaffected member spoiled the supper, and we dispatched it in angry silence and got away as soon as we could. Here we were in beautiful France —in a vast stone house of quaint architecture—surrounded by all manner of curiously worded French signs—stared at by strangely habited, bearded French people—everything gradually and surely forcing upon us the coveted consciousness that at last, and beyond all question, we *were* in beautiful France and absorbing its nature to the forgetfulness of everything else, and coming to feel the happy romance of the thing in all its enchanting delightfulness—and to think of this skinny veteran intruding with her vile English, at such a moment, to blow the fair vision to the winds! It was exasperating.

We set out to find the center of the city, inquiring the direction every now and then. We never did succeed in making anybody understand just exactly what we wanted, and neither did we ever succeed in comprehending just exactly what they said in reply, but then they always pointed —they always did that—and we bowed politely and said, "Merci, monsieur," and so it was a blighting triumph over the disaffected member anyway. He was restive under these victories and often asked:

"What did that pirate say?"

"Why, he told us which way to go to find the Grand Casino."

"Yes, but what did he *say?*"

"Oh, it don't matter what he said—*we* understood him. These are educated people—not like that absurd boatman."

"Well, I wish they were educated enough to tell a man a direction that goes *some*where—for we've been going around in a circle for an hour. I've passed this same old drugstore seven times."

We said it was a low, disreputable falsehood (but we knew it was not). It was plain that it would not do to pass that drugstore again, though—we might go on asking directions, but we must cease from following finger-pointings if we hoped to check the suspicions of the disaffected member.

A long walk through smooth, asphaltum-paved streets bordered by blocks of vast new mercantile houses of cream-colored stone—every house and every block precisely like all the other houses and all the other blocks for a mile, and all brilliantly lighted—brought us at last to the principal thoroughfare. On every hand were bright colors, flashing constellations of gas burners, gaily dressed men and women thronging the sidewalks—hurry, life, activity, cheerfulness, conversation, and laughter everywhere! We found the Grand Hotel du Louvre et de la Paix, and wrote down who we were, where we were born, what our occupations were, the place we came from last, whether we were married or single, how we liked it, how old we were, where we were bound for and when we expected to get there, and a great deal of information of similar importance—all for the benefit of the landlord and the secret police. We hired a guide and began the business of sightseeing immediately. That first night on French soil was a stirring one. I cannot think of half the places we went to or what we particularly saw; we had no disposition to examine carefully into anything at all—we only wanted to glance and go—to move, keep moving! The spirit of the country was upon us. We sat down, finally, at a late hour, in the great Casino, and called for unstinted champagne. It is so easy to be bloated aristocrats where it costs nothing of consequence! There were about five hundred people in that dazzling place, I suppose, though the walls being papered entirely with mirrors, so to speak, one could not really tell but that there were a hundred thousand. Young, daintily dressed exquisites and young, stylishly dressed women, and also old gentlemen and old ladies, sat in couples and groups about innumerable marble-topped tables and ate fancy suppers, drank wine, and kept up a chattering din of conversation that was dazing to the senses. There was a stage at the far end and a large orchestra; and every now and then actors and actresses in preposterous comic dresses came out and sang the most extravagantly funny songs, to judge by their absurd actions; but that audience merely suspended its chatter, stared cynically, and never once smiled, never once applauded! I had always thought that Frenchmen were ready to laugh at anything.

11

We are getting foreignized rapidly and with facility. We are getting reconciled to halls and bedchambers with unhomelike stone floors and no carpets—floors that ring to the tread of one's heels with a sharpness that is death to sentimental musing. We are getting used to tidy, noiseless waiters, who glide hither and thither, and hover about your back and your elbows like butterflies, quick to comprehend orders, quick to fill them; thankful for a gratuity without regard to the amount; and always polite—never otherwise than polite. That is the strangest curiosity yet—a really polite hotel waiter who isn't an idiot. We are getting used to driving right into the central court of the hotel, in the midst of a fragrant circle of vines and flowers, and in the midst also of parties of gentlemen sitting quietly reading the paper and smoking. We are getting used to ice frozen by artificial process in ordinary bottles—the only kind of ice they have here. We are getting used to all these things, but we are *not* getting used to carrying our own soap. We are sufficiently civilized to carry our own combs and toothbrushes, but this thing of having to ring for soap every time we wash is new to us and not pleasant at all. We think of it just after we get our heads and faces thoroughly wet or just when we think we have been in the bathtub long enough, and then, of course, an annoying delay follows. These Marseillaises make Marseillaise hymns and Marseilles vests and Marseilles soap for all the world, but they never sing their hymns or wear their vests or wash with their soap themselves.

We have learned to go through the lingering routine of the table d'hôte with patience, with serenity, with satisfaction. We take soup, then wait a few minutes for the fish; a few minutes more and the plates are changed, and the roast beef comes; another change and we take peas; change again and take lentils; change and take snail patties (I prefer grasshoppers); change and take roast chicken and salad; then strawberry pie and ice cream; then green figs, pears, oranges, green almonds, etc.; finally coffee. Wine with every course, of course, being in France. With such a cargo on board, digestion is a slow process, and we must sit long in the cool chambers and smoke—and read French newspapers, which have a strange fashion of telling a perfectly straight story till you get to the "nub" of it, and then a word drops in that no man can translate, and that story is ruined. An embankment fell on some Frenchmen yesterday, and the papers are full of it today—but whether those sufferers were killed, or crippled, or bruised, or only scared is more than I can possibly make out, and yet I would just give anything to know.

We were troubled a little at dinner today by the conduct of an American, who talked very loudly and coarsely and laughed boisterously where all others were so quiet and well behaved. He ordered wine with a royal flourish and said: "I never dine without wine, sir" (which was a pitiful falsehood), and looked around upon the company to bask in the admiration he expected to find in their faces. All these airs in a land where they would as soon expect to leave the soup out of the bill of fare as the wine!—in a land where wine is nearly as common among all ranks as water! This fellow said: "I am a freeborn sovereign, sir, an American, sir, and I want everybody to know it!" He did not mention that he was a lineal descendant of Balaam's ass, but everybody knew that without his telling it.

We have driven in the Prado—that superb avenue bordered with patrician mansions and noble shade trees—and have visited the Château Boarely and its curious museum. They showed us a miniature cemetery there—a copy of the first graveyard that was ever in Marseilles, no doubt. The delicate little skeletons were lying in broken vaults and had their household gods and kitchen utensils with them. The original of this cemetery was dug up in the principal street of the city a few years ago. It had remained there, only twelve feet underground, for a matter of twenty-five hundred years or thereabouts. Romulus was here before he built Rome, and thought something of founding a city on this spot, but gave up the idea. He may have been personally acquainted with some of these Phoenicians whose skeletons we have been examining.

In the great Zoological Gardens we found specimens of all the animals the world produces, I think, including a drome-dary, a monkey ornamented with tufts of brilliant blue and carmine hair—a very gorgeous monkey he was—a hippopot-amus from the Nile, and a sort of tall, long-legged bird with a beak like a powder horn and close-fitting wings like the tails of a dress coat. This fellow stood up with his eyes shut and his shoulders stooped forward a little, and looked as if he had his hands under his coattails. Such tranquil stupidity, such supernatural gravity, such self-righteousness, and such ineffable self-complacency as were in the countenance and attitude of that gray-bodied, dark-winged, bald-headed, and preposterously uncomely bird! He was so ungainly, so pimply about the head, so scaly about the legs, yet so serene, so unspeakably satisfied! He was the most comical-looking creature that can be imagined. It was good to hear Dan and the doctor laugh—such natural and such enjoyable laughter had not been heard among our excursionists since our ship sailed away from America. This bird was a godsend to us, and I should be an ingrate if I forgot to make honorable mention of him in these pages. Ours was a pleasure ex-cursion; therefore we stayed with that bird an hour and made the most of him. We stirred him up occasionally, but he only unclosed an eye and slowly closed it again, abating no jot of his stately piety of demeanor or his tremendous seriousness. He only seemed to say, "Defile not Heaven's anointed with unsanctified hands." We did not know his name, and so we called him "The Pilgrim." Dan said:

"All he wants now is a *Plymouth Collection*."

The boon companion of the colossal elephant was a common cat! This cat had a fashion of climbing up the elephant's hind legs and roosting on his back. She would sit up there, with her paws curved under her breast, and sleep in the sun half the afternoon. It used to annoy the elephant at first, and he would reach up and take her down, but she would go aft and climb up again. She persisted until she finally conquered the elephant's prejudices, and now they are inseparable friends. The cat plays about her comrade's forefeet or his trunk often, until dogs approach, and then she goes aloft out of danger. The elephant has annihilated several dogs lately that pressed his companion too closely.

We hired a sailboat and a guide and made an excursion to one of the small islands in the harbor to visit the Castle d'If. This ancient fortress has a melancholy history. It has been used as a prison for political offenders for two or three hundred years, and its dungeon walls are scarred with the rudely carved names of many and many a captive who fretted his life away here and left no record of himself but these sad epitaphs wrought with his own hands. How thick the names were! And their long-departed owners seemed to throng the gloomy cells and corridors with their phantom shapes. We loitered through dungeon after dungeon, away down into the living rock below the level of the sea, it seemed. Names everywhere!—some plebeian, some noble, some even princely. Plebeian, prince, and noble had one solicitude in common—they would not be forgotten! They could suffer solitude, inactivity, and the horrors of a silence that no sound ever disturbed, but they could not bear the thought of being utterly forgotten by the world. Hence the carved names. In one cell, where a little light penetrated, a man had lived twenty-seven years without seeing the face of a human being—lived in filth and wretchedness, with no companionship but his own thoughts, and they were sorrowful enough and hopeless enough, no doubt. Whatever his jailers considered that he needed was conveyed to his cell by night through a wicket. This man carved the walls of his prison house from floor to roof with all manner of figures of men and animals grouped in intricate designs. He had toiled there year after year, at his self-appointed task, while

infants grew to boyhood—to vigorous youth—idled through
school and college—acquired a profession—claimed man's
mature estate—married and looked back to infancy as to a
thing of some vague, ancient time almost. But who shall tell
how many ages it seemed to this prisoner? With the one,
time flew sometimes; with the other, never—it crawled always. To the one, nights spent in dancing had seemed made
of minutes instead of hours; to the other, those selfsame
nights had been like all other nights of dungeon life and
seemed made of slow, dragging weeks instead of hours and
minutes.

One prisoner of fifteen years had scratched verses upon
his walls, and brief prose sentences—brief, but full of pathos.
These spoke not of himself and his hard estate, but only of
the shrine where his spirit fled the prison to worship—of
home and the idols that were templed there. He never lived
to see them.

The walls of these dungeons are as thick as some bedchambers at home are wide—fifteen feet. We saw the damp,
dismal cells in which two of Dumas' heroes passed their
confinement—heroes of *Monte Cristo*. It was here that the
brave Abbé wrote a book with his own blood, with a pen
made of a piece of iron hoop, and by the light of a lamp
made out of shreds of cloth soaked in grease obtained from
his food; and then dug through the thick wall with some
trifling instrument which he wrought himself out of a stray
piece of iron or table cutlery and freed Dantés from his
chains. It was a pity that so many weeks of dreary labor
should have come to naught at last.

They showed us the noisome cell where the celebrated
"Iron Mask"—that ill-starred brother of a hardhearted king
of France—was confined for a season before he was sent
to hide the strange mystery of his life from the curious in the
dungeons of Ste. Marguerite. The place had a far greater interest for us than it could have had if we had known beyond all question who the Iron Mask was, and what his history
had been, and why this most unusual punishment had been
meted out to him. Mystery! That was the charm. That speechless tongue, those prisoned features, that heart so freighted
with unspoken troubles, and that breast so oppressed with
its piteous secret had been here. These dank walls had known
the man whose dolorous story is a sealed book forever!
There was fascination in the spot.

12

We have come five hundred miles by rail through the heart of France. What a bewitching land it is! What a garden! Surely the leagues of bright green lawns are swept and brushed and watered every day and their grasses trimmed by the barber. Surely the hedges are shaped and measured and their symmetry preserved by the most architectural of gardeners. Surely the long straight rows of stately poplars that divide the beautiful landscape like the squares of a checkerboard are set with line and plummet, and their uniform height determined with a spirit level. Surely the straight, smooth, pure white turnpikes are jack-planed and sandpapered every day. How else are these marvels of symmetry, cleanliness, and order attained? It is wonderful. There are no unsightly stone walls and never a fence of any kind. There is no dirt, no decay, no rubbish anywhere—nothing that even hints at untidiness—nothing that ever suggests neglect. All is orderly and beautiful—everything is charming to the eye.

We had such glimpses of the Rhone gliding along between its grassy banks; of cosy cottages buried in flowers and shrubbery; of quaint old red-tiled villages with mossy medieval cathedrals looming out of their midst; of wooded hills with ivy-grown towers and turrets of feudal castles projecting above the foliage; such glimpses of Paradise, it seemed to us, such visions of fabled fairyland!

We knew then what the poet meant when he sang of:

> —thy cornfields green, and sunny vines,
> O pleasant land of France!

And it *is* a pleasant land. No word describes it so felicitously as that one. They say there is no word for "home" in the French language. Well, considering that they have the article itself in such an attractive aspect, they ought to manage to get along without the word. Let us not waste too much pity on "homeless" France. I have observed that Frenchmen abroad seldom wholly give up the idea of going back to France some time or other. I am not surprised at it now.

We are not infatuated with these French railway cars, though. We took first-class passage, not because we wished to attract attention by doing a thing which is uncommon in Europe but because we could make our journey quicker by so doing. It is hard to make railroading pleasant in any country. It is too tedious. Stagecoaching is infinitely more delightful. Once I crossed the plains and deserts and mountains of the West in a stagecoach, from the Missouri line to California, and since then all my pleasure trips must be measured to that rare holiday frolic. Two thousand miles of ceaseless rush and rattle and clatter, by night and by day, and never a weary moment, never a lapse of interest! The first seven hundred miles a level continent, its grassy carpet greener and softer and smoother than any sea and figured with designs fitted to its magnitude—the shadows of the clouds. Here were no scenes but summer scenes, and no disposition inspired by them but to lie at full length on the mail sacks in the grateful breeze and dreamily smoke the pipe of peace—what other, where all was repose and contentment? In cool mornings, before the sun was fairly up, it was worth a lifetime of city toiling and moiling to perch in the foretop with the driver and see the six mustangs scamper under the sharp snapping of the whip that never touched them; to scan the blue distances of a world that knew no lords but us; to cleave the wind with uncovered head and feel the sluggish pulses rousing to the spirit of a speed that pretended to the resistless rush of a typhoon! Then thirteen hundred miles of desert solitudes; of limitless panoramas of bewildering perspective; of mimic cities, of pinnacled cathedrals, of massive fortresses, counterfeited in the eternal rocks and splendid with the crimson and gold of the setting sun; of dizzy altitudes among fog-wreathed peaks and never-melting snows, where thunders and lightnings and tempests warred magnificently at our feet and the storm clouds above swung their shredded banners in our very faces!

But I forgot. I am in elegant France now, and not skurrying through the great South Pass and the Wind River Mountains, among antelopes and buffaloes and painted Indians on the warpath. It is not meet that I should make too disparaging comparisons between humdrum travel on a railway and that royal summer flight across a continent in a stagecoach. I meant in the beginning to say that railway journeying is tedious and tiresome, and so it is—though at the time I was thinking particularly of a dismal fifty-hour pilgrimage between New York and St. Louis. Of course our trip through France was not really tedious because all its scenes and experiences were new and strange; but as Dan says, it had its "discrepancies."

The cars are built in compartments that hold eight persons each. Each compartment is partially subdivided, and so there are two tolerably distinct parties of four in it. Four face the other four. The seats and backs are thickly padded and cushioned and are very comfortable; you can smoke if you wish; there are no bothersome peddlers; you are saved the infliction of a multitude of disagreeable fellow passengers. So far, so well. But then the conductor locks you in when the train starts; there is no water to drink in the car; there is no heating apparatus for night travel; if a drunken rowdy should get in, you could not remove a matter of twenty seats from him or enter another car; but above all, if you are worn out and must sleep, you must sit up and do it in naps, with cramped legs and in a torturing misery that leaves you withered and lifeless the next day—for behold they have not that culmination of all charity and human kindness, a sleeping car, in all France. I prefer the American system. It has not so many grievous "discrepancies."

In France, all is clockwork, all is order. They make no mistakes. Every third man wears a uniform, and whether he be a marshal of the empire or a brakeman, he is ready and perfectly willing to answer all your questions with tireless politeness, ready to tell you which car to take, yea, and ready to go and put you into it to make sure that you shall not go astray. You cannot pass into the waiting room of the depot till you have secured your ticket, and you cannot pass from its only exit till the train is at its threshold to receive you. Once on board, the train will not start till your ticket has been examined—till every passenger's ticket has been inspected. This is chiefly for your own good. If by any possibility you have managed to take the wrong train, you will be handed over to a polite official who will take you whither you belong and bestow you with many an affable bow. Your ticket will be inspected every now and then along the route, and when it is time to change cars you will know it. You are in the hands of officials who zealously study your welfare and your interest, instead of turning their talents to the invention of new methods of discommoding and snubbing you, as is very often the main employment of that exceedingly self-satisfied monarch, the railroad conductor of America.

But the happiest regulation in French railway government is—thirty minutes to dinner! No five-minute boltings of flabby rolls, muddy coffee, questionable eggs, gutta-percha beef, and pies whose conception and execution are a dark and bloody mystery to all save the cook that created them! No, we sat calmly down—it was in old Dijon, which is so easy to spell and so impossible to pronounce except when you civilize it and call it Demijohn—and poured out rich Burgundian wines and munched calmly through a long table d'hôte bill of fare, snail patties, delicious fruits and all, then paid the trifle it cost and stepped happily aboard the train again, without once cursing the railroad company. A rare experience and one to be treasured forever.

They say they do not have accidents on these French roads, and I think it must be true. If I remember rightly, we passed high above wagon roads or through tunnels under them, but never crossed them on their own level. About every quarter of a mile, it seemed to me, a man came out and held up a club till the train went by, to signify that everything was safe ahead. Switches were changed a mile in advance by pulling a wire rope that passed along the ground by the rail from station to station. Signals for the day and signals for the night gave constant and timely notice of the position of switches.

No, they have no railroad accidents to speak of in France. But why? Because when one occurs, *somebody* has to hang for it! [1] Not hang, maybe, but be punished at least with such vigor of emphasis as to make negligence a thing to be shuddered at by railroad officials for many a day thereafter. "No blame attached to the officers"—that lying and disaster-breeding verdict so common to our softhearted juries is seldom rendered in France. If the trouble occurred in the conductor's department, that officer must suffer if his subordinate cannot be proven guilty; if in the engineer's department and the case be similar, the engineer must answer.

---

[1] They go on the principle that it is better that one innocent man should suffer than five hundred.

The Old Travelers—those delightful parrots who have "been here before" and know more about the country than Louis Napoleon knows now or ever will know—tell us these things, and we believe them because they are pleasant things to believe and because they are plausible and savor of the rigid subjection to law and order which we behold about us everywhere.

But we love the Old Travelers. We love to hear them prate and drivel and lie. We can tell them the moment we see them. They always throw out a few feelers; they never cast themselves adrift till they have sounded every individual and know that he has not traveled. Then they open their throttle valves, and how they do brag, and sneer, and swell, and soar, and blaspheme the sacred name of Truth! Their central idea, their grand aim, is to subjugate you, keep you down, make you feel insignificant and humble in the blaze of their cosmopolitan glory! They will not let you know anything. They sneer at your most inoffensive suggestions; they laugh unfeelingly at your treasured dreams of foreign lands; they brand the statements of your traveled aunts and uncles as the stupidest absurdities; they deride your most trusted authors and demolish the fair images they have set up for your willing worship with the pitiless ferocity of the fanatic inconoclast! But still I love the Old Travelers. I love them for their witless platitudes, for their supernatural ability to bore, for their delightful asinine vanity, for their luxuriant fertility of imagination, for their startling, their brilliant, their overwhelming mendacity!

By Lyons and the Saône (where we saw the lady of Lyons and thought little of her comeliness), by Villa Franca, Tonnere, venerable Sens, Melun, Fontainebleau, and scores of other beautiful cities, we swept, always noting the absence of hog wallows, broken fences, cow lots, unpainted houses, and mud, and always noting, as well, the presence of cleanliness, grace, taste in adorning and beautifying, even to the disposition of a tree or the turning of a hedge, the marvel of roads in perfect repair, void of ruts and guiltless of even an inequality of surface—we bowled along, hour after hour, that brilliant summer day, and as nightfall approached we entered a wilderness of odorous flowers and shrubbery, sped through it, and then, excited, delighted, and half persuaded that we were only the sport of a beautiful dream, lo, we stood in magnificent Paris!

What excellent order they kept about that vast depot! There was no frantic crowding and jostling, no shouting and swearing, and no swaggering intrusion of services by rowdy hackmen. These latter gentry stood outside—stood quietly by their long line of vehicles and said never a word. A kind of hackman general seemed to have the whole matter of transportation in his hands. He politely received the passengers and ushered them to the kind of conveyance they wanted, and told the driver where to deliver them. There was no "talking back," no dissatisfaction about overcharging, no grumbling about anything. In a little while we were speeding through the streets of Paris and delightfully recognizing certain names and places with which books had long ago made us familiar. It was like meeting an old friend when we read "Rue de Rivoli" on the street corner; we knew the genuine vast palace of the Louvre as well as we knew its picture; when we passed by the Column of July we needed no one to tell us what it was or to remind us that on its site once stood the grim Bastile, that grave of human hopes and happiness, that dismal prison house within whose dungeons so many young faces put on the wrinkles of age, so many proud spirits grew humble, so many brave hearts broke.

We secured rooms at the hotel, or rather, we had three beds put into one room, so that we might be together, and then we went out to a restaurant, just after lamplighting, and ate a comfortable, satisfactory, lingering dinner. It was a pleasure to eat where everything was so tidy, the food so well cooked, the waiters so polite, and the coming and departing company so moustached, so frisky, so affable, so fearfully and wonderfully Frenchy! All the surroundings were gay and enlivening. Two hundred people sat at little tables on the sidewalk, sipping wine and coffee; the streets were thronged with light vehicles and with joyous pleasure-seekers; there was music in the air, life and action all about us, and a conflagration of gaslight everywhere!

After dinner we felt like seeing such Parisian specialties as we might see without distressing exertion, and so we sauntered through the brilliant streets and looked at the dainty trifles in variety stores and jewelry shops. Occasionally, merely for the pleasure of being cruel, we put unoffending Frenchmen on the rack with questions framed in the incomprehensible jargon of their native language, and while they writhed we impaled them, we peppered them, we scarified them, with their own vile verbs and participles.

We noticed that in the jewelry stores they had some of the articles marked "gold" and some labeled "imitation." We wondered at this extravagance of honesty and inquired into the matter. We were informed that inasmuch as most people are not able to tell false gold from the genuine article, the government compels jewelers to have their gold work assayed and stamped officially according to its fineness and their imitation work duly labeled with the sign of its falsity. They told us the jewelers would not dare to violate this law, and that whatever a stranger bought in one of their stores might be depended upon as being strictly what it was represented to be. Verily, a wonderful land is France!

Then we hunted for a barbershop. From earliest infancy it had been a cherished ambition of mine to be shaved some day in a palatial barbershop in Paris. I wished to recline at full length in a cushioned invalid chair, with pictures about me and sumptuous furniture; with frescoed walls and gilded arches above me and vistas of Corinthian columns stretching far before me; with perfumes of Araby to intoxicate my senses and the slumbrous drone of distant noises to soothe me to sleep. At the end of an hour I would wake up regretfully and find my face as smooth and as soft as an infant's. Departing, I would lift my hands above that barber's head and say, "Heaven bless you, my son!"

So we searched high and low, for a matter of two hours, but never a barbershop could we see. We saw only wigmaking establishments, with shocks of dead and repulsive hair bound upon the heads of painted waxen brigands who stared out from glass boxes upon the passerby with their stony eyes and scared him with the ghostly white of their countenances. We shunned these signs for a time, but finally we concluded that the wigmakers must of necessity be the barbers as well, since we could find no single legitimate representative of the fraternity. We entered and asked, and found that it was even so.

I said I wanted to be shaved. The barber inquired where my room was. I said never mind where my room was, I wanted to be shaved—there, on the spot. The doctor said he would be shaved also. Then there was an excitement among those two barbers! There was a wild consultation, and afterwards a hurrying to and fro and a feverish gathering up of razors from obscure places and a ransacking for soap. Next they took us into a little mean, shabby back room; they got two ordinary sitting-room chairs and placed us in them with our coats on. My old, old dream of bliss vanished into thin air!

I sat bolt upright, silent, sad, and solemn. One of the wig-making villains lathered my face for ten terrible minutes and finished by plastering a mass of suds into my mouth. I expelled the nasty stuff with a strong English expletive and said, "Foreigner, beware!" Then this outlaw strapped his razor on his boot, hovered over me ominously for six fearful seconds, and then swooped down upon me like the genius of destruction. The first rake of his razor loosened the very hide from my face and lifted me out of the chair. I stormed and raved, and the other boys enjoyed it. Their beards are not strong and thick. Let us draw the curtain over this harrowing scene. Suffice it that I submitted and went through with the cruel infliction of a shave by a French barber; tears of exquisite agony coursed down my cheeks now and then, but I survived. Then the incipient assassin held a basin of water under my chin and slopped its contents over my face, and into my bosom, and down the back of my neck, with a mean pretense of washing away the soap and blood. He dried my features with a towel and was going to comb my hair, but I asked to be excused. I said, with withering irony, that it was sufficient to be skinned—I declined to be scalped.

I went away from there with my handkerchief about my face, and never, never, never desired to dream of palatial Parisian barbershops anymore. The truth is, as I believe I have since found out, that they have no barbershops worthy of the name in Paris—and no barbers, either, for that matter. The impostor who does duty as a barber brings his pans and napkins and implements of torture to your residence and deliberately skins you in your private apartments. Ah, I have suffered, suffered, suffered, here in Paris, but never mind—the time is coming when I shall have a dark and bloody revenge. Someday a Parisian barber will come to my room to skin me, and from that day forth that barber will never be heard of more.

At eleven o'clock we alighted upon a sign which manifestly referred to billiards. Joy! We had played billiards in the Azores with balls that were not round and on an ancient table that was very little smoother than a brick pavement—

one of those wretched old things with dead cushions, and with patches in the faded cloth and invisible obstructions that made the balls describe the most astonishing and unsuspected angles and perform feats in the way of unlooked-for and almost impossible "scratches" that were perfectly bewildering. We had played at Gibraltar with balls the size of a walnut on a table like a public square—and in both instances we achieved far more aggravation than amusement. We expected to fare better here, but we were mistaken. The cushions were a good deal higher than the balls, and as the balls had a fashion of always stopping under the cushions, we accomplished very little in the way of caroms. The cushions were hard and unelastic, and the cues were so crooked that in making a shot you had to allow for the curve or you would infallibly put the "English" on the wrong side of the ball. Dan was to mark while the doctor and I played. At the end of an hour neither of us had made a count, and so Dan was tired of keeping tally with nothing to tally, and we were heated and angry and disgusted. We paid the heavy bill— about six cents—and said we would call around sometime when we had a week to spend, and finish the game.

We adjourned to one of those pretty cafés and took supper and tested the wines of the country, as we had been instructed to do, and found them harmless and unexciting. They might have been exciting, however, if we had chosen to drink a sufficiency of them.

To close our first day in Paris cheerfully and pleasantly, we now sought our grand room in the Grand Hotel du Louvre and climbed into our sumptuous bed to read and smoke—but alas!

> It was pitiful,
> In a whole city-full,
> Gas we had none.

No gas to read by—nothing but dismal candles. It was a shame. We tried to map out excursions for the morrow; we puzzled over French "guides to Paris"; we talked disjointedly in a vain endeavor to make head or tail of the wild chaos of the day's sights and experiences; we subsided to indolent smoking; we gaped and yawned and stretched—then feebly wondered if we were really and truly in renowned Paris, and drifted drowsily away into that vast mysterious void which men call sleep.

13

The next morning we were up and dressed at ten o'clock. We went to the *commissionaire* of the hotel—I don't know what a *commissionaire* is, but that is the man we went to —and told him we wanted a guide. He said the great International Exposition had drawn such multitudes of Englishmen and Americans to Paris that it would be next to impossible to find a good guide unemployed. He said he usually kept a dozen or two on hand, but he only had three now. He called them. One looked so like a very pirate that we let him go at once. The next one spoke with a simpering precision of pronunciation that was irritating and said:

"If ze zhentlemans will to me make ze grande honneur to me rattain in hees serveece, I shall show to him everysing zat is magnifique to look upon in ze beautiful Parree. I speaky ze Angleesh pairfaitemaw."

He would have done well to have stopped there, because he had that much by heart and said it right off without making a mistake. But his self-complacency seduced him into attempting a flight into regions of unexplored English, and the reckless experiment was his ruin. Within ten seconds he was so tangled up in a maze of mutilated verbs and torn and bleeding forms of speech that no human ingenuity could ever have gotten him out of it with credit. It was plain enough that he could not "speaky" the English quite as "pairfaitemaw" as he had pretended he could.

The third man captured us. He was plainly dressed, but he had a noticeable air of neatness about him. He wore a high silk hat which was a little old, but had been carefully brushed. He wore secondhand kid gloves, in good repair, and carried a small rattan cane with a curved handle—a female leg—of ivory. He stepped as gently and as daintily as a cat crossing a muddy street; and oh, he was urbanity; he was quiet, unobtrusive self-possession; he was deference itself! He spoke softly and guardedly; and when he was about to make a statement on his sole responsibility or offer a suggestion, he weighed it by drachms and scruples first, with the crook of his little stick placed meditatively to his teeth. His opening speech was perfect. It was perfect in construction, in phraseology, in grammar, in emphasis, in pronunciation—everything. He spoke little and guardedly after that. We were charmed. We were more than charmed—we were overjoyed. We hired him at once. We never even asked him his price. This man—our lackey, our servant, our unquestioning slave though he was—was still a gentleman—we could see that—while of the other two one was coarse and awkward and the other was a born pirate. We asked our man Friday's name. He drew from his pocketbook a snowy little card and passed it to us with a profound bow:

A. BILLFINGER
Guide to Paris, France, Germany,
Spain, &c., &c.
Grande Hotel du Louvre

"Billfinger! Oh, carry me home to die!"

That was an "aside" from Dan. The atrocious name grated harshly on my ear, too. The most of us can learn to forgive, and even to like, a countenance that strikes us unpleasantly at first, but few of us, I fancy, become reconciled to a jarring name so easily. I was almost sorry we had hired this man, his name was so unbearable. However, no matter. We were impatient to start. Billfinger stepped to the door to call a carriage, and then the doctor said:

"Well, the guide goes with the barbershop, with the billiard table, with the gasless room, and maybe with many another pretty romance of Paris. I expected to have a guide named Henri de Montmorency or Armand de la Chartreuse or something that would sound grand in letters to the villagers at home, but to think of a Frenchman by the name of Billfinger! Oh! This is absurd, you know. This will never do. We can't say Billfinger; it is nauseating. Name him over again; what had we better call him? Alexis du Caulain-court?"

"Alphonse Henri Gustave de Hauteville," I suggested.

"Call him Ferguson," said Dan.

That was practical, unromantic good sense. Without debate, we expunged Billfinger *as* Billfinger and called him Ferguson.

The carriage—an open barouche—was ready. Ferguson mounted beside the driver, and we whirled away to breakfast. As was proper, Mr. Ferguson stood by to transmit our orders and answer questions. By and by, he mentioned casually— the artful adventurer—that he would go and get his breakfast as soon as we had finished ours. He knew we could not get along without him and that we would not want to loiter about and wait for him. We asked him to sit down and eat with us. He begged, with many a bow, to be excused. It was not proper, he said; he would sit at another table. We ordered him peremptorily to sit down with us.

Here endeth the first lesson. It was a mistake.

As long as we had that fellow after that, he was always hungry; he was always thirsty. He came early; he stayed late; he could not pass a restaurant; he looked with a lecherous eye upon every wineshop. Suggestions to stop, excuses to eat and to drink, were forever on his lips. We tried all we could to fill him so full that he would have no room to spare for a fortnight, but it was a failure. He did not hold enough to smother the cravings of his superhuman appetite.

He had another "discrepancy" about him. He was always wanting us to buy things. On the shallowest pretenses he would inveigle us into shirt stores, boot stores, tailor shops, glove shops—anywhere under the broad sweep of the heavens that there seemed a chance of our buying anything. Anyone could have guessed that the shopkeepers paid him a percentage on the sales, but in our blessed innocence we didn't until this feature of his conduct grew unbearably prominent. One day Dan happened to mention that he thought of buying three or four silk dress patterns for presents. Ferguson's hungry eye was upon him in an instant. In the course of twenty minutes the carriage stopped.

"What's this?"

"Zis is ze finest silk *magasin* in Paris—ze most celebrate."

"What did you come here for? We told you to take us to the palace of the Louvre."

"I suppose ze gentleman say he wish to buy some silk."

"You are not required to 'suppose' things for the party,

Ferguson. We do not wish to tax your energies too much. We will bear some of the burden and heat of the day ourselves. We will endeavor to do such 'supposing' as is really necessary to be done. Drive on." So spake the doctor.

Within fifteen minutes the carriage halted again, and before another silk store. The doctor said:

"Ah, the palace of the Louvre—beautiful, beautiful edifice! Does the Emperor Napoleon live here now, Ferguson?"

"Ah, Doctor! You do jest; zis is not ze palace; we come there directly. But since we pass right by zis store, where is such beautiful silk——"

"Ah! I see, I see. I meant to have told you that we did not wish to purchase any silks today, but in my absentmindedness I forgot it. I also meant to tell you we wished to go directly to the Louvre, but I forgot that also. However, we will go there now. Pardon my seeming carelessness, Ferguson. Drive on."

Within the half hour we stopped again—in front of another silk store. We were angry; but the doctor was always serene, always smooth-voiced. He said:

"At last! How imposing the Louvre is, and yet how small! How exquisitely fashioned! How charmingly situated! Venerable, venerable pile——"

"Pairdon, Doctor, zis is not ze Louvre—it is——"

"*What* is it?"

"I have ze idea—it come to me in a moment—zat ze silk in zis *magasin*——"

"Ferguson, how heedless I am. I fully intended to tell you that we did not wish to buy any silks today, and I also intended to tell you that we yearned to go immediately to the palace of the Louvre, but enjoying the happiness of seeing you devour four breakfasts this morning has so filled me with pleasurable emotions that I neglect the commonest interests of the time. However, we will proceed now to the Louvre, Ferguson."

"But, Doctor" (excitedly), "it will take not a minute—not but one small minute! Ze gentleman need not to buy if he not wish to—but only *look* at ze silk—*look* at ze beautiful fabric. [Then pleadingly.] *Sair*—just only one *leetle* moment!"

Dan said, "Confound the idiot! I don't want to see any silks today, and I *won't* look at them. Drive on."

And the doctor: "We need no silks now, Ferguson. Our

hearts yearn for the Louvre. Let us journey on—let us journey on."

"But, *Doctor!* It is only one moment—one leetle moment. And ze time will be save—entirely save! Because zere is nothing to see now—it is too late. It want ten minute to four and ze Louvre close at four—*only* one leetle moment, Doctor!"

The treacherous miscreant! After four breakfasts and a gallon of champagne, to serve us such a scurvy trick. We got no sight of the countless treasures of art in the Louvre galleries that day, and our only poor little satisfaction was in the reflection that Ferguson sold not a solitary silk dress pattern.

I am writing this chapter partly for the satisfaction of abusing that accomplished knave Billfinger, and partly to show whosoever shall read this how Americans fare at the hands of the Paris guides and what sort of people Paris guides are. It need not be supposed that we were a stupider or an easier prey than our countrymen generally are, for we were not. The guides deceive and defraud every American who goes to Paris for the first time and sees its sights alone or in company with others as little experienced as himself. I shall visit Paris again someday, and then let the guides beware! I shall go in my war paint—I shall carry my tomahawk along.

I think we have lost but little time in Paris. We have gone to bed every night tired out. Of course we visited the renowned International Exposition. All the world did that. We went there on our third day in Paris—and we stayed there *nearly two hours*. That was our first and last visit. To tell the truth, we saw at a glance that one would have to spend weeks—yea, even months—in that monstrous establishment to get an intelligible idea of it. It was a wonderful show, but the moving masses of people of all nations we saw there were a still more wonderful show. I discovered that if I were to stay there a month, I should still find myself looking at the people instead of the inanimate objects on exhibition. I got a little interested in some curious old tapestries of the thirteenth century, but a party of Arabs came by, and their dusky faces and quaint costumes called my attention away at once. I watched a silver swan, which had a living grace about his movements and a living intelligence in his eyes—watched him swimming about as com-

fortably and as unconcernedly as if he had been born in a
morass instead of a jeweler's shop—watched him seize a
silver fish from under the water and hold up his head and go
through all the customary and elaborate motions of swal-
lowing it—but the moment it disappeared down his throat
some tattooed South Sea Islanders approached and I yielded
to their attractions. Presently I found a revolving pistol several hundred years old which looked strangely like a modern
Colt, but just then I heard that the Empress of the French
was in another part of the building, and hastened away to
see what she might look like. We heard martial music—we
saw an unusual number of soldiers walking hurriedly about
—there was a general movement among the people. We inquired what it was all about and learned that the Emperor
of the French and the Sultan of Turkey were about to review twenty-five thousand troops at the Arc de l'Etoile. We
immediately departed. I had a greater anxiety to see these
men than I could have had to see twenty expositions.

We drove away and took up a position in an open space
opposite the American minister's house. A speculator bridged
a couple of barrels with a board and we hired standing places
on it. Presently there was a sound of distant music; in another minute a pillar of dust came moving slowly toward
us; a moment more and then, with colors flying and a grand
crash of military music, a gallant array of cavalrymen
emerged from the dust and came down the street on a gentle
trot. After them came a long line of artillery; then more
cavalry, in splendid uniforms; and then their imperial
majesties Napoleon III and Abdul-Aziz. The vast concourse
of people swung their hats and shouted—the windows and
housetops in the wide vicinity burst into a snowstorm of
waving handkerchiefs, and the wavers of the same mingled
their cheers with those of the masses below. It was a stirring
spectacle.

But the two central figures claimed all my attention. Was
ever such a contrast set up before a multitude till then?
Napoleon in military uniform—a long-bodied, short-legged
man, fiercely moustached, old, wrinkled, with eyes half
closed, and *such* a deep, crafty, scheming expression about
them! Napoleon bowing ever so gently to the loud plaudits,
and watching everything and everybody with his cat eyes
from under his depressed hat brim, as if to discover any
sign that those cheers were not heartfelt and cordial.

Abdul-Aziz, absolute lord of the Ottoman empire—clad in dark green European clothes, almost without ornament or insignia of rank; a red Turkish fez on his head; a short, stout, dark man, black-bearded, black-eyed, stupid, unprepossessing—a man whose whole appearance somehow suggested that if he only had a cleaver in his hand and a white apron on, one would not be at all surprised to hear him say: "A mutton roast today, or will you have a nice porterhouse steak?"

Napoleon III, the representative of the highest modern civilization, progress, and refinement; Abdul-Aziz, the representative of a people by nature and training filthy, brutish, ignorant, unprogressive, superstitious—and a government whose Three Graces are Tyranny, Rapacity, Blood. Here in brilliant Paris, under this majestic Arch of Triumph, the first century greets the nineteenth!

Napoleon III, Emperor of France! Surrounded by shouting thousands, by military pomp, by the splendors of his capital city, and companioned by kings and princes—this is the man who was sneered at and reviled and called Bastard —yet who was dreaming of a crown and an empire all the while; who was driven into exile—but carried his dreams with him; who associated with the common herd in America and ran foot races for a wager—but still sat upon a throne in fancy; who braved every danger to go to his dying mother —and grieved that she could not be spared to see him cast aside his plebeian vestments for the purple of royalty; who kept his faithful watch and walked his weary beat a common policeman of London—but dreamed the while of a coming night when he should tread the long-drawn corridors of the Tuileries; who made the miserable fiasco of Strasbourg; saw his poor, shabby eagle, forgetful of its lesson, refuse to perch upon his shoulder; delivered his carefully prepared, sententious burst of eloquence unto unsympathetic ears; found himself a prisoner, the butt of small wits, a mark for the pitiless ridicule of all the world—yet went on dreaming of coronations and splendid pageants as before; who lay a forgotten captive in the dungeons of Ham—and still schemed and planned and pondered over future glory and future power; President of France at last! a *coup d'état*, and surrounded by applauding armies, welcomed by the thunders of cannon, he mounts a throne and waves before an astounded world the scepter of a mighty empire! Who talks of the marvels of fiction? Who speaks of the wonders of romance? Who prates of the tame achievements of Aladdin and the Magii of Arabia?

Abdul-Aziz, Sultan of Turkey, Lord of the Ottoman Empire! Born to a throne; weak, stupid, ignorant, almost, as his meanest slave; chief of a vast royalty, yet the puppet of his premier and the obedient child of a tyrannical mother; a man who sits upon a throne—the beck of whose finger moves navies and armies—who holds in his hands the power of life and death over millions—yet who sleeps, sleeps, eats, eats, idles with his eight hundred concubines, and when he is surfeited with eating and sleeping and idling, and would rouse up and take the reins of government and threaten to *be* a sultan, is charmed from his purpose by wary Fuad Pasha with a pretty plan for a new palace or a new ship— charmed away with a new toy, like any other restless child; a man who sees his people robbed and oppressed by soulless tax gatherers, but speaks no word to save them; who believes in gnomes and genii and the wild fables of *The Arabian Nights*, but has small regard for the mighty magicians of today and is nervous in the presence of their mysterious railroads and steamboats and telegraphs; who would see undone in Egypt all that great Mehemet Ali achieved and would prefer rather to forget than emulate him; a man who found his great empire a blot upon the earth—a degraded, poverty-stricken, miserable, infamous agglomeration of ignorance, crime, and brutality—and will idle away the allotted days of his trivial life and then pass to the dust and the worms and leave it so!

Napoleon has augmented the commercial prosperity of France in ten years to such a degree that figures can hardly compute it. He has rebuilt Paris and has partly rebuilt every city in the state. He condemns a whole street at a time, assesses the damages, pays them, and rebuilds superbly. Then speculators buy up the ground and sell, but the original owner is given the first choice by the government at a stated price before the speculator is permitted to purchase. But above all things, he has taken the sole control of the empire of France into his hands and made it a tolerably free land— for people who will not attempt to go too far in meddling with government affairs. No country offers greater security to life and property than France, and one has all the freedom he wants, but no license—no license to interfere with anybody or make anyone uncomfortable.

As for the Sultan, one could set a trap anywhere and catch a dozen abler men in a night.

The bands struck up, and the brilliant adventurer, Napoleon III, the genius of Energy, Persistence, Enterprise, and the feeble Abdul-Aziz, the genius of Ignorance, Bigotry, and Indolence, prepared for the Forward—March!

We saw the splendid review, we saw the white-moustached old Crimean soldier Canrobert, marshal of France, we saw—well, we saw everything, and then we went home satisfied.

14

We went to see the Cathedral of Notre Dame. We had heard of it before. It surprises me sometimes to think how much we *do* know and how intelligent we are. We recognized the brown old Gothic pile in a moment; it was like the pictures. We stood at a little distance and changed from one point of observation to another and gazed long at its lofty square towers and its rich front, clustered thick with stony, mutilated saints who had been looking calmly down from their perches for ages. The Patriarch of Jerusalem stood under them in the old days of chivalry and romance, and preached the third Crusade, more than six hundred years ago; and since that day they have stood there and looked quietly down upon the most thrilling scenes, the grandest pageants, the most extraordinary spectacles that have grieved or delighted Paris. These battered and broken-nosed old fellows saw many and many a cavalcade of mail-clad knights come marching home from Holy Land; they heard the bells above them toll the signal for the St. Bartholomew's Massacre, and they saw the slaughter that followed; later they saw the Reign of Terror, the carnage of the Revolution, the overthrow of a king, the coronation of two Napoleons, the christening of the young prince that lords it over a regiment of servants in the Tuileries today—and they may possibly continue to stand there until they see the Napoleon dynasty swept away and the banners of a great republic floating above its ruins. I wish these old parties could speak. They could tell a tale worth the listening to.

They say that a pagan temple stood where Notre Dame now stands, in the old Roman days, eighteen or twenty centuries ago—remains of it are still preserved in Paris; and that a Christian church took its place about A.D. 300; another took the place of that in A.D. 500; and that the foundations of the present cathedral were laid about A.D. 1100. The ground ought to be measurably sacred by this time, one would think. One portion of this noble old edifice is suggestive of the quaint fashions of ancient times. It was built by Jean Sans-Peur, Duke of Burgundy, to set his conscience at rest—he had assassinated the Duke of Orleans. Alas! Those good old times are gone when a murderer could wipe the stain from his name and soothe his troubles to sleep simply by getting out his bricks and mortar and building an addition to a church.

The portals of the great western front are bisected by square pillars. They took the central one away in 1852, on the occasion of thanksgivings for the reinstitution of the presidential power—but precious soon they had occasion to reconsider that motion and put it back again! And they did.

We loitered through the grand aisles for an hour or two, staring up at the rich stained-glass windows embellished with blue and yellow and crimson saints and martyrs, and trying to admire the numberless great pictures in the chapels, and then we were admitted to the sacristy and shown the magnificent robes which the pope wore when he crowned Napoleon I; a wagonload of solid gold and silver utensils used in the great public processions and ceremonies of the church; some nails of the true cross, a fragment of the cross itself, a part of the crown of thorns. We had already seen a large piece of the true cross in a church in the Azores, but no nails. They showed us likewise the bloody robe which that archbishop of Paris wore who exposed his sacred person and braved the wrath of the insurgents of 1848, to mount the barricades and hold aloft the olive branch of peace in the hope of stopping the slaughter. His noble effort cost him his life. He was shot dead. They showed us a cast of his face taken after death, the bullet that killed him, and the two vertebrae in which it lodged. These people have a somewhat singular taste in the matter of relics. Ferguson told us that the silver cross which the good archbishop wore at his girdle was seized and thrown into the Seine, where it lay embedded in the mud for fifteen years, and then an angel appeared to a priest and told him where to dive for it; he *did* dive for it and got it, and now it is there on exhibition at Notre Dame, to be inspected by anybody who feels an interest in inanimate objects of miraculous intervention.

Next we went to visit the Morgue, that horrible receptacle for the dead who die mysteriously and leave the manner of their taking off a dismal secret. We stood before a grating and looked through into a room which was hung all about with the clothing of dead men; coarse blouses, water-soaked; the delicate garments of women and children; patrician vestments, hacked and stabbed and stained with red; a hat that was crushed and bloody. On a slanting stone lay a drowned man, naked, swollen, purple; clasping the fragment of a broken bush with a grip which death had so petrified that human strength could not unloose it—mute witness of the last despairing effort to save the life that was doomed beyond all help. A stream of water trickled ceaselessly over the hideous face. We knew that the body and the clothing were there for identification by friends, but still we wondered if anybody could love that repulsive object or grieve for its loss. We grew meditative and wondered if, some forty years ago, when the mother of that ghastly thing was dandling it upon her knee, and kissing it and petting it and displaying it with satisfied pride to the passersby, a prophetic vision of this dread ending ever flitted through her brain. I half feared that the mother or the wife or a brother of the dead man might come while we stood there, but nothing of the kind occurred. Men and women came, and some looked eagerly in and pressed their faces against the bars; others glanced carelessly at the body and turned away with a disappointed look—people, I thought, who live upon strong excitements and who attend the exhibitions of the Morgue regularly, just as other people go to see theatrical spectacles every night. When one of these looked in and passed on, I could not help thinking:

"Now this don't afford you any satisfaction—a party with his head shot off is what *you* need."

One night we went to the celebrated Jardin Mabille, but only stayed a little while. We wanted to see some of this kind of Paris life, however, and therefore the next night we went to a similar place of entertainment in a great garden in the suburb of Asnières. We went to the railroad depot toward evening, and Ferguson got tickets for a second-class carriage. Such a perfect jam of people I have not often seen—but there was no noise, no disorder, no rowdyism. Some of the women and young girls that entered the train we knew to be of the demimonde, but others we were not at all sure about.

The girls and women in our carriage behaved themselves modestly and becomingly all the way out, except that they smoked. When we arrived at the garden in Asnières, we paid a franc or two admission and entered a place which had flower beds in it, and grass plots, and long, curving rows of ornamental shrubbery, with here and there a secluded bower convenient for eating ice cream in. We moved along the sinuous gravel walks, with the great concourse of girls and young men, and suddenly a domed and filigreed white temple, starred over and over and over again with brilliant gas jets, burst upon us like a fallen sun. Nearby was a large, handsome house with its ample front illuminated in the same way, and above its roof floated the Star-Spangled Banner of America.

"Well!" I said. "How is this?" It nearly took my breath away.

Ferguson said an American—a New Yorker—kept the place, and was carrying on quite a stirring opposition to the Jardin Mabille.

Crowds composed of both sexes and nearly all ages were frisking about the garden or sitting in the open air in front of the flagstaff and the temple, drinking wine and coffee or smoking. The dancing had not begun yet. Ferguson said there was to be an exhibition. The famous Blondin was going to perform on a tightrope in another part of the garden. We went thither. Here the light was dim, and the masses of people were pretty closely packed together. And now I made a mistake which any donkey might make, but a sensible man never. I committed an error which I find myself repeating every day of my life. Standing right before a young lady, I said:

"Dan, just look at this girl, how beautiful she is!"

"I thank you more for the evident sincerity of the compliment, sir, than for the extraordinary publicity you have given to it!" This in good, pure English.

We took a walk, but my spirits were very, very sadly dampened. I did not feel right comfortable for some time afterward. Why *will* people be so stupid as to suppose themselves the only foreigners among a crowd of ten thousand persons?

But Blondin came out shortly. He appeared on a stretched cable, far away above the sea of tossing hats and handkerchiefs, and in the glare of the hundreds of rockets that whizzed heavenward by him he looked like a wee insect. He balanced his pole and walked the length of his rope—two or three hundred feet; he came back and got a man and carried him across; he returned to the center and danced a jig; next he performed some gymnastic and balancing feats too perilous to afford a pleasant spectacle; and he finished by fastening to his person a thousand Roman candles, Catherine wheels, serpents and rockets of all manner of brilliant colors, setting them on fire all at once and walking and waltzing across his rope again in a blinding blaze of glory that lit up the garden and the people's faces like a great conflagration at midnight.

The dance had begun, and we adjourned to the temple. Within it was a drinking saloon, and all around it was a broad circular platform for the dancers. I backed up against the wall of the temple and waited. Twenty sets formed, the music struck up, and then—I placed my hands before my face for very shame. But I looked through my fingers. They were dancing the renowned "Cancan." A handsome girl in the set before me tripped forward lightly to meet the opposite gentleman, tripped back again, grasped her dresses vigorously on both sides with her hands, raised them pretty high, danced an extraordinary jig that had more activity and exposure about it than any jig I ever saw before, and then, drawing her clothes still higher, she advanced gaily to the center and launched a vicious kick full at her *vis-à-vis* that must infallibly have removed his nose if he had been seven feet high. It was a mercy he was only six.

That is the cancan. The idea of it is to dance as wildly, as noisily, as furiously as you can; expose yourself as much as possible if you are a woman; and kick as high as you can, no matter which sex you belong to. There is no word of exaggeration in this. Any of the staid, respectable, aged people who were there that night can testify to the truth of that statement. There were a good many such people present. I suppose French morality is not of that straight-laced description which is shocked at trifles.

I moved aside and took a general view of the cancan. Shouts, laughter, furious music, a bewildering chaos of darting and intermingling forms, stormy jerking and snatching of gay dresses, bobbing heads, flying arms, lightning flashes of white-stockinged calves and dainty slippers in the air, and then a grand final rush, riot, a terrific hubbub, and a wild stampede! Heavens! Nothing like it has been seen on earth since trembling Tam O'Shanter saw the devil and the witches at their orgies that stormy night in "Alloway's auld haunted kirk."

We visited the Louvre, at a time when we had no silk purchases in view, and looked at its miles of paintings by the old masters. Some of them were beautiful, but at the same time they carried such evidences about them of the cringing spirit of those great men that we found small pleasure in examining them. Their nauseous adulation of princely patrons was more prominent to me and chained my attention more surely than the charms of color and expression which are claimed to be in the pictures. Gratitude for kindnesses is well, but it seems to me that some of those artists carried it so far that it ceased to be gratitude and became worship. If there is a plausible excuse for the worship of men, then by all means let us forgive Rubens and his brethren.

But I will drop the subject, lest I say something about the old masters that might as well be left unsaid.

Of course we drove in the Bois de Boulogne, that limitless park, with its forests, its lakes, its cascades, and its broad avenues. There were thousands upon thousands of vehicles abroad, and the scene was full of life and gaiety. There were very common hacks, with father and mother and all the children in them; conspicuous little open carriages with celebrated ladies of questionable reputation in them; there were dukes and duchesses abroad, with gorgeous footmen perched behind, and equally gorgeous outriders perched on each of the six horses; there were blue and silver, and green and gold, and pink and black, and all sorts and descriptions of stunning and startling liveries out, and I almost yearned to be a flunky myself, for the sake of the fine clothes.

But presently the Emperor came along and he outshone them all. He was preceded by a bodyguard of gentlemen on horseback in showy uniforms, his carriage horses (there appeared to be somewhere in the remote neighborhood of a thousand of them) were bestridden by gallant-looking fellows, also in stylish uniforms, and after the carriage followed another detachment of bodyguards. Everybody got out of the way; everybody bowed to the Emperor and his friend the Sultan; and they went by on a swinging trot and disappeared.

I will not describe the Bois de Boulogne. I cannot do it. It is simply a beautiful, cultivated, endless, wonderful wilderness. It is an enchanting place. It is in Paris now, one may say, but a crumbling old cross in one portion of it reminds one that it was not always so. The cross marks the spot where a celebrated troubadour was waylaid and murdered in the fourteenth century. It was in this park that that fellow with an unpronounceable name made the attempt upon the Russian czar's life last spring with a pistol. The bullet struck a tree. Ferguson showed us the place. Now in America that interesting tree would be chopped down or forgotten within the next five years, but it will be treasured here. The guides will point it out to visitors for the next eight hundred years, and when it decays and falls down they will put up another there and go on with the same old story just the same.

15

One of our pleasantest visits was to Père la Chaise, the national burying ground of France, the honored resting place of some of her greatest and best children, the last home of scores of illustrious men and women who were born to no titles, but achieved fame by their own energy

and their own genius. It is a solemn city of winding streets
and of miniature marble temples and mansions of the dead
gleaming white from out a wilderness of foliage and fresh
flowers. Not every city is so well peopled as this or has so
ample an area within its walls. Few palaces exist in any
city that are so exquisite in design, so rich in art, so costly
in material, so graceful, so beautiful.

We had stood in the ancient church of St. Denis, where
the marble effigies of thirty generations of kings and queens
lay stretched at length upon the tombs, and the sensations
invoked were startling and novel; the curious armor, the ob-
solete costumes, the placid faces, the hands placed palm to
palm in eloquent supplication—it was a vision of gray antiquity. It seemed curious enough to be standing face to face, as
it were, with old Dagobert I, and Clovis and Charlemagne,
those vague, colossal heroes, those shadows, those myths of
a thousand years ago! I touched their dust-covered faces
with my finger, but Dagobert was deader than the sixteen
centuries that have passed over him, Clovis slept well after
his labor for Christ, and old Charlemagne went on dreaming
of his paladins, of bloody Roncesvalles, and gave no heed to
me.

The great names of Père la Chaise impress one, too, but
differently. There the suggestion brought constantly to his
mind is that this place is sacred to a nobler royalty—the
royalty of heart and brain. Every faculty of mind, every
noble trait of human nature, every high occupation which
men engage in, seems represented by a famous name. The
effect is a curious medley. Davoust and Massena, who
wrought in many a battle tragedy, are here, and so also is
Rachel, of equal renown in mimic tragedy on the stage. The
Abbé Sicard sleeps here—the first great teacher of the
deaf and dumb—a man whose heart went out to every
unfortunate, and whose life was given to kindly offices in
their service; and not far off, in repose and peace at last,
lies Marshal Ney, whose stormy spirit knew no music like
the bugle call to arms. The man who originated public gas-
lighting, and that other benefactor who introduced the cultivation of the potato and thus blessed millions of his starving countrymen, lie with the Prince of Masserano, and with
exiled queens and princes of Further India. Gay-Lussac
the chemist, Laplace the astronomer, Larrey the surgeon, De
Seze the advocate, are here, and with them are Talma,

Bellini, Rubini; de Balzac, Beaumarchais, Beranger; Molière and La Fontaine, and scores of other men whose names and whose worthy labors are as familiar in the remote byplaces of civilization as are the historic deeds of the kings and princes that sleep in the marble vaults of St. Denis.

But among the thousands and thousands of tombs in Père la Chaise, there is one that no man, no woman, no youth of either sex, ever passes by without stopping to examine. Every visitor has a sort of indistinct idea of the history of its dead and comprehends that homage is due there, but not one in twenty thousand clearly remembers the story of that tomb and its romantic occupants. This is the grave of Abelard and Héloïse—a grave which has been more revered, more widely known, more written and sung about and wept over, for seven hundred years, than any other in Christendom save only that of the Saviour. All visitors linger pensively about it; all young people capture and carry away keepsakes and mementos of it; all Parisian youths and maidens who are disappointed in love come there to bail out when they are full of tears; yea, many stricken lovers make pilgrimages to this shrine from distant provinces to weep and wail and "grit" their teeth over their heavy sorrows, and to purchase the sympathies of the chastened spirits of that tomb with offerings of immortelles and budding flowers.

Go when you will, you find somebody snuffling over that tomb. Go when you will, you find it furnished with those bouquets and immortelles. Go when you will, you find a gravel train from Marseilles arriving to supply the deficiencies caused by memento-cabbaging vandals whose affections have miscarried.

Yet who really knows the story of Abelard and Héloïse? Precious few people. The names are perfectly familiar to everybody, and that is about all. With infinite pains I have acquired a knowledge of that history, and I propose to narrate it here, partly for the honest information of the public and partly to show that public that they have been wasting a good deal of marketable sentiment very unnecessarily.

STORY OF ABELARD

Héloïse was born seven hundred and sixty-six years ago. She may have had parents. There is no telling. She lived with her uncle Fulbert, a canon of the cathedral of Paris. I do not know what a canon of a cathedral is, but that is what he was. He was nothing more than a sort of a mountain howitzer, likely, because they had no heavy artillery in those days. Suffice it, then, that Héloïse lived with her uncle the howitzer and was happy. She spent the most of her childhood in the convent of Argenteuil—never heard of Argenteuil before, but suppose there was really such a place. She then returned to her uncle, the old gun, or son of a gun, as the case may be, and he taught her to write and speak Latin, which was the language of literature and polite society at that period.

Just at this time, Pierre Abelard, who had already made himself widely famous as a rhetorician, came to found a school of rhetoric in Paris. The originality of his principles, his eloquence, and his great physical strength and beauty created a profound sensation. He saw Héloïse, and was captivated by her blooming youth, her beauty, and her charming disposition. He wrote to her; she answered. He wrote again; she answered again. He was now in love. He longed to know her—to speak to her face to face.

His school was near Fulbert's house. He asked Fulbert to allow him to call. The good old swivel saw here a rare opportunity: his niece, whom he so much loved, would absorb knowledge from this man, and it would not cost him a cent. Such was Fulbert—penurious.

Fulbert's first name is not mentioned by any author, which is unfortunate. However, George W. Fulbert will answer for him as well as any other. We will let him go at that. He asked Abelard to teach her.

Abelard was glad enough of the opportunity. He came often and stayed long. A letter of his shows in its very first sentence that he came under that friendly roof like a cold-hearted villain as he was, with the deliberate intention of debauching a confiding, innocent girl. This is the letter:

I cannot cease to be astonished at the simplicity of Fulbert; I was as much surprised as if he had placed a lamb in the power of a hungry wolf. Héloïse and I, under pretext of study, gave ourselves up wholly to love, and the solitude that love seeks our studies procured for us. Books were open before us, but we spoke oftener of love than philosophy, and kisses came more readily from our lips than words.

And so, exulting over an honorable confidence which to

his degraded instinct was a ludicrous "simplicity," this un-
manly Abelard seduced the niece of the man whose guest he
was. Paris found it out. Fulbert was told of it—told often—
but refused to believe it. He could not comprehend how a
man could be so depraved as to use the sacred protection
and security of hospitality as a means for the commission of
such a crime as that. But when he heard the rowdies in the
streets singing the lovesongs of Abelard to Héloïse, the
case was too plain—lovesongs come not properly within the
teachings of rhetoric and philosophy.

He drove Abelard from his house. Abelard returned secretly and carried Héloïse away to Palais, in Brittany, his
native country. Here, shortly afterward, she bore a son,
who, from his rare beauty, was surnamed Astrolabe—William
G. The girl's flight enraged Fulbert, and he longed for
vengeance, but feared to strike lest retaliation visit Héloïse
—for he still loved her tenderly. At length Abelard offered
to marry Héloïse—but on a shameful condition: that the
marriage should be kept secret from the world, to the end
that (while her good name remained a wreck, as before)
his priestly reputation might be kept untarnished. It was
like that miscreant. Fulbert saw his opportunity and con-
sented. He would see the parties married and then violate
the confidence of the man who had taught him that trick;
he would divulge the secret and so remove somewhat of the
obloquy that attached to his niece's fame. But the niece
suspected his scheme. She refused the marriage at first; she
said Fulbert would betray the secret to save her, and besides, she did not wish to drag down a lover who was so
gifted, so honored by the world, and who had such a
splendid career before him. It was noble, self-sacrificing love,
and characteristic of the pure-souled Héloïse, but it was
not good sense.

But she was overruled, and the private marriage took
place. Now for Fulbert! The heart so wounded should be
healed at last; the proud spirit so tortured should find rest
again; the humbled head should be lifted up once more. He
proclaimed the marriage in the high places of the city and
rejoiced that dishonor had departed from his house. But lo!
Abelard denied the marriage! Héloïse denied it! The people, knowing the former circumstances, might have believed
Fulbert had only Abelard denied it, but when the person

chiefly interested—the girl herself—denied it, they laughed, despairing Fulbert to scorn.

The poor canon of the cathedral of Paris was spiked again. The last hope of repairing the wrong that had been done his house was gone. What next? Human nature suggested revenge. He compassed it. The historian says:

Ruffians, hired by Fulbert, fell upon Abelard by night, and inflicted upon him a terrible and nameless mutilation.

I am seeking the last resting place of those "ruffians." When I find it I shall shed some tears on it, and stack up some bouquets and immortelles, and cart away from it some gravel whereby to remember that howsoever blotted by crime their lives may have been, these ruffians did one just deed, at any rate, albeit it was not warranted by the strict letter of the law.

Héloïse entered a convent and gave good-bye to the world and its pleasures for all time. For twelve years she never heard of Abelard—never even heard his name mentioned. She had become prioress of Argenteuil and led a life of complete seclusion. She happened one day to see a letter written by him, in which he narrated his own history. She cried over it and wrote him. He answered, addressing her as his "sister in Christ." They continued to correspond, she in the unweighed language of unwavering affection, he in the chilly phraseology of the polished rhetorician. She poured out her heart in passionate, disjointed sentences; he replied with finished essays, divided deliberately into heads and subheads, premises and argument. She showered upon him the tenderest epithets that love could devise, he addressed her from the North Pole of his frozen heart as the "Spouse of Christ"! The abandoned villain!

On account of her too easy government of her nuns, some disreputable irregularities were discovered among them, and the Abbot of St. Denis broke up her establishment. Abelard was the official head of the monastery of St. Gildas de Ruys at that time, and when he heard of her homeless condition a sentiment of pity was aroused in his breast (it is a wonder the unfamiliar emotion did not blow his head off), and he placed her and her troop in the little oratory of the Paraclete, a religious establishment which he had founded. She had many privations and sufferings to undergo at first, but her worth and her gentle disposition

won influential friends for her, and she built up a wealthy
and flourishing nunnery. She became a great favorite with
the heads of the church, and also the people, though she
seldom appeared in public. She rapidly advanced in esteem,
in good report, and in usefulness, and Abelard as rapidly
lost ground. The Pope so honored her that he made her the
head of her order. Abelard, a man of splendid talents, and
ranking as the first debater of his time, became timid, ir-
resolute, and distrustful of his powers. He only needed a
great misfortune to topple him from the high position he held
in the world of intellectual excellence, and it came. Urged
by kings and princes to meet the subtle St. Bernard in debate and crush him, he stood up in the presence of a royal
and illustrious assemblage, and when his antagonist had
finished he looked about him and stammered a commence-
ment; but his courage failed him, the cunning of his tongue
was gone; with his speech unspoken, he trembled and sat
down, a disgraced and vanquished champion.

He died a nobody, and was buried at Cluny, A.D. 1144.
They removed his body to the Paraclete afterward, and
when Héloïse died, twenty years later, they buried her
with him, in accordance with her last wish. He died at the
ripe age of 64, and she at 63. After the bodies had remained
entombed three hundred years, they were removed once
more. They were removed again in 1800, and finally, seventeen years afterward, they were taken up and transferred
to Père la Chaise, where they will remain in peace and
quiet until it comes time for them to get up and move again.

History is silent concerning the last acts of the mountain
howitzer. Let the world say what it will about him, I, at
least, shall always respect the memory and sorrow for the
abused trust and the broken heart and the troubled spirit of
the old smooth bore. Rest and repose be his!

Such is the story of Abelard and Héloïse. Such is the history that Lamartine has shed such cataracts of tears over.
But that man never could come within the influence of a subject in the least pathetic without overflowing his banks. He
ought to be dammed—or leveed, I should more properly say.
Such is the history—not as it is usually told, but as it is when
stripped of the nauseous sentimentality that would enshrine
for our loving worship a dastardly seducer like Pierre Abelard. I have not a word to say against the misused, faithful
girl, and would not withhold from her grave a single one of

those simple tributes which blighted youths and maidens offer to her memory, but I am sorry enough that I have not time and opportunity to write four or five volumes of my opinion of her friend the founder of the Parachute, or the Paraclete, or whatever it was.

The tons of sentiment I have wasted on that unprincipled humbug in my ignorance! I shall throttle down my emotions hereafter, about this sort of people, until I have read them up and know whether they are entitled to any tearful attentions or not. I wish I had my immortelles back now, and that bunch of radishes.

In Paris we often saw in shop windows the sign *"English Spoken Here,"* just as one sees in the windows at home the sign *"Ici on parle française."* We always invaded these places at once—and invariably received the information, framed in faultless French, that the clerk who did the English for the establishment had just gone to dinner and would be back in an hour. Would monsieur buy something? We wondered why those parties happened to take their dinners at such erratic and extraordinary hours, for we never called at a time when an exemplary Christian would be in the least likely to be abroad on such an errand. The truth was, it was a base fraud—a snare to trap the unwary—chaff to catch fledglings with. They had no English-murdering clerk. They trusted to the sign to inveigle foreigners into their lairs, and trusted to their own blandishments to keep them there till they bought something.

We ferreted out another French imposition—a frequent sign to this effect: "ALL MANNER OF AMERICAN DRINKS ARTISTICALLY PREPARED HERE." We procured the services of a gentleman experienced in the nomenclature of the American bar, and moved upon the works of one of these impostors. A bowing, aproned Frenchman skipped forward and said:

"Que voulez les messieurs?" I do not know what *"Que voulez les messieurs?"* means, but such was his remark.

Our general said, "We will take a whiskey straight."

[A stare from the Frenchman.]

"Well, if you don't know what that is, give us a champagne cocktail."

[A stare and a shrug.]

"Well, then, give us a sherry cobbler."

The Frenchman was checkmated. This was all Greek to him.

"Give us a brandy smash!"

The Frenchman began to back away, suspicious of the ominous vigor of the last order—began to back away, shrugging his shoulders and spreading his hands apologetically.

The general followed him up and gained a complete victory. The uneducated foreigner could not even furnish a Santa Cruz Punch, an Eye-Opener, a Stone Fence, or an Earthquake. It was plain that he was a wicked impostor.

An acquaintance of mine said the other day that he was doubtless the only American visitor to the Exposition who had had the high honor of being escorted by the Emperor's bodyguard. I said with unobtrusive frankness that I was astonished that such a long-legged, lantern-jawed, unprepossessing-looking specter as he should be singled out for a distinction like that, and asked how it came about. He said he had attended a great military review in the Champ de Mars some time ago, and while the multitude about him was growing thicker and thicker every moment he observed an open space inside the railing. He left his carriage and went into it. He was the only person there, and so he had plenty of room, and the situation being central, he could see all the preparations going on about the field. By and by there was a sound of music, and soon the Emperor of the French and the Emperor of Austria, escorted by the famous *Cent Gardes,* entered the enclosure. They seemed not to observe him, but directly, in response to a sign from the commander of the guard, a young lieutenant came toward him with a file of his men following, halted, raised his hand, and gave the military salute, and then said in a low voice that he was sorry to have to disturb a stranger and a gentleman, but the place was sacred to royalty. Then this New Jersey phantom rose up and bowed and begged pardon, then with the officer beside him, the file of men marching behind him, and with every mark of respect, he was escorted to his carriage by the imperial *Cent Gardes!* The officer saluted again and fell back, the New Jersey sprite bowed in return and had presence of mind enough to pretend that he had simply called on a matter of private business with those emperors, and so waved them an adieu and drove from the field!

Imagine a poor Frenchman ignorantly intruding upon a

public rostrum sacred to some sixpenny dignitary in America. The police would scare him to death first with a storm of their elegant blasphemy, and then pull him to pieces getting him away from there. We are measurably superior to the French in some things, but they are immeasurably our betters in others.

Enough of Paris for the present. We have done our whole duty by it. We have seen the Tuileries, the Napoleon Column, the Madeleine, that wonder of wonders the tomb of Napoleon, all the great churches and museums, libraries, imperial palaces, and sculpture and picture galleries, the Panthéon, Jardin des Plantes, the opera, the circus, the legislative body, the billiard rooms, the barbers, the grisettes—

Ah, the grisettes! I had almost forgotten. They are another romantic fraud. They were (if you let the books of travel tell it) always so beautiful—so neat and trim, so graceful—so naïve and trusting—so gentle, so winning—so faithful to their shop duties, so irresistible to buyers in their prattling importunity—so devoted to their poverty-stricken students of the Latin Quarter—so lighthearted and happy on their Sunday picnics in the suburbs—and oh, so charmingly, so delightfully immoral!

Stuff! For three or four days I was constantly saying:

"Quick, Ferguson! Is that a grisette?"

And he always said, "No."

He comprehended at last that I wanted to see a grisette. Then he showed me dozens of them. They were like nearly all the Frenchwomen I ever saw—homely. They had large hands, large feet, large mouths; they had pug noses as a general thing, and moustaches that not even good breeding could overlook; they combed their hair straight back without parting; they were ill-shaped, they were not winning, they were not graceful; I knew by their looks that they ate garlic and onions; and lastly and finally, to my thinking it would be base flattery to call them immoral.

Aroint thee, wench! I sorrow for the vagabond student of the Latin Quarter now, even more than formerly I envied him. Thus topples to earth another idol of my infancy.

We have seen everything, and tomorrow we go to Versailles. We shall see Paris only for a little while as we come back to take up our line of march for the ship, and so I may as well bid the beautiful city a regretful farewell. We shall travel many thousands of miles after we leave here and visit many great cities, but we shall find none so enchanting as this.

Some of our party have gone to England, intending to take a roundabout course and rejoin the vessel at Leghorn or Naples several weeks hence. We came near going to Geneva, but have concluded to return to Marseilles and go up through Italy from Genoa.

I will conclude this chapter with a remark that I am sincerely proud to be able to make—and glad, as well, that my comrades cordially endorse it, to wit: by far the handsomest women we have seen in France were born and reared in America.

I feel now like a man who has redeemed a failing reputation and shed luster upon a dimmed escutcheon by a single just deed done at the eleventh hour.

Let the curtain fall, to slow music.

16

Versailles! It is wonderfully beautiful! You gaze and stare and try to understand that it is real, that it is on the earth, that it is not the Garden of Eden—but your brain grows giddy, stupefied by the world of beauty around you, and you half believe you are the dupe of an exquisite dream. The scene thrills one like military music! A noble palace, stretching its ornamented front, block upon block away, till it seemed that it would never end; a grand promenade before it, whereon the armies of an empire might parade; all about it rainbows of flowers, and colossal statues that were almost numberless and yet seemed only scattered over the ample space; broad flights of stone steps leading down from the promenade to lower grounds of the park—stairways that whole regiments might stand to arms upon and have room to spare; vast fountains whose great bronze effigies discharged rivers of sparkling water into the air and mingled a hundred curving jets together in forms of matchless beauty; wide grass-carpeted

avenues that branched hither and thither in every direction
and wandered to seemingly interminable distances, walled all
the way on either side with compact ranks of leafy trees
whose branches met above and formed arches as faultless
and as symmetrical as ever were carved in stone; and here
and there were glimpses of sylvan lakes with miniature ships
glassed in their surfaces. And everywhere—on the palace
steps, and the great promenade, around the fountains, among
the trees, and far under the arches of the endless avenues—
hundreds and hundreds of people in gay costumes walked
or ran or danced, and gave to the fairy picture the life and
animation which was all of perfection it could have lacked.

It was worth a pilgrimage to see. Everything is on so gigantic a scale. Nothing is small—nothing is cheap. The statues
are all large; the palace is grand; the park covers a fair-
sized county; the avenues are interminable. All the distances
and all the dimensions about Versailles are vast. I used to
think the pictures exaggerated these distances and these
dimensions beyond all reason, and that they made Versailles
more beautiful than it was possible for any place in the
world to be. I know now that the pictures never came up to
the subject in any respect, and that no painter could represent
Versailles on canvas as beautiful as it is in reality. I used to
abuse Louis XIV for spending two hundred millions of
dollars in creating this marvelous park when bread was so
scarce with some of his subjects, but I have forgiven him
now. He took a tract of land sixty miles in circumference
and set to work to make this park and build this palace and
a road to it from Paris. He kept 36,000 men employed daily
on it, and the labor was so unhealthy that they used to die
and be hauled off by cartloads every night. The wife of a
nobleman of the time speaks of this as an *"inconvenience,"*
but naïvely remarks that "it does not seem worthy of attention in the happy state of tranquillity we now enjoy."

I always thought ill of people at home who trimmed their
shrubbery into pyramids and squares and spires and all
manner of unnatural shapes, and when I saw the same thing
being practiced in this great park I began to feel dissatisfied.
But I soon saw the idea of the thing and the wisdom of it.
They seek the *general* effect. We distort a dozen sickly trees
into unaccustomed shapes in a little yard no bigger than a
dining room, and then surely they look absurd enough. But
here they take two hundred thousand tall forest trees and set

them in a double row; allow no sign of leaf or branch to
grow on the trunk lower down than six feet above the ground;
from that point the boughs begin to project, and very gradually they extend outward further and further till they meet
overhead, and a faultless tunnel of foliage is formed. The
arch is mathematically precise. The effect is then very fine.
They make trees take fifty different shapes, and so these
quaint effects are infinitely varied and picturesque. The trees
in no two avenues are shaped alike, and consequently the eye
is not fatigued with anything in the nature of monotonous
uniformity. I will drop this subject now, leaving it to others
to determine how these people manage to make endless ranks
of lofty forest trees grow to just a certain thickness of
trunk (say a foot and two-thirds); how they make them spring
to precisely the same height for miles; how they make them
grow so close together; how they compel one huge limb to
spring from the same identical spot on each tree and form
the main sweep of the arch; and how all these things are kept
exactly in the same condition and in the same exquisite shape-
liness and symmetry month after month and year after year—
for I have tried to reason out the problem and have failed.

We walked through the great hall of sculpture and the
one hundred and fifty galleries of paintings in the palace of
Versailles, and felt that to be in such a place was useless
unless one had a whole year at his disposal. These pictures
are all battle scenes, and only one solitary little canvas among
them all treats of anything but great French victories. We
wandered, also, through the Grand Trianon and the Petit
Trianon, those monuments of royal prodigality, and with histories so mournful—filled, as it is, with souvenirs of Napoleon the First, and three dead kings and as many queens. In
one sumptuous bed they had all slept in succession, but no
one occupies it now. In a large dining room stood the table at
which Louis XIV and his mistress Madame Maintenon, and
after them Louis XV, and Pompadour, had sat at their meals
naked and unattended—for the table stood upon a trapdoor,
which descended with it to regions below when it was necessary to replenish its dishes. In a room of the Petit Trianon
stood the furniture, just as poor Marie Antoinette left it
when the mob came and dragged her and the King to Paris,
never to return. Near at hand, in the stables, were prodigious
carriages that showed no color but gold—carriages used by
former kings of France on state occasions, and never used

now save when a kingly head is to be crowned or an imperial
infant christened. And with them were some curious sleighs,
whose bodies were shaped like lions, swans, tigers, etc.—
vehicles that had once been handsome with pictured designs
and fine workmanship, but were dusty and decaying now.
They had their history. When Louis XIV had finished the
Grand Trianon, he told Maintenon he had created a paradise
for her, and asked if she could think of anything now to wish
for. He said he wished the Trianon to be perfection—nothing less. She said she could think of but one thing—it was
summer, and it was balmy France—yet she would like well to
sleigh ride in the leafy avenues of Versailles! The next morning found miles and miles of grassy avenues spread thick
with snowy salt and sugar, and a procession of those quaint
sleighs waiting to receive the chief concubine of the gaiest
and most unprincipled court that France has ever seen!

From sumptuous Versailles, with its palaces, its statues, its
gardens, and its fountains, we journeyed back to Paris and
sought its antipodes—the Faubourg St. Antoine. Little, narrow streets; dirty children blockading them; greasy, slovenly
women capturing and spanking them; filthy dens on first
floors, with rag stores in them (the heaviest business in the
Faubourg is the chiffonier's); other filthy dens where whole
suits of second- and third-hand clothing are sold at prices that
would ruin any proprietor who did not steal his stock; still
other filthy dens where they sold groceries—sold them by the
halfpennyworth—five dollars would buy the man out, goodwill and all. Up these little crooked streets they will murder
a man for seven dollars and dump the body in the Seine.
And up some other of these streets—most of them, I should
say—live *lorettes*.

All through this Faubourg St. Antoine, misery, poverty,
vice, and crime go hand in hand, and the evidences of it stare
one in the face from every side. Here the people live who
begin the revolutions. Whenever there is anything of that
kind to be done, they are always ready. They take as much
genuine pleasure in building a barricade as they do in cutting
a throat or shoving a friend into the Seine. It is these savage-
looking ruffians who storm the splendid halls of the Tuileries
occasionally, and swarm into Versailles when a king is to be
called to account.

But they will build no more barricades; they will break no
more soldiers' heads with paving stones. Louis Napoleon has

taken care of all that. He is annihilating the crooked streets and building in their stead noble boulevards as straight as an arrow—avenues which a cannon ball could traverse from end to end without meeting an obstruction more irresistible than the flesh and bones of men—boulevards whose stately edifices will never afford refuges and plotting places for starving, discontented revolution breeders. Five of these great thorough-fares radiate from one ample center—a center which is ex-ceedingly well adapted to the accommodation of heavy artil-lery. The mobs used to riot there, but they must seek another rallying place in future. And this ingenious Napoleon paves the streets of his great cities with a smooth, compact composi-tion of asphaltum and sand. No more barricades of flagstones —no more assaulting his majesty's troops with cobbles. I cannot feel friendly toward my quondam fellow American Napoleon III, especially at this time,* when in fancy I see his credulous victim, Maximilian, lying stark and stiff in Mexico, and his maniac widow watching eagerly from her French asylum for the form that will never come—but I do admire his nerve, his calm self-reliance, his shrewd good sense.

17

We had a pleasant journey of it seaward again. We found that for the three past nights our ship had been in a state of war. The first night the sailors of a British ship, being happy with grog, came down on the pier and challenged our sailors to a free fight. They accepted with alacrity, repaired to the pier, and gained—their share of a drawn battle. Several bruised and bloody members of both parties were carried off by the police and imprisoned until the following morning. The next night the British boys came again to renew the fight, but our men had had strict orders to remain on board and out of sight. They did so, and the besieging party grew noisy and more and more abusive as the fact became

* July, 1867.

apparent (to them) that our men were afraid to come out. They went away finally with a closing burst of ridicule and offensive epithets. The third night they came again and were more obstreperous than ever. They swaggered up and down the almost deserted pier and hurled curses, obscenity, and stinging sarcasms at our crew. It was more than human nature could bear. The executive officer ordered our men ashore—with instructions not to fight. They charged the British and gained a brilliant victory. I probably would not have mentioned this war had it ended differently. But I travel to learn, and I still remember that they picture no French defeats in the battle galleries of Versailles.

It was like home to us to step on board the comfortable ship again and smoke and lounge about her breezy decks. And yet it was not altogether like home, either, because so many members of the family were away. We missed some pleasant faces which we would rather have found at dinner, and at night there were gaps in the euchre parties which could not be satisfactorily filled. "Moult" was in England, Jack in Switzerland, Charley in Spain. Blucher was gone, none could tell where. But we were at sea again, and we had the stars and the ocean to look at, and plenty of room to meditate in.

In due time the shores of Italy were sighted, and as we stood gazing from the decks, early in the bright summer morning, the stately city of Genoa rose up out of the sea and flung back the sunlight from her hundred palaces.

Here we rest for the present—or rather, here we have been trying to rest, for some little time, but we run about too much to accomplish a great deal in that line.

I would like to remain here. I had rather not go any further. There may be prettier women in Europe, but I doubt it. The population of Genoa is 120,000; two-thirds of these are women, I think, and at least two-thirds of the women are beautiful. They are as dressy and as tasteful and as graceful as they could possibly be without being angels. However, angels are not very dressy, I believe. At least the angels in pictures are not—they wear nothing but wings. But these Genoese women do look so charming. Most of the young demoiselles are robed in a cloud of white from head to foot, though many trick themselves out more elaborately. Nine-tenths of them wear nothing on their heads but a filmy sort of veil, which falls down their backs like a white mist. They are very fair, and many of them have blue eyes, but black and dreamy dark brown ones are met with oftenest.

The ladies and gentlemen of Genoa have a pleasant fashion of promenading in a large park on the top of a hill in the center of the city, from six till nine in the evening, and then eating ices in a neighboring garden an hour or two longer. We went to the park on Sunday evening. Two thousand persons were present, chiefly young ladies and gentlemen. The gentlemen were dressed in the very latest Paris fashions, and the robes of the ladies glinted among the trees like so many snowflakes. The multitude moved round and round the park in a great procession. The bands played, and so did the fountains; the moon and the gas lamps lit up the scene, and altogether it was a brilliant and an animated picture. I scanned every female face that passed, and it seemed to me that all were handsome. I never saw such a freshet of loveliness before. I did not see how a man of only ordinary decision of character could marry here, because before he could get his mind made up he would fall in love with somebody else.

Never smoke any Italian tobacco. Never do it on any account. It makes me shudder to think what it must be made of. You cannot throw an old cigar "stub" down anywhere, but some vagabond will pounce upon it on the instant. I like to smoke a good deal, but it wounds my sensibilities to see one of these stub-hunters watching me out of the corners of his hungry eyes and calculating how long my cigar will be likely to last. It reminded me too painfully of that San Francisco undertaker who used to go to sickbeds with his watch in his hand and time the corpse. One of these stub-hunters followed us all over the park last night, and we never had a smoke that was worth anything. We were always moved to appease him with the stub before the cigar was half gone, because he looked so viciously anxious. He regarded us as his own legitimate prey, by right of discovery, I think, because he drove off several other professionals who wanted to take stock in us.

Now, they surely must chew up those old stubs and dry and sell them for smoking tobacco. Therefore, give your custom to other than Italian brands of the article.

"The Superb" and the "City of Palaces" are names which Genoa has held for centuries. She is full of palaces, certainly, and the palaces are sumptuous inside, but they are very rusty without and make no pretensions to architectural magnificence. "Genoa the Superb" would be a felicitous title if it referred to the women.

We have visited several of the palaces—immense thick-walled piles, with great stone staircases, tessellated marble pavement on the floors (sometimes they make a mosaicwork of intricate designs, wrought in pebbles or little fragments of marble laid in cement), and grand *salons* hung with pictures by Rubens, Guido, Titian, Paul Veronese, and so on, and portraits of heads of the family in plumed helmets and gallant coats of mail, and patrician ladies in stunning costumes of centuries ago. But, of course, the folks were all out in the country for the summer, and might not have known enough to ask us to dinner if they had been at home, and so all the grand empty *salons*, with their resounding pavements, their grim pictures of dead ancestors, and tattered banners with the dust of bygone centuries upon them seemed to brood solemnly of death and the grave, and our spirits ebbed away, and our cheerfulness passed from us. We never went up to the eleventh story. We always began to suspect ghosts. There was always an undertaker-looking servant along, too, who handed us a program, pointed to the picture that began the list of the *salon* he was in, and then stood stiff and stark and unsmiling in his petrified livery till we were ready to move on to the next chamber, whereupon he marched sadly ahead and took up another malignantly respectful position as before. I wasted so much time praying that the roof would fall in on these dispiriting flunkies that I had but little left to bestow upon palace and pictures.

And besides, as in Paris, we had a guide. Perdition catch all the guides. This one said he was the most gifted linguist in Genoa, as far as English was concerned, and that only two persons in the city beside himself could talk the language at all. He showed us the birthplace of Christopher Columbus, and after we had reflected in silent awe before it for fifteen minutes, he said it was not the birthplace of Columbus, but of Columbus' grandmother! When we demanded an explanation of his conduct he only shrugged his shoulders and answered in barbarous Italian. I shall speak further of this guide in a future chapter. All the information we got out of him we shall be able to carry along with us, I think.

I have not been to church so often in a long time as I have in the last few weeks. The people in these old lands seem to make churches their specialty. Especially does this

seem to be the case with the citizens of Genoa. I think there
is a church every three or four hundred yards all over town.
The streets are sprinkled from end to end with shovel-hatted,
long-robed, well-fed priests, and the church bells by dozens
are pealing all the day long, nearly. Every now and then one
comes across a friar of orders gray, with shaven head, long,
coarse robe, rope girdle and beads, and with feet cased in
sandals or entirely bare. These worthies suffer in the flesh and
do penance all their lives, I suppose, but they look like consummate famine-breeders. They are all fat and serene.

The old Cathedral of San Lorenzo is about as notable a
building as we have found in Genoa. It is vast, and has
colonnades of noble pillars, and a great organ, and the customary pomp of gilded moldings, pictures, frescoed ceilings,
and so forth. I cannot describe it, of course—it would require a good many pages to do that. But it is a curious
place. They said that half of it—from the front door halfway down to the altar—was a Jewish synagogue before the
Saviour was born, and that no alteration had been made in
it since that time. We doubted the statement, but did it
reluctantly. We would much rather have believed it. The
place looked in too perfect repair to be so ancient.

The main point of interest about the cathedral is the little
Chapel of St. John the Baptist. They only allow women to
enter it on one day in the year, on account of the animosity
they still cherish against the sex because of the murder of the
saint to gratify a caprice of Herodias. In this chapel is a
marble chest, in which, they told us, were the ashes of
St. John; and around it was wound a chain, which, they said,
had confined him when he was in prison. We did not desire
to disbelieve these statements, and yet we could not feel
certain that they were correct—partly because we could
have broken that chain, and so could St. John, and partly
because we had seen St. John's ashes before, in another church.
We could not bring ourselves to think St. John had two sets
of ashes.

They also showed us a portrait of the Madonna which
was painted by St. Luke, and it did not look half as old
and smoky as some of the pictures by Rubens. We could
not help admiring the Apostle's modesty in never once mentioning in his writings that he could paint.

But isn't this relic matter a little overdone? We find a
piece of the true cross in every old church we go into, and

some of the nails that held it together. I would not like to be positive, but I think we have seen as much as a keg of these nails. Then there is the crown of thorns; they have part of one in Sainte Chapelle, in Paris, and part of one also in Notre Dame. And as for bones of St. Denis, I feel certain we have seen enough of them to duplicate him if necessary.

I only meant to write about the churches, but I keep wandering from the subject. I could say that the Church of the Annunciation is a wilderness of beautiful columns, of statues, gilded moldings, and pictures almost countless, but that would give no one an entirely perfect idea of the thing, and so where is the use? One family built the whole edifice and have got money left. There is where the mystery lies. We had an idea at first that only a mint could have survived the expense.

These people here live in the heaviest, highest, broadest, darkest, solidest houses one can imagine. Each one might "laugh a siege to scorn." A hundred feet front and a hundred high is about the style, and you go up three flights of stairs before you begin to come upon signs of occupancy. Everything is stone, and stone of the heaviest—floors, stairways, mantels, benches—everything. The walls are four to five feet thick. The streets generally are four or five to eight feet wide and as crooked as a corkscrew. You go along one of these gloomy cracks, and look up and behold the sky like a mere ribbon of light, far above your head, where the tops of the tall houses on either side of the street bend almost together. You feel as if you were at the bottom of some tremendous abyss, with all the world far above you. You wind in and out and here and there, in the most mysterious way, and have no more idea of the points of the compass than if you were a blind man. You can never persuade yourself that these are actually streets, and the frowning, dingy, monstrous houses dwellings, till you see one of these beautiful, prettily dressed women emerge from them—see her emerge from a dark, dreary-looking den that looks dungeon all over, from the ground away halfway up to heaven. And then you wonder that such a charming moth could come from such a forbidding shell as that. The streets are wisely made narrow and the houses heavy and thick and stony, in order that the people may be cool in this roasting climate. And they are cool, and stay so. And while I think of it—the men wear hats and have very dark complexions, but the women wear no headgear but a flimsy veil like a gossamer's web, and yet are exceedingly fair as a general thing. Singular, isn't it?

The huge palaces of Genoa are each supposed to be occupied by one family, but they could accommodate a hundred, I should think. They are relics of the grandeur of Genoa's palmy days—the days when she was a great commercial and maritime power several centuries ago. These houses, solid marble palaces though they be, are in many cases of a dull pinkish color, outside, and from pavement to eaves are pictured with Genoese battle scenes, with monstrous Jupiters and Cupids, and with familiar illustrations from Grecian mythology. Where the paint has yielded to age and exposure and is peeling off in flakes and patches, the effect is not happy. A noseless Cupid or a Jupiter with an eye out or a Venus with a fly blister on her breast are not attractive features in a picture. Some of these painted walls reminded me somewhat of the tall van, plastered with fanciful bills and posters, that follows the bandwagon of a circus about a country village. I have not read or heard that the outsides of the houses of any other European city are frescoed in this way.

I cannot conceive of such a thing as Genoa in ruins. Such massive arches, such ponderous substructions as support these towering broad-winged edifices, we have seldom seen before; and surely the great blocks of stone of which these edifices are built can never decay; walls that are as thick as an ordinary American doorway is high cannot crumble.

The republics of Genoa and Pisa were very powerful in the Middle Ages. Their ships filled the Mediterranean, and they carried on an extensive commerce with Constantinople and Syria. Their warehouses were the great distributing depots from whence the costly merchandise of the East was sent abroad over Europe. They were warlike little nations and defied, in those days, governments that overshadow them now as mountains overshadow molehills. The Saracens captured and pillaged Genoa nine hundred years ago, but during the following century Genoa and Pisa entered into an offensive and defensive alliance and besieged the Saracen colonies in Sardinia and the Balearic Isles with an obstinacy that maintained its pristine vigor and held to its purpose for forty long years. They were victorious at last and divided their conquests equably among their great patrician families.

Descendants of some of those proud families still inhabit the palaces of Genoa, and trace in their own features a resemblance to the grim knights whose portraits hang in their stately halls, and to pictured beauties with pouting lips and merry eyes whose originals have been dust and ashes for many a dead and forgotten century.

The hotel we live in belonged to one of those great orders of knights of the Cross in the times of the Crusades, and its mailed sentinels once kept watch and ward in its massive turrets and woke the echoes of these halls and corridors with their iron heels.

But Genoa's greatness has degenerated into an unostentatious commerce in velvets and silver filagreework. They say that each European town has its specialty. These filagree things are Genoa's specialty. Her smiths take silver ingots and work them up into all manner of graceful and beautiful forms. They make bunches of flowers, from flakes and wires of silver, that counterfeit the delicate creations the frost weaves upon a windowpane; and we were shown a miniature silver temple whose fluted columns, whose Corinthian capitals and rich entablatures, whose spire, statues, bells, and ornate lavishness of sculpture were wrought in polished silver, and with such matchless art that every detail was a fascinating study and the finished edifice a wonder of beauty.

We are ready to move again, though we are not really tired yet of the narrow passages of this old marble cave. Cave is a good word—when speaking of Genoa under the stars. When we have been prowling at midnight through the gloomy crevices they call streets, where no footfalls but ours were echoing, where only ourselves were abroad, and lights appeared only at long intervals and at a distance, and mysteriously disappeared again, and the houses at our elbows seemed to stretch upward farther than ever toward the heavens, the memory of a cave I used to know at home was always in my mind, with its lofty passages, its silence and solitude, its shrouding gloom, its sepulchral echoes, its flitting lights, and more than all, its sudden revelations of branching crevices and corridors where we least expected them.

We are not tired of the endless processions of cheerful, chattering gossipers that throng these courts and streets all day long, either; nor of the coarse-robed monks; nor of the "Asti" wines, which that old doctor (whom we call the Ora-

cle), with customary felicity in the matter of getting everything wrong, misterms "nasty." But we must go, nevertheless.

Our last sight was the cemetery (a burial place intended
to accommodate 60,000 bodies), and we shall continue to
remember it after we shall have forgotten the palaces. It is a
vast marble colonnaded corridor extending around a
great unoccupied square of ground; its broad floor is marble,
and on every slab is an inscription—for every slab covers a
corpse. On either side, as one walks down the middle of the
passage, are monuments, tombs, and sculptured figures that
are exquisitely wrought and are full of grace and beauty.
They are new and snowy; every outline is perfect, every
feature guiltless of mutilation, flaw, or blemish; and therefore, to us these far-reaching ranks of bewitching forms are
a hundredfold more lovely than the damaged and dingy
statuary they have saved from the wreck of ancient art and
set up in the galleries of Paris for the worship of the world.

Well provided with cigars and other necessaries of life,
we are now ready to take the cars for Milan.

18

All day long we sped through a mountainous country whose
peaks were bright with sunshine, whose hillsides were dotted
with pretty villas sitting in the midst of gardens and shrubbery, and whose deep ravines were cool and shady and
looked ever so inviting from where we and the birds were
winging our flight through the sultry upper air.

We had plenty of chilly tunnels wherein to check our
perspiration, though. We timed one of them. We were twenty
minutes passing through it, going at the rate of thirty to
thirty-five miles an hour.

Beyond Alessandria we passed the battlefield of Marengo.

Toward dusk we drew near Milan and caught glimpses of
the city and the blue mountain peaks beyond. But we were
not caring for these things—they did not interest us in the

least. We were in a fever of impatience; we were dying to see the renowned cathedral! We watched—in this direction and that—all around—everywhere. We needed no one to point it out—we did not wish anyone to point it out—we would recognize it even in the desert of the great Sahara.

At last, a forest of graceful needles, shimmering in the amber sunlight, rose slowly above the pygmy housetops, as one sometimes sees, in the far horizon, a gilded and pinnacled mass of cloud lift itself above the waste of waves, at sea—the cathedral! We knew it in a moment.

Half of that night and all of the next day this architectural autocrat was our sole object of interest.

What a wonder it is! So grand, so solemn, so vast! And yet so delicate, so airy, so graceful! A very world of solid weight, and yet it seems in the soft moonlight only a fairy delusion of frostwork that might vanish with a breath! How sharply its pinnacled angles and its wilderness of spires were cut against the sky, and how richly their shadows fell upon its snowy roof! It was a vision!—a miracle!—an anthem sung in stone, a poem wrought in marble!

Howsoever you look at the great cathedral, it is noble, it is beautiful! Wherever you stand in Milan or within seven miles of Milan, it is visible—and when it is visible, no other object can chain your whole attention. Leave your eyes unfettered by your will but a single instant and they will surely turn to seek it. It is the first thing you look for when you rise in the morning, and the last your lingering gaze rests upon at night. Surely it must be the princeliest creation that ever brain of man conceived.

At nine o'clock in the morning we went and stood before this marble colossus. The central one of its five great doors is bordered with a bas-relief of birds and fruits and beasts and insects, which have been so ingeniously carved out of the marble that they seem like living creatures—and the figures are so numerous and the design so complex that one might study it a week without exhausting its interest. On the great steeple—surmounting the myriad of spires—inside of the spires—over the doors, the windows—in nooks and corners —everywhere that a niche or a perch can be found about the enormous building, from summit to base, there is a marble statue, and every statue is a study in itself! Raphael, Angelo, Canova—giants like these gave birth to the designs, and their own pupils carved them. Every face is eloquent with ex-

pression, and every attitude is full of grace. Away above, on
the lofty roof, rank on rank of carved and fretted spires
spring high in the air, and through their rich tracery one
sees the sky beyond. In their midst the central steeple towers
proudly up like the mainmast of some great Indiaman among
a fleet of coasters.

We wished to go aloft. The sacristan showed us a marble
stairway (of course it was marble, and of the purest and
whitest—there is no other stone, no brick, no wood, among
its building materials) and told us to go up one hundred
and eighty-two steps and stop till he came. It was not necessary to say stop—we should have done that anyhow. We
were tired by the time we got there. This was the roof.
Here, springing from its broad marble flagstones, were the long
files of spires, looking very tall close at hand, but diminishing in the distance like the pipes of an organ. We could see
now that the statue on the top of each was the size of a
large man, though they all looked like dolls from the street.
We could see also that from the inside of each and every
one of these hollow spires, from sixteen to thirty-one beautiful
marble statues looked out upon the world below.

From the eaves to the comb of the roof stretched in endless succession great curved marble beams, like the fore-
and-aft braces of a steamboat, and along each beam from
end to end stood up a row of richly carved flowers and fruits
—each separate and distinct in kind, and over 15,000 species
represented. At a little distance these rows seem to close
together like the ties of a railroad track, and then the mingling
together of the buds and blossoms of this marble garden
forms a picture that is very charming to the eye.

We descended and entered. Within the church, long rows
of fluted columns, like huge monuments, divided the building
into broad aisles, and on the figured pavement fell many a
soft blush from the painted windows above. I knew the
church was very large, but I could not fully appreciate its
great size until I noticed that the men standing far down by
the altar looked like boys, and seemed to glide, rather than
walk. We loitered about gazing aloft at the monster windows
all aglow with brilliantly colored scenes in the lives of the
Saviour and his followers. Some of these pictures are mosaics,
and so artistically are their thousand particles of tinted glass
or stone put together that the work has all the smoothness
and finish of a painting. We counted sixty panes of glass in

one window, and each pane was adorned with one of these master achievements of genius and patience.

The guide showed us a coffee-colored piece of sculpture which he said was considered to have come from the hand of Phidias, since it was not possible that any other artist, of any epoch, could have copied nature with such faultless accuracy. The figure was that of a man without a skin; with every vein, artery, muscle, every fiber and tendon and tissue of the human frame represented in minute detail. It looked natural, because somehow it looked as if it were in pain. A skinned man would be likely to look that way unless his attention were occupied with some other matter. It was a hideous thing, and yet there was a fascination about it somewhere. I am very sorry I saw it, because I shall always see it now. I shall dream of it sometimes. I shall dream that it is resting its corded arms on the bed's head and looking down on me with its dead eyes; I shall dream that it is stretched between the sheets with me and touching me with its exposed muscles and its stringy cold legs.

It is hard to forget repulsive things. I remember yet how I ran off from school once, when I was a boy, and then, pretty late at night, concluded to climb into the window of my father's office and sleep on a lounge, because I had a delicacy about going home and getting thrashed. As I lay on the lounge and my eyes grew accustomed to the darkness, I fancied I could see a long, dusky, shapeless thing stretched upon the floor. A cold shiver went through me. I turned my face to the wall. That did not answer. I was afraid that that thing would creep over and seize me in the dark. I turned back and stared at it for minutes and minutes—they seemed hours. It appeared to me that the lagging moonlight never, never would get to it. I turned to the wall and counted twenty, to pass the feverish time away. I looked—the pale square was nearer. I turned again and counted fifty—it was almost touching it. With desperate will I turned again and counted one hundred, and faced about, all in a tremble. A white human hand lay in the moonlight! Such an awful sinking at the heart—such a sudden gasp for breath! I felt —I cannot tell *what* I felt. When I recovered strength enough, I faced the wall again. But no boy could have remained so with that mysterious hand behind him. I counted again and looked—the most of a naked arm was exposed. I put my hands over my eyes and counted till I could stand it no longer, and then—the pallid face of a man was there, with the corners of the mouth drawn down, and the eyes fixed and glassy in death! I raised to a sitting posture and glowered on that corpse till the light crept down the bare breast— line by line—inch by inch—past the nipple—and then it disclosed a ghastly stab!

I went away from there. I do not say that I went away in any sort of a hurry, but I simply went—that is sufficient. I went out at the window, and I carried the sash along with me. I did not need the sash, but it was handier to take it than it was to leave it, and so I took it. I was not scared, but I was considerably agitated.

When I reached home, they whipped me, but I enjoyed it. It seemed perfectly delightful. That man had been stabbed near the office that afternoon, and they carried him in there to doctor him, but he only lived an hour. I have slept in the same room with him often since then—in my dreams.

Now we will descend into the crypt, under the grand altar of Milan Cathedral, and receive an impressive sermon from lips that have been silent and hands that have been gestureless for three hundred years.

The priest stopped in a small dungeon and held up his candle. This was the last resting place of a good man, a warmhearted, unselfish man; a man whose whole life was given to succoring the poor, encouraging the fainthearted, visiting the sick; in relieving distress whenever and wherever he found it. His heart, his hand, and his purse were always open. With his story in one's mind we can almost see his benignant countenance moving calmly among the haggard faces of Milan in the days when the plague swept the city, brave where all others were cowards, full of compassion where pity had been crushed out of all other breasts by the instinct of self-preservation gone mad with terror, cheering all, praying with all, helping all, with hand and brain and purse, at a time when parents forsook their children, the friend deserted the friend, and the brother turned away from the sister while her pleadings were still wailing in his ears.

This was good St. Charles Borromeo, Bishop of Milan. The people idolized him; princes lavished uncounted treasures upon him. We stood in his tomb. Nearby was the sarcophagus, lighted by the dripping candles. The walls were faced with bas-reliefs representing scenes in his life done in massive silver. The priest put on a short white lace garment over his black robe, crossed himself, bowed reverently, and began to turn a windlass slowly. The sarcophagus separated in two parts, lengthwise, and the lower part sank down and disclosed a coffin of rock crystal as clear as the atmosphere. Within lay the body, robed in costly habiliments covered with gold embroidery and starred with scintillating gems. The decaying head was black with age, the dry skin was drawn tight to the bones, the eyes were gone, there was a hole in the temple and another in the cheek, and the skinny lips were parted as in a ghastly smile! Over this dreadful face, its dust and decay and its mocking grin, hung a crown sown thick with flashing brilliants; and upon the breast lay crosses and crosiers of solid gold that were splendid with emeralds and diamonds.

How poor and cheap and trivial these gewgaws seemed in presence of the solemnity, the grandeur, the awful majesty of Death! Think of Milton, Shakespeare, Washington, standing before a reverent world tricked out in the glass beads, the brass earrings, and tin trumpery of the savages of the plains!

Dead Borromeo preached his pregnant sermon, and its burden was: You that worship the vanities of earth—you that long for worldly honor, worldly wealth, worldly fame—behold their worth!

To us it seemed that so good a man, so kind a heart, so simple a nature, deserved rest and peace in a grave sacred from the intrusion of prying eyes, and believed that he himself would have preferred to have it so, but peradventure our wisdom was at fault in this regard.

As we came out upon the floor of the church again, another priest volunteered to show us the treasures of the church. What, more? The furniture of the narrow chamber of death we had just visited weighed six millions of francs in ounces and carats alone, without a penny thrown into the account for the costly workmanship bestowed upon them! But we followed into a large room filled with tall wooden presses like wardrobes. He threw them open, and behold, the cargoes of "crude bullion" of the assay offices of Nevada faded out of my memory. There were Virgins and bishops there, above their natural size, made of solid silver, each worth, by weight, from eight hundred thousand to two millions of francs, and bearing gemmed books in their hands worth eighty thousand; there were bas-reliefs that weighed six hundred pounds, carved in solid silver; crosiers and crosses, and candlesticks six and eight feet high, all of virgin gold and brilliant with precious stones; and beside these were all manner of cups and vases and such things, rich in proportion. It was an Aladdin's palace. The treasures here, by simple weight, without counting workmanship, were valued at fifty millions of francs! If I could get the custody of them for a while, I fear me the market price of silver bishops would advance shortly, on account of their exceeding scarcity in the Cathedral of Milan.

The priests showed us two of St. Paul's fingers and one of St. Peter's; a bone of Judas Iscariot (it was black) and also bones of all the other disciples; a handkerchief in which the Saviour had left the impression of his face. Among the most precious of the relics were a stone from the Holy Sepulchre, part of the crown of thorns (they have a whole one at Notre Dame), a fragment of the purple robe worn by the Saviour, a nail from the Cross, and a picture of the Virgin and Child painted by the veritable hand of St. Luke. This is the second of St. Luke's Virgins we have seen. Once a year all these holy relics are carried in procession through the streets of Milan.

I like to revel in the dryest details of the great cathedral. The building is five hundred feet long by one hundred and eighty wide, and the principal steeple is in the neighborhood of four hundred feet high. It has 7,148 marble statues, and will have upwards of three thousand more when it is finished. In addition it has one thousand five hundred bas-reliefs. It has one hundred and thirty-six spires—twenty-one more are to be added. Each spire is surmounted by a statue six and a half feet high. Everything about the church is marble, and all from the same quarry; it was bequeathed to the Archbishopric for this purpose centuries ago. So nothing but the mere workmanship costs; still, that is expensive—the bill foots up six hundred and eighty-four millions of francs thus far (considerably over a hundred millions of dollars), and it is estimated that it will take a hundred and twenty years yet to finish the cathedral. It looks complete, but is far from being so. We saw a new statue put in its niche yesterday, alongside of one which had been standing these four hundred years, they said. There are four staircases leading up to the main steeple, each of which cost a hundred thousand dollars, with the four hundred and eight statues which adorn them. Marco Compioni was the architect who designed the wonderful structure more than five hundred years ago, and it took him forty-six years to work out the plan and get it ready to hand over to the builders. He is dead now. The building was begun a little less than five hundred years ago, and the third generation hence will not see it completed.

The building looks best by moonlight, because the older portions of it, being stained with age, contrast unpleasantly with the newer and whiter portions. It seems somewhat too broad for its height, but maybe familiarity with it might dissipate this impression.

They say that the Cathedral of Milan is second only to St. Peter's at Rome. I cannot understand how it can be second to anything made by human hands.

We bid it good-bye now—possibly for all time. How surely, in some future day, when the memory of it shall have lost its vividness, shall we half believe we have seen it in a wonderful dream, but never with waking eyes!

19

"Do you wis zo haut can be?"

This was what the guide asked when we were looking up at the bronze horses on the Arch of Peace. It meant, do you wish to go up there? I give it as a specimen of guide-English. These are the people that make life a burthen to the tourist. Their tongues are never still. They talk forever and forever, and that is the kind of billingsgate they use. Inspiration itself could hardly comprehend them. If they would only show you a masterpiece of art, or a venerable tomb, or a prison house, or a battlefield, hallowed by touching memories or historical reminiscences, or grand traditions, and then step aside and hold still for ten minutes and let you think, it would not be so bad. But they interrupt every dream, every pleasant train of thought, with their tiresome cackling. Sometimes when I have been standing before some cherished old idol of mine that I remembered years and years ago in pictures in the geography at school, I have thought I would give a whole world if the human parrot at my side would suddenly perish where he stood and leave me to gaze and ponder and worship.

No, we did not "wis zo haut can be." We wished to go to La Scala, the largest theater in the world, I think they call it. We did so. It was a large place. Seven separate and distinct masses of humanity—six great circles and a monster par-quette.

We wished to go to the Ambrosian Library, and we did that also. We saw a manuscript of Vergil, with annotations in the handwriting of Petrarch, the gentleman who loved another man's Laura and lavished upon her all through life a love which was a clear waste of the raw material. It was sound sentiment, but bad judgment. It brought both parties fame and created a fountain of commiseration for them in sentimental breasts that is running yet. But who says a word in behalf of poor Mr. Laura? (I do not know his other name.) Who glorifies him? Who bedews him with tears? Who writes poetry about him? Nobody. How do you suppose *he* liked the state of things that has given the world so much pleasure? How did he enjoy having another man following his wife everywhere and making her name a fa-miliar word in every garlic-exterminating mouth in Italy with his sonnets to her preempted eyebrows? *They* got fame and sympathy—he got neither. This is a peculiarly felicitous instance of what is called poetical justice. It is all very fine, but it does not chime with my notions of right. It is too one-sided—too ungenerous. Let the world go on fretting about Laura and Petrarch if it will; but as for me, my tears and my lamentations shall be lavished upon the unsung de-fendant.

We saw also an autograph letter of Lucrezia Borgia, a lady for whom I have always entertained the highest respect, on account of her rare histrionic capabilities, her opulence in solid gold goblets made of gilded wood, her high distinction as an operatic screamer, and the facility with which she could order a sextuple funeral and get the corpses ready for it. We saw one single coarse yellow hair from Lucrezia's head, likewise. It awoke emotions, but we still live. In this

same library we saw some drawings by Michelangelo (these
Italians call him Mickelangelo) and Leonardo da Vinci.
(They spell it Vinci and pronounce it Vinchy; foreigners
always spell better than they pronounce.) We reserve our
opinion of these sketches.

In another building they showed us a fresco representing
some lions and other beasts drawing chariots; and they
seemed to project so far from the wall that we took them
to be sculptures. The artist had shrewdly heightened the
delusion by painting dust on the creatures' backs, as if it had
fallen there naturally and properly. Smart fellow—if it be
smart to deceive strangers.

Elsewhere we saw a huge Roman amphitheater, with its
stone seats still in good preservation. Modernized, it is now
the scene of more peaceful recreations than the exhibition of
a party of wild beasts with Christians for dinner. Part of
the time the Milanese use it for a racetrack, and at other
seasons they flood it with water and have spirited yachting
regattas there. The guide told us these things, and he would
hardly try so hazardous an experiment as the telling of a
falsehood, when it is all he can do to speak the truth in
English without getting the lockjaw.

In another place we were shown a sort of summer arbor
with a fence before it. We said that was nothing. We looked
again and saw, through the arbor, an endless stretch of
garden and shrubbery and grassy lawn. We were perfectly
willing to go in there and rest, but it could not be done.
It was only another delusion—a painting by some ingenious
artist with little charity in his heart for tired folk. The
deception was perfect. No one could have imagined the park
was not real. We even thought we smelled the flowers at
first.

We got a carriage at twilight and drove in the shaded
avenues with the other nobility, and after dinner we took
wine and ices in a fine garden with the great public. The
music was excellent, the flowers and shrubbery were pleasant
to the eye, the scene was vivacious, everybody was genteel
and well behaved, and the ladies were slightly moustached,
and handsomely dressed, but very homely.

We adjourned to a café and played billiards an hour, and
I made six or seven points by the doctor pocketing his ball,
and he made as many by my pocketing my ball. We came
near making a carom sometimes, but not the one we were

trying to make. The table was of the usual European style—cushions dead and twice as high as the balls; the cues in bad repair. The natives play only a sort of pool on them. We have never seen anybody playing the French three-ball game yet, and I doubt if there is any such game known in France or that there lives any man mad enough to try to play it on one of these European tables. We had to stop playing finally because Dan got to sleeping fifteen minutes between the counts and paying no attention to his marking.

Afterward we walked up and down one of the most popular streets for some time, enjoying other people's comfort and wishing we could export some of it to our restless, driving, vitality-consuming marts at home. Just in this one matter lies the main charm of life in Europe—comfort. In America we hurry—which is well; but when the day's work is done, we go on thinking of losses and gains, we plan for the morrow, we even carry our business cares to bed with us, and toss and worry over them when we ought to be restoring our racked bodies and brains with sleep. We burn up our energies with these excitements, and either die early or drop into a lean and mean old age at a time of life which they call a man's prime in Europe. When an acre of ground has produced long and well, we let it lie fallow and rest for a season; we take no man clear across the continent in the same coach he started in—the coach is stabled somewhere on the plains and its heated machinery allowed to cool for a few days; when a razor has seen long service and refuses to hold an edge, the barber lays it away for a few weeks, and the edge comes back of its own accord. We bestow thoughtful care upon inanimate objects, but none upon ourselves. What a robust people, what a nation of thinkers we might be, if we would only lay ourselves on the shelf occasionally and renew our edges!

I do envy these Europeans the comfort they take. When the work of the day is done, they forget it. Some of them go, with wife and children, to a beer hall and sit quietly and genteelly drinking a mug or two of ale and listening to music; others walk the streets, others drive in the avenues; others assemble in the great ornamental squares in the early evening to enjoy the sight and the fragrance of flowers and to hear the military bands play—no European city being without its fine military music at eventide; and yet others of the populace sit in the open air in front of the refreshment houses and eat ices and drink mild beverages that could not harm a child. They go to bed moderately early and sleep well. They are always quiet, always orderly, always cheerful, comfortable, and appreciative of life and its manifold blessings. One never sees a drunken man among them. The change that has come over our little party is surprising. Day by day we lose some of our restlessness and absorb some of the spirit of quietude and ease that is in the tranquil atmosphere about us and in the demeanor of the people. We grow wise apace. We begin to comprehend what life is for.

We have had a bath in Milan, in a public bathhouse. They were going to put all three of us in one bathtub, but we objected. Each of us had an Italian farm on his back. We could have felt affluent if we had been officially surveyed and fenced in. We chose to have three bathtubs, and large ones—tubs suited to the dignity of aristocrats who had real estate and brought it with them. After we were stripped and had taken the first chilly dash, we discovered that haunting atrocity that has embittered our lives in so many cities and villages of Italy and France—there was no soap. I called. A woman answered, and I barely had time to throw myself against the door—she would have been in, in another second. I said:

"Beware, woman! Go away from here—go away now or it will be the worse for you. I am an unprotected male, but I will preserve my honor at the peril of my life!"

These words must have frightened her, for she skurried away very fast.

Dan's voice rose on the air:

"Oh, bring some soap, why don't you!"

The reply was Italian. Dan resumed:

"Soap, you know—soap. That is what I want—soap. S-o-a-p, soap; s-o-p-e, soap; s-o-u-p, soap. Hurry up! I don't know how you Irish spell it, but I want it. Spell it to suit yourself, but fetch it. I'm freezing."

I heard the doctor say impressively:

"Dan, how often have we told you that these foreigners cannot understand English? Why will you not depend upon us? Why will you not tell *us* what you want, and let us ask for it in the language of the country? It would save us a great deal of the humiliation your reprehensible ignorance causes us. I will address this person in his mother tongue: 'Here, cospetto! Corpo di Bacco! Sacramento! Solferino!

Soap, you son of a gun!' Dan, if you would let *us* talk for you, you would never expose your ignorant vulgarity."

Even this fluent discharge of Italian did not bring the soap at once, but there was a good reason for it. There was not such an article about the establishment. It is my belief that there never had been. They had to send far uptown and to several different places before they finally got it, so they said. We had to wait twenty or thirty minutes. The same thing had occurred the evening before at the hotel. I think I have divined the reason for this state of things at last. The English know how to travel comfortably, and they carry soap with them; other foreigners do not use the article.

At every hotel we stop at we always have to send out for soap, at the last moment, when we are grooming ourselves for dinner, and they put it in the bill along with the candles and other nonsense. In Marseilles they make half the fancy toilet soap we consume in America, but the Marseillaises only have a vague theoretical idea of its use, which they have obtained from books of travel, just as they have acquired an uncertain notion of clean shirts and the peculiarities of the gorilla and other curious matters. This reminds me of poor Blucher's note to the landlord in Paris:

PARIS, le 7 Juillet.

Monsieur le Landlord—Sir: *Pourquoi* don't you *mettez* some *savon* in your bedchambers? *Est-ce que vous pensez* I will steal it? *La nuit passée* you charged me *pour deux chandelles* when I only had one; *hier vous avez* charged me *avec glace* when I had none at all; *tout les jours* you are coming some fresh game or other on me, *mais vous ne pouvez pas* play this *savon* dodge on me twice. *Savon* is a necessary *de la vie* to anybody but a Frenchman, *et je l'aurai hors de cet hôtel* or make trouble. You hear *me. Allons*.

BLUCHER.

I remonstrated against the sending of this note, because it was so mixed up that the landlord would never be able to make head or tail of it; but Blucher said he guessed the old man could read the French of it and average the rest.

Blucher's French is bad enough, but it is not much worse than the English one finds in advertisements all over Italy every day. For instance, observe the printed card of the hotel we shall probably stop at on the shores of Lake Como:

NOTISH

This hotel which the best it is in Italy and most superb, is handsome locate on the best situation of the lake, with the most splendid view near the Villas Melzy, to the King of Belgian, and Serbelloni. This hotel have recently enlarge, do offer all commodities on moderate price, at the strangers gentlemen who whish spend the seasons on the Lake Como.

How is that for a specimen? In the hotel is a handsome little chapel where an English clergyman is employed to preach to such of the guests of the house as hail from England and America, and this fact is also set forth in barbarous English in the same advertisement. Wouldn't you have supposed that the adventurous linguist who framed the card would have known enough to submit it to that clergyman before he sent it to the printer?

Here in Milan, in an ancient tumbledown ruin of a church, is the mournful wreck of the most celebrated painting in the world—"The Last Supper," by Leonardo da Vinci. We are not infallible judges of pictures, but of course we went there to see this wonderful painting, once so beautiful, always so worshiped by masters in art, and forever to be famous in song and story. And the first thing that occurred was the infliction on us of a placard fairly reeking with wretched English. Take a morsel of it:

Bartholomew (that is the first figure on the left hand side at the spectator) uncertain and doubtful about what he thinks to have heard, and upon which he wants to be assured by himself at Christ and by no others.

Good, isn't it? And then Peter is described as "argumenting in a threatening and angrily condition at Judas Iscariot."

This paragraph recalls the picture. "The Last Supper" is painted on the dilapidated wall of what was a little chapel attached to the main church in ancient times, I suppose. It is battered and scarred in every direction, and stained and discolored by time, and Napoleon's horses kicked the legs off most the disciples when they (the horses, not the disciples) were stabled there more than half a century ago.

I recognized the old picture in a moment—the Saviour with bowed head seated at the center of a long, rough table with scattering fruits and dishes upon it, and six disciples on either side in their long robes, talking to each other—the picture from which all engravings and all copies have been made for three centuries. Perhaps no living man has ever known an attempt to paint the Lord's Supper differently. The world seems to have become settled in the belief, long ago, that it is not possible for human genius to outdo this creation of da Vinci's. I suppose painters will go on copying it as long as any of the original is left visible to the eye. There were a dozen easels in the room, and as many artists transferring the great picture to their canvases. Fifty proofs of steel engravings and lithographs were scattered around, too. And as usual, I could not help noticing how superior the copies were to the original, that is, to my inexperienced eye. Wherever you find a Raphael, a Rubens, a Michelangelo, a Carracci, or a da Vinci (and we see them every day), you find artists copying them, and the copies are always the handsomest. Maybe the originals were handsome when they were new, but they are not now.

This picture is about thirty feet long and ten or twelve high, I should think, and the figures are at least life-size. It is one of the largest paintings in Europe.

The colors are dimmed with age; the countenances are scaled and marred, and nearly all expression is gone from them; the hair is a dead blur upon the wall, and there is no life in the eyes. Only the attitudes are certain.

People come here from all parts of the world and glorify this masterpiece. They stand entranced before it with bated breath and parted lips, and when they speak, it is only in the catchy ejaculations of rapture:

"Oh, wonderful!"

"Such expression!"

"Such grace of attitude!"

"Such dignity!"

"Such faultless drawing!"

"Such matchless coloring!"

"Such feeling!"

"What delicacy of touch!"

"What sublimity of conception!"

"A vision! A vision!"

I only envy these people; I envy them their honest admiration, if it be honest—their delight, if they feel delight. I harbor no animosity toward any of them. But at the same time the thought *will* intrude itself upon me: How can they see what is not visible? What would you think of a man who looked at some decayed, blind, toothless, pock-marked Cleopatra and said: "What matchless beauty! What soul! What expression!" What would you think of a man who gazed upon a dingy, foggy sunset and said: "What sublimity! What feeling! What richness of coloring!" What would you think of a man who stared in ecstasy upon a desert of stumps and said: "Oh, my soul, my beating heart, what a noble forest is here!"

You would think that those men had an astonishing talent for seeing things that had already passed away. It was what I thought when I stood before "The Last Supper" and heard men apostrophizing wonders and beauties and perfections which had faded out of the picture and gone a hundred years before they were born. We can imagine the beauty that was once in an aged face; we can imagine the forest if we see the stumps; but we cannot absolutely *see* these things when they are not there. I am willing to believe that the eye of the practiced artist can rest upon "The Last Supper" and renew a luster where only a hint of it is left, supply a tint that has faded away, restore an expression that is gone; patch and color and add to the dull canvas until at last its figures shall stand before him aglow with the life, the feeling, the freshness, yea, with all the noble beauty that was theirs when first they came from the hand of the master. But *I* cannot work this miracle. Can those other uninspired visitors do it, or do they only happily imagine they do?

After reading so much about it, I am satisfied that "The Last Supper" was a very miracle of art once. But it was three hundred years ago.

It vexes me to hear people talk so glibly of "feeling," "expression," "tone," and those other easily acquired and inexpensive technicalities of art that make such a fine show in conversations concerning pictures. There is not one man in seventy-five hundred that can tell *what* a pictured face is intended to express. There is not one man in five hundred that can go into a courtroom and be sure that he will not mistake some harmless innocent of a juryman for the black-hearted assassin on trial. Yet such people talk of "character" and presume to interpret "expression" in pictures. There is an old story that Matthews, the actor, was once lauding the ability of the human face to express the passions and emotions hidden in the breast. He said the countenance could disclose what was passing in the heart plainer than the tongue could.

"Now," he said, "observe my face—what does it express?"

"Despair!"

"Bah, it expresses peaceful resignation! What does *this* express?"

"Rage!"

"Stuff! It means terror! *This!*"

"Imbecility!"

"Fool! It is smothered ferocity! Now *this!*"

"Joy!"

"Oh, perdition! *Any* ass can see it means insanity!"

Expression! People coolly pretend to read it who would think themselves presumptuous if they pretended to interpret the hieroglyphics on the obelisks of Luxor—yet they are fully as competent to do the one thing as the other. I have heard two very intelligent critics speak of Murillo's "Immaculate Conception" (now in the museum at Seville) within the past few days. One said:

"Oh, the Virgin's face is full of the ecstasy of a joy that is complete—that leaves nothing more to be desired on earth!"

The other said:

"Ah, that wonderful face is so humble, so pleading—it says as plainly as words could say it: 'I fear; I tremble; I am unworthy. But Thy will be done; sustain Thou Thy servant!' "

The reader can see the picture in any drawing room; it can be easily recognized: the Virgin (the only young and really beautiful Virgin that was ever painted by one of the old masters, some of us think) stands in the crescent of the new moon, with a multitude of cherubs hovering about her, and more coming; her hands are crossed upon her breast, and upon her uplifted countenance falls a glory out of the heavens. The reader may amuse himself, if he chooses, in trying to determine which of these gentlemen read the Virgin's "expression" aright or if either of them did it.

Anyone who is acquainted with the old masters will comprehend how much "The Last Supper" is damaged when I say that the spectator cannot really tell now whether the disciples are Hebrews or Italians. These ancient painters never succeeded in denationalizing themselves. The Italian artists painted Italian Virgins, the Dutch painted Dutch Virgins, the Virgins of the French painters were Frenchwomen—none of them ever put into the face of the Madonna that indescribable something which proclaims the Jewess, whether you find her in New York, in Constantinople, in Paris, Jerusalem, or in the empire of Morocco. I saw in the Sandwich Islands, once, a picture copied by a talented German artist from an engraving in one of the American illustrated papers. It was an allegory, representing Mr. Davis in the act of signing a secession act or some such document. Over him hovered the ghost of Washington in warning attitude, and in the background a troop of shadowy soldiers in Continental uniform were limping with shoeless, bandaged feet through a driving snowstorm. Valley Forge was suggested, of course. The copy seemed accurate, and yet there was a discrepancy somewhere. After a long examination I discovered what it was—the shadowy soldiers were all Germans! Jeff Davis was a German! Even the hovering ghost was a German ghost! The artist had unconsciously worked his nationality into the picture. To tell the truth, I am getting a little perplexed about John the Baptist and his portraits. In France I finally grew reconciled to him as a Frenchman; here he is unquestionably an Italian. What next? Can it be possible that the painters make John the Baptist a Spaniard in Madrid and an Irishman in Dublin?

We took an open barouche and drove two miles out of Milan to "see ze echo," as the guide expressed it. The road was smooth, it was bordered by trees, fields, and grassy meadows, and the soft air was filled with the odor of flowers. Troops of picturesque peasant girls, coming from work, hooted at us, shouted at us, made all manner of game of us, and entirely delighted me. My long-cherished judgment was confirmed. I always did think those frowzy, romantic, unwashed peasant girls I had read so much about in poetry were a glaring fraud.

We enjoyed our jaunt. It was an exhilarating relief from tiresome sightseeing.

We distressed ourselves very little about the astonishing echo the guide talked so much about. We were growing accustomed to encomiums on wonders that too often proved no wonders at all. And so we were most happily disappointed to find in the sequel that the guide had even failed to rise to the magnitude of his subject.

We arrived at a tumbledown old rookery called the Palazzo Simonetti—a massive hewn-stone affair occupied by a family of ragged Italians. A good-looking young girl conducted us to a window on the second floor which looked out on a court walled on three sides by tall buildings. She put her head out at the window and shouted. The echo answered more times than we could count. She took a speaking trumpet and through it she shouted, sharp and quick, a single

"Ha!" The echo answered:

"Ha!——ha!——ha!——ha!—ha!-ha! ha! h-a-a-a-a-a!" and finally went off into a rollicking convulsion of the jolliest laughter that could be imagined. It was so joyful— so long continued—so perfectly cordial and hearty that everybody was forced to join in. There was no resisting it.

Then the girl took a gun and fired it. We stood ready to count the astonishing clatter of reverberations. We could not say one, two, three, fast enough, but we could dot our notebooks with our pencil points almost rapidly enough to take down a sort of shorthand report of the result. My page revealed the following account. I could not keep up, but I did as well as I could.

I set down fifty-two distinct repetitions, and then the echo got the advantage of me. The doctor set down sixty-four, and thenceforth the echo moved too fast for him also. After the separate concussions could no longer be noted, the reverberations dwindled to a wild, long-sustained clatter of sounds such as a watchman's rattle produces. It is likely that this is the most remarkable echo in the world.

The doctor, in jest, offered to kiss the young girl, and was taken a little aback when she said he might for a franc! The commonest gallantry compelled him to stand by his offer, and so he paid the franc and took the kiss. She was a philosopher. She said a franc was a good thing to have, and she did not care anything for one paltry kiss, because she had a million left. Then our comrade, always a shrewd businessman, offered to take the whole cargo at thirty days, but that little financial scheme was a failure.

20

We left Milan by rail. The cathedral six or seven miles behind us; vast, dreamy, bluish, snow-clad mountains twenty miles in front of us—these were the accented points in the scenery. The more immediate scenery consisted of fields and farmhouses outside the car and a monster-headed dwarf and a moustached woman inside it. These latter were not show people. Alas, deformity and female beards are too common in Italy to attract attention.

We passed through a range of wild, picturesque hills, steep, wooded, cone-shaped, with rugged crags projecting here and there, and with dwellings and ruinous castles perched away up toward the drifting clouds. We lunched at the curious old town of Como, at the foot of the lake, and then took the small steamer and had an afternoon's pleasure excursion to this place—Bellaggio.

When we walked ashore, a party of policemen (people whose cocked hats and showy uniforms would shame the

finest uniform in the military service of the United States)
put us into a little stone cell and locked us in. We had the
whole passenger list for company, but their room would have
been preferable, for there was no light, there were no windows,
no ventilation. It was close and hot. We were much crowded. It
was the Black Hole of Calcutta on a small scale. Presently a
smoke rose about our feet—a smoke that smelled of all
the dead things of earth, of all the putrefaction and corruption imaginable.

We were there five minutes, and when we got out it was
hard to tell which of us carried the vilest fragrance.

These miserable outcasts called that "fumigating" us, and
the term was a tame one indeed. They fumigated us to guard
themselves against the cholera, though we hailed from no
infected port. We had left the cholera far behind us all the
time. However, they must keep epidemics away somehow or
other, and fumigation is cheaper than soap. They must either
wash themselves or fumigate other people. Some of the lower
classes had rather die than wash, but the fumigation of strangers causes them no pangs. They need no fumigation themselves. Their habits make it unnecessary. They carry their
preventive with them; they sweat and fumigate all the day
long. I trust I am a humble and a consistent Christian. I
try to do what is right. I know it is my duty to "pray for
them that despitefully use me"; and therefore, hard as it is,
I shall still try to pray for these fumigating, maccaroni-
stuffing organ-grinders.

Our hotel sits at the water's edge—at least its front
garden does—and we walk among the shrubbery and smoke at
twilight; we look afar off at Switzerland and the Alps and
feel an indolent willingness to look no closer; we go down
the steps and swim in the lake; we take a shapely little boat
and sail abroad among the reflections of the stars, lie on
the thwarts and listen to the distant laughter, the singing,
the soft melody of flutes and guitars that comes floating
across the water from pleasuring gondolas; we close the
evening with exasperating billiards on one of those same old
execrable tables. A midnight luncheon in our ample bedchamber; a final smoke in its contracted veranda facing the
water, the gardens, and the mountains; a summing up of
the day's events. Then to bed, with drowsy brains harassed
with a mad panorama that mixes up pictures of France, of
Italy, of the ship, of the ocean, of home, in grotesque and

bewildering disorder. Then a melting away of familiar faces, of cities, and of tossing waves, into a great calm of forgetfulness and peace.

After which, the nightmare.

Breakfast in the morning, and then the lake.

I did not like it yesterday. I thought Lake Tahoe was *much* finer. I have to confess now, however, that my judgment erred somewhat, though not extravagantly. I always had an idea that Como was a vast basin of water, like Tahoe, shut in by great mountains. Well, the border of huge mountains is here, but the lake itself is not a basin. It is as crooked as any brook, and only from one-quarter to two-thirds as wide as the Mississippi. There is not a yard of low ground on either side of it—nothing but endless chains of mountains that spring abruptly from the water's edge and tower to altitudes varying from a thousand to two thousand feet. Their craggy sides are clothed with vegetation, and white specks of houses peep out from the luxuriant foliage everywhere; they are even perched upon jutting and picturesque pinnacles a thousand feet above your head.

Again, for miles along the shores, handsome country seats, surrounded by gardens and groves, sit fairly in the water, sometimes in nooks carved by Nature out of the vine-hung precipices, and with no ingress or egress save by boats. Some have great broad stone staircases leading down to the water, with heavy stone balustrades ornamented with statuary and fancifully adorned with creeping vines and bright-colored flowers—for all the world like a drop curtain in a theater— and lacking nothing but long-waisted, high-heeled women and plumed gallants in silken tights coming down to go serenading in the splendid gondola in waiting.

A great feature of Como's attractiveness is the multitude of pretty houses and gardens that cluster upon its shores and on its mountainsides. They look so snug and so homelike, and at eventide, when everything seems to slumber and the music of the vesper bells comes stealing over the water, one almost believes that nowhere else than on the lake of Como can there be found such a paradise of tranquil repose.

From my window here in Bellaggio I have a view of the other side of the lake now, which is as beautiful as a picture. A scarred and wrinkled precipice rises to a height of eighteen hundred feet; on a tiny bench halfway up its vast wall sits a little snowflake of a church, no bigger than a

martin box apparently; skirting the base of the cliff are a
hundred orange groves and gardens, flecked with glimpses of
the white dwellings that are buried in them; in front, three
or four gondolas lie idle upon the water—and in the bur-
nished mirror of the lake, mountain, chapel, houses, groves,
and boats are counterfeited so brightly and so clearly
that one scarce knows where the reality leaves off and the
reflection begins!

The surroundings of this picture are fine. A mile away a
grove-plumed promontory juts far into the lake and glasses
its palace in the blue depths; in midstream a boat is cutting
the shining surface and leaving a long track behind like a
ray of light; the mountains beyond are veiled in a dreamy
purple haze; far in the opposite direction a tumbled mass
of domes and verdant slopes and valleys bars the lake, and
here indeed does distance lend enchantment to the view—
for on this broad canvas, sun and clouds and the richest
of atmospheres have blended a thousand tints together,
and over its surface the filmy lights and shadows drift, hour
after hour, and glorify it with a beauty that seems reflected
out of heaven itself. Beyond all question, this is the most
voluptuous scene we have yet looked upon.

Last night the scenery was striking and picturesque. On
the other side crags and trees and snowy houses were reflected in the lake with a wonderful distinctness, and streams
of light from many a distant window shot far abroad over
the still waters. On this side, near at hand, great mansions,
white with moonlight, glared out from the midst of masses
of foliage that lay black and shapeless in the shadows that
fell from the cliff above—and down in the margin of the lake
every feature of the weird vision was faithfully repeated.

Today we have idled through a wonder of a garden attached to a ducal estate—but enough of description is enough,
I judge. I suspect that this was the same place the gardener's
son deceived the Lady of Lyons with, but I do not know.
You may have heard of the passage somewhere:

A deep vale,
Shut out by Alpine hills from the rude world,
Near a clear lake margined by fruits of gold
And whispering myrtles:
Glassing softest skies, cloudless,
Save with rare and roseate shadows;
A palace, lifting to eternal heaven its marbled walls,
From out a glossy bower of coolest foliage musical with birds.

That is all very well, except the "clear" part of the lake. It certainly is clearer than a great many lakes, but how dull its waters are compared with the wonderful transparence of Lake Tahoe! I speak of the north shore of Tahoe, where one can count the scales on a trout at a depth of a hundred and eighty feet. I have tried to get this statement off at par here, but with no success; so I have been obliged to negotiate it at fifty percent discount. At this rate I find some takers; perhaps the reader will receive it on the same terms —ninety feet instead of one hundred and eighty. But let it be remembered that those are forced terms—sheriff's sale prices. As far as I am privately concerned, I abate not a jot of the original assertion that in those strangely magnifying waters one may count the scales on a trout (a trout of the large kind) at a depth of a hundred and eighty feet—may see every pebble on the bottom—might even count a paper of dray pins. People talk of the transparent waters of the Mexican Bay of Acapulco, but in my own experience I know they cannot compare with those I am speaking of. I have fished for trout in Tahoe, and at a measured depth of eighty-four feet I have seen them put their noses to the bait and I could see their gills open and shut. I could hardly have seen the trout themselves at that distance in the open air.

As I go back in spirit and recall that noble sea, reposing among the snow peaks six thousand feet above the ocean, the conviction comes strong upon me again that Como would only seem a bedizened little courtier in that august presence.

Sorrow and misfortune overtake the legislature that still from year to year permits Tahoe to retain its unmusical cognomen! Tahoe! It suggests no crystal waters, no picturesque shores, no sublimity. Tahoe for a sea in the clouds: a sea that has character and asserts it in solemn calms at times, at times in savage storms; a sea whose royal seclusion is guarded by a cordon of sentinel peaks that lift their frosty fronts nine thousand feet above the level world; a sea whose every aspect is impressive, whose belongings are all beautiful, whose lonely majesty types the Deity!

Tahoe means grasshoppers. It means grasshopper soup. It is Indian and suggestive of Indians. They say it is Paiute —possibly it is Digger. I am satisfied it was named by the Diggers—those degraded savages who roast their dead relatives, then mix the human grease and ashes of bones with tar and "gaum" it thick all over their heads and foreheads

and ears, and go caterwauling about the hills and call it
mourning. *These* are the gentry that named the lake.

People say that Tahoe means "silver lake"—"limpid
water"—"falling leaf." Bosh. It means grasshopper soup, the
favorite dish of the Digger tribe—and of the Paiutes as well.
It isn't worthwhile, in these practical times, for people to
talk about Indian poetry—there never was any in them—except in the Fenimore Cooper Indians. But *they* are an ex-
tinct tribe that never existed. I know the Noble Red Man.
I have camped with the Indians; I have been on the warpath
with them, taken part in the chase with them—for grasshoppers; helped them steal cattle; I have roamed with them,
scalped them, had them for breakfast. I would gladly eat the
whole race if I had a chance.

But I am growing unreliable. I will return to my comparison of the lakes. Como is a little deeper than Tahoe, if people
here tell the truth. They say it is eighteen hundred feet deep
at this point, but it does not look a dead enough blue for
that. Tahoe is one thousand five hundred and twenty-five
feet deep in the center, by the state geologist's measurement.
They say the great peak opposite this town is five thousand
feet high, but I feel sure that three thousand feet of that
statement is a good honest lie. The lake is a mile wide here
and maintains about that width from this point to its northern
extremity—which is distant sixteen miles, from here to its
southern extremity—say fifteen miles—it is not over half a
mile wide in any place, I should think. Its snow-clad mountains one hears so much about are only seen occasionally,
and then in the distance, the Alps. Tahoe is from ten to
eighteen miles wide, and its mountains shut it in like a
wall. Their summits are never free from snow the year
round. One thing about it is very strange: it never has even
a skim of ice upon its surface, although lakes in the same
range of mountains, lying in a lower and warmer temperature,
freeze over in winter.

It is cheerful to meet a shipmate in these out-of-the-way
places and compare notes with him. We have found one of
ours here—an old soldier of the war, who is seeking bloodless
adventures and rest from his campaigns in these sunny lands.*

* Colonel J. Heron Foster, editor of a Pittsburgh journal, and a
most estimable gentleman. As these sheets are being prepared for
the press I am pained to learn of his decease shortly after his return home.—M.T.

21

We voyaged by steamer down the Lago di Lecco, through wild mountain scenery, and by hamlets and villas, and disembarked at the town of Lecco. They said it was two hours by carriage to the ancient city of Bergamo and that we would arrive there in good season for the railway train. We got an open barouche and a wild, boisterous driver and set out. It was delightful. We had a fast team and a perfectly smooth road. There were towering cliffs on our left and the pretty Lago di Lecco on our right, and every now and then it rained on us. Just before starting, the driver picked up, in the street, a stump of a cigar an inch long and put it in his mouth. When he had carried it thus about an hour, I thought it would be only Christian charity to give him a light. I handed him my cigar, which I had just lit, and he put it in his mouth and returned his stump to his pocket! I never saw a more sociable man. At least I never saw a man who was more sociable on a short acquaintance.

We saw interior Italy now. The houses were of solid stone, and not often in good repair. The peasants and their children were idle, as a general thing, and the donkeys and chickens made themselves at home in drawing room and bedchamber, and were not molested. The drivers of each and every one of the slow-moving market carts we met were stretched in the sun upon their merchandise, sound asleep. Every three or four hundred yards, it seemed to me, we came upon the shrine of some saint or other—a rude picture of him built into a huge cross or a stone pillar by the roadside. Some of the pictures of the Saviour were curiosities in their way. They represented him stretched upon the Cross, his countenance distorted with agony. From the wounds of the crown of thorns, from the pierced side, from the mutilated hands and feet, from the scourged body—from every hand-breadth of his person streams of blood were flowing! Such a gory, ghastly spectacle would frighten the children out of their senses, I should think. There were some unique auxiliaries to the painting which added to its spirited effect. These were genuine wooden and iron implements, and were prominently disposed round about the figure; a bundle of nails; the hammer to drive them; the sponge; the reed that supported it; the cup of vinegar; the ladder for the ascent of the Cross; the spear that pierced the Saviour's side. The crown of thorns was made of real thorns, and was nailed to the sacred head. In some Italian church paintings, even by the old masters, the Saviour and the Virgin wear silver or gilded crowns that are fastened to the pictured head with nails. The effect is as grotesque as it is incongruous.

Here and there, on the fronts of roadside inns, we found huge, coarse frescoes of suffering martyrs like those in the shrines. It could not have diminished their sufferings any to be so uncouthly represented. We were in the heart and home of priestcraft—of a happy, cheerful, contented ignorance, superstition, degradation, poverty, indolence, and everlasting unaspiring worthlessness. And we said fervently: It suits these people precisely; let them enjoy it, along with the other animals, and heaven forbid that they be molested. *We* feel no malice toward these fumigators.

We passed through the strangest, funniest, undreamt-of old towns, wedded to the customs and steeped in the dreams of the elder ages, and perfectly unaware that the world turns round! And perfectly indifferent, too, as to whether it turns around or stands still. *They* have nothing to do but eat and sleep and sleep and eat, and toil a little when they can get a friend to stand by and keep them awake. *They* are not paid for thinking—*they* are not paid to fret about the world's concerns. They were not respectable people—they were not worthy people—they were not learned and wise and brilliant people—but in their breasts, all their stupid lives long, resteth a peace that passeth understanding! How can men, calling themselves men, consent to be so degraded and happy.

We whisked by many a gray old medieval castle, clad thick with ivy that swung its green banners down from towers and turrets where once some old Crusader's flag had floated. The driver pointed to one of these ancient fortresses and said (I translate):

"Do you see that great iron hook that projects from the wall just under the highest window in the ruined tower?"

We said we could not see it at such a distance, but had no doubt it was there.

"Well," he said, "there is a legend connected with that iron hook. Nearly seven hundred years ago that castle was the property of the noble Count Luigi Gennaro Guido Alphonso di Genova———"

"What was his other name?" said Dan.

"He had no other name. The name I have spoken was all the name he had. He was the son of———"

"Poor but honest parents—that is all right—never mind the particulars—go on with the legend."

THE LEGEND

Well, then, all the world at that time was in a wild excitement about the Holy Sepulcher. All the great feudal lords in Europe were pledging their lands and pawning their plate to fit out men-at-arms so that they might join the grand armies of Christendom and win renown in the Holy Wars. The Count Luigi raised money, like the rest, and one mild September morning, armed with battle-ax, portcullis, and thundering culverin, he rode through the greaves and bucklers of his donjon keep with as gallant a troop of Christian bandits as ever stepped in Italy. He had his sword, Excalibur, with him. His beautiful countess and her young daughter waved him a tearful adieu from the battering rams and buttresses of the fortress, and he galloped away with a happy heart.

He made a raid on a neighboring baron and completed his outfit with the booty secured. He then razed the castle to the ground, massacred the family, and moved on. They were hardy fellows in the grand old days of chivalry. Alas! Those days will never come again.

Count Luigi grew high in fame in the Holy Land. He plunged into the carnage of a hundred battles, but his good Excalibur always brought him out alive, albeit often sorely wounded. His face became browned by exposure to the Syrian sun in long marches; he suffered hunger and thirst; he pined in prisons, he languished in loathsome plague hospitals. And many and many a time he thought of his loved ones at home and wondered if all was well with them. But his heart said, "Peace, is not thy brother watching over thy household?"

* * *

Forty-two years waxed and waned; the good fight was won; Godfrey reigned in Jerusalem—the Christian hosts reared the banner of the cross above the Holy Sepulcher!

Twilight was approaching. Fifty harlequins, in flowing robes, approached this castle wearily, for they were on foot, and the dust upon their garments betokened that they had traveled far. They overtook a peasant and asked him if it were likely they could get food and a hospitable bed there, for love of Christian charity, and if perchance a moral parlor entertainment might meet with generous countenance—"for," said they, "this exhibition hath no feature that could offend the most fastidious taste."

"Marry," quoth the peasant, "an' it please your worships, ye had better journey many a good rood hence with your juggling circus than trust your bones in yonder castle."

"How now, sirrah!" exclaimed the chief monk. "Explain thy ribald speech, or by'r Lady it shall go hard with thee."

"Peace, good mountebank, I did but utter the truth that was in my heart. San Paolo be my witness that did ye but find the stout Count Leonardo in his cups, sheer from the castle's topmost battlements would he hurl ye all! Alack-a-day, the good Lord Luigi reigns not here in these sad times."

"The good Lord Luigi?"

"Aye, none other, please your worship. In his day the poor rejoiced in plenty and the rich he did oppress; taxes were not known, the fathers of the Church waxed fat upon his bounty; travelers went and came, with none to interfere; and whosoever would, might tarry in his halls in cordial welcome, and eat his bread and drink his wine withal. But woe is me! Some two-and-forty years agone the good count rode hence to fight for Holy Cross, and many a year hath flown since word or token have we had of him. Men say his bones lie bleaching in the fields of Palestine."

"And now?"

"*Now!* God 'a mercy, the cruel Leonardo lords it in the castle. He wrings taxes from the poor; he robs all travelers that journey by his gates; he spends his days in feuds and murders and his nights in revel and debauch; he roasts the fathers of the Church upon his kitchen spits and enjoyeth the same, calling it pastime. These thirty years Luigi's countess hath not been seen by any he in all this land, and many whisper that she pines in the dungeons of the castle for that she will not wed with Leonardo, saying her dear lord still liveth and that she will die ere she prove false to him. They whisper likewise that her daughter is a prisoner as well. Nay, good jugglers, seek ye refreshment other wheres. 'Twere better that ye perished in a Christian way than that ye plunged from off yon dizzy tower. Give ye good day."

"God keep ye, gentle knave—farewell."

But heedless of the peasant's warning, the players moved straightway toward the castle.

Word was brought to Count Leonardo that a company of mountebanks besought his hospitality.

" 'Tis well. Dispose of them in the customary manner. Yet stay! I have need of them. Let them come hither. Later cast them from the battlements—or—how many priests have ye on hand?"

"The day's results are meager, good my lord. An abbot and a dozen beggarly friars is all we have."

"Hell and furies! Is the estate going to seed? Send hither the mountebanks. Afterward broil them with the priests."

The robed and close-cowled harlequins entered. The grim Leonardo sate in state at the head of his council board. Ranged up and down the hall on either hand stood near a hundred men-at-arms.

"Ha, villains!" quoth the count. "What can ye do to earn the hospitality ye crave?"

"Dread lord and mighty, crowded audiences have greeted our humble efforts with rapturous applause. Among our body count we the versatile and talented Ugolino; the justly celebrated Rodolpho; the gifted and accomplished Roderigo; the management have spared neither pains nor expense——"

" 'Sdeath! What can ye *do?* Curb thy prating tongue."

"Good my lord, in acrobatic feats, in practice with the dumbbells, in balancing and ground and lofty tumbling are we versed—and sith your highness asketh me, I venture here to publish that in the truly marvelous and entertaining Zampillaerostation——"

"Gag him! Throttle him! Body of Bacchus! Am I a dog that I am to be assailed with polysyllabled blasphemy like to this? But hold! Lucretia, Isabel, stand forth! Sirrah, behold this dame, this weeping wench. The first I marry within the hour; the other shall dry her tears or feed the vultures. Thou and thy vagabonds shall crown the wedding with thy merry-makings. Fetch hither the priest!"

The dame sprang toward the chief player.

"Oh, save me!" she cried. "Save me from a fate far worse than death! Behold these sad eyes, these sunken cheeks, this withered frame! See thou the wreck this fiend hath made, and let thy heart be moved with pity! Look upon this damosel; note her wasted form, her halting step, her bloomless cheeks where youth should blush and happiness exult in smiles! Hear us and have compassion. This monster was my husband's brother. He who should have been our shield against all harm hath kept us shut within the noisome caverns of his donjon keep for lo these thirty years. And for what crime? None other than that I would not belie my troth, root out my strong love for him who marches with the legions of the Cross in Holy Land (for oh, he is not dead!), and wed with him! Save us, oh, save thy persecuted suppliants!"

She flung herself at his feet and clasped his knees.

"Ha! Ha! Ha!" shouted the brutal Leonardo. Priest, to thy work!" And he dragged the weeping dame from her refuge. "Say, once for all, *will* you be mine? For by my halidome, that breath that uttereth thy refusal shall be thy last on earth!"

"Ne-ver!"

"Then die!" And the sword leaped from its scabbard.

Quicker than thought, quicker than the lightning's flash, fifty monkish habits disappeared, and fifty knights in splendid armor stood revealed! Fifty falchions gleamed in air above the men-at-arms, and brighter, fiercer than them all, flamed Excalibur aloft, and cleaving downward, struck the brutal Leonardo's weapon from his grasp!

"A Luigi to the rescue! Whoop!"

"A Leonardo! Tare an ouns!"

"Oh, God, Oh, God, my husband!"

"Oh, God, Oh, God, my wife!"

"My father!"

"My precious!" [Tableau.]

Count Luigi bound his usurping brother hand and foot. The practiced knights from Palestine made holiday sport of carving the awkward men-at-arms into chops and steaks. The victory was complete. Happiness reigned. The knights all married the daughter. Joy! Wassail! Finis!

"But what did they do with the wicked brother?"

"Oh, nothing—only hanged him on the iron hook I was speaking of. By the chin."

"As how?"

"Passed it up through his gills into his mouth."

"Leave him there?"

"Couple of years."

"Ah—is—is he dead?"

"Six hundred and fifty years ago, or such a matter."

"Splendid legend—splendid lie—drive on."

We reached the quaint old fortified city of Bergamo, the renowned in history, some three-quarters of an hour before the train was ready to start. The place has thirty or forty thousand inhabitants and is remarkable for being the birthplace of harlequin. When we discovered that, that legend of our driver took to itself a new interest in our eyes.

Rested and refreshed, we took the rail happy and contented. I shall not tarry to speak of the handsome Lago di Gardi; its stately castle that holds in its stony bosom the secrets of an age so remote that even tradition goeth not back to it; the imposing mountain scenery that ennobles the landscape thereabouts; nor yet of ancient Padua or haughty Verona; nor of their Montagues and Capulets, their famous balconies and tombs of Juliet and Romeo et al., but hurry straight to the ancient city of the sea, the widowed bride of the Adriatic. It was a long, long ride. But toward evening, as we sat silent and hardly conscious of where we were—subdued into that meditative calm that comes so surely after a conversational storm —someone shouted:

"VENICE!"

And sure enough, afloat on the placid sea a league away lay a great city, with its towers and domes and steeples drowsing in a golden mist of sunset.

22

This Venice, which was a haughty, invincible, magnificent republic for nearly fourteen hundred years, whose armies compelled the world's applause whenever and wherever they attled, whose navies well-nigh held dominion of the seas, nd whose merchant fleets whitened the remotest oceans with their sails and loaded these piers with the products of very clime, is fallen a prey to poverty, neglect, and melancholy decay. Six hundred years ago Venice was the Autocrat of Commerce; her mart was the great commercial center, the distributing house from whence the enormous trade of the Orient was spread abroad over the Western world. Today her piers are deserted, her warehouses are empty, her merchant fleets are vanished, her armies and her navies are but memories. Her glory is departed, and with her crumbling grandeur of wharves and palaces about her, she sits among her stagnant lagoons, forlorn and beggared, forgotten of the world. She that in her palmy days commanded the commerce of a hemisphere, and made the weal or woe of nations with a beck of her puissant finger, is become the humblest among the peoples of the earth—a peddler of glass beads for women and trifling toys and trinkets for schoolgirls and children.

The venerable Mother of the Republics is scarce a fit subject for flippant speech or the idle gossiping of tourists. It seems a sort of sacrilege to disturb the glamour of old romance that pictures her to us softly from afar off as through a tinted mist, and curtains her ruin and her desolation from our view. One ought, indeed, to turn away from her rags, her poverty, and her humiliation and think of her only as she was when she sunk the fleets of Charlemagne, when she humbled Frederick Barbarossa or waved her victorious banners above the battlements of Constantinople.

We reached Venice at eight in the evening and entered a hearse belonging to the Grand Hôtel d'Europe. At any rate, it was more like a hearse than anything else, though to speak by the card, it was a gondola. And this was the storied gondola of Venice!—the fairy boat in which the princely cavaliers of the olden time were wont to cleave the waters of the moonlit canals and look the eloquence of love into the soft eyes of patrician beauties, while the gay gondolier in silken doublet touched his guitar and sang as only gondoliers can sing! This the famed gondola and this the gorgeous gondolier!—the one an inky, rusty old canoe with a sable hearse body clapped onto the middle of it, and the other a mangy, barefooted guttersnipe with a portion of his

raiment on exhibition which should have been sacred from
public scrutiny. Presently, as he turned a corner and shot
his hearse into a dismal ditch between two long rows of
towering, untenanted buildings, the gay gondolier began to
sing, true to the traditions of his race. I stood it a little
while. Then I said:

"Now, here, Roderigo Gonzales Michelangelo, I'm a pilgrim and I'm a stranger, but I am not going to have my
feelings lacerated by any such caterwauling as that. If that
goes on, one of us has got to take water. It is enough that
my cherished dreams of Venice have been blighted forever as
to the romantic gondola and the gorgeous gondolier; this
system of destruction shall go no farther; I will accept the
hearse under protest, and you may fly your flag of truce in
peace, but here I register a dark and bloody oath that you
shan't sing. Another yelp, and overboard you go."

I began to feel that the old Venice of song and story had
departed forever. But I was too hasty. In a few minutes we
swept gracefully out into the Grand Canal, and under the
mellow moonlight the Venice of poetry and romance stood
revealed. Right from the water's edge rose long lines of
stately palaces of marble; gondolas were gliding swiftly hither
and thither and disappearing suddenly through unsuspected
gates and alleys; ponderous stone bridges threw their shadows
athwart the glittering waves. There was life and motion everywhere, and yet everywhere there was a hush, a stealthy sort
of stillness, that was suggestive of secret enterprises of bravos
and of lovers; and clad half in moonbeams and half in mysterious shadows, the grim old mansions of the republic seemed
to have an expression about them of having an eye out
for just such enterprises as these at that same moment.
Music came floating over the waters—Venice was complete.

It was a beautiful picture—very soft and dreamy and beautiful. But what was this Venice to compare with the Venice
of midnight? Nothing. There was a fete—a grand fete in
honor of some saint who had been instrumental in checking
the cholera three hundred years ago, and all Venice was
abroad on the water. It was no common affair, for the Venetians did not know how soon they might need the saint's
services again, now that the cholera was spreading everywhere. So in one vast space—say a third of a mile wide and
two miles long—were collected two thousand gondolas, and
every one of them had from two to ten, twenty, and even

thirty colored lanterns suspended about it, and from four to a dozen occupants. Just as far as the eye could reach, these painted lights were massed together—like a vast garden of many-colored flowers, except that these blossoms were never still; they were ceaselessly gliding in and out, and mingling together, and seducing you into bewildering attempts to follow their mazy evolutions. Here and there a strong red, green, or blue glare from a rocket that was struggling to get away splendidly illuminated all the boats around it. Every gondola that swam by us, with its crescents and pyramids and circles of colored lamps hung aloft, and lighting up the faces of the young and the sweet-scented and lovely below, was a picture; and the reflections of those lights, so long, so slender, so numberless, so many-colored, and so distorted and wrinkled by the waves, was a picture likewise, and one that was enchantingly beautiful. Many and many a party of young ladies and gentlemen had their state gondolas handsomely decorated, and ate supper on board, bringing their swallow-tailed, white-cravatted varlets to wait upon them and having their tables tricked out as if for a bridal supper. They had brought along the costly globe lamps from their drawing rooms, and the lace and silken curtains from the same places, I suppose. And they had also brought pianos and guitars, and they played and sang operas, while the plebeian paper-lanterned gondolas from the suburbs and the back alleys crowded around to stare and listen.

There was music everywhere—choruses, string bands, brass bands, flutes, everything. I was so surrounded, walled in, with music, magnificence, and loveliness that I became inspired with the spirit of the scene and sang one tune myself. However, when I observed that the other gondolas had sailed away, and my gondolier was preparing to go overboard, I stopped.

The fete was magnificent. They kept it up the whole night long, and I never enjoyed myself better than I did while it lasted.

What a funny old city this Queen of the Adriatic is! Narrow streets, vast, gloomy marble palaces, black with the corroding damps of centuries, and all partly submerged; no dry land visible anywhere, and no sidewalks worth mentioning; if you want to go to church, to the theater, or to the restaurant, you must call a gondola. It must be a paradise for cripples, for verily a man has no use for legs here.

For a day or two the place looked so like an overflowed Arkansas town, because of its currentless waters laving the very doorsteps of all the houses, and the cluster of boats made fast under the windows or skimming in and out of the alleys and byways, that I could not get rid of the impression that there was nothing the matter here but a spring freshet, and that the river would fall in a few weeks and leave a dirty high-water mark on the houses and the streets full of mud and rubbish.

In the glare of day there is little poetry about Venice, but under the charitable moon her stained palaces are white again, their battered sculptures are hidden in shadows, and the old city seems crowned once more with the grandeur that was hers five hundred years ago. It is easy then in fancy to people these silent canals with plumed gallants and fair ladies —with Shylocks in gaberdine and sandals, venturing loans upon the rich argosies of Venetian commerce—with Othellos and Desdemonas, with Iagos and Roderigos—with noble fleets and victorious legions returning from the wars. In the treacherous sunlight we see Venice decayed, forlorn, poverty-stricken, and commerceless—forgotten and utterly insignificant. But in the moonlight her fourteen centuries of greatness fling their glories about her, and once more is she the princeliest among the nations of the earth.

> There is a glorious city in the sea;
> The sea is in the broad, the narrow streets,
> Ebbing and flowing; and the salt-sea weed
> Clings to the marble of her palaces.
> No track of men, no footsteps to and fro,
> Lead to her gates! The path lies o'er the sea,
> Invisible: and from the land we went,
> As to a floating city—steering in,
> And gliding up her streets, as in a dream,
> So smoothly, silently—by many a dome,
> Mosque-like, and many a stately portico,
> The statues ranged along an azure sky;
> By many a pile, in more than Eastern pride,
> Of old the residence of merchant kings;
> The fronts of some, tho' time had shatter'd them,
> Still glowing with the richest hues of art,
> As tho' the wealth within them had run o'er.

What would one naturally wish to see first in Venice? The Bridge of Sighs, of course—and next the Church and the

Great Square of St. Mark, the Bronze Horses, and the famous Lion of St. Mark.

We intended to go to the Bridge of Sighs, but happened into the Ducal Palace first—a building which necessarily figures largely in Venetian poetry and tradition. In the Senate Chamber of the ancient republic we wearied our eyes with staring at acres of historical paintings by Tintoretto and Paul Veronese, but nothing struck us forcibly except the one thing that strikes *all* strangers forcibly—a black square in the midst of a gallery of portraits. In one long row, around the great hall, were painted the portraits of the doges of Venice (venerable fellows, with flowing white beards, for of the three hundred Senators eligible to the office, the oldest was usually chosen Doge), and each had its complimentary inscription attached—till you came to the place that should have had Marino Faliero's picture in it, and that was blank and black—blank except that it bore a terse inscription saying that the conspirator had died for his crime. It seemed cruel to keep that pitiless inscription still staring from the walls after the unhappy wretch had been in his grave five hundred years.

At the head of the Giant's Staircase, where Marino Faliero was beheaded, and where the doges were crowned in ancient times, two small slits in the stone wall were pointed out, two harmless, insignificant orifices that would never attract a stranger's attention—yet these were the terrible Lions' Mouths! The heads were gone (knocked off by the French during their occupation of Venice), but these were the throats down which went the anonymous accusation, thrust in secretly at dead of night by an enemy, that doomed many an innocent man to walk the Bridge of Sighs and descend into the dungeon which none entered and hoped to see the sun again. This was in the old days when the patricians alone governed Venice—the common herd had no vote and no voice. There were one thousand five hundred patricians; from these, three hundred Senators were chosen; from the Senators a Doge and a Council of Ten were selected, and by secret ballot the Ten chose from their own number a Council of Three. All these were government spies then, and every spy was under surveillance himself—men spoke in whispers in Venice, and no man trusted his neighbor; not always his own brother. No man knew who the Council of Three were—not even the Senate, not even the Doge; the members of that dread tribunal met at night in a chamber to themselves, masked, and robed from head to foot in scarlet cloaks, and did not even know each other unless by voice. It was their duty to judge heinous political crimes, and from their sentence there was no appeal. A nod to the executioner was sufficient. The doomed man was marched down a hall and out at a doorway into the covered Bridge of Sighs, through it and into the dungeon and unto his death. At no time in his transit was he visible to any save his conductor. If a man had an enemy in those old days, the cleverest thing he could do was to slip a note for the Council of Three into the Lion's mouth, saying, "This man is plotting against the government." If the awful Three found no proof, ten to one they would drown him anyhow, because he was a deep rascal, since his plots were unsolvable. Masked judges and masked executioners, with unlimited power and no appeal from their judgments, in that hard, cruel age, were not likely to be lenient with men they suspected yet could not convict.

We walked through the hall of the Council of Ten and presently entered the infernal den of the Council of Three.

The table around which they had sat was there still, and likewise the stations where the masked inquisitors and executioners formerly stood, frozen, upright, and silent, till they received a bloody order, and then, without a word, moved off, like the inexorable machines they were, to carry it out. The frescoes on the walls were startlingly suited to the place. In all the other saloons, the halls, the great state chambers of the palace, the walls and ceilings were bright with gilding, rich with elaborate carving, and resplendent with gallant pictures of Venetian victories in war and Venetian display in foreign courts, and hallowed with portraits of the Virgin, the Saviour of men, and the holy saints that preached the gospel of peace upon earth, but here, in dismal contrast, were none but pictures of death and dreadful suffering!—not a living figure but was writhing in torture, not a dead one but was smeared with blood, gashed with wounds, and distorted with the agonies that had taken away its life!

From the palace to the gloomy prison is but a step—one might almost jump across the narrow canal that intervenes. The ponderous stone Bridge of Sighs crosses it at the second story—a bridge that is a covered tunnel—you cannot be seen when you walk in it. It is partitioned lengthwise, and through one compartment walked such as bore light sentences in an-

cient times, and through the other marched sadly the
wretches whom the Three had doomed to lingering misery
and utter oblivion in the dungeons or to sudden and mysterious death. Down below the level of the water, by the light
of smoking torches, we were shown the damp, thick-walled
cells where many a proud patrician's life was eaten away by
the long-drawn miseries of solitary imprisonment—without
light, air, books; naked, unshaven, uncombed, covered with
vermin; his useless tongue forgetting its office, with none to
speak to; the days and nights of his life no longer marked,
but merged into one eternal eventless night; far away from
all cheerful sounds, buried in the silence of a tomb; forgotten
by his helpless friends, and his fate a dark mystery to them
forever; losing his own memory at last, and knowing no more
who he was or how he came there; devouring the loaf of
bread and drinking the water that were thrust into the cell by
unseen hands, and troubling his worn spirit no more with
hopes and fears and doubts and longings to be free; ceasing
to scratch vain prayers and complainings on walls where none,
not even himself, could see them, and resigning himself to
hopeless apathy, driveling childishness, lunacy! Many and
many a sorrowful story like this these stony walls could tell
if they could but speak.

In a little narrow corridor nearby they showed us where
many a prisoner, after lying in the dungeons until he was forgotten by all save his persecutors, was brought by masked
executioners and garroted or sewed up in a sack, passed
through a little window to a boat, at dead of night, and
taken to some remote spot and drowned.

They used to show to visitors the implements of torture
wherewith the Three were wont to worm secrets out of the
accused—villainous machines for crushing thumbs; the stocks
where a prisoner sat immovable while water fell drop by
drop upon his head till the torture was more than humanity
could bear; and a devilish contrivance of steel, which enclosed
a prisoner's head like a shell and crushed it slowly by means
of a screw. It bore the stains of blood that had trickled
through its joints long ago, and on one side it had a projection whereon the torturer rested his elbow comfortably and
bent down his ear to catch the moanings of the sufferer
perishing within.

Of course we went to see the venerable relic of the ancient
glory of Venice, with its pavements worn and broken by the

passing feet of a thousand years of plebeians and patricians—the Cathedral of St. Mark. It is built entirely of
precious marbles brought from the Orient—nothing in its
composition is domestic. Its hoary traditions make it an object of absorbing interest to even the most careless stranger,
and thus far it had interest for me; but no further. I could
not go into ecstasies over its coarse mosaics, its unlovely
Byzantine architecture, or its five hundred curious interior
columns from as many distant quarries. Everything was worn
out—every block of stone was smooth and almost shapeless
with the polishing hands and shoulders of loungers who
devoutly idled here in bygone centuries and have died and
gone to the dev—no, simply died, I mean.

Under the altar repose the ashes of St. Mark—and Matthew, Luke, and John, too, for all I know. Venice reveres
those relics above all things earthly. For fourteen hundred
years St. Mark has been her patron saint. Everything about
the city seems to be named after him or so named as to refer
to him in some way—so named or some purchase rigged in
some way to scrape a sort of hurrahing acquaintance with
him. That seems to be the idea. To be on good terms with St.
Mark seems to be the very summit of Venetian ambition.
They say St. Mark had a tame lion and used to travel with
him—and everywhere that St. Mark went, the lion was sure
to go. It was his protector, his friend, his librarian. And so
the Winged Lion of St. Mark, with the open Bible under his
paw, is a favorite emblem in the grand old city. It casts its
shadow from the most ancient pillar in Venice, in the Grand
Square of St. Mark, upon the throngs of free citizens below,
and has so done for many a long century. The winged lion
is found everywhere—and doubtless here, where the winged
lion is, no harm can come.

St. Mark died at Alexandria, in Egypt. He was martyred,
I think. However, that has nothing to do with my legend.
About the founding of the city of Venice—say four hundred
and fifty years after Christ (for Venice is much younger than
any other Italian city)—a priest dreamed that an angel told
him that until the remains of St. Mark were brought to
Venice, the city could never rise to high distinction among
the nations; that the body must be captured, brought to the
city, and a magnificent church built over it; and that if
ever the Venetians allowed the saint to be removed from his
new resting place, in that day Venice would perish from off

the face of the earth. The priest proclaimed his dream, and forthwith Venice set about procuring the corpse of St. Mark. One expedition after another tried and failed, but the project was never abandoned during four hundred years. At last it was secured by stratagem, in the year eight hundred and something. The commander of a Venetian expedition disguised himself, stole the bones, separated them, and packed them in vessels filled with lard. The religion of Muhammad causes its devotees to abhor anything that is in the nature of pork, and so when the Christian was stopped by the officers at the gates of the city, they only glanced once into his precious baskets, then turned up their noses at the unholy lard, and let him go. The bones were buried in the vaults of the grand cathedral, which had been waiting long years to receive them, and thus the safety and the greatness of Venice were secured. And to this day there be those in Venice who believe that if those holy ashes were stolen away, the ancient city would vanish like a dream and its foundations be buried forever in the unremembering sea.

23

The Venetian gondola is as free and graceful in its gliding movement as a serpent. It is twenty or thirty feet long, and is narrow and deep like a canoe; its sharp bow and stern sweep upward from the water like the horns of a crescent with the abruptness of the curve slightly modified.

The bow is ornamented with a steel comb with a battle-ax attachment which threatens to cut passing boats in two occasionally, but never does. The gondola is painted black because in the zenith of Venetian magnificence the gondolas became too gorgeous altogether, and the Senate decreed that all such display must cease, and a solemn, unembellished black be substituted. If the truth were known, it would doubtless appear that rich plebeians grew too prominent in their affectation of patrician show on the Grand Canal, and required a wholesome snubbing. Reverence for the hallowed Past and its traditions keeps the dismal fashion in force now that the compulsion exists no longer. So let it remain. It is the color of mourning. Venice mourns. The stern of the boat is decked over and the gondolier stands there. He uses a single oar—a long blade, of course, for he stands nearly erect. A wooden peg, a foot and a half high, with two slight crooks or curves in one side of it and one in the other, projects above the starboard gunwale. Against that peg the gondolier takes a purchase with his oar, changing it at intervals to the other side of the peg or dropping it into another of the crooks, as the steering of the craft may demand—and how in the world he can back and fill, shoot straight ahead, or flirt suddenly around a corner, and make the oar stay in those insignificant notches is a problem to me and a never-diminishing matter of interest. I am afraid I study the gondolier's marvelous skill more than I do the sculptured palaces we glide among. He cuts a corner so closely, now and then, or misses another gondola by such an imperceptible hairbreadth that I feel myself "scrooching," as the children say, just as one does when a buggy wheel grazes his elbow. But he makes all his calculations with the nicest precision, and goes darting in and out among a Broadway confusion of busy craft with the easy confidence of the educated hackman. He never makes a mistake.

Sometimes we go flying down the great canals at such a gait that we can get only the merest glimpses into front doors, and again, in obscure alleys in the suburbs, we put on a solemnity suited to the silence, the mildew, the stagnant waters, the clinging weeds, the deserted houses, and the general lifelessness of the place, and move to the spirit of grave meditation.

The gondolier *is* a picturesque rascal for all he wears no satin harness, no plumed bonnet, no silken tights. His attitude is stately; he is lithe and supple; all his movements are full of grace. When his long canoe and his fine figure, towering from its high perch on the stern, are cut against the evening sky, they make a picture that is very novel and striking to a foreign eye.

We sit in the cushioned carriage body of a cabin, with the curtains drawn, and smoke or read or look out upon the passing boats, the houses, the bridges, the people, and enjoy ourselves much more than we could in a buggy jolting over our

cobblestone pavements at home. This is the gentlest, pleasantest locomotion we have ever known.

But it seems queer—ever so queer—to see a boat doing
duty as a private carriage. We see businessmen come to the
front door, step into a gondola instead of a streetcar, and go
off downtown to the counting room.

We see visiting young ladies stand on the stoop, and laugh,
and kiss good-bye, and flirt their fans, and say, "Come soon—
now *do*—you've been just as mean as ever you can be—
Mother's dying to see you—and we've moved into the new
house, oh such a love of a place!—so convenient to the post
office and the church, and the Young Men's Christian Asso-
ciation; and we do have such fishing, and such carrying on,
and *such* swimming matches in the backyard—oh, you *must*
come—no distance at all, and if you go down through by St.
Mark's and the Bridge of Sighs, and cut through the alley and
come up by the Church of Santa Maria dei Frari and into the
Grand Canal, there isn't a *bit* of current—now *do* come, Sally
Maria—bye-bye!" And then the little humbug trips down the
steps, jumps into the gondola, says under her breath, "Disagreeable old thing, I hope she *won't!*" goes skimming away,
round the corner; and the other girl slams the street door and
says, "Well, *that* infliction's over, anyway—but I suppose I've
got to go and see her—tiresome, stuck-up thing!" Human
nature appears to be just the same all over the world. We see
the diffident young man, mild of moustache, affluent of hair,
indigent of brain, elegant of costume, drive up to *her*
father's mansion, tell his hackman to bail out and wait, start
fearfully up the steps and meet "the old gentleman" right on
the threshold!—hear him ask what street the new British bank
is in—as if *that* were what he came for—and then bounce
into his boat and skurry away with his coward heart in his
boots!—see him come sneaking around the corner again
directly, with a crack of the curtain open toward the old
gentleman's disappearing gondola, and out scampers his
Susan with a flock of little Italian endearments fluttering
from her lips, and goes to drive with him in the watery
avenues down toward the Rialto.

We see the ladies go out shopping in the most natural way,
and flit from street to street and from store to store, just in
the good old fashion, except that they leave the gondola, instead of a private carriage, waiting at the curbstone a couple
of hours for them—waiting while they make the nice young

clerks pull down tons and tons of silks and velvets and moire antiques and those things; and then they buy a paper of pins and go paddling away to confer the rest of their disastrous patronage on some other firm. And they always have their purchases sent home just in the good old way. Human nature is *very* much the same all over the world; and it is *so* like my dear native home to see a Venetian lady go into a store and buy ten cents' worth of blue ribbon and have it sent home in a scow. Ah, it is these little touches of nature that move one to tears in these far-off foreign lands.

We see little girls and boys go out in gondolas with their nurses for an airing. We see staid families, with prayer book and beads, enter the gondola dressed in their Sunday best and float away to church. And at midnight we see the theater break up and discharge its swarm of hilarious youth and beauty; we hear the cries of the hackman-gondoliers and behold the struggling crowd jump aboard, and the black multitude of boats go skimming down the moonlit avenues; we see them separate here and there and disappear up divergent streets; we hear the faint sounds of laughter and of shouted farewells floating up out of the distance; and then, the strange pageant being gone, we have lonely stretches of glittering water—of stately buildings—of blotting shadows—of weird stone faces creeping into the moonlight—of deserted bridges—of motionless boats at anchor. And over all broods that mysterious stillness, that stealthy quiet, that befits so well this old dreaming Venice.

We have been pretty much everywhere in our gondola. We have bought beads and photographs in the stores and wax matches in the Great Square of St. Mark. The last remark suggests a digression. Everybody goes to this vast square in the evening. The military bands play in the center of it and countless couples of ladies and gentlemen promenade up and down on either side, and platoons of them are constantly drifting away toward the old cathedral, and by the venerable column with the Winged Lion of St. Mark on its top, and out to where the boats lie moored; and other platoons are as constantly arriving from the gondolas and joining the great throng. Between the promenaders and the sidewalks are seated hundreds and hundreds of people at small tables, smoking and taking *granita* (a first cousin to ice cream); on the sidewalks are more employing themselves in the same way. The shops in the first floor of the tall rows of buildings that wall in three sides of the square are brilliantly lighted, the air is filled with music and merry voices, and altogether the scene is as bright and spirited and full of cheerfulness as any man could desire. We enjoy it thoroughly. Very many of the young women are exceedingly pretty and dress with rare good taste. We are gradually and laboriously learning the ill manners of staring them unflinchingly in the face—not because such conduct is agreeable to us, but because it is the custom of the country and they say the girls like it. We wish to learn all the curious, outlandish ways of all the different countries, so that we can "show off" and astonish people when we get home. We wish to excite the envy of our untraveled friends with our strange foreign fashions which we can't shake off. All our passengers are paying strict attention to this thing, with the end in view which I have mentioned. The gentle reader will never, never know what a consummate ass he can become until he goes abroad. I speak now, of course, in the supposition that the gentle reader has not been abroad, and therefore is not already a consummate ass. If the case be otherwise, I beg his pardon and extend to him the cordial hand of fellowship and call him brother. I shall always delight to meet an ass after my own heart when I have finished my travels.

On this subject let me remark that there are Americans abroad in Italy who have actually forgotten their mother tongue in three months—forgot it in France. They cannot even write their address in English in a hotel register. I append these evidences, which I copied verbatim from the register of a hotel in a certain Italian city:

John P. Whitcomb, *Etats Unis*.

Wm. L. Ainsworth, *travailleur* (he meant traveler, I suppose) *Etats Unis*.

George P. Morton, *et fils, d'Amerique*.

Lloyd B. Williams, *et trois amis, ville de* Boston, *Amerique*.

J. Ellsworth Baker, *tout de suite de France, place de naissance Amerique, destination la Grand Bretagne*.

I love this sort of people. A lady passenger of ours tells of a fellow citizen of hers who spent eight weeks in Paris and then returned home and addressed his dearest old bosom friend Herbert as Mr. "Er-bare!" He apologized, though, and said, " 'Pon my soul, it is aggravating, but I cahn't help it—I have got so used to speaking nothing but French, my dear Erbare—damme, there it goes again!—got so used to French pronunciation that I cahn't get rid of it—it is positively annoying, I assure you." This entertaining idiot, whose name was Gordon, allowed himself to be hailed three times in the street before he paid any attention, and then begged a thousand pardons and said he had grown so accustomed to hearing himself addressed as 'M'sieu Gor-r-*dong*,'" with a roll to the r, that he had forgotten the legitimate sound of his name! He wore a rose in his buttonhole; he gave the French salutation—two flips of the hand in front of the face; he called Paris *Pairree* in ordinary English conversation; he carried envelopes bearing foreign postmarks protruding from his breast pocket; he cultivated a moustache and imperial, and did what else he could to suggest to the beholder his pet fancy that he resembled Louis Napoleon—and in a spirit of thankfulness which is entirely unaccountable, considering the slim foundation there was for it, he praised his Maker that he was *as* he was, and went on enjoying his little life just the same as if he really *had* been deliberately designed and erected by the great Architect of the Universe.

Think of our Whitcombs and our Ainsworths and our Williamses writing themselves down in dilapidated French in foreign hotel registers! We laugh at Englishmen, when we are at home, for sticking so sturdily to their national ways and customs, but we look back upon it from abroad very forgivingly. It is not pleasant to see an American thrusting his nationality forward *obtrusively* in a foreign land, but oh, it is pitiable to see him making of himself a thing that is neither male nor female, neither fish, flesh, nor fowl—a poor, miserable, hermaphrodite Frenchman!

Among a long list of churches, art galleries, and such things visited by us in Venice, I shall mention only one—the Church of Santa Maria dei Frari. It is about five hundred years old, I believe, and stands on twelve hundred thousand piles. In it lie the body of Canova and the heart of Titian, under magnificent monuments. Titian died at the age of almost one hundred years. A plague which swept away fifty thousand lives was raging at the time, and there is notable evidence of the reverence in which the great painter was held, in the fact that to him alone the state permitted a public funeral in all that season of terror and death.

In this church, also, is a monument to the doge Foscari,

whose name a once resident of Venice, Lord Byron, has made permanently famous.

The monument to the doge Giovanni Pesaro, in this church, is a curiosity in the way of mortuary adornment. It is eighty feet high and is fronted like some fantastic pagan temple. Against it stand four colossal Nubians, as black as night, dressed in white marble garments. The black legs are bare, and through rents in sleeves and breeches, the skin, of shiny black marble, shows. The artist was as ingenious as his funeral designs were absurd. There are two bronze skeletons bearing scrolls, and two great dragons uphold the sarcophagus. On high, amid all this grotesqueness, sits the departed doge.

In the conventional buildings attached to this church are the state archives of Venice. We did not see them, but they are said to number millions of documents. "They are the records of centuries of the most watchful, observant, and suspicious government that ever existed—in which everything was written down and nothing spoken out." They fill nearly three hundred rooms. Among them are manuscripts from the archives of nearly two thousand families, monasteries, and convents. The secret history of Venice for a thousand years is here—its plots, its hidden trials, its assassinations, its commissions of hireling spies and masked bravos— food, ready to hand, for a world of dark and mysterious romances.

Yes, I think we have seen all of Venice. We have seen, in these old churches, a profusion of costly and elaborate sepulcher ornamentation such as we never dreamt of before. We have stood in the dim religious light of these hoary sanctuaries, in the midst of long ranks of dusty monuments and effigies of the great dead of Venice, until we seemed drifting back, back, back, into the solemn past, and looking upon the scenes and mingling with the peoples of a remote antiquity. We have been in a half-waking sort of dream all the time. I do not know how else to describe the feeling. A part of our being has remained still in the nineteenth century, while another part of it has seemed in some unaccountable way walking among the phantoms of the tenth.

We have seen famous pictures until our eyes are weary with looking at them and refuse to find interest in them any longer. And what wonder, when there are twelve hundred pictures by Palma the Younger in Venice and fifteen hun-

dred by Tintoretto? And behold there are Titians and the
works of other artists in proportion. We have seen Titian's
celebrated "Cain and Abel," his "David and Goliath," his
"Abraham's Sacrifice." We have seen Tintoretto's monster
picture, which is seventy-four feet long and I do not know
how many feet high, and thought it a very commodious picture. We have seen pictures of martyrs enough and saints
enough to regenerate the world. I ought not to confess it,
but still, since one has no opportunity in America to acquire
a critical judgment in art, and since I could not hope to
become educated in it in Europe in a few short weeks, I may
therefore as well acknowledge, with such apologies as may
be due, that to me it seemed that when I had seen one of
these martyrs I had seen them all. They all have a marked
family resemblance to each other, they dress alike, in coarse
monkish robes and sandals, they are all bald-headed, they all
stand in about the same attitude, and without exception they
are gazing heavenward with countenances which the Ainsworths, the Mortons, and the Williamses *et fils* inform me
are full of "expression." To me there is nothing tangible
about these imaginary portraits, nothing that I can grasp and
take a living interest in. If great Titian had only been gifted
with prophecy, and had skipped a martyr, and gone over to
England and painted a portrait of Shakespeare, even as a
youth, which we could all have confidence in now, the
world down to the latest generations would have forgiven
him the lost martyr in the rescued seer. I think posterity
could have spared one more martyr for the sake of a great
historical picture of Titian's time and painted by his brush
—such as Columbus returning in chains from the discovery
of a world, for instance. The old masters did paint some
Venetian historical pictures, and these we did not tire of
looking at, notwithstanding representations of the formal introduction of defunct doges to the Virgin Mary in regions
beyond the clouds clashed rather harshly with the proprie-
ties, it seemed to us.

But humble as we are, and unpretending, in the matter of
art, our researches among the painted monks and martyrs
have not been wholly in vain. We have striven hard to learn.
We have had some success. We have mastered some things,
possibly of trifling import in the eyes of the learned, but to
us they give pleasure, and we take as much pride in our
little acquirements as do others who have learned far more,

and we love to display them full as well. When we see a
monk going about with a lion and looking tranquilly up to
heaven, we know that that is St. Mark. When we see a monk
with a book and a pen, looking tranquilly up to heaven,
trying to think of a word, we know that that is St. Matthew.
When we see a monk sitting on a rock, looking tranquilly
up to heaven, with a human skull beside him, and without
other baggage, we know that that is St. Jerome. Because
we know that he always went flying light in the matter of
baggage. When we see a party looking tranquilly up to
heaven, unconscious that his body is shot through and
through with arrows, we know that that is St. Sebastian.
When we see other monks looking tranquilly up to heaven,
but having no trademark, we always ask who those parties
are. We do this because we humbly wish to learn. We
have seen thirteen thousand St. Jeromes, and twenty-two
thousand St. Marks, and sixteen thousand St. Matthews, and
sixty thousand St. Sebastians, and four millions of assorted
monks, undesignated, and we feel encouraged to believe that
when we have seen some more of these various pictures
and had a larger experience, we shall begin to take an absorbing interest in them like our cultivated countrymen
from *Amerique*.

Now it does give me real pain to speak in this almost
unappreciative way of the old masters and their martyrs,
because good friends of mine in the ship—friends who do
thoroughly and conscientiously appreciate them and are in
every way competent to discriminate between good pictures and inferior ones—have urged me for my own sake
not to make public the fact that I lack this appreciation
and this critical discrimination myself. I believe that what I
have written and may still write about pictures will give
them pain, and I am honestly sorry for it. I even promised
that I would hide my uncouth sentiments in my own breast.
But alas! I never could keep a promise. I do not blame
myself for this weakness, because the fault must lie in my
physical organization. It is likely that such a very liberal
amount of space was given to the organ which enables me
to *make* promises that the organ which should enable me to
keep them was crowded out. But I grieve not. I like no
halfway things. I had rather have one faculty nobly de-
veloped than two faculties of mere ordinary capacity. I
certainly meant to keep that promise, but I find I cannot do

it. It is impossible to travel through Italy without speaking of pictures, and can I see them through others' eyes?

If I did not so delight in the grand pictures that are spread before me every day of my life by that monarch of all the old masters, Nature, I should come to believe sometimes that I had in me no appreciation of the beautiful whatsoever.

It seems to me that whenever I glory to think that for once I have discovered an ancient painting that is beautiful and worthy of all praise, the pleasure it gives me is an infallible proof that it is *not* a beautiful picture and not in any wise worthy of commendation. This very thing has occurred more times than I can mention in Venice. In every single instance the guide has crushed out my swelling enthusiasm with the remark:

"It is nothing—it is of the *Renaissance*."

I did not know what in the mischief the Renaissance was, and so always I had to simply say:

"Ah! So it is—I had not observed it before."

I could not bear to be ignorant before a cultivated Negro, the offspring of a South Carolina slave. But it occurred too often for even my self-complacency, did that exasperating "It is nothing—it is of the *Renaissance*." I said at last:

"*Who* is this Renaissance? Where did he come from? Who gave him permission to cram the republic with his execrable daubs?"

We learned then that Renaissance was not a man; that *renaissance* was a term used to signify what was at best but an imperfect rejuvenation of art. The guide said that after Titian's time and the time of the other great names we had grown so familiar with, high art declined; then it partially rose again—an inferior sort of painters sprang up, and these shabby pictures were the work of their hands. Then I said, in my heat, that I "wished to goodness high art had declined five hundred years sooner." The Renaissance pictures suit me very well, though sooth to say its school were too much given to painting real men and did not indulge enough in martyrs.

The guide I have spoken of is the only one we have had yet who knew anything. He was born in South Carolina, of slave parents. They came to Venice while he was an infant. He has grown up here. He is well educated. He reads, writes, and speaks English, Italian, Spanish, and French with perfect facility; is a worshiper of art and thoroughly conversant with it; knows the history of Venice by heart and never tires of talking of her illustrious career. He dresses better than any of us, I think, and is daintily polite. Negroes are deemed as good as white people in Venice, and so this man feels no desire to go back to his native land. His judgment is correct.

I have had another shave. I was writing in our front room this afternoon and trying hard to keep my attention on my work and refrain from looking out upon the canal. I was resisting the soft influences of the climate as well as I could, and endeavoring to overcome the desire to be indolent and happy. The boys sent for a barber. They asked me if I would be shaved. I reminded them of my tortures in Genoa, Milan, Como; of my declaration that I would suffer no more on Italian soil. I said, "Not any for me, if you please."

I wrote on. The barber began on the doctor. I heard him say:

"Dan, this is the easiest shave I have had since we left the ship."

He said again, presently:

"Why, Dan, a man could go to sleep with this man shaving him."

Dan took the chair. Then he said:

"Why, this is Titian. This is one of the old masters."

I wrote on. Directly Dan said:

"Doctor, it is perfect luxury. The ship's barber isn't anything to him."

My rough beard was distressing me beyond measure. The barber was rolling up his apparatus. The temptation was too strong. I said:

"Hold on, please. Shave me also."

I sat down in the chair and closed my eyes. The barber soaped my face and then took his razor and gave me a rake that well-nigh threw me into convulsions. I jumped out of the chair: Dan and the doctor were both wiping blood off their faces and laughing.

I said it was a mean, disgraceful fraud.

They said that the misery of this shave had gone so far beyond anything they had ever experienced before that they could not bear the idea of losing such a chance of hearing a cordial opinion from me on the subject.

It was shameful. But there was no help for it. The

skinning was begun and had to be finished. The tears flowed with every rake, and so did the fervent execrations. The barber grew confused, and brought blood every time. I think the boys enjoyed it better than anything they have seen or heard since they left home.

We have seen the Campanile and Byron's house and Balbi's the geographer, and the palaces of all the ancient dukes and doges of Venice, and we have seen their effeminate descendants airing their nobility in fashionable French attire in the Grand Square of St. Mark, and eating ices and drinking cheap wines, instead of wearing gallant coats of mail and destroying fleets and armies as their great ancestors did in the days of Venetian glory. We have seen no bravos with poisoned stilettos, no masks, no wild carnival; but we have seen the ancient pride of Venice, the grim bronze horses that figure in a thousand legends. Venice may well cherish them, for they are the only horses she ever had. It is said there are hundreds of people in this curious city who never have seen a living horse in their lives. It is entirely true, no doubt.

And so, having satisfied ourselves, we depart tomorrow and leave the venerable Queen of the Republics to summon her vanished ships, and marshal her shadowy armies, and know again in dreams the pride of her old renown.

24

Some of the *Quaker City's* passengers had arrived in Venice from Switzerland and other lands before we left there, and others were expected every day. We heard of no casualties among them and no sickness.

We were a little fatigued with sightseeing, and so we rattled through a good deal of country by rail without caring to stop. I took few notes. I find no mention of Bologna in my memorandum book, except that we arrived there in good season, but saw none of the sausages for which the place is so justly celebrated.

Pistoia awoke but a passing interest.

Florence pleased us for a while. I think we appreciated the great figure of David in the grand square, and the sculptured group they call the Rape of the Sabines. We wandered through the endless collections of paintings and statues of the Pitti and Ufizzi galleries, of course. I make that statement in self-defense; there let it stop. I could not rest under the imputation that I visited Florence and did not traverse its weary miles of picture galleries. We tried indolently to recollect something about the Guelphs and Ghibellines and the other historical cutthroats whose quarrels and assassinations make up so large a share of Florentine history, but the subject was not attractive. We had been robbed of all the fine mountain scenery on our little journey by a system of railroading that had three miles of tunnel to a hundred yards of daylight, and we were not inclined to be sociable with Florence. We had seen the spot, outside the city somewhere, where these people had allowed the bones of Galileo to rest in unconsecrated ground for an age because his great discovery that the world turned around was regarded as a damning heresy by the Church; and we know that long after the world had accepted his theory and raised his name high in the list of its great men, they had still let him rot there. That we had lived to see his dust in honored sepulture in the Church of Santa Croce we owed to a society of *literati,* and not to Florence or her rulers. We saw Dante's tomb in that church also, but we were glad to know that his body was not in it; that the ungrateful city that had exiled him and persecuted him would give much to have it there, but need not hope to ever secure that high honor to herself. Medicis are good enough for Florence. Let her plant Medicis and build grand monuments over them to testify how gratefully she was wont to lick the hand that scourged her.

Magnanimous Florence! Her jewelry marts are filled with artists in mosaic. Florentine mosaics are the choicest in all the world. Florence loves to have that said. Florence is proud of it. Florence would foster this specialty of hers. She is grateful to the artists that bring to her this high credit and fill her coffers with foreign money, and so she encourages them with pensions. With pensions! Think of the lavishness of it. She knows that people who piece together the beautiful trifles die early because the labor is so confining and so exhausting to hand and brain, and so she has decreed that all these people who reach the age of sixty shall have a pension after that! I have not heard that any of them have called for their dividends yet. One man did fight along till he was sixty and started after his pension, but it appeared that there had been a mistake of a year in his family record, and so he gave it up and died.

These artists will take particles of stone or glass no larger than a mustard seed, and piece them together on a sleeve button or a shirt stud, so smoothly and with such nice adjustment of the delicate shades of color the pieces bear as to form a pygmy rose with stem, thorn, leaves, petals complete, and all as softly and as truthfully tinted as though Nature had builded it herself. They will counterfeit a fly or a high-toned bug or the ruined Coliseum, within the cramped circle of a breast pin, and do it so deftly and so neatly that any man might think a master painted it.

I saw a little table in the great mosaic school in Florence— a little trifle of a center table—whose top was made of some sort of precious polished stone, and in the stone was inlaid the figure of a flute, with bell mouth and a mazy complication of keys. No painting in the world could have been softer or richer; no shading out of one tint into another could have been more perfect; no work of art of any kind could have been more faultless than this flute, and yet to count the multitude of little fragments of stone of which they swore it was formed would bankrupt any man's arithmetic! I do not think one could have seen where two particles joined each other with eyes of ordinary shrewdness. Certainly *we* could detect no such blemish. This tabletop cost the labor of one man for ten long years, so they said, and it was for sale for thirty-five thousand dollars.

We went to the Church of Santa Croce, from time to time, in Florence, to weep over the tombs of Michelangelo, Raphael, and Machiavelli (I suppose they are buried there, but it may be that they reside elsewhere and rent their tombs to other parties—such being the fashion in Italy), and between times we used to go and stand on the bridges and admire the Arno. It is popular to admire the Arno. It is a great historical creek with four feet in the channel and some scows floating around. It would be a very plausible river if they would pump some water into it. They all call it a river, and they honestly think it *is* a river, do these dark and bloody Florentines. They even help out the delusion by building bridges over it. I do not see why they are too good to wade.

How the fatigues and annoyances of travel fill one with bitter prejudices sometimes! I might enter Florence under happier auspices a month hence and find it all beautiful, all attractive. But I do not care to think of it now at all, nor of its roomy shops filled to the ceiling with snowy marble and alabaster copies of all the celebrated sculptures in Europe —copies so enchanting to the eye that I wonder how they can really be shaped like the dingy petrified nightmares they are the portraits of. I got lost in Florence at nine o'clock one night, and stayed lost in that labyrinth of narrow streets and long rows of vast buildings that look all alike until toward three o'clock in the morning. It was a pleasant night and at first there were a good many people abroad, and there were cheerful lights about. Later I grew accustomed to prowling about mysterious drifts and tunnels and astonishing and interesting myself with coming around corners expecting to find the hotel staring me in the face, and not finding it doing anything of the kind. Later still, I felt tired. I soon felt remarkably tired. But there was no one abroad now— not even a policeman. I walked till I was out of all patience and very hot and thirsty. At last, somewhere after one o'clock, I came unexpectedly to one of the city gates. I knew then that I was very far from the hotel. The soldiers thought I wanted to leave the city, and they sprang up and barred the way with their muskets. I said:

"Hotel d'Europe!"

It was all the Italian I knew, and I was not certain whether that was Italian or French. The soldiers looked stupidly at each other and at me, and shook their heads and took me into custody. I said I wanted to go home. They did not understand me. They took me into the guardhouse and searched me, but they found no sedition on me. They found a small piece of soap (we carry soap with us now), and I made them a present of it, seeing that they regarded it as a curiosity. I continued to say Hotel d'Europe and they continued to shake their heads, until at last a young soldier nodding in the corner roused up and said something. He said he knew where the hotel was, I suppose, for the officer of the guard sent him away with me. We walked a hundred or a hundred and fifty miles, it appeared to me, and then *he* got lost. He turned this way and that, and finally gave it up and signified that he was going to spend the remainder of the morning trying to find the city gate again. At that moment it struck me that there was something familiar about the house over the way. It was the hotel!

It was a happy thing for me that there happened to be a soldier there that knew even as much as he did; for they say that the policy of the government is to change the soldiery from one place to another constantly and from country to city, so that they cannot become acquainted with the people and grow lax in their duties and enter into plots and conspiracies with friends. My experiences of Florence were chiefly unpleasant. I will change the subject.

At Pisa we climbed up to the top of the strangest structure the world has any knowledge of—the Leaning Tower. As everyone knows, it is in the neighborhood of one hundred and eighty feet high—and I beg to observe that one hundred and eighty feet reach to about the height of four ordinary three-story buildings piled one on top of the other and is a very considerable altitude for a tower of uniform thickness to aspire to, even when it stands upright, yet this one leans more than thirteen feet out of the perpendicular. It is seven hundred years old, but neither history or tradition say whether it was built as it is purposely or whether one of its sides has settled. There is no record that it ever stood straight up. It is built of marble. It is an airy and a beautiful structure, and each of its eight stories is encircled by fluted columns, some of marble and some of granite, with Corinthian capitals that were handsome when they were new. It is a bell tower, and in its top hangs a chime of ancient bells. The winding staircase within is dark, but one always knows which side of the tower he is on because of his naturally gravitating from one side to the other of the staircase with the rise or dip of the tower. Some of the stones steps are footworn only on one end; others only on the other end; others only in the middle. To look down into the tower from the top is like looking down into a tilted well. A rope that hangs from the center of the top touches the wall before it reaches the bottom. Standing on the summit, one does not feel altogether comfortable when he looks down from the high side; but to crawl on your breast to the verge on the lower side and try to stretch your neck out far enough to see the base of the tower makes your flesh creep, and convinces you for a single moment, in spite of all your philosophy, that the building is falling. You handle yourself very carefully all the time, under the silly impression that if it is *not* falling, your trifling weight will start it unless you are particular not to "bear down" on it.

The Duomo, close at hand, is one of the finest cathedrals in Europe. It is eight hundred years old. Its grandeur has outlived the high commercial prosperity and the political importance that made it a necessity, or rather, a possibility. Surrounded by poverty, decay, and ruin, it conveys to us a more tangible impression of the former greatness of Pisa than books could give us.

The Baptistery, which is a few years older than the Leaning Tower, is a stately rotunda of huge dimensions, and was a costly structure. In it hangs the lamp whose measured swing suggested to Galileo the pendulum. It looked an insignificant thing to have conferred upon the world of science and mechanics such a mighty extension of their dominions as it has. Pondering, in its suggestive presence, I seemed to see a crazy universe of swinging disks, the toiling children of this sedate parent. He appeared to have an intelligent expression about him of knowing that he was not a lamp at all; that he was a Pendulum; a pendulum disguised, for prodigious and inscrutable purposes of his own deep devising, and not a common pendulum either, but the old original patriarchal Pendulum—the Abraham Pendulum of the world.

This Baptistery is endowed with the most pleasing echo of all the echoes we have read of. The guide sounded two sonorous notes, about half an octave apart; the echo answered with the most enchanting, the most melodious, the richest blending of sweet sounds that one can imagine. It was like a long-drawn chord of a church organ, infinitely softened by distance. I may be extravagant in this matter, but if this be the case my ear is to blame—not my pen. I am describing a memory—and one that will remain long with me.

The peculiar devotional spirit of the olden time, which placed a higher confidence in outward forms of worship than in the watchful guarding of the heart against sinful thoughts and the hands against sinful deeds, and which believed in the protecting virtues of inanimate objects made holy by contact with holy things, is illustrated in a striking manner in one of the cemeteries of Pisa. The tombs are set in soil brought in ships from the Holy Land ages ago. To be buried in such ground was regarded by the ancient Pisans as being more potent for salvation than many masses purchased of the Church and the vowing of many candles to the Virgin.

Pisa is believed to be about three thousand years old. It was one of the twelve great cities of ancient Etruria, that commonwealth which has left so many monuments in testimony of its extraordinary advancement and so little history of itself that is tangible and comprehensible. A Pisan antiquarian gave me an ancient tear jug which he averred was full four thousand years old. It was found among the ruins of one of the oldest of the Etruscan cities. He said it came from a tomb, and was used by some bereaved family in that remote age when even the pyramids of Egypt were young, Damascus a village, Abraham a prattling infant, and ancient Troy not yet dreamt of, to receive the tears wept for some lost idol of a household. It spoke to us in a language of its own; and with a pathos more tender than any words might bring, its mute eloquence swept down the long roll of the centuries with its tale of a vacant chair, a familiar footstep missed from the threshold, a pleasant voice gone from the chorus, a vanished form!—a tale which is always so new to us, so startling, so terrible, so benumbing to the senses, and behold how threadbare and old it is! No shrewdly worded history could have brought the myths and shadows of that old dreamy age before us clothed with human flesh and warmed with human sympathies so vividly as did this poor little unsentient vessel of pottery.

Pisa was a republic in the Middle Ages, with a government of her own, armies and navies of her own, and a great commerce. She was a warlike power and inscribed upon her banners many a brilliant fight with Genoese and Turks. It is said that the city once numbered a population of four hundred thousand; but her scepter has passed from her grasp now, her ships and her armies are gone, her commerce is dead. Her battle flags bear the mold and the dust of centuries, her marts are deserted, she has shrunken far within her crumbling walls, and her great population has diminished to twenty thousand souls. She has but one thing left to boast of, and that is not much, viz.: she is the second city of Tuscany.

We reached Leghorn in time to see all we wished to see of

it long before the city gates were closed for the evening,
and then came on board the ship.

We felt as though we had been away from home an age.
We never entirely appreciated before what a very pleasant
den our stateroom is, nor how jolly it is to sit at dinner in
one's own seat in one's own cabin and hold familiar conversation with friends in one's own language. Oh, the rare happiness of comprehending every single word that is said, and
knowing that every word one says in return will be understood as well! We would talk ourselves to death now, only
there are only about ten passengers out of the sixty-
five to talk to. The others are wandering we hardly know
where. We shall not go ashore in Leghorn. We are surfeited
with Italian cities for the present, and much prefer to walk
the familiar quarterdeck and view this one from a distance.

The stupid magnates of this Leghorn government cannot
understand that so large a steamer as ours could cross the
broad Atlantic with no other purpose than to indulge a party
of ladies and gentlemen in a pleasure excursion. It looks too
improbable. It is suspicious, they think. Something more important must be hidden behind it all. They cannot understand it, and they scorn the evidence of the ship's papers.
They have decided at last that we are a battalion of incendiary, bloodthirsty Garibaldians in disguise! And in all seriousness they have set a gunboat to watch the vessel night
and day, with orders to close down on any revolutionary
movement in a twinkling! Police boats are on patrol duty
about us all the time, and it is as much as a sailor's liberty
is worth to show himself in a red shirt. These policemen follow the executive officer's boat from shore to ship and from
ship to shore and watch his dark maneuvers with a vigilant
eye. They will arrest him yet unless he assumes an expression
of countenance that shall have less of carnage, insurrection,
and sedition in it. A visit paid in a friendly way to General
Garibaldi yesterday (by cordial invitation) by some of our
passengers has gone far to confirm the dread suspicions the
government harbors toward us. It is thought the friendly
visit was only the cloak of a bloody conspiracy. These people
draw near and watch us when we bathe in the sea from the
ship's side. Do they think we are communing with a reserve
force of rascals at the bottom?

It is said that we shall probably be quarantined at Naples.
Two or three of us prefer not to run this risk. Therefore,

when we are rested, we propose to go in a French steamer to
Civitavecchia, and from thence to Rome, and by rail to
Naples. They do not quarantine the cars, no matter where
they got their passengers from.

25

There are a good many things about this Italy which I
do not understand—and more especially I cannot understand
how a bankrupt government can have such palatial railroad
depots and such marvels of turnpikes. Why, these latter are as
hard as adamant, as straight as a line, as smooth as a floor,
and as white as snow. When it is too dark to see any other
object, one can still see the white turnpikes of France and
Italy; and they are clean enough to eat from without a tablecloth. And yet no tolls are charged.

As for the railways—we have none like them. The cars
slide as smoothly along as if they were on runners. The
depots are vast palaces of cut marble, with stately colonnades
of the same royal stone traversing them from end to end,
and with ample walls and ceilings richly decorated with
frescoes. The lofty gateways are graced with statues, and the
broad floors are all laid in polished flags of marble.

These things win me more than Italy's hundred galleries
of priceless art treasures, because I can understand the
one and am not competent to appreciate the other. In the
turnpikes, the railways, the depots, and the new boulevards
of uniform houses in Florence and other cities here, I see
the genius of Louis Napoleon, or rather, I see the works of
that statesman imitated. But Louis has taken care that in
France there shall be a foundation for these improvements—
money. He has always the wherewithal to back up his projects; they strengthen France and never weaken her. Her
material prosperity is genuine. But here the case is different.
This country is bankrupt. There is no real foundation for
these great works. The prosperity they would seem to in-

dicate is a pretense. There is no money in the treasury, and
so they enfeeble her instead of strengthening. Italy has
achieved the dearest wish of her heart and become an in-
dependent state—and in so doing she has drawn an elephant in the political lottery. She has nothing to feed it on.
Inexperienced in government, she plunged into all manner
of useless expenditure and swamped her treasury almost in
a day. She squandered millions of francs on a navy which
she did not need, and the first time she took her new toy
into action she got it knocked higher than Gilderoy's kite—
to use the language of the Pilgrims.

But it is an ill wind that blows nobody good. A year ago,
when Italy saw utter ruin staring her in the face and her
greenbacks hardly worth the paper they were printed on,
her Parliament ventured upon a *coup de main* that would
have appalled the stoutest of her statesmen under less desperate circumstances. They, in a manner, confiscated the
domains of the Church! This in priest-ridden Italy! This in a
land which has groped in the midnight of priestly superstition
for sixteen hundred years! It was a rare good fortune for
Italy, the stress of weather that drove her to break from this
prison house.

They do not call it *confiscating* the Church property. That
would sound too harshly yet. But it amounts to that. There
are thousands of churches in Italy, each with untold millions
of treasures stored away in its closets, and each with its
battalion of priests to be supported. And then there are the
estates of the Church—league on league of the richest lands
and the noblest forests in all Italy—all yielding immense
revenues to the Church, and none paying a cent in taxes to
the State. In some great districts the Church owns *all* the
property—lands, watercourses, woods, mills, and factories.
They buy, they sell, they manufacture, and since they pay no
taxes, who can hope to compete with them?

Well, the government has seized all this in effect, and will
yet seize it in rigid and unpoetical reality, no doubt. Something must be done to feed a starving treasury, and there is
no other resource in all Italy—none but the riches of the
Church. So the government intends to take to itself a great
portion of the revenues arising from priestly farms, factories,
etc., and also intends to take possession of the churches and
carry them on, after its own fashion and upon its own
responsibility. In a few instances it will leave the establish-

ments of great pet churches undisturbed, but in all others only a handful of priests will be retained to preach and pray, a few will be pensioned, and the balance turned adrift.

Pray glance at some of these churches and their embellishments, and see whether the government is doing a righteous thing or not. In Venice today, a city of a hundred thousand inhabitants, there are twelve hundred priests. Heaven only knows how many there were before the Parliament reduced their numbers. There was the great Jesuit Church. Under the old regime it required sixty priests to engineer it—the government does it with five now, and the others are discharged from service. All about that church wretchedness and poverty abound. At its door a dozen hats and bonnets were doffed to us, as many heads were humbly bowed, and as many hands extended, appealing for pennies—appealing with foreign words we could not understand, but appealing mutely, with sad eyes, and sunken cheeks, and ragged raiment, that no words were needed to translate. Then we passed within the great doors, and it seemed that the riches of the world were before us! Huge columns carved out of single masses of marble, and inlaid from top to bottom with a hundred intricate figures wrought in costly verd antique; pulpits of the same rich materials, whose draperies hung down in many a pictured fold, the stony fabric counterfeiting the delicate work of the loom; the grand altar brilliant with polished facings and balustrades of oriental agate, jasper, verd antique, and other precious stones, whose names, even, we seldom hear—and slabs of priceless lapis lazuli lavished everywhere as recklessly as if the church had owned a quarry of it. In the midst of all this magnificence, the solid gold and silver furniture of the altar seemed cheap and trivial. Even the floors and ceilings cost a princely fortune.

Now, where is the use of allowing all those riches to lie idle while half of that community hardly know from day to day how they are going to keep body and soul together? And where is the wisdom in permitting hundreds upon hundreds of millions of francs to be locked up in the useless trumpery of churches all over Italy, and the people ground to death with taxation to uphold a perishing government?

As far as I can see, Italy for fifteen hundred years has turned all her energies, all her finances, and all her industry to the building up of a vast array of wonderful church edifices, and starving half her citizens to accomplish it. She is today one vast museum of magnificence and misery. All the churches in an ordinary American city put together could hardly buy the jeweled frippery in one of her hundred cathedrals. And for every beggar in America, Italy can show a hundred—and rags and vermin to match. It is the wretchedest, princeliest land on earth.

Look at the grand Duomo of Florence—a vast pile that has been sapping the purses of her citizens for five hundred years, and is not nearly finished yet. Like all other men, I fell down and worshiped it, but when the filthy beggars swarmed around me the contrast was too striking, too suggestive, and I said, "O sons of classic Italy, *is* the spirit of enterprise, of self-reliance, of noble endeavor, utterly dead within ye? Curse your indolent worthlessness, why don't you rob your church?"

Three hundred happy, comfortable priests are employed in that cathedral.

And now that my temper is up, I may as well go on and abuse everybody I can think of. They have a grand mausoleum in Florence, which they built to bury our Lord and Saviour and the Medici family in. It sounds blasphemous, but it is true, and here they *act* blasphemy. The dead and damned Medicis, who cruelly tyrannized over Florence and were her curse for over two hundred years, are salted away in a circle of costly vaults, and in their midst the Holy Sepulchre was to have been set up. The expedition sent to Jerusalem to seize it got into trouble and could not accomplish the burglary, and so the center of the mausoleum is vacant now. They say the entire mausoleum was intended for the Holy Sepulchre, and was only turned into a family burying place after the Jerusalem expedition failed—but you will excuse me. Some of those Medicis would have smuggled themselves in sure. What *they* had not the effrontery to do was not worth doing. Why, they had their trivial, forgotten exploits on land and sea pictured out in grand frescoes (as did also the ancient doges of Venice) with the Saviour and the Virgin throwing bouquets to them out of the clouds, and the Deity himself applauding from his throne in heaven! And who painted these things? Why, Titian, Tintoretto, Paul Veronese, Raphael—none other than the world's idols, the "old masters."

Andrea del Sarto glorified his princes in pictures that must save them forever from the oblivion they merited, and they let him starve. Served him right. Raphael pictured such infernal villains as Catherine and Marie de Médicis seated in heaven and conversing familiarly with the Virgin Mary and the angels (to say nothing of higher personages), and yet my friends abuse me because I am a little prejudiced against the old masters—because I fail sometimes to see the beauty that is in their productions. I cannot help but see it now and then, but I keep on protesting against the groveling spirit that could persuade those masters to prostitute their noble talents to the adulation of such monsters as the French, Venetian, and Florentine princes of two and three hundred years ago, all the same.

I am told that the old masters had to do these shameful things for bread, the princes and potentates being the only patrons of art. If a grandly gifted man may drag his pride and his manhood in the dirt for bread rather than starve with the nobility that is in him untainted, the excuse is a valid one. It would excuse theft in Washingtons and Wellingtons, and unchastity in women as well.

But somehow I cannot keep that Medici mausoleum out of my memory. It is as large as a church; its pavement is rich enough for the pavement of a king's palace; its great dome is gorgeous with frescoes; its walls are made of—what? Marble? Plaster? Wood? Paper? No. Red porphyry—verd antique—jasper—oriental agate—alabaster—mother-of-pearl—chalcedony—red coral—lapis lazuli! All the vast walls are made wholly of these precious stones, worked in, and in and in together in elaborate patterns and figures, and polished till they glow like great mirrors with the pictured splendors reflected from the dome overhead. And before a statue of one of those dead Medicis reposes a crown that blazes with diamonds and emeralds enough to buy a ship-of-the-line almost. These are the things the government has its evil eye upon, and a happy thing it will be for Italy when they melt away in the public treasury.

And now— However, another beggar approaches. I will go out and destroy him and then come back and write another chapter of vituperation.

Having eaten the friendless orphan—having driven away his comrades—having grown calm and reflective at length—I now feel in a kindlier mood. I feel that after talking so freely about the priests and the churches, justice demands that if I know anything good about either I ought to say it. I *have* heard of many things that redound to the credit of the priesthood, but the most notable matter that occurs to me now is the devotion one of the mendicant orders showed during the prevalence of the cholera last year. I speak of the Dominican friars—men who wear a coarse, heavy brown robe and a cowl, in this hot climate, and go barefoot. They live on alms altogether, I believe. They must unquestionably love their religion to suffer so much for it. When the cholera was raging in Naples, when the people were dying by hundreds and hundreds every day, when every concern for the public welfare was swallowed up in selfish private interest, and every citizen made the taking care of himself his sole object, these men banded themselves together and went about nursing the sick and burying the dead. Their noble efforts cost many of them their lives. They laid them down cheerfully, and well they might. Creeds mathematically precise and hair-splitting niceties of doctrine are absolutely necessary for the salvation of some kinds of souls, but surely the charity, the purity, the unselfishness that are in the hearts of men like these would save their souls though they were bankrupt in the true religion—which is ours.

One of these fat barefooted rascals came here to Civitavecchia with us in the little French steamer. There were only half a dozen of us in the cabin. He belonged in the steerage. He was the life of the ship, the bloody-minded son of the Inquisition! He and the leader of the marine band of a French man-of-war played on the piano and sang opera turn about; they sang duets together; they rigged impromptu theatrical costumes and gave us extravagant farces and pantomimes. We got along first-rate with the friar, and were excessively conversational, albeit he could not understand what we said, and certainly he never uttered a word that we could guess the meaning of.

This Civitavecchia is the finest nest of dirt, vermin, and ignorance we have found yet except that African perdition they call Tangier, which is just like it. The people here live in alleys two yards wide, which have a smell about them which is peculiar but not entertaining. It is well the alleys are not wider, because they hold as much smell now as a person can stand, and of course if they were wider they would hold more, and then the people would die. These alleys are paved with stone and carpeted with deceased cats and decayed rags and decomposed vegetable tops and remnants of old boots, all soaked with dishwater, and the people sit around on stools and enjoy it. They are indolent, as a general thing, and yet have few pastimes. They work two or three hours at a time, but not hard, and then they knock off and catch flies. This does not require any talent, because they only have to grab—if they do not get the one they are after, they get another. It is all the same to them. They have no partialities. Whichever one they get is the one they want.

They have other kinds of insects, but it does not make them arrogant. They are very quiet, unpretending people. They have more of these kind of things than other communities, but they do not boast.

They are very uncleanly—these people—in face, in person, and dress. When they see anybody with a clean shirt on, it arouses their scorn. The women wash clothes half the day, at the public tanks in the streets, but they are probably somebody else's. Or maybe they keep one set to wear and another to wash; because they never put on any that have ever been washed. When they get done washing, they sit in the alleys and nurse their cubs. They nurse one ash cat at a time, and the others scratch their backs against the doorpost and are happy.

All this country belongs to the Papal States. They do not appear to have any schools here, and only one billiard table. Their education is at a very low stage. One portion of the men go into the military, another into the priesthood, and the rest into the shoemaking business.

They keep up the passport system here, but so they do in Turkey. This shows that the Papal States are as far advanced as Turkey. This fact will be alone sufficient to silence the tongues of malignant calumniators. I had to get my passport *vised* for Rome in Florence, and then they would not let me come ashore here until a policeman had examined it on the wharf and sent me a permit. They did not even dare to let me take my passport in my hands for twelve hours, I looked so formidable. They judged it best to let me cool down. They thought I wanted to take the town, likely. Little did they know me. I wouldn't have it. They examined my baggage at the depot. They took one of my ablest jokes and read it over carefully twice and then read it backwards. But it was too deep for them. They passed it around, and everybody speculated on it awhile, but it mastered them all.

It was no common joke. At length a veteran officer spelled it over deliberately and shook his head three or four times and said that in his opinion it was seditious. That was the first time I felt alarmed. I immediately said I would explain the document, and they crowded around. And so I explained and explained and explained, and they took notes of all I said, but the more I explained, the more they could not understand it, and when they desisted at last, I could not even understand it myself. They said they believed it was an incendiary document leveled at the government. I declared solemnly that it was not, but they only shook their heads and would not be satisfied. Then they consulted a good while, and finally they confiscated it. I was very sorry for this, because I had worked a long time on that joke and took a good deal of pride in it, and now I suppose I shall never see it anymore. I suppose it will be sent up and filed away among the criminal archives of Rome, and will always be regarded as a mysterious infernal machine which would have blown up like a mine and scattered the good Pope all around but for a miraculous providential interference. And I suppose that all the time I am in Rome the police will dog me about from place to place because they think I am a dangerous character.

It is fearfully hot in Civitavecchia. The streets are made very narrow and the houses built very solid and heavy and high, as a protection against the heat. This is the first Italian town I have seen which does not appear to have a patron saint. I suppose no saint but the one that went up in the chariot of fire could stand the climate.

There is nothing here to see. They have not even a cathedral, with eleven tons of solid silver archbishops in the back room; and they do not show you any moldy buildings that are seven thousand years old; nor any smoke-dried old fire-screens which are *chef d'œuvres* of Rubens or Simpson, or Titian or Ferguson, or any of those parties; and they haven't any bottled fragments of saints and not even a nail from the true Cross. We are going to Rome. There is nothing to see here.

26

What is it that confers the noblest delight? What is that
which swells a man's breast with pride above that which any
other experience can bring to him? Discovery! To know that
you are walking where none others have walked, that you are
beholding what human eye has not seen before, that you are
breathing a virgin atmosphere. To give birth to an idea—to
discover a great thought—an intellectual nugget, right under
the dust of a field that many a brain plow had gone over
before. To find a new planet, to invent a new hinge, to find
the way to make the lightnings carry your messages. To be
the *first*—that is the idea. To do something, say something,
see something, before *anybody* else—these are the things that
confer a pleasure compared with which other pleasures are
tame and commonplace, other ecstasies cheap and trivial.
Morse, with his first message, brought by his servant, the
lightning; Fulton, in that long-drawn century of suspense,
when he placed his hand upon the throttle valve and lo, the
steamboat moved; Jenner, when his patient with the cow's
virus in his blood walked through the smallpox hospitals
unscathed; Howe, when the idea shot through his brain that
for a hundred and twenty generations the eye had been bored
through the wrong end of the needle; the nameless lord of art
who laid down his chisel in some old age that is forgotten
now and gloated upon the finished Laocoön; Daguerre,
when he commanded the sun, riding in the zenith, to print
the landscape upon his insignificant silvered plate, and he
obeyed; Columbus, in the *Pinta's* shrouds, when he swung
his hat above a fabled sea and gazed abroad upon an unknown world! These are the men who have really *lived*—who
have actually comprehended what pleasure is—who have
crowded long lifetimes of ecstasy into a single moment.

What is there in Rome for me to see that others have not
seen before me? What is there for me to touch that others

have not touched? What is there for me to feel, to learn, to
hear, to know, that shall thrill me before it pass to others?
What can I discover? Nothing. Nothing whatsoever. One
charm of travel dies here. But if I were only a Roman! If,
added to my own, I could be gifted with modern Roman
sloth, modern Roman superstition, and modern Roman
boundlessness of ignorance, what bewildering worlds of unsuspected wonders I would discover! Ah, if I were only a
habitant of the Campagna five-and-twenty miles from Rome!
Then I would travel.

I would go to America and see and learn and return to the
Campagna and stand before my countrymen an illustrious
discoverer. I would say:

"I saw there a country which has no overshadowing
Mother Church, and yet the people survive. I saw a government which never was protected by foreign soldiers at a cost
greater than that required to carry on the government itself.
I saw common men and common women who could read; I
even saw small children of common country people reading
from books; if I dared think you would believe it, I would
say they could write also. In the cities I saw people drinking
a delicious beverage made of chalk and water, but never
once saw goats driven through their Broadway or their
Pennsylvania Avenue or their Montgomery Street and milked
at the doors of the houses. I saw real glass windows in the
houses of even the commonest people. Some of the houses
are not of stone nor yet of bricks; I solemnly swear they
are made of wood. Houses there will take fire and burn
sometimes—actually burn entirely down and not leave a
single vestige behind. I could state that for a truth, upon my
deathbed. And as a proof that the circumstance is not rare, I
aver that they have a thing which they call a fire engine,
which vomits forth great streams of water, and is kept always
in readiness, by night and by day, to rush to houses that are
burning. You would think one engine would be sufficient,
but some great cities have a hundred; they keep men hired,
and pay them by the month to do nothing but put out fires.
For a certain sum of money other men will insure that your
house shall not burn down; and if it burns they will pay you
for it. There are hundreds and thousands of schools, and
anybody may go and learn to be wise, like a priest. In that
singular country if a rich man dies a sinner, he is damned;
he cannot buy salvation with money for masses. There is

really not much use in being rich there. Not much use as far
as the other world is concerned, but much, very much use,
as concerns this; because there, if a man be rich he is very
greatly honored, and can become a legislator, a governor, a
general, a senator, no matter how ignorant an ass he is—
just as in our beloved Italy the nobles hold all the great
places, even though sometimes they are born noble idiots.
There, if a man be rich they give him costly presents, they
ask him to feasts, they invite him to drink complicated beverages; but if he be poor and in debt, they require him to do
that which they term to 'settle.' The women put on a
different dress almost every day; the dress is usually fine, but
absurd in shape; the very shape and fashion of it changes
twice in a hundred years; and did I but covet to be called
an extravagant falsifier, I would say it changed even oftener.
Hair does not grow upon the American women's heads; it
is made for them by cunning workmen in the shops, and is
curled and frizzled into scandalous and ungodly forms. Some
persons wear eyes of glass which they see through with
facility perhaps, else they would not use them; and in the
mouths of some are teeth made by the sacrilegious hand of
man. The dress of the men is laughably grotesque. They
carry no musket in ordinary life, nor no long-pointed pole;
they wear no wide green-lined cloak; they wear no peaked
black felt hat, no leathern gaiters reaching to the knee, no
goatskin breeches with the hair side out, no hobnailed shoes,
no prodigious spurs. They wear a conical hat termed a
'nail-kag'; a coat of saddest black; a shirt which shows dirt
so easily that it has to be changed every month, and is very
troublesome; things called pantaloons, which are held up by
shoulder straps, and on their feet they wear boots which are
ridiculous in pattern and can stand no wear. Yet dressed
in this fantastic garb, these people laughed at *my* costume. In
that country, books are so common that it is really no curiosity
to see one. Newspapers also. They have a great machine
which prints such things by thousands every hour.

"I saw common men there—men who were neither priests
nor princes—who yet absolutely owned the land they tilled.
It was not rented from the Church nor from the nobles. I am
ready to take my oath of this. In that country you might fall
from a third-story window three several times, and not mash
either a soldier or a priest. The scarcity of such people is
astonishing. In the cities you will see a dozen civilians for

every soldier, and as many for every priest or preacher. Jews there are treated just like human beings, instead of dogs. They can work at any business they please; they can sell brand-new goods if they want to; they can keep drugstores; they can practice medicine among Christians; they can even shake hands with Christians if they choose; they can associate with them just the same as one human being does with another human being; they don't have to stay shut up in one corner of the towns; they can live in any part of a town they like best; it is said they even have the privilege of buying land and houses, and owning them themselves, though I doubt that, myself; they never have had to run races naked through the public streets, against jackasses, to please the people in carnival time; there they never have been driven by the soldiers into a church every Sunday for hundreds of years to hear themselves and their religion especially and particularly cursed; at this very day, in that curious country, a Jew is allowed to vote, hold office, yea, get up on a rostrum in the public street and express his opinion of the government if the government don't suit him! Ah, it is wonderful. The common people there know a great deal; they even have the effrontery to complain if they are not properly governed, and to take hold and help conduct the government themselves; if they had laws like ours, which give one dollar of every three a crop produces to the government for taxes, they would have that law altered; instead of paying thirty-three dollars in taxes out of every one hundred they receive, they complain if they have to pay seven. They are curious people. They do not know when they are well off. Mendicant priests do not prowl among them with baskets begging for the Church and eating up their substance. One hardly ever sees a minister of the gospel going around there in his bare feet, with a basket, begging for subsistence. In that country the preachers are not like our mendicant orders of friars—they have two or three suits of clothing, and they wash sometimes. In that land are mountains far higher than the Alban Mountains; the vast Roman Campagna, a hundred miles long and full forty broad, is really small compared to the United States of America; the Tiber, that celebrated river of ours, which stretches its mighty course almost two hundred miles, and which a lad can scarcely threw a stone across at Rome, is not so long nor yet so wide as the American Mississippi—nor yet the Ohio nor even the Hudson. In

America the people are absolutely wiser and know much more than their grandfathers did. *They* do not plow with a sharpened stick, nor yet with a three-cornered block of wood that merely scratches the top of the ground. We do that because our fathers did three thousand years ago, I suppose. But those people have no holy reverence for their ancestors. They plow with a plow that is a sharp, curved blade of iron, and it cuts into the earth full five inches. And this is not all. They cut their grain with a horrid machine that mows down whole fields in a day. If I dared, I would say that sometimes they use a blasphemous plow that works by fire and vapor and tears up an acre of ground in a single hour—but—but— I see by your looks that you do not believe the things I am telling you. Alas, my character is ruined, and I am a branded speaker of untruths!"

Of course we have been to the monster Church of St. Peter frequently. I knew its dimensions. I knew it was a prodigious structure. I knew it was just about the length of the Capitol at Washington—say seven hundred and thirty feet. I knew it was three hundred and sixty-four feet wide, and consequently wider than the Capitol. I knew that the cross on the top of the dome of the church was four hundred and thirty-eight feet above the ground, and therefore about a hundred or maybe a hundred and twenty-five feet higher than the dome of the Capitol. Thus I had one gauge. I wished to come as near forming a correct idea of how it was going to look as possible; I had a curiosity to see how much I would err. I erred considerably. St. Peter's did not look nearly so large as the Capitol, and certainly not a twentieth part as beautiful, from the outside.

When we reached the door and stood fairly within the church, it was impossible to comprehend that it was a *very* large building. I had to *cipher* a comprehension of it. I had to ransack my memory for some more similes. St. Peter's is bulky. Its height and size would represent two of the Washington Capitol set one on top of the other—if the Capitol were wider; or two blocks or two blocks and a half of ordinary buildings set one on top of the other. St. Peter's *was* that large, but it could and would not look so. The trouble was that everything in it and about it was on such a scale of uniform vastness that there were no contrasts to judge by —none but the people, and I had not noticed them. They were insects. The statues of children holding vases of holy water were immense, according to the tables of figures, but so was everything else around them. The mosaic pictures in the dome were huge, and were made of thousands and thousands of cubes of glass as large as the end of my little finger, but those pictures looked smooth, and gaudy of color, and in good proportion to the dome. Evidently they would not answer to measure by. Away down toward the far end of the church (I thought it was really clear at the far end, but discovered afterward that it was in the center, under the dome) stood the thing they call the baldachino—a great bronze pyramidal framework like that which upholds a mosquito bar. It only looked like a considerably magnified bedstead—nothing more. Yet I knew it was a good deal more than half as high as Niagara Falls. It was overshadowed by a dome so mighty that its own height was snubbed. The four great square piers or pillars that stand equidistant from each other in the church and support the roof, I could not work up to their real dimensions by any method of comparison. I knew that the faces of each were about the width of a very large dwelling house front (fifty or sixty feet) and that they were twice as high as an ordinary three-story dwelling, but still they looked small. I tried all the different ways I could think of to compel myself to understand how large St. Peter's was, but with small success. The mosaic portrait of an Apostle who was writing with a pen six feet long seemed only an ordinary Apostle.

But the people attracted my attention after a while. To stand in the door of St. Peter's and look at men down toward its further extremity, two blocks away, has a diminishing effect on them; surrounded by the prodigious pictures and statues, and lost in the vast spaces, they look very much smaller than they would if they stood two blocks away in the open air. I "averaged" a man as he passed me and watched him as he drifted far down by the baldachino and beyond—watched him dwindle to an insignificant schoolboy, and then, in the midst of the silent throng of human pygmies gliding about him, I lost him. The church had lately been decorated, on the occasion of a great ceremony in honor of St. Peter, and men were engaged now in removing the flowers and gilt paper from the walls and pillars. As no ladders could reach the great heights, the men swung themselves down from balustrades and the capitals of pilasters by ropes to do this work. The upper gallery, which encircles the inner sweep of the dome, is two hundred and forty feet above the floor of the church—very few steeples in America could reach up to it. Visitors always go up there to look down into the church because one gets the best idea of some of the heights and distances from that point. While we stood on the floor one of the workmen swung loose from that gallery at the end of a long rope. I had not supposed before that a man *could* look so much like a spider. He was insignificant in size, and his rope seemed only a thread. Seeing that he took up so little space, I could believe the story then that ten thousand troops went to St. Peter's once to hear mass, and their commanding officer came afterward and, not finding them, supposed they had not yet arrived. But they were in the church, nevertheless—they were in one of the transepts. Nearly fifty thousand persons assembled in St. Peter's to hear the publishing of the dogma of the Immaculate Conception. It is estimated that the floor of the church affords standing room for—for a large number of people; I have forgotten the exact figures. But it is no matter—it is near enough.

They have twelve small pillars in St. Peter's, which came from Solomon's Temple. They have also—which was far more interesting to me—a piece of the true Cross, and some nails, and a part of the crown of thorns.

Of course we ascended to the summit of the dome, and of course we also went up into the gilt copper ball which is above it. There was room there for a dozen persons, with a little crowding, and it was as close and hot as an oven. Some of those people who are so fond of writing their names in prominent places had been there before us—a million or two, I should think. From the dome of St. Peter's one can see every notable object in Rome, from the Castle of St. Angelo to the Coliseum. He can discern the seven hills upon which Rome is built. He can see the Tiber, and the locality of the bridge which Horatius kept "in the brave days of old" when Lars Porsena attempted to cross it with his invading host. He can see the spot where the Horatii and the Curatii fought their famous battle. He can see the broad green Campagna, stretching away toward the mountains, with its scattered arches and broken aqueducts of the olden time, so picturesque in their gray ruin, and so daintily festooned with vines. He can see the Alban Mountains, the Appenines, the Sabine Hills, and the blue Mediterranean. He can see a panorama that is varied, extensive, beautiful to the eye, and more il-

lustrious in history than any other in Europe. About his feet
is spread the remnant of a city that once had a population of
four million souls; and among its massed edifices stand the
ruins of temples, columns, and triumphal arches that knew
the Caesars and the noonday of Roman splendor; and close
by them, in unimpaired strength, is a drain of arched and
heavy masonry that belonged to that older city which stood
here before Romulus and Remus were born or Rome thought
of. The Appian Way is here yet, and looking much as it did,
perhaps, when the triumphal processions of the emperors
moved over it in other days bringing fettered princes from
the confines of the earth. We cannot see the long array of
chariots and mail-clad men laden with the spoils of conquest,
but we can imagine the pageant, after a fashion. We look out
upon many objects of interest from the dome of St. Peter's;
and last of all, almost at our feet, our eyes rest upon the
building which was once the Inquisition. How times changed,
between the older ages and the new! Some seventeen or eighteen centuries ago the ignorant men of Rome were wont to
put Christians in the arena of the Coliseum yonder and turn
the wild beasts in upon them for a show. It was for a
lesson as well. It was to teach the people to abhor and fear
the new doctrine the followers of Christ were teaching. The
beasts tore the victims limb from limb and made poor
mangled corpses of them in the twinkling of an eye. But
when the Christians came into power, when the holy Mother
Church became mistress of the barbarians, she taught them
the error of their ways by no such means. No, she put them
in this pleasant Inquisition and pointed to the Blessed Redeemer, who was so gentle and so merciful toward all men,
and they urged the barbarians to love him; and they did all
they could to persuade them to love and honor him—first
by twisting their thumbs out of joint with a screw; then by
nipping their flesh with pincers—red-hot ones, because they
are the most comfortable in cold weather; then by skinning
them alive a little; and finally by roasting them in public.
They always convinced those barbarians. The true religion,
properly administered, as the good Mother Church used to
administer it, is very, very soothing. It is wonderfully persuasive also. There is a great difference between feeding parties to wild beasts and stirring up their finer feelings in an
Inquisition. One is the system of degraded barbarians, the

other of enlightened, civilized people. It is a great pity the playful Inquisition is no more.

I prefer not to describe St. Peter's. It has been done before. The ashes of Peter, the disciple of the Saviour, repose in a crypt under the baldachino. We stood reverently in that place; so did we also in the Mamertine Prison, where he was confined, where he converted the soldiers, and where tradition says he caused a spring of water to flow in order that he might baptize them. But when they showed us the print of Peter's face in the hard stone of the prison wall and said he made that by falling up against it, we doubted. And when, also, the monk at the Church of San Sebastian showed us a paving stone with two great footprints in it and said that Peter's feet made those, we lacked confidence again. Such things do not impress one. The monk said that angels came and liberated Peter from prison by night, and he started away from Rome by the Appian Way. The Saviour met him and told him to go back, which he did. Peter left those footprints in the stone upon which he stood at the time. It was not stated how it was ever discovered whose footprints they were, seeing the interview occurred secretly and at night. The print of the face in the prison was that of a man of common size; the footprints were those of a man ten or twelve feet high. The discrepancy confirmed our unbelief.

We necessarily visited the Forum, where Caesar was assassinated, and also the Tarpeian Rock. We saw the Dying Gladiator at the Capitol, and I think that even we appreciated that wonder of art, as much perhaps as we did that fearful story wrought in marble in the Vatican—the Laocoön. And then the Coliseum.

Everybody knows the picture of the Coliseum; everybody recognizes at once that "looped and windowed" bandbox with a side bitten out. Being rather isolated, it shows to better advantage than any other of the monuments of ancient Rome. Even the beautiful Pantheon, whose pagan altars uphold the cross now, and whose Venus, tricked out in consecrated gimcracks, does reluctant duty as a Virgin Mary today, is built about with shabby houses and its stateliness sadly marred. But the monarch of all European ruins, the Coliseum, maintains that reserve and that royal seclusion which is proper to majesty. Weeds and flowers spring from its massy arches and its circling seats, and vines hang their fringes from its lofty walls. An impressive silence broods

over the monstrous structure where such multitudes of men
and women were wont to assemble in other days. The butterflies have taken the places of the queens of fashion and
beauty of eighteen centuries ago, and the lizards sun themselves in the sacred seat of the emperor. More vividly than
all the written histories, the Coliseum tells the story of
Rome's grandeur and Rome's decay. It is the worthiest type
of both that exists. Moving about the Rome of today, we
might find it hard to believe in her old magnificence and her
millions of population; but with this stubborn evidence before us that she was obliged to have a theater with sitting
room for eighty thousand persons and standing room for
twenty thousand more, to accommodate such of her citizens
as required amusement, we find belief less difficult. The
Coliseum is over one thousand six hundred feet long, seven
hundred and fifty wide, and one hundred and sixty-five high.
Its shape is oval.

In America we make convicts useful at the same time that
we punish them for their crimes. We farm them out and
compel them to earn money for the State by making barrels
and building roads. Thus we combine business with retribution, and all things are lovely. But in ancient Rome they
combined religious duty with pleasure. Since it was necessary
that the new sect called Christians should be exterminated,
the people judged it wise to make this work profitable to the
State at the same time, and entertaining to the public. In addition to the gladiatorial combats and other shows, they
sometimes threw members of the hated sect into the arena of
the Coliseum and turned wild beasts in upon them. It is estimated that seventy thousand Christians suffered martyrdom
in this place. This has made the Coliseum holy ground in the
eyes of the followers of the Saviour. And well it might; for
if the chain that bound a saint and the footprints a saint has
left upon a stone he chanced to stand upon be holy, surely
the spot where a man gave up his life for his faith is holy.

Seventeen or eighteen centuries ago this Coliseum was *the*
theater of Rome, and Rome was mistress of the world.
Splendid pageants were exhibited here, in presence of the
emperor, the great ministers of State, the nobles, and vast
audiences of citizens of smaller consequence. Gladiators
fought with gladiators and at times with warrior prisoners
from many a distant land. It was *the* theater of Rome—of
the world—and the man of fashion who could not let fall in

a casual and unintentional manner something about "my private box at the Coliseum" could not move in the first circles. When the clothing-store merchant wished to consume the corner grocery man with envy, he bought secured seats in the front row and let the thing be known. When the irresistible dry-goods clerk wished to blight and destroy, according to his native instinct, he got himself up regardless of expense and took some other fellow's young lady to the Coliseum, and then accented the affront by cramming her with ice cream between the acts or by approaching the cage and stirring up the martyrs with his whalebone cane for her edification. The Roman swell was in his true element only when he stood up against a pillar and fingered his moustache unconscious of the ladies; when he viewed the bloody combats through an opera glass two inches long; when he excited the envy of provincials by criticisms which showed that he had been to the Coliseum many and many a time and was long ago over the novelty of it; when he turned away with a yawn at last and said:

"*He* a star! Handles his sword like an apprentice brigand! He'll do for the country maybe, but he don't answer for the metropolis!"

Glad was the contraband that had a seat in the pit at the Saturday matinee, and happy the Roman street boy who ate his peanuts and guyed the gladiators from the dizzy gallery.

For me was reserved the high honor of discovering among the rubbish of the ruined Coliseum the only playbill of that establishment now extant. There was a suggestive smell of mint drops about it still, a corner of it had evidently been chewed, and on the margin, in choice Latin, these words were written in a delicate female hand:

Meet me on the Tarpeian Rock tomorrow evening, dear, at sharp seven. Mother will be absent on a visit to her friends in the Sabine Hills.

Claudia

Ah, where is that lucky youth today, and where the little hand that wrote those dainty lines? Dust and ashes these seventeen hundred years!

Thus reads the bill:

ROMAN COLISEUM

UNPARALLELED ATTRACTION!

NEW PROPERTIES! NEW LIONS! NEW GLADIATORS!

Engagement of the renowned

MARCUS MARCELLUS VALERIAN!

FOR SIX NIGHTS ONLY!

The management beg leave to offer to the public an entertainment surpassing in magnificence anything that has hereto-
fore been attempted on any stage. No expense has been
spared to make the opening season one which shall be worthy
the generous patronage which the management feel sure will
crown their efforts. The management beg leave to state that
they have succeeded in securing the services of a

GALAXY OF TALENT!

such as has not been beheld in Rome before.
The performance will commence this evening with a

GRAND BROADSWORD COMBAT!

between two young and promising amateurs and a celebrated
Parthian gladiator who has just arrived a prisoner from the
Camp of Verus.
This will be followed by a grand moral

BATTLE-AX ENGAGEMENT!

between the renowned Valerian (with one hand tied behind
him) and two gigantic savages from Britain.
After which the renowned Valerian (if he survive) will fight
with the broadsword
LEFT-HANDED!

against six sophomores and a freshman from the Gladiatorial
College!
A long series of brilliant engagements will follow, in which
the finest talent of the empire will take part.
After which the celebrated Infant Prodigy, known as

"THE YOUNG ACHILLES,"

will engage four tiger whelps in combat, armed with no other weapon than his little spear!

The whole to conclude with a chaste and elegant

GENERAL SLAUGHTER!

in which thirteen African lions and twenty-two barbarian prisoners will war with each other until all are exterminated.

BOX OFFICE NOW OPEN

Dress Circle One Dollar; Children and Servants half price.

An efficient police force will be on hand to preserve order and keep the wild beasts from leaping the railings and discommoding the audience.

Doors open at 7; performance begins at 8.

POSITIVELY NO FREE LIST.

Diodorus Job Press

It was as singular as it was gratifying that I was also so fortunate as to find among the rubbish of the arena a stained and mutilated copy of the *Roman Daily Battle-Ax,* containing a critique upon this very performance. It comes to hand too late by many centuries to rank as news, and therefore I translate and publish it simply to show how very little the general style and phraseology of dramatic criticism has altered in the ages that have dragged their slow length along since the carriers laid this one damp and fresh before their Roman patrons:

THE OPENING SEASON. COLISEUM. Notwithstanding the inclemency of the weather, quite a respectable number of the rank and fashion of the city assembled last night to witness the debut upon metropolitan boards of the young tragedian who has of late been winning such golden opinions in the amphitheaters of the provinces. Some sixty thousand persons were present, and but for the fact that the streets were almost impassable, it is fair to presume that the house would have been full. His august Majesty, the Emperor Aurelius, occupied the imperial box, and was the cynosure of all eyes. Many illustrious nobles and generals of the empire graced the occasion with their presence, and not the least among them was the young patrician lieutenant whose laurels, won in the ranks of the "Thundering Legion," are still so green upon his brow. The cheer which greeted his entrance was heard beyond the Tiber!

The late repairs and decorations add both to the comeliness and the comfort of the Coliseum. The new cushions are a great improvement upon the hard marble seats we have been so long accustomed to. The present management deserve well of the public. They have restored to the Coliseum the gilding, the rich upholstery, and the uniform magnificence which old Coliseum frequenters tell us Rome was so proud of fifty years ago.

The opening scene last night—the broadsword combat between two young amateurs and a famous Parthian gladiator who was sent here a prisoner—was very fine. The elder of the two young gentlemen handled his weapon with a grace that marked the possession of extraordinary talent. His feint of thrusting, followed instantly by a happily delivered blow which unhelmeted the Parthian, was received with hearty applause. He was not thoroughly up in the backhanded stroke, but it was very gratifying to his numerous friends to know that, in time, practice would have overcome this defect. However, he was killed. His sisters, who were present, expressed considerable regret. His mother left the Coliseum. The other youth maintained the contest with such spirit as to call forth enthusiastic bursts of applause. When at last he fell a corpse, his aged mother ran screaming, with hair disheveled and tears streaming from her eyes, and swooned away just as her hands were clutching at the railings of the arena. She was promptly removed by the police. Under the circumstances, the woman's conduct was pardonable, perhaps, but we suggest that such exhibitions interfere with the decorum which should be preserved during the performances, and are highly improper in the presence of the Emperor. The Parthian prisoner fought bravely and well; and well he might, for he was fighting for both life and liberty. His wife and children were there to nerve his arm with their love, and to remind him of the old home he should see again if he conquered. When his second assailant fell, the woman clasped her children to her breast and wept for joy. But it was only a transient happiness. The captive staggered toward her and she saw that the liberty he had earned was earned too late. He was wounded unto death. Thus the first act closed in a manner which was entirely satisfactory. The manager was called before the curtain and returned his thanks for the honor done him, in a speech which was replete with wit and humor, and closed by hoping that his humble efforts to afford cheerful and instructive entertainment would continue to meet with the approbation of the Roman public.

The star now appeared, and was received with vociferous applause and the simultaneous waving of sixty thousand handkerchiefs. Marcus Marcellus Valerian (stage name—his real name is Smith) is a splendid specimen of physical development and an artist of rare merit. His management of the battle-ax is wonderful. His gaiety and his playfulness are irresistible in his comic parts, and yet they are inferior to his sublime conceptions in the grave realm of tragedy. When his ax was describing fiery circles about the heads of the bewildered barbarians, in exact time with his springing body and his prancing legs, the audience gave way to uncontrollable bursts of laughter; but when the back of his weapon broke the skull of one and almost in the same instant its edge clove the other's body in twain, the howl of enthusiastic applause that shook the building was the acknowledgment of a critical assemblage that he was a master of the noblest department of his profession. If he has a fault (and we are sorry to even intimate that he has), it is that of glancing at the audience in the midst of the most exciting moments of the performance, as if seeking admiration. The pausing in a fight to bow when bouquets are thrown to him is also in bad taste. In the great left-handed combat he appeared to be looking at the audience half the time instead of carving his adversaries; and when he had slain all the sophomores and was dallying with the freshman, he stooped and snatched a bouquet as it fell, and offered it to his adversary at a time when a blow was descending which promised favorably to be his death warrant. Such levity is proper enough in the provinces, we make no doubt, but it ill suits the dignity of the metropolis. We trust our young friend will take these remarks in good part, for we mean them solely for his benefit. All who know us are aware that although we are at times justly severe upon tigers and martyrs, we never intentionally offend gladiators.

The Infant Prodigy performed wonders. He overcame his four tiger whelps with ease, and with no other hurt than the loss of a portion of his scalp. The General Slaughter was rendered with a faithfulness to details which reflects the highest credit upon the late participants in it.

Upon the whole, last night's performances shed honor not only upon the management but upon the city that encourages and sustains such wholesome and instructive entertainments. We would simply suggest that the practice of vulgar young boys in the gallery of shying peanuts and paper pellets at the tigers, and saying "Hi-yi!" and manifesting approbation or dissatisfaction by such observations as "Bully for the lion!" "Go it, Gladdy!" "Boots!" "Speech!" "Take a walk round the block!" and so on, are extremely reprehensible when the Emperor is present, and ought to be stopped by the police. Several times last night, when the supernumeraries entered the arena to drag out the bodies, the young ruffians in the gallery shouted, "Supe! Supe!" and also, "Oh, what a coat!" and "Why don't you pad them shanks?" and made use of various other remarks expressive of derision. These things are very annoying to the audience.

A matinee for the little folks is promised for this afternoon, on which occasion several martyrs will be eaten by the tigers. The regular performance will continue every night till further notice. Material change of program every evening. Benefit of Valerian, Tuesday, 29th, if he lives.

I have been a dramatic critic myself, in my time, and I was often surprised to notice how much more I knew about Hamlet than Forrest did; and it gratifies me to observe now how much better my brethren of ancient times knew how a broadsword battle ought to be fought than the gladiators.

27

So far, good. If any man has a right to feel proud of himself and satisfied, surely it is I. For I have written about the Coliseum and the gladiators, the martyrs and the lions, and yet have never once used the phrase "butchered to make a Roman holiday." I am the only free white man of mature age who has accomplished this since Byron originated the expression.

Butchered to make a Roman holiday sounds well for the first seventeen or eighteen hundred thousand times one sees it in print, but after that it begins to grow tiresome. I find it in all the books concerning Rome—and here latterly it reminds me of Judge Oliver. Oliver was a young lawyer, fresh from the schools, who had gone out to the deserts of Nevada to begin life. He found that country and our ways of life there, in those early days, different from life in New England or Paris. But he put on a woolen shirt and strapped a navy revolver to his person, took to the bacon and beans of the country, and determined to do in Nevada as Nevada did. Oliver accepted the situation so completely that although he must have sorrowed over many of his trials, he never complained —that is, he never complained but once. He, two others, and myself started to the new silver mines in the Humboldt Mountains—he to be Probate Judge of Humboldt County and we to mine. The distance was two hundred miles. It was dead of winter. We bought a two-horse wagon and put eighteen hundred pounds of bacon, flour, beans, blasting powder, picks, and shovels in it; we bought two sorry-looking Mexican "plugs," with the hair turned the wrong way and more corners on their bodies than there are on the Mosque of Omar; we hitched up and started. It was a dreadful trip. But Oliver did not complain. The horses dragged the wagon two miles from town and then gave out. Then we three pushed the wagon seven miles, and Oliver moved ahead and pulled the horses after him by the bits. We complained, but Oliver did not. The ground was frozen, and it froze our backs while we slept; the wind swept across our faces and froze our noses. Oliver did not complain. Five days of pushing the wagon by day and freezing by night brought us to the bad part of the journey—the Forty-Mile Desert, or the Great American Desert, if you please. Still, this mildest-mannered man that ever was had not complained. We started across at eight in the morning, pushing through sand that had no bottom; toiling all day long by the wrecks of a thousand wagons, the skeletons of ten thousand oxen; by wagon tires enough to hoop the Washington Monument to the top, and ox chains enough to girdle Long Island; by human graves; with our throats parched always with thirst; lips bleeding from the alkali dust; hungry, perspiring, and very, very weary—so weary that when we dropped in the sand every fifty yards to rest the horses, we could hardly keep from going to sleep—no complaints from Oliver; none the next morning at three o'clock, when we got across, tired to death. Awakened two or three nights afterward at midnight, in a narrow canyon, by the snow falling on our faces, and appalled at the imminent danger of being "snowed in," we harnessed up and pushed on till eight in the morning, passed the "Divide," and knew we were saved. No complaints. Fifteen days of hardship and fatigue brought us to the end of the two hundred miles, and the judge had not complained. We wondered if anything *could* exasperate him. We built a Humboldt house. It is done in this way. You dig a square in the steep base of the mountain and set up two uprights and top them with two joists. Then you stretch a great sheet of "cotton domestic" from the point where the joists join the hillside down over the joists to the ground; this makes the roof and the front of the mansion; the sides and back are the dirt walls your digging has left. A chimney is easily made by turning up one corner of the roof. Oliver was sitting alone in this dismal den one night, by a sagebrush fire, writing poetry; he was very fond of digging poetry out of himself—or blasting it out when it came hard. He heard an animal's footsteps close to the roof; a stone or two and some dirt came through and fell by him. He grew uneasy and said, "Hi! Clear out from there, can't you!"—from time to time. But by and by he fell asleep where he sat, and pretty soon a mule fell down the chimney! The fire flew in every direction, and Oliver went over backwards. About ten nights after that, he recovered confidence enough to go to writing poetry again. Again he dozed off to sleep, and again a mule fell down the chimney. This time about half of that side of the house came in with the mule. Struggling to get up, the mule kicked the candle out and smashed most of the kitchen furniture, and raised considerable dust. These violent awakenings must have been annoying to Oliver, but he never complained. He moved to a mansion on the opposite side of the canyon because he had noticed the mules did not go there. One night about eight o'clock he was endeavoring to finish his poem, when a stone rolled in—then a hoof appeared below the canvas—then part of a cow—the after part. He leaned back in dread and shouted, "Hooy! Hooy! Get out of this!" And the cow struggled manfully—lost ground steadily—dirt and dust streamed down—and before Oliver could get well away, the entire cow crashed through onto the table and made a shapeless wreck of everything!

Then, for the first time in his life, I think, Oliver complained. He said:

"This thing is growing monotonous!"

Then he resigned his judgeship and left Humboldt County. "Butchered to make a Roman holiday" has grown monotonous to me.

In this connection I wish to say one word about Michelangelo Buonarroti. I used to worship the mighty genius of Michelangelo—that man who was great in poetry, painting, sculpture, architecture—great in everything he undertook. But I do not want Michelangelo for breakfast—for luncheon—for dinner—for tea—for supper—for between meals. I like a change occasionally. In Genoa he designed everything; in Milan he or his pupils designed everything; he designed the Lake of Como; in Padua, Verona, Venice, Bologna, who did we ever hear of from guides but Michelangelo? In Florence he painted everything, designed everything nearly, and what he did not design he used to sit on a favorite stone and look at, and they showed us the stone. In Pisa he designed everything but the old shot tower, and they would have attributed that to him if it had not been so awfully out of the perpendicular. He designed the piers of Leghorn and the customhouse regulations of Civitavecchia. But here—here it is frightful. He designed St. Peter's; he designed the Pope; he designed the Pantheon, the uniform of the Pope's soldiers, the Tiber, the Vatican, the Coliseum, the Capitol, the Tarpeian Rock, the Barberini Palace, St. John Lateran, the Campagna, the Appian Way, the Seven Hills, the Baths of Caracalla, the Claudian Aqueduct, the Cloaca Maxima—the eternal bore designed the Eternal City, and unless all men and books do lie, he painted everything in it! Dan said the other day to the guide, "Enough, enough, enough! Say no more! Lump the whole thing! Say that the Creator made Italy from designs by Michelangelo!"

I never felt so fervently thankful, so soothed, so tranquil, so filled with a blessed peace as I did yesterday when I learned that Michelangelo was dead.

But we have taken it out of this guide. He has marched us through miles of pictures and sculpture in the vast corridors of the Vatican, and through miles of pictures and sculpture in twenty other palaces; he has shown us the great picture in the Sistine Chapel, and frescoes enough to fresco the heavens—pretty much all done by Michelangelo. So with him we have played that game which has vanquished so many guides for us—imbecility and idiotic questions. These creatures never suspect—they have no idea of a sarcasm.

He shows us a figure and says: "Statoo brunzo." (Bronze statue.)

We look at it indifferently and the doctor asks: "By Michelangelo?"

"No—not know who."

Then he shows us the ancient Roman Forum. The doctor asks: "Michelangelo?"

A stare from the guide. "No—thousan' year before he is born."

Then an Egyptian obelisk. Again: "Michelangelo?"

"Oh, *mon dieu*, genteelmen! Zis is *two* thousan' year before he is born!"

He grows so tired of that unceasing question sometimes that he dreads to show us anything at all. The wretch has tried all the ways he can think of to make us comprehend that Michelangelo is only responsible for the creation of a *part* of the world, but somehow he has not succeeded yet. Relief for overtasked eyes and brain from study and sightseeing is necessary or we shall become idiotic sure enough. Therefore this guide must continue to suffer. If he does not enjoy it, so much the worse for him. We do.

In this place I may as well jot down a chapter concerning those necessary nuisances, European guides. Many a man has wished in his heart he could do without his guide, but, knowing he could not, has wished he could get some amusement out of him as a remuneration for the affliction of his society. We accomplished this latter matter, and if our experience can be made useful to others they are welcome to it.

Guides know about enough English to tangle everything up so that a man can make neither head nor tail of it. They know their story by heart—the history of every statue, painting, cathedral, or other wonder they show you. They know it and tell it as a parrot would—and if you interrupt and throw them off the track, they have to go back and begin over again. All their lives long they are employed in showing strange things to foreigners and listening to their bursts of admiration. It is human nature to take delight in exciting admiration. It is what prompts children to say "smart" things, and do absurd ones, and in other ways "show off" when company is present. It is what makes gossips turn out in rain and storm to go and be the first to tell a startling bit of news. Think, then, what a passion it becomes with a guide, whose privilege it is, every day, to show to strangers wonders that throw them into perfect ecstasies of admiration! He gets so that he could not by any possibility live in a soberer atmosphere. After we discovered this, we *never* went into ecstasies anymore—we never admired anything—we never showed any but impassible faces and stupid indifference in the presence of the sublimest wonders a guide had to display. We had found their weak point. We have made good use of it ever since. We have made some of those people savage at times, but we have never lost our own serenity.

The doctor asks the questions generally because he can keep his countenance, and look more like an inspired idiot, and throw more imbecility into the tone of his voice than any man that lives. It comes natural to him.

The guides in Genoa are delighted to secure an American party, because Americans so much wonder and deal so much in sentiment and emotion before any relic of Columbus. Our guide there fidgeted about as if he had swallowed a spring mattress. He was full of animation—full of impatience. He said:

"Come wis me, genteelmen! Come! I show you ze letter-writing by Christopher Colombo! Write it himself! Write it wis his own hand! Come!"

He took us to the municipal palace. After much impressive fumbling of keys and opening of locks, the stained and aged document was spread before us. The guide's eyes sparkled. He danced about us and tapped the parchment with his finger:

"What I tell you, genteelmen! Is it not so? See! Handwriting Christopher Colombo! Write it himself!"

We looked indifferent—unconcerned. The doctor examined the document very deliberately, during a painful pause. Then he said, without any show of interest:

"Ah—Ferguson—what—what did you say was the name of the party who wrote this?"

"Christopher Colombo! Ze great Christopher Colombo!"

Another deliberate examination.

"Ah—did he write it himself or—or how?"

"He write it himself! Christopher Colombo! His own handwriting, write by himself!"

Then the doctor laid the document down and said:

"Why, I have seen boys in America only fourteen years old that could write better than that."

"But zis is ze great Christo——"

"I don't care who it is! It's the worst writing I ever saw. Now you mustn't think you can impose on us because we are strangers. We are not fools, by a good deal. If you have got any specimens of penmanship of real merit, trot them out! And if you haven't, drive on!"

We drove on. The guide was considerably shaken up, but he made one more venture. He had something which he thought would overcome us. He said:

"Ah, genteelmen, you come wis me! I show you beautiful, oh, magnificent bust Christopher Colombo! Splendid, grand, magnificent!"

He brought us before the beautiful bust—for it *was* beautiful—and sprang back and struck an attitude:

"Ah, look, genteelmen! Beautiful, grand—bust Christopher Colombo! Beautiful bust, beautiful pedestal!"

The doctor put up his eyeglass—procured for such occasions:

"Ah—what did you say this gentleman's name was?"

"Christopher Colombo! Ze great Christopher Colombo!"

"Christopher Colombo—the great Christopher Colombo. Well, what did *he* do?"

"Discover America! Discover America, oh, ze devil!"

"Discover America. No—that statement will hardly wash. We are just from America ourselves. We heard nothing about it. Christopher Colombo—pleasant name—is—is he dead?"

"Oh, corpo di Baccho! Three hundred year!"

"What did he die of?"

"I do not know! I cannot tell."

"Smallpox, think?"

"I do not know, genteelmen! I do not know *what* he die of!"

"Measles, likely?"

"Maybe—maybe—I do *not* know—I think he die of somethings."

"Parents living?"

"Im-posseeble!"

"Ah—which is the bust and which is the pedestal?"

"Santa Maria! *Zis* ze bust! *Zis* ze pedestal!"

"Ah, I see, I see—happy combination—very happy combination indeed. Is—is this the first time this gentleman was ever on a bust?"

That joke was lost on the foreigner—guides cannot master the subtleties of the American joke.

We have made it interesting for this Roman guide. Yesterday we spent three or four hours in the Vatican again, that wonderful world of curiosities. We came very near expressing interest sometimes—even admiration—it was very hard to keep from it. We succeeded, though. Nobody else ever did in the Vatican museums. The guide was bewildered—nonplussed. He walked his legs off nearly, hunting up extraordinary things, and exhausted all his ingenuity on us, but it was a failure; we never showed any interest in anything. He had reserved what he considered to be his greatest wonder till the last—a royal Egyptian mummy, the best preserved

in the world, perhaps. He took us there. He felt so sure this
time that some of his old enthusiasm came back to him:

"See, genteelmen! Mummy! Mummy!"

The eyeglass came up as calmly, as deliberately as ever.

"Ah—Ferguson—what did I understand you to say the
gentleman's name was?"

"Name? He got no name! Mummy! 'Gyptian mummy!"

"Yes, yes. Born here?"

"No! *'Gyptian* mummy!"

"Ah, just so. Frenchman, I presume?"

"No! *Not* Frenchman, not Roman! Born in Egypta!"

"Born in Egypta. Never heard of Egypta before. Foreign
locality, likely. Mummy—mummy. How calm he is—how
self-possessed. Is, ah—is he dead?"

"Oh, *sacre bleu*, been dead three thousan' year!"

The doctor turned on him savagely.

"Here, now, what do you mean by such conduct as this!
Playing us for Chinamen because we are strangers and trying
to learn! Trying to impose your vile secondhand carcasses on
us! Thunder and lightning, I've a notion to—to—if you've
got a nice *fresh* corpse, fetch him out! Or, by George, we'll
brain you!"

We make it exceedingly interesting for this Frenchman.
However, he has paid us back partly, without knowing it.
He came to the hotel this morning to ask if we were up, and
he endeavored as well as he could to describe us, so that the
landlord would know which persons he meant. He finished
with the casual remark that we were lunatics. The observation was so innocent and so honest that it amounted to a very
good thing for a guide to say.

There is one remark (already mentioned) which never yet
has failed to disgust these guides. We use it always when
we can think of nothing else to say. After they have exhausted their enthusiasm pointing out to us and praising the
beauties of some ancient bronze image or broken-legged
statue, we look at it stupidly and in silence for five, ten,
fifteen minutes—as long as we can hold out, in fact—and
then ask:

"Is—is he dead?"

That conquers the serenest of them. It is not what they
are looking for—especially a new guide. Our Roman Ferguson is the most patient, unsuspecting, long-suffering subject
we have had yet. We shall be sorry to part with him. We

have enjoyed his society very much. We trust he has enjoyed ours, but we are harassed with doubts.

We have been in the catacombs. It was like going down into a very deep cellar, only it was a cellar which had no end to it. The narrow passages are roughly hewn in the rock, and on each hand as you pass along, the hollowed shelves are carved out, from three to fourteen deep; each held a corpse once. There are names and Christian symbols and prayers or sentences expressive of Christian hopes carved upon nearly every sarcophagus. The dates belong away back in the dawn of the Christian era, of course. Here, in these holes in the ground, the first Christians sometimes burrowed to escape persecution. They crawled out at night to get food, but remained undercover in the daytime. The priest told us that St. Sebastian lived underground for some time while he was being hunted; he went out one day, and the soldiery discovered and shot him to death with arrows. Five or six of the early popes—those who reigned about sixteen hundred years ago—held their papal courts and advised with their clergy in the bowels of the earth. During seventeen years—from A.D. 235 to A.D. 252—the popes did not appear aboveground. Four were raised to the great office during that period. Four years apiece, or thereabouts. It is very suggestive of the unhealthiness of underground graveyards as places of residence. One pope afterward spent his entire pontificate in the catacombs—eight years. Another was discovered in them and murdered in the episcopal chair. There was no satisfaction in being a pope in those days. There were too many annoyances. There are one hundred and sixty catacombs under Rome, each with its maze of narrow passages crossing and recrossing each other and each passage walled to the top with scooped graves its entire length. A careful estimate makes the length of the passages of all the catacombs combined foot up nine hundred miles, and their graves number seven millions. We did not go through all the passages of all the catacombs. We were very anxious to do it, and made the necessary arrangements, but our too limited time obliged us to give up the idea. So we only groped through the dismal labyrinth of St. Callixtus, under the Church of St. Sebastian. In the various catacombs are small chapels rudely hewn in the stones, and here the early Christians often held their religious services by dim, ghostly lights. Think of mass and a sermon away down in those tangled caverns underground!

In the catacombs were buried St. Cecilia, St. Agnes, and several other of the most celebrated of the saints. In the catacomb of St. Callixtus, St. Bridget used to remain long hours in holy contemplation, and St. Charles Borromeo was wont to spend whole nights in prayer there. It was also the scene of a very marvelous thing.

Here the heart of St. Philip Neri was so inflamed with divine love as to burst his ribs.

I find that grave statement in a book published in New York in 1858 and written by "Rev. William H. Neligan, LL.D., M.A., Trinity College, Dublin; Member of the Archaeological Society of Great Britain." Therefore I believe it. Otherwise I could not. Under other circumstances I should have felt a curiosity to know what Philip had for dinner.

This author puts my credulity on its mettle every now and then. He tells of one St. Joseph Calasanctius whose house in Rome he visited; he visited only the house—the priest has been dead two hundred years. He says the Virgin Mary appeared to this saint. Then he continues:

His tongue and his heart, which were found after nearly a century to be whole, when the body was disinterred before his canonization, are still preserved in a glass case, and after two centuries the heart is still whole. When the French troops came to Rome, and when Pius VII was carried away prisoner, blood dropped from it.

To read that in a book written by a monk far back in the Middle Ages would surprise no one; it would sound natural and proper; but when it is seriously stated in the middle of the nineteenth century, by a man of finished education, an LL.D., M.A., and an archaeological magnate, it sounds strangely enough. Still, I would gladly change my unbelief for Neligan's faith, and let him make the conditions as hard as he pleased.

The old gentleman's undoubting, unquestioning simplicity has a rare freshness about it in these matter-of-fact railroading and telegraphing days. Hear him concerning the Church of Ara Coeli:

In the roof of the church, directly above the high altar, is engraved, *"Regina Coeli laetare Alleluia."* In the sixth century Rome was visited by a fearful pestilence. Gregory the

Great urged the people to do penance, and a general procession was formed. It was to proceed from Ara Coeli to St.
Peter's. As it passed before the mole of Adrian, now the Castle of St. Angelo, the sound of heavenly voices was heard
singing (it was Easter morn), *"Regina Coeli, laetare! alleluia!
quia quem meruisti portare, alleluia! resurrexit sicut dixit;
alleluia!"* The Pontiff, carrying in his hands the portrait of
the Virgin (which is over the high altar and is said to have
been painted by St. Luke), answered, with the astonished people, *"Ora pro nobis Deum, alleluia!"* At the same time an
angel was seen to put up a sword in a scabbard, and the
pestilence ceased on the same day. There are four circumstances which *confirm**this miracle: the annual procession
which takes place in the western church on the feast of St.
Mark; the statue of St. Michael, placed on the mole of
Adrian, which has since that time been called the Castle of
St. Angelo; the antiphon Regina Coeli, which the Catholic
church sings during paschal time; and the inscription in the
church.

28

From the sanguinary sports of the Holy Inquisition, the
slaughter of the Coliseum, and the dismal tombs of the
catacombs, I naturally pass to the picturesque horrors of the
Capuchin Convent. We stopped a moment in a small chapel
in the church to admire a picture of St. Michael vanquishing
Satan—a picture which is so beautiful that I cannot but think
it belongs to the reviled "Renaissance," notwithstanding I believe they told us one of the ancient old masters painted it—
and then we descended into the vast vault underneath.

Here was a spectacle for sensitive nerves! Evidently the old
masters had been at work in this place. There were six divi-
sions in the apartment, and each division was ornamented with
a style of decoration peculiar to itself—and these decorations
were in every instance formed of human bones! There were
shapely arches, built wholly of thighbones; there were start-

* The italics are mine.—M.T.

ling pyramids, built wholly of grinning skulls; there were quaint architectural structures of various kinds, built of shin-bones and the bones of the arm; on the wall were elaborate frescoes, whose curving vines were made of knotted human vertebrae, whose delicate tendrils were made of sinews and tendons, whose flowers were formed of kneecaps and toe-nails. Every lasting portion of the human frame was represent-ed in these intricate designs (they were by Michelangelo, I think), and there was a careful finish about the work and an attention to details that betrayed the artist's love of his labors as well as his schooled ability. I asked the good-natured monk who accompanied us, "Who did this?" And he said, "*We* did it"—meaning himself and his brethren upstairs. I could see that the old friar took a high pride in his curious show. We made him talkative by exhibiting an interest we never betrayed to guides.

"Who were these people?"

"We—upstairs—monks of the Capuchin order—my breth-ren."

"How many departed monks were required to upholster these six parlors?"

"These are the bones of four thousand."

"It took a long time to get enough?"

"Many, many centuries."

"Their different parts are well separated—skulls in one room, legs in another, ribs in another—there would be stirring times here for a while if the last trump should blow. Some of the brethren might get hold of the wrong leg in the confu-sion, and the wrong skull, and find themselves limping, and looking through eyes that were wider apart or closer together than they were used to. You cannot tell any of these parties apart, I suppose?"

"Oh, yes, I know many of them."

He put his finger on a skull. "This was Brother Anselmo—dead three hundred years—a good man."

He touched another. "This was Brother Alexander—dead two hundred and eighty years. This was Brother Carlo—dead about as long."

Then he took a skull and held it in his hand and looked re-flectively upon it, after the manner of the gravedigger when he discourses of Yorick.

"This," he said, "was Brother Thomas. He was a young prince, the scion of a proud house that traced its lineage back to the grand old days of Rome well-nigh two thousand years ago. He loved beneath his estate. His family persecuted him, persecuted the girl as well. They drove her from Rome; he followed; he sought her far and wide; he found no trace of her. He came back and offered his broken heart at our altar and his weary life to the service of God. But look you. Shortly his father died, and likewise his mother. The girl returned, rejoicing. She sought everywhere for him whose eyes had used to look tenderly into hers out of this poor skull, but she could not find him. At last, in this coarse garb we wear, she recognized him in the street. He knew her. It was too late. He fell where he stood. They took him up and brought him here. He never spoke afterward. Within the week he died. You can see the color of his hair—faded somewhat— by this thin shred that clings still to the temple. This [taking up a thighbone] was his. The veins of this leaf in the decorations over your head were his finger joints a hundred and fifty years ago."

This businesslike way of illustrating a touching story of the heart by laying the several fragments of the lover before us and naming them was as grotesque a performance, and as ghastly, as any I ever witnessed. I hardly knew whether to smile or shudder. There are nerves and muscles in our frames whose functions and whose methods of working it seems a sort of sacrilege to describe by cold physiological names and surgical technicalities, and the monk's talk suggested to me something of this kind. Fancy a surgeon, with his nippers lifting tendons, muscles, and such things into view, out of the complex machinery of a corpse, and observing, "Now this little nerve quivers—the vibration is imparted to this muscle —from here it is passed to this fibrous substance; here its ingredients are separated by the chemical action of the blood —one part goes to the heart and thrills it with what is popularly termed emotion, another part follows this nerve to the brain and communicates intelligence of a startling character, the third part glides along this passage and touches the spring connected with the fluid receptacles that lie in the rear of the eye. Thus, by this simple and beautiful process, the party is informed that his mother is dead, and he weeps." Horrible!

I asked the monk if all the brethren upstairs expected to be put in this place when they died. He answered quietly:

"We must all lie here at last."

See what one can accustom himself to. The reflection that

he must someday be taken apart like an engine or a clock or like a house whose owner is gone, and worked up into arches and pyramids and hideous frescoes, did not distress this monk in the least. I thought he even looked as if he were thinking, with complacent vanity, that his own skull would look well on top of the heap and his own ribs add a charm to the frescoes which possibly they lacked at present.

Here and there, in ornamental alcoves, stretched upon beds of bones, lay dead and dried-up monks, with lank frames dressed in the black robes one sees ordinarily upon priests. We examined one closely. The skinny hands were clasped upon the breast; two lusterless tufts of hair stuck to the skull; the skin was brown and sunken; it stretched tightly over the cheekbones and made them stand out sharply; the crisp, dead eyes were deep in the sockets; the nostrils were painfully prominent, the end of the nose being gone; the lips had shriveled away from the yellow teeth; and brought down to us through the circling years, and petrified there, was a weird laugh a full century old!

It was the jolliest laugh, but yet the most dreadful, that one can imagine. Surely, I thought, it must have been a most extraordinary joke this veteran produced with his latest breath that he has not got done laughing at it yet. At this moment I saw that the old instinct was strong upon the boys, and I said we had better hurry to St. Peter's. They were trying to keep from asking, "Is—is he dead?"

It makes me dizzy to think of the Vatican—of its wilderness of statues, paintings, and curiosities of every description and every age. The "old masters" (especially in sculpture) fairly swarm there. I cannot write about the Vatican. I think I shall never remember anything I saw there distinctly but the mummies, and "The Transfiguration," by Raphael, and some other things it is not necessary to mention now. I shall remember "The Transfiguration" partly because it was placed in a room almost by itself, partly because it is acknowledged by all to be the first oil painting in the world, and partly because it was wonderfully beautiful. The colors are fresh and rich, the "expression," I am told, is fine, the "feeling" is lively, the "tone" is good, the "depth" is profound, and the width is about four and a half feet, I should judge. It is a picture that really holds one's attention; its beauty is fascinating. It is fine enough to be a "Renaissance." A remark I made awhile ago suggests a thought—and a hope. Is it not possible that the reason I find such charms in this picture is because it is out of the crazy chaos of the galleries? If some of the others were set apart, might not they be beautiful? If this were set in the midst of the tempest of pictures one finds in the vast galleries of the Roman palaces, would I think it so handsome? If, up to this time, I had seen only one "old master" in each palace, instead of acres and acres of walls and ceilings fairly papered with them, might I not have a more civilized opinion of the old masters than I have now? I think so. When I was a schoolboy and was to have a new knife, I could not make up my mind as to which was the prettiest in the showcase, and I did not think any of them were particularly pretty; and so I chose with a heavy heart. But when I looked at my purchase at home, where no glittering blades came into competition with it, I was astonished to see how handsome it was. To this day my new hats look better out of the shop than they did in it with other new hats. It begins to dawn upon me now that possibly what I have been taking for uniform ugliness in the galleries may be uniform beauty after all. I honestly hope it is to others, but certainly it is not to me. Perhaps the reason I used to enjoy going to the Academy of Fine Arts in New York was because there were but a few hundred paintings in it, and it did not surfeit me to go through the list. I suppose the academy was bacon and beans in the Forty-Mile Desert, and a European gallery is a state dinner of thirteen courses. One leaves no sign after him of the one dish, but the thirteen frighten away his appetite and give him no satisfaction.

There is one thing I am certain of, though. With all the Michelangelos, the Raphaels, the Guidos, and the other old masters, the sublime history of Rome remains unpainted! They painted Virgins enough and popes enough and saintly scarecrows enough to people paradise almost, and these things are all they did paint. "Nero fiddling o'er burning Rome," the assassination of Caesar, the stirring spectacle of a hundred thousand people bending forward with rapt interest, in the Coliseum, to see two skillful gladiators hacking away each other's lives, a tiger springing upon a kneeling martyr—these and a thousand other matters which we read of with a living interest must be sought for only in books, not among the rubbish left by the old masters—who are no more, I have the satisfaction of informing the public.

They did paint, and they did carve in marble, one historical scene, and one only (of any great historical consequence).

And what was it and why did they choose it particularly? It was the Rape of the Sabines, and they chose it for the legs and busts.

I like to look at statues, however, and I like to look at pictures also—even of monks looking up in sacred ecstacy, and monks looking down in meditation, and monks skirmishing for something to eat—and therefore I drop ill nature to thank the papal government for so jealously guarding and so industriously gathering up these things, and for permitting me, a stranger and not an entirely friendly one, to roam at will and unmolested among them, charging me nothing and only requiring that I shall behave myself simply as well as I ought to behave in any other man's house. I thank the Holy Father right heartily, and I wish him long life and plenty of happiness.

The popes have long been the patrons and preservers of art, just as our new, practical republic is the encourager and upholder of mechanics. In their Vatican is stored up all that is curious and beautiful in art; in our Patent Office is hoarded all that is curious or useful in mechanics. When a man invents a new style of horse collar or discovers a new and superior method of telegraphing, our government issues a patent to him that is worth a fortune; when a man digs up an ancient statue in the Campagna, the Pope gives him a fortune in gold coin. We can make something of a guess at a man's character by the style of nose he carries on his face. The Vatican and the Patent Office are governmental noses, and they bear a deal of character about them.

The guide showed us a colossal statue of Jupiter in the Vatican, which he said looked so damaged and rusty—so like the god of the Vagabonds—because it had but recently been dug up in the Campagna. He asked how much we supposed this Jupiter was worth. I replied, with intelligent promptness, that he was probably worth about four dollars—maybe four and a half. "A hundred thousand dollars!" Ferguson said. Ferguson said, further, that the Pope permits no ancient work of this kind to leave his dominions. He appoints a commission to examine discoveries like this and report upon the value; then the Pope pays the discoverer one-half of that assessed value and takes the statue. He said this Jupiter was dug from a field which had just been bought for thirty-six thousand dollars, so the first crop was a good one for the new farmer. I do not know whether Ferguson always tells the truth or not, but I suppose he does. I know that an exorbitant export duty is exacted upon all pictures painted by the old masters, in order to discourage the sale of those in the private collections. I am satisfied also that genuine old masters hardly exist at all in America, because the cheapest and most insignificant of them are valued at the price of a fine farm. I proposed to buy a small trifle of a Raphael myself, but the price of it was eighty thousand dollars, the export duty would have made it considerably over a hundred, and so I studied on it awhile and concluded not to take it.

I wish here to mention an inscription I have seen, before I forget it:

"Glory to God in the highest, peace on earth TO MEN OF GOOD WILL!" It is not good scripture, but it is sound Catholic and human nature.

This is in letters of gold around the apsis of a mosaic group at the side of the *scala santa*, Church of St. John Lateran, the mother and mistress of all the Catholic churches of the world. The group represents the Saviour, St. Peter, Pope Leo, St. Silvester, Constantine, and Charlemagne. Peter is giving the *pallium* to the Pope and a standard to Charlemagne. The Saviour is giving the keys to St. Silvester and a standard to Constantine. No prayer is offered to the Saviour, who seems to be of little importance anywhere in Rome; but an inscription below says, "*Blessed Peter, give life to Pope Leo and victory to King Charles.*" It does not say, "*Intercede for us*, through the Saviour, with the Father, for this boon," but, "*Blessed Peter, give it us.*"

In all seriousness—without meaning to be frivolous—without meaning to be irreverent, and more than all, without meaning to be blasphemous—I state as my simple deduction from the things I have seen and the things I have heard that the Holy Personages rank thus in Rome:

First: "The Mother of God"—otherwise the Virgin Mary.

Second: The Deity.

Third: Peter.

Fourth: Some twelve or fifteen canonized popes and martyrs.

Fifth: Jesus Christ the Saviour (but always as an infant in arms).

I may be wrong in this—my judgment errs often, just as is the case with other men's—but it *is* my judgment, be it good or bad.

Just here I will mention something that seems curious to

me. There are no "Christ's churches" in Rome and no "churches of the Holy Ghost" that I can discover. There are some four hundred churches, but about a fourth of them seem to be named for the Madonna and St. Peter. There are so many named for Mary that they have to be distinguished by all sorts of affixes, if I understand the matter rightly. Then we have churches of St. Louis, St. Augustine, St. Agnes, St. Calixtus, St. Lorenzo in Lucina, St. Lorenzo in Damaso, St. Cecilia, St. Athanasius, St. Philip Neri, St. Catherine, St. Dominico, and a multitude of lesser saints whose names are not familiar in the world—and away down, clear out of the list of the churches, comes a couple of hospitals: one of them is named for the Saviour and the other for the Holy Ghost!

Day after day and night after night we have wandered among the crumbling wonders of Rome; day after day and night after night we have fed upon the dust and decay of five-and-twenty centuries—have brooded over them by day and dreamt of them by night till sometimes we seemed moldering away ourselves, and growing defaced and cornerless, and liable at any moment to fall a prey to some antiquary and be patched in the legs, and "restored" with an unseemly nose, and labeled wrong and dated wrong, and set up in the Vatican for poets to drivel about and vandals to scribble their names on forever and forevermore.

But the surest way to stop writing about Rome is to stop. I wished to write a real "guidebook" chapter on this fascinating city, but I could not do it because I have felt all the time like a boy in a candy shop—there was everything to choose from and yet no choice. I have drifted along hopelessly for a hundred pages of manuscript without knowing where to commence. I will not commence at all. Our passports have been examined. We will go to Naples.

29

The ship is lying here in the harbor of Naples—quarantined. She has been here several days and will remain several more.

We that came by rail from Rome have escaped this misfortune. Of course no one is allowed to go on board the ship or come ashore from her. She is a prison now. The passengers probably spend the long, blazing days looking out from under the awnings at Vesuvius and the beautiful city—and in swearing. Think of ten days of this sort of pastime! We go out every day in a boat and request them to come ashore. It soothes them. We lie ten steps from the ship and tell them how spendid the city is, and how much better the hotel fare is here than anywhere else in Europe, and how cool it is, and what frozen continents of ice cream there are, and what a time we are having cavorting about the country and sailing to the islands in the bay. This tranquilizes them.

ASCENT OF VESUVIUS

I shall remember our trip to Vesuvius for many a day—partly because of its sightseeing experiences, but chiefly on account of the fatigue of the journey. Two or three of us had been resting ourselves among the tranquil and beautiful scenery of the island of Ischia, eighteen miles out in the harbor, for two days; we called it "resting," but I do not remember now what the resting consisted of, for when we got back to Naples we had not slept for forty-eight hours. We were just about to go to bed early in the evening, and catch up on some of the sleep we had lost, when we heard of this Vesuvius expedition. There was to be eight of us in the party, and we were to leave Naples at midnight. We laid in some provisions for the trip, engaged carriages to take us to Annuciation, and then moved about the city, to keep awake, till twelve. We got away punctually, and in the course of an hour and a half arrived at the town of Annunciation. Annunciation is the very last place under the sun. In other towns in Italy the people lie around quietly and wait for you to ask them a question or do some overt act that can be charged for—but in Annunciation they have lost even that fragment of delicacy; they seize a lady's shawl from a chair and hand it to her and charge a penny; they open a carriage door and charge for it —shut it when you get out and charge for it; they help you to take off a duster—two cents; brush your clothes and make them worse than they were before—two cents; smile upon you—two cents; bow, with a lick-spittle smirk, hat in hand —two cents; they volunteer all information, such as that the mules will arrive presently—two cents; warm day, sir—two cents; take you four hours to make the ascent—two cents. And so they go. They crowd you—infest you—swarm about you, and sweat and smell offensively, and look sneaking and mean and obsequious. There is no office too degrading for them to perform for money. I have had no opportunity to find out anything about the upper classes by my own observation, but from what I hear said about them, I judge that what they lack in one or two of the bad traits the *canaille* have, they make up in one or two others that are worse. How the people beg! Many of them very well dressed, too.

I said I knew nothing against the upper classes by personal observation. I must recall it! I had forgotten. What I saw their bravest and their fairest do last night, the lowest multitude that could be scraped up out of the purlieus of Christendom would blush to do, I think. They assembled by hundreds, and even thousands, in the great Theater of San Carlo to do—what? Why, simply to make fun of an old woman—to deride, to hiss, to jeer at an actress they once worshiped, but whose beauty is faded now and whose voice has lost its former richness. Everybody spoke of the rare sport there was to be. They said the theater would be crammed because Frezzolini was going to sing. It was said she could not sing well now, but then the people liked to see her anyhow. And so we went. And every time the woman sang they hissed and laughed—the whole magnificent house—and as soon as she left the stage they called her on again with applause. Once or twice she was encored five and six times in succession, and received with hisses when she appeared and discharged with hisses and laughter when she had finished—then instantly encored and insulted again! And how the high-born knaves enjoyed it! White-kidded gentlemen and ladies laughed till the tears came, and clapped their hands in very ecstasy when that unhappy old woman would come meekly out for the sixth time, with uncomplaining patience, to meet a storm of hisses! It was the cruelest exhibition—the most wanton, the most unfeeling. The singer would have conquered an audience of American rowdies by her brave, unflinching tranquility (for she answered encore after encore, and smiled and bowed pleasantly, and sang the best she possibly could, and went bowing off, through all the jeers and hisses, without ever losing countenance or temper), and surely in any other land than Italy her sex and her helplessness must have been an ample protection to her—she could have needed no other. Think what a multitude of small souls were crowded into that theater last night. If the manager could have filled his theater with Neapolitan souls alone, without the bodies, he could not have cleared less than ninety millions of dollars. What traits of character must a man have to enable him to help three thousand miscreants to hiss and jeer and laugh at one friendless old woman, and shamefully humiliate her? He must have *all* the vile, mean traits there are. My observation persuades me (I do not like to venture beyond my own personal observation) that the upper classes of Naples possess those traits of character. Otherwise they may be very good people; I cannot say.

ASCENT OF VESUVIUS—CONTINUED

In this city of Naples they believe in and support one of the wretchedest of all the religious impostures one can find in Italy—the miraculous liquefaction of the blood of St. Januarius. Twice a year the priests assemble all the people at the cathedral, and get out this vial of clotted blood and let them see it slowly dissolve and become liquid—and every day for eight days this dismal farce is repeated while the priests go among the crowd and collect money for the exhibition. The first day the blood liquefies in forty-seven minutes—the church is crammed then, and time must be allowed the collectors to get around; after that it liquefies a little quicker and a little quicker every day, as the houses grow smaller, till on the eighth day, with only a few dozens present to see the miracle, it liquefies in four minutes.

And here also they used to have a grand procession of priests, citizens, soldiers, sailors, and the high dignitaries of the city government once a year, to shave the head of a made-up Madonna—a stuffed and painted image like a milliner's dummy—whose hair miraculously grew and restored itself every twelve months. They still kept up this shaving procession as late as four or five years ago. It was a source of great profit to the church that possessed the remarkable effigy, and the ceremony of the public barbering of her was always carried out with the greatest possible éclat and display—the more the better, because the more excitement there was about it, the larger the crowds it drew and the heavier the revenues it produced; but at last a day came when the Pope and his servants were unpopular in Naples, and the city government stopped the Madonna's annual show.

There we have two specimens of these Neapolitans—two of the silliest possible frauds, which half the population religiously and faithfully believed, and the other half either believed also or else said nothing about, and thus lent themselves to the support of the imposture. I am very well satisfied to think the whole population believed in those poor, cheap miracles—a people who want two cents every time they bow to you and who abuse a woman are capable of it, I think.

ASCENT OF VESUVIUS—CONTINUED

These Neapolitans always ask four times as much money as they intend to take, but if you give them what they first demand, they feel ashamed of themselves for aiming so low and immediately ask more. When money is to be paid and received, there is always some vehement jawing and gesticulating about it. One cannot buy and pay for two cents' worth of clams without trouble and a quarrel. One "course," in a two-horse carriage, costs a franc—that is law—but the hackman always demands more, on some pretense or other, and if he gets it he makes a new demand. It is said that a stranger took a one-horse carriage for a course—tariff, half a franc. He gave the man five francs, by way of experiment. He demanded more and received another franc. Again he demanded more and got a franc—demanded more and it was refused. He grew vehement, was again refused, and became noisy. The stranger said, "Well, give me the seven francs again, and I will see what I can do"—and when he got them, he handed the hackman half a franc, and he immediately asked for two cents to buy a drink with. It may be thought that I am prejudiced. Perhaps I am. I would be ashamed of myself if I were not.

ASCENT OF VESUVIUS—CONTINUED

Well, as I was saying, we got our mules and horses, after an hour and a half of bargaining with the population of Annunciation, and started sleepily up the mountain, with a vagrant at each mule's tail who pretended to be driving the brute along, but was really holding on and getting himself dragged up instead. I made slow headway at first, but I began to get dissatisfied at the idea of paying my minion five francs to hold my mule back by the tail and keep him from going up the hill, and so I discharged him. I got along faster then.

We had one magnificent picture of Naples from a high point on the mountainside. We saw nothing but the gas lamps, of course—two-thirds of a circle, skirting the great bay—a necklace of diamonds glinting up through the darkness from the remote distance—less brilliant than the stars overhead, but more softly, richly beautiful—and over all the great city the lights crossed and recrossed each other in many and many a sparkling line and curve. And back of the town, far around and abroad over the miles of level campagna, were scattered rows and circles and clusters of lights, all glowing like so many gems and marking where a score of villages were sleeping. About this time the fellow who was hanging onto the tail of the horse in front of me and practicing all sorts of unnecessary cruelty upon the animal got kicked some fourteen rods, and this incident, together with the fairy spectacle of the lights far in the distance, made me serenely happy, and I was glad I started to Vesuvius.

ASCENT OF MOUNT VESUVIUS—CONTINUED

This subject will be excellent matter for a chapter, and tomorrow or next day I will write it.

30

ASCENT OF VESUVIUS—CONTINUED

"See Naples and die." Well, I do not know that one would necessarily die after merely seeing it, but to attempt to live there might turn out a little differently. To see Naples as we saw it, in the early dawn from far up on the side of Vesuvius, is to see a picture of wonderful beauty. At that distance its dingy buildings looked white—and so, rank on rank of balconies, windows, and roofs, they piled themselves up from the blue ocean till the colossal castle of St. Elmo topped the grand white pyramid and gave the picture symmetry, emphasis, and completeness. And when its lilies turned to roses—when it blushed under the sun's first kiss—it was beautiful beyond all description. One might well say then, "See Naples and die." The frame of the picture was charming, itself. In front the smooth sea—a vast mosaic of many colors; the lofty islands swimming in a dreamy haze in the distance; at our end of the city the stately double peak of Vesuvius, and its strong black ribs and seams of lava stretching down to the limitless level campagna—a green carpet that enchants the eye and leads it on and on, past clusters of trees and isolated houses and snowy villages, until it shreds out in a fringe of mist and general vagueness far away. It is from the Hermitage, there on the side of Vesuvius, that one should "see Naples and die."

But do not go within the walls and look at it in detail. That takes away some of the romance of the thing. The people are filthy in their habits, and this makes filthy streets and breeds disagreeable sights and smells. There never was a community so prejudiced against the cholera as these Neapolitans are. But they have good reason to be. The cholera generally vanquishes a Neapolitan when it seizes him, because, you understand, before the doctor can dig through the dirt and get at the disease the man dies. The upper classes take a sea bath every day, and are pretty decent.

The streets are generally about wide enough for one wagon, and how they do swarm with people! It is Broadway repeated in every street, in every court, in every alley! Such masses, such throngs, such multitudes of hurrying, bustling, struggling humanity! We never saw the like of it, hardly even in New York, I think. There are seldom any sidewalks, and when there are, they are not often wide enough to pass a man on without caroming on him. So everybody walks in the street—and where the street is wide enough, carriages are forever dashing along. Why a thousand people are not run over and crippled every day is a mystery that no man can solve.

But if there is an eighth wonder in the world, it must be the dwelling houses of Naples. I honestly believe a good majority of them are a hundred feet high! And the solid brick walls are seven feet through. You go up nine flights of stairs before you get to the "first" floor. No, not nine, but there or thereabouts. There is a little birdcage of an iron railing in front of every window clear away up, up, up, among the eternal clouds, where the roof is, and there is always somebody looking out of every window—people of ordinary size looking out from the first floor, people a shade smaller from the second, people that look a little smaller yet from the third, and from thence upward they grow smaller and smaller by a regularly graduated diminution till the folks in the topmost windows seem more like birds in an uncommonly tall martin box than anything else. The perspective of one of these narrow cracks of streets, with its rows of tall houses stretching away till they come together in the distance like railway tracks, its clotheslines crossing over at all altitudes and waving their bannered raggedness over the swarms of people below, and the white-dressed women perched in balcony railings all the way from the pavement up to the heavens—a perspective like that is really worth going into Neapolitan details to see.

ASCENT OF VESUVIUS—CONTINUED

Naples, with its immediate suburbs, contains six hundred and twenty-five thousand inhabitants, but I am satisfied it covers no more ground than an American city of one hundred and fifty thousand. It reaches up into the air infinitely higher than three American cities, though, and there is where the secret of it lies. I will observe here in passing that the contrasts between opulence and poverty, and magnificence and misery, are more frequent and more striking in Naples than in Paris even. One must go to the Bois de Boulogne to see fashionable dressing, splendid equipages and stunning liveries, and to the Faubourg St. Antoine to see vice, misery, hunger, rags, dirt—but in the thoroughfares of Naples these things are all mixed together. Naked boys of nine years and the fancy-dressed children of luxury; shreds and tatters, and brilliant uniforms; jackass carts and state carriages; beggars, princes, and bishops jostle each other in every street. At six o'clock every evening all Naples turns out to drive on the Riviere di Chiaja (whatever that may mean), and for two hours one may stand there and see the motliest and the worst mixed procession go by that ever eyes beheld. Princes (there are more princes than policemen in Naples—the city is infested with them)—princes who live up seven flights of stairs and don't own any principalities will keep a carriage and go hungry; and clerks, mechanics, milliners, and strumpets will go without their dinners and squander the money on a hack ride in the Chiaja; the ragtag and rubbish of the city stack themselves up, to the number of twenty or thirty, on a rickety little go-cart hauled by a donkey not much bigger than a cat, and *they* drive in the Chiaja; dukes and bankers, in sumptuous carriages and with gorgeous drivers and footmen, turn out also, and so the furious procession goes. For two hours rank and wealth, and obscurity and poverty, clatter along side by side in the wild procession, and then go home serene, happy, covered with glory!

I was looking at a magnificent marble staircase in the King's palace the other day, which, it was said, cost five million francs, and I suppose it did cost half a million maybe. I felt as if it must be a fine thing to live in a country where there was such comfort and such luxury as this. And then I stepped out musing, and almost walked over a vagabond who was eating his dinner on the curbstone—a piece of bread and a bunch of grapes. When I found that this mustang was clerking in a fruit establishment (he had the establishment along with him in a basket) at two cents a day, and that he had no palace at home where he lived, I lost some of my enthusiasm concerning the happiness of living in Italy.

This naturally suggests to me a thought about wages here. Lieutenants in the army get about a dollar a day and common soldiers a couple of cents. I only know one clerk—he gets four dollars a month. Printers get six dollars and a half a month, but I have heard of a foreman who gets thirteen. To be growing suddenly and violently rich, as this man is, naturally makes him a bloated aristocrat. The airs he puts on are insufferable.

And speaking of wages reminds me of prices of merchandise. In Paris you pay twelve dollars a dozen for Jouvin's best kid gloves; gloves of about as good quality sell here at three or four dollars a dozen. You pay five and six dollars apiece for fine linen shirts in Paris; here and in Leghorn you pay two and a half. In Marseilles you pay forty dollars for a first-class dress coat made by a good tailor, but in Leghorn you can get a full dress suit for the same money. Here you get handsome business suits at from ten to twenty dollars, and in Leghorn you can get an overcoat for fifteen dollars that would cost you seventy in New York. Fine kid boots are worth eight dollars in Marseilles and four dollars here. Lyons velvets rank higher in America than those of Genoa. Yet the bulk of Lyons velvets you buy in the States are made in Genoa and imported into Lyons, where they receive the Lyons stamp and are then exported to America. You can buy enough velvet in Genoa for twenty-five dollars to make a five-hundred-dollar cloak in New York—so the ladies tell me. Of course these things bring me back, by a natural and easy transition, to the

ASCENT OF VESUVIUS—CONTINUED

And thus the wonderful blue grotto is suggested to me. It is situated on the island of Capri, twenty-two miles from Naples. We chartered a little steamer and went out there. Of course the police boarded us, and put us through a health examination and inquired into our politics before they would let us land. The airs these little insect governments put on are in the last degree ridiculous. They even put a policeman on board of our boat to keep an eye on us as long as we were in the Capri dominions. They thought we wanted to steal the grotto, I suppose. It was worth stealing. The entrance to the cave is four feet high and four feet wide, and is in the face of a lofty perpendicular cliff—the seawall. You enter in small boats—and a tight squeeze it is, too. You cannot go in at all when the tide is up. Once within, you find yourself in an arched cavern about one hundred and sixty feet long, one hundred and twenty wide, and about seventy high. How deep it is no man knows. It goes down to the bottom of the ocean. The waters of this placid subterranean lake are the brightest, loveliest blue that can be imagined. They are as transparent as plate glass, and their coloring would shame the richest sky that ever bent over Italy. No tint could be more ravishing, no luster more superb. Throw a stone into the water, and the myriad of tiny bubbles that are created flash out a brilliant glare like blue theatrical fires. Dip an oar, and its blade turns to splendid frosted silver, tinted with blue. Let a man jump in, and instantly he is cased in an armor more gorgeous than ever kingly Crusader wore.

Then we went to Ischia, but I had already been to that island and tired myself to death "resting" a couple of days

and studying human villainy, with the landlord of the Grande
Sentinelle for a model. So we went to Procida, and from
thence to Pozzuoli, where St. Paul landed after he sailed
from Samos. I landed at precisely the same spot where St.
Paul landed, and so did Dan and the others. It was a remarkable coincidence. St. Paul preached to these people seven
days before he started to Rome.

Nero's Baths, the ruins of Baiae, the Temple of Serapis;
Cumae, where the Cumaen Sybil interpreted the oracles;
the Lake Agnano, with its ancient submerged city still visible
far down in its depths—these and a hundred other points of
interest we examined with critical imbecility, but the Grotto
of the Dog claimed our chief attention, because we had
heard and read so much about it. Everybody has written
about the Grotto del Cane and its poisonous vapors, from
Pliny down to Smith, and every tourist has held a dog over
its floor by the legs to test the capabilities of the place. The
dog dies in a minute and a half—a chicken instantly. As a
general thing, strangers who crawl in there to sleep do not
get up until they are called. And then they don't, either.
The stranger that ventures to sleep there takes a permanent
contract. I longed to see this grotto. I resolved to take a dog
and hold him myself; suffocate him a little and time him;
suffocate him some more and then finish him. We reached
the grotto at about three in the afternoon and proceeded at
once to make the experiments. But now an important difficulty presented itself. We had no dog.

ASCENT OF VESUVIUS—CONTINUED

At the Hermitage we were about fifteen or eighteen hundred feet above the sea, and thus far a portion of the ascent
had been pretty abrupt. For the next two miles the road was
a mixture—sometimes the ascent was abrupt and sometimes
it was not; but one characteristic it possessed all the time,
without failure—without modification: it was all uncompromisingly and unspeakably infamous. It was a rough, narrow
trail and led over an old lava flow—a black ocean which was
tumbled into a thousand fantastic shapes—a wild chaos of
ruin, desolation, and barrenness—a wilderness of billowy
upheavals, of furious whirlpools, of miniature mountains rent
asunder—of gnarled and knotted, wrinkled and twisted
masses of blackness that mimicked branching roots, great

vines, trunks of trees, all interlaced and mingled together: and all these weird shapes, all this turbulent panorama, all this stormy, far-stretching waste of blackness, with its thrilling suggestiveness of life, of action, of boiling, surging, furious motion, was petrified!—all stricken dead and cold in the instant of its maddest rioting!—fettered, paralyzed, and left to glower at heaven in impotent rage forevermore!

Finally we stood in a level, narrow valley (a valley that had been created by the terrific march of some old-time eruption), and on either hand towered the two steep peaks of Vesuvius. The one we had to climb—the one that contains the active volcano—seemed about eight hundred or one thousand feet high, and looked almost too straight-up-and-down for any man to climb, and certainly no mule could climb it with a man on his back. Four of these native pirates will carry you to the top in a sedan chair if you wish it, but suppose they were to slip and let you fall—is it likely that you would ever stop rolling? Not this side of eternity, perhaps. We left the mules, sharpened our finger-nails, and began the ascent I have been writing about so long, at twenty minutes to six in the morning. The path led straight up a rugged sweep of loose chunks of pumice stone, and for about every two steps forward we took, we slid back one. It was so excessively steep that we had to stop every fifty or sixty steps and rest a moment. To see our comrades we had to look very nearly straight up at those above us and very nearly straight down at those below. We stood on the summit at last—it had taken an hour and fifteen minutes to make the trip.

What we saw there was simply a circular crater—a circular ditch, if you please—about two hundred feet deep and four or five hundred feet wide, whose inner wall was about half a mile in circumference. In the center of the great circus ring thus formed was a torn and ragged upheaval a hundred feet high, all snowed over with a sulfur crust of many and many a brilliant and beautiful color, and the ditch enclosed this like the moat of a castle, or surrounded it as a little river does a little island, if the simile is better. The sulfur coating of that island was gaudy in the extreme —all mingled together in the richest confusion were red, blue, brown, black, yellow, white—I do not know that there was a color or shade of a color or combination of colors unrepresented—and when the sun burst through the morning

mists and fired this tinted magnificence, it topped imperial
Vesuvius like a jeweled crown!

The crater itself—the ditch—was not so variegated in
coloring, but yet, in its softness, richness, and unpretentious
elegance it was more charming, more fascinating to the eye.
There was nothing "loud" about its well-bred and well-dressed
look. Beautiful? One could stand and look down upon it for a
week without getting tired of it. It had the semblance of a
pleasant meadow, whose slender grasses and whose velvety
mosses were frosted with a shining dust, and tinted with
palest green that deepened gradually to the darkest hue of
the orange leaf, and deepened yet again into gravest brown,
then faded into orange, then into brightest gold, and culminated in the delicate pink of a new-blown rose. Where portions of the meadow had sunk, and where other portions
had been broken up like an ice floe, the cavernous openings
of the one and the ragged upturned edges exposed by the
other were hung with a lacework of soft-tinted crystals of
sulfur that changed their deformities into quaint shapes and
figures that were full of grace and beauty.

The walls of the ditch were brilliant with yellow banks
of sulfur and with lava and pumice stone of many colors.
No fire was visible anywhere, but gusts of sulfurous steam
issued silently and invisibly from a thousand little cracks
and fissures in the crater and were wafted to our noses
with every breeze. But so long as we kept our nostrils buried
in our handkerchiefs, there was small danger of suffocation.

Some of the boys thrust long slips of paper down into
holes and set them on fire, and so achieved the glory of
lighting their cigars by the flames of Vesuvius, and others
cooked eggs over fissures in the rocks and were happy.

The view from the summit would have been superb but
for the fact that the sun could only pierce the mists at
long intervals. Thus the glimpses we had of the grand panorama below were only fitful and unsatisfactory.

THE DESCENT

The descent of the mountain was a labor of only four
minutes. Instead of stalking down the rugged path we ascended, we chose one which was bedded knee-deep in loose
ashes, and plowed our way with prodigious strides that

would almost have shamed the performance of him of the seven-league boots.

The Vesuvius of today is a very poor affair compared to the mighty volcano of Kilauea, in the Sandwich Islands, but I am glad I visited it. It was well worth it.

It is said that during one of the grand eruptions of Vesuvius it discharged massy rocks, weighing many tons, a thousand feet into the air, its vast jets of smoke and steam ascended thirty miles toward the firmament, and clouds of its ashes were wafted abroad and fell upon the decks of ships seven hundred and fifty miles at sea! I will take the ashes at a moderate discount if anyone will take the thirty miles of smoke, but I do not feel able to take a commanding interest in the whole story by myself.

31

They pronounce it Pom-*pay*-e. I always had an idea that you went down into Pompeii with torches by the way of damp, dark stairways, just as you do in silver mines, and traversed gloomy tunnels with lava overhead and something on either hand like dilapidated prisons gouged out of the solid earth that faintly resembled houses. But you do nothing of the kind. Fully one-half of the buried city, perhaps, is completely exhumed and thrown open freely to the light of day; and there stand the long rows of solidly built brick houses (roofless) just as they stood eighteen hundred years ago, hot with the flaming sun; and there lie their floors, clean swept, and not a bright fragment tarnished or wanting of the labored mosaics that pictured them with the beasts and birds and flowers which we copy in perishable carpets today; and there are the Venuses and Bacchuses and Adonises making love and getting drunk in many-hued frescoes on the walls of saloon and bedchamber; and there are the narrow streets and narrower sidewalks, paved with flags of good hard lava, the one deeply rutted with the chariot wheels and the other with the passing feet of the Pompeiians of bygone centuries; and there are the bakeshops, the temples, the halls of justice, the baths, the theaters—all clean scraped and neat, and suggesting nothing of the nature of a silver mine away down in the bowels of the earth. The broken pillars lying about, the doorless doorways, and the crumbled tops of the wilderness of walls were wonderfully suggestive of the "burnt district" in one of our cities, and if there had been any charred timbers, shattered windows, heaps of debris, and general blackness and smokiness about the place, the resemblance would have been perfect. But no—the sun shines as brightly down on old Pompeii today as it did when Christ was born in Bethlehem, and its streets are cleaner a hundred times than ever Pompeiian saw them in her prime. I know whereof I speak—for in the great, chief thoroughfares (Merchant Street and the Street of Fortune) have I not seen with my own eyes how for two hundred years at least the pavements were not repaired!—how ruts five and even ten inches deep were worn into the thick flagstones by the chariot wheels of generations of swindled taxpayers? And do I not know by these signs that street commissioners of Pompeii never attended to their business, and that if they never mended the pavements they never cleaned them? And besides, is it not the inborn nature of street commissioners to avoid their duty whenever they get a chance? I wish I knew the name of the last one that held office in Pompeii so that I could give him a blast. I speak with feeling on this subject, because I caught my foot in one of those ruts, and the sadness that came over me when I saw the first poor skeleton, with ashes and lava sticking to it, was tempered by the reflection that maybe that party was the street commissioner.

No—Pompeii is no longer a buried city. It is a city of hundreds and hundreds of roofless houses, and a tangled maze of streets where one could easily get lost without a guide, and have to sleep in some ghostly palace that had known no living tenant since that awful November night of eighteen centuries ago.

We passed through the gate which faces the Mediterranean (called the "Marine Gate") and by the rusty, broken image of Minerva, still keeping tireless watch and ward over the possessions it was powerless to save, and went up a long street and stood in the broad court of the Forum of Justice.

The floor was level and clean, and up and down either side was a noble colonnade of broken pillars, with their beautiful Ionic and Corinthian columns scattered about them. At the upper end were the vacant seats of the judges, and behind them we descended into a dungeon where the ashes and cinders had found two prisoners chained on that memorable November night and tortured them to death. How they must have tugged at the pitiless fetters as the fierce fires surged around them!

Then we lounged through many and many a sumptuous private mansion which we could not have entered without a formal invitation in incomprehensible Latin, in the olden time, when the owners lived there—and we probably wouldn't have got it. These people built their houses a good deal alike. The floors were laid in fanciful figures wrought in mosaics of many-colored marbles. At the threshold your eyes fall upon a Latin sentence of welcome sometimes, or a picture of a dog with the legend "Beware of the Dog," and sometimes a picture of a bear or a faun with no inscription at all. Then you enter a sort of vestibule, where they used to keep the hat rack, I suppose; next a room with a large marble basin in the midst and the pipes of a fountain; on either side are bedrooms; beyond the fountain is a reception room, then a little garden, dining room, and so forth and so on. The floors were all mosaic, the walls were stuccoed or frescoed or ornamented with bas-reliefs, and here and there were statues large and small, and little fish pools, and cascades of sparkling water that sprang from secret places in the colonnade of handsome pillars that surrounded the court and kept the flower beds fresh and the air cool. Those Pompeiians were very luxurious in their tastes and habits. The most exquisite bronzes we have seen in Europe came from the exhumed cities of Herculaneum and Pompeii, and also the finest cameos and the most delicate engravings on precious stones; their pictures, eighteen or nineteen centuries old, are often much more pleasing than the celebrated rubbish of the old masters of three centuries ago. They were well up in art. From the creation of these works of the first, clear up to the eleventh, century, art seems hardly to have existed at all—at least no remnants of it are left—and it was curious to see how far (in some things, at any rate) these old-time pagans excelled the remote generations of masters that came after them. The pride of the world in sculptures seem to be the Laocoön and the Dying Gladiator, in Rome. They are as old as Pompeii, were dug from the earth like Pompeii; but their exact age or who made them can only be conjectured. But worn and cracked, without a history, and with the blemishing stains of numberless centuries upon them, they still mutely mock at all efforts to rival their perfections.

It was a quaint and curious pastime, wandering through this old silent city of the dead—lounging through utterly deserted streets where thousands and thousands of human beings once bought and sold, and walked and rode, and made the place resound with the noise and confusion of traffic and pleasure. They were not lazy. They hurried in those days. We had evidence of that. There was a temple on one corner, and it was a shorter cut to go between the columns of that temple from one street to the other than to go around—and behold that pathway had been worn deep into the heavy flagstone floor of the building by generations of time-saving feet! They would not go around when it was quicker to go through. We do that way in our cities.

Everywhere you see things that make you wonder how old these old houses were before the night of destruction came —things, too, which bring back those long-dead inhabitants and place them living before your eyes. For instance: The steps (two feet thick—lava blocks) that lead up out of the school and the same kind of steps that lead up into the dress circle of the principal theater are almost worn through! For ages the boys hurried out of that school, and for ages their parents hurried into that theater, and the nervous feet that have been dust and ashes for eighteen centuries have left their record for us to read today. I imagined I could see crowds of gentlemen and ladies thronging into the theater, with tickets for secured seats in their hands, and on the wall I read the imaginary placard, in infamous grammar, "POSITIVELY NO FREE LIST EXCEPT MEMBERS OF THE PRESS!" Hanging about the doorway (I fancied) were slouchy Pompeiian street boys uttering slang and profanity, and keeping a wary eye out for checks. I entered the theater and sat down in one of the long rows of stone benches in the dress circle, and looked at the place for the orchestra and the ruined stage and around at the wide sweep of empty boxes, and thought to myself, "This house won't pay." I tried to imagine the music in full blast, the leader of the orchestra beating time, and the "versatile" So-and-So (who had "just returned from a most successful tour in the provinces to play his last and farewell engagement of positively six nights only, in Pompeii, previous to his departure for Herculaneum") charging around the stage and piling the agony mountains high—but I could not do it with such a "house" as that; those empty benches tied my fancy down to dull reality. I said, these people that ought to be here have been dead and still and moldering to dust for ages and ages, and will never care for the trifles and follies of life anymore forever—"Owing to circumstances, etc., etc., there will not be any performance tonight." Close down the curtain. Put out the lights.

And so I turned away and went through shop after shop and store after store, far down the long street of the merchants, and called for the wares of Rome and the East, but the tradesmen were gone, the marts were silent, and nothing was left but the broken jars all set in cement of cinders and ashes; the wine and the oil that once had filled them were gone with their owners.

In a bakeshop was a mill for grinding the grain and the furnaces for baking the bread; and they say that here, in the same furnaces, the exhumers of Pompeii found nice, well-baked loaves which the baker had not found time to remove from the ovens the last time he left his shop, because circumstances compelled him to leave in such a hurry.

In one house (the only building in Pompeii which no woman is now allowed to enter) were the small rooms and short beds of solid masonry, just as they were in the old times, and on the walls were pictures which looked almost as fresh as if they were painted yesterday, but which no pen could have the hardihood to describe; and here and there were Latin inscriptions—obscene scintillations of wit —scratched by hands that possibly were uplifted to heaven for succor in the midst of a driving storm of fire before the night was done.

In one of the principal streets was a ponderous stone tank and a water spout that supplied it, and where the tired, heated toilers from the Campagna used to rest their right hands when they bent over to put their lips to the spout, the thick stone was worn down to a broad groove an inch or two deep. Think of the countless thousands of hands that had pressed that spot in the ages that are gone, to so reduce a stone that is as hard as iron!

They had a great public bulletin board in Pompeii—a place where announcements for gladiatorial combats, elections, and such things were posted—not on perishable paper, but carved in enduring stone. One lady, who, I take it, was rich and well brought up, advertised a dwelling or so to rent, with baths and all the modern improvements, and several hundred shops, stipulating that the dwellings should not be put to immoral purposes. You can find out who lived in many a house in Pompeii by the carved stone doorplates affixed to them; and in the same way you can tell who they were that occupy the tombs. Everywhere around are things that reveal to you something of the customs and history of this forgotten people. But what would a volcano leave of an American city if it once rained its cinders on it? Hardly a sign or a symbol to tell its story.

In one of these long Pompeiian halls the skeleton of a man was found with ten pieces of gold in one hand and a large key in the other. He had seized his money and started toward the door, but the fiery tempest caught him at the very threshold, and he sank down and died. One more minute of precious time would have saved him. I saw the skeletons of a man, a woman, and two young girls. The woman had her hands spread wide apart, as if in mortal terror, and I imagined I could still trace upon her shapeless face something of the expression of wild despair that distorted it when the heavens rained fire in these streets so many ages ago. The girls and the man lay with their faces upon their arms, as if they had tried to shield them from the enveloping cinders. In one apartment eighteen skeletons were found, all in sitting postures, and blackened places on the walls still mark their shapes and show their attitudes, like shadows. One of them, a woman, still wore upon her skeleton throat a necklace with her name engraved upon it: JULIE DI DIOMEDE.

But perhaps the most poetical thing Pompeii has yielded to modern research was that grand figure of a Roman soldier clad in complete armor, who, true to his duty, true to his proud name of a soldier of Rome, and full of the stern courage which had given to that name its glory, stood to his post by the city gate, erect and unflinching, till the hell that raged around him *burned out* the dauntless spirit it could not conquer.

We never read of Pompeii but we think of that soldier; we cannot write of Pompeii without the natural impulse to grant to him the mention he so well deserves. Let us remember that he was a soldier—not a policeman—and so praise him. Being a soldier, he stayed—because the warrior instinct forbade him to fly. Had he been a policeman, he would have stayed also—because he would have been asleep.

There are not half a dozen flights of stairs in Pompeii, and no other evidences that the houses were more than one story high. The people did not live in the clouds, as do the Venetians, the Genoese, and Neapolitans of today.

We came out from under the solemn mysteries of this city of the Venerable Past—this city which perished, with all its old ways and its quaint old fashions about it, remote centuries ago, when the Disciples were preaching the new religion, which is as old as the hills to us now—and went dreaming among the trees that grow over acres and acres of its still-buried streets and squares, till a shrill whistle and the cry of *"All aboard—last train for Naples!"* woke me up and reminded me that I belonged in the nineteenth century, and was not a dusty mummy, caked with ashes and cinders, eighteen hundred years old. The transition was startling. The idea of a railroad train actually running to old dead Pompeii, and whistling irreverently, and calling for passengers in the most bustling and businesslike way, was as strange a thing as one could imagine, and as unpoetical and disagreeable as it was strange.

Compare the cheerful life and the sunshine of this day with the horrors the younger Pliny saw here, the 9th of November, A.D. 79, when he was so bravely striving to remove his mother out of reach of harm while she begged him, with all a mother's unselfishness, to leave her to perish and save himself.

By this time the murky darkness had so increased that one might have believed himself abroad in a black and moonless night, or in a chamber where all the lights had been extinguished. On every hand was heard the complaints of women, the wailing of children, and the cries of men. One called his father, another his son, and another his wife, and only by their voices could they know each other. Many in their despair begged that death would come and end their distress.

Some implored the gods to succor them, and some believed that this night was the last, the eternal night which should engulf the universe!

Even so it seemed to me—and I consoled myself for the coming death with the reflection: BEHOLD, THE WORLD IS PASSING AWAY!

*   *   *

After browsing among the stately ruins of Rome, of Baiae, of Pompeii, and after glancing down the long marble ranks of battered and nameless imperial heads that stretch down the corridors of the Vatican, one thing strikes me with a force it never had before: the unsubstantial, unlasting character of fame. Men lived long lives in the olden time, and struggled feverishly through them, toiling like slaves, in oratory, in generalship, or in literature, and then laid them down and died, happy in the possession of an enduring history and a deathless name. Well, twenty little centuries flutter away, and what is left of these things? A crazy inscription on a block of stone, which snuffy antiquaries bother over and tangle up and make nothing out of but a bare name (which they spell wrong)—no history, no tradition, no poetry—nothing that can give it even a passing interest. What may be left of General Grant's great name forty centuries hence? This—in the encyclopedia for A.D. 5868, possibly:

URIAH S. (or Z.) GRAUNT—popular poet of ancient times in the Aztec provinces of the United States of British America. Some authors say flourished about A.D. 742; but the learned Ah-ah Foo-foo states that he was a contemporary of Scharkspyre, the English poet, and flourished about A. D. 1328, some three centuries *after* the Trojan war instead of before it. He wrote "Rock Me to Sleep, Mother."

These thoughts sadden me. I will to bed.

32

Home, again! For the first time in many weeks the ship's entire family met and shook hands on the quarterdeck. They had gathered from many points of the compass and from many lands, but not one was missing; there was no tale of sickness or death among the flock to dampen the pleasure of the reunion. Once more there was a full audience on deck to listen to the sailors' chorus as they got the anchor up, and to wave an adieu to the land as we sped away from Naples. The seats were full at dinner again, the domino parties were complete, and the life and bustle on the upper deck in the fine moonlight at night was like old times—old times that had been gone weeks only, but yet they were weeks so crowded with incident, adventure, and excitement that they seemed almost like years. There was no lack of cheerfulness on board the *Quaker City*. For once her title was a misnomer.

At seven in the evening, with the western horizon all golden from the sunken sun and specked with distant ships, the full moon sailing high over head, the dark blue of the sea under foot, and a strange sort of twilight affected by all these different lights and colors around us and about us, we sighted superb Stromboli. With what majesty the monarch held his lonely state above the level sea! Distance clothed him in a purple gloom and added a veil of shimmering mist that so softened his rugged features that we seemed to see him through a web of silver gauze. His torch was out; his fires were smoldering; a tall column of smoke that rose up and lost itself in the growing moonlight was all the sign he gave that he was a living Autocrat of the Sea and not the specter of a dead one.

At two in the morning we swept through the Straits of Messina, and so bright was the moonlight that Italy on the one hand and Sicily on the other seemed almost as distinctly visible as though we looked at them from the middle of a street we were traversing. The city of Messina, milk-white, and starred and spangled all over with gaslights, was a fairy spectacle. A great party of us were on deck, smoking and making a noise and waiting to see famous Scylla and Charybdis. And presently the Oracle stepped out with his eternal spyglass and squared himself on the deck like another Colossus of Rhodes. It was a surprise to see him abroad at such an hour. Nobody supposed he cared anything about an old fable like that of Scylla and Charybdis. One of the boys said:

"Hello, Doctor, what are you doing up here at this time of night? What do you want to see this place for?"

"What do *I* want to see this place for? Young man, little do you know me, or you wouldn't ask such a question. I wish to see *all* the places that's mentioned in the Bible."

"Stuff—this place isn't mentioned in the Bible."

"It ain't mentioned in the Bible! *This* place ain't— Well, now, what place *is* this, since you know so much about it?"

"Why, it's Scylla and Charybdis."

"Scylla and Cha— Confound it, I thought it was Sodom and Gomorrah!"

And he closed up his glass and went below. The above is the ship story. Its plausibility is marred a little by the fact that the Oracle was not a biblical student and did not spend much of his time instructing himself about Scriptural localities. They say the Oracle complains in this hot weather lately that the only beverage in the ship that is passable is the butter. He did not mean butter, of course, but inasmuch as that article remains in a melted state now since we are out of ice, it is fair to give him the credit of getting one long word in the right place, anyhow, for once in his life. He said in Rome that the Pope was a noble-looking old man, but he never *did* think much of his Iliad.

We spent one pleasant day skirting along the isles of Greece. They are very mountainous. Their prevailing tints are gray and brown, approaching to red. Little white villages surrounded by trees nestle in the valleys or roost upon the lofty perpendicular seawalls.

We had one fine sunset—a rich carmine flush that suffused the western sky and cast a ruddy glow far over the sea. Fine sunsets seem to be rare in this part of the world—or at least striking ones. They are soft, sensuous, lovely—they are exquisite, refined, effeminate—but we have seen no sunsets here yet like the gorgeous conflagrations that flame in the track of the sinking sun in our high northern latitudes.

But what were sunsets to us, with the wild excitement upon us of approaching the most renowned of cities! What cared we for outward visions when Agamemnon, Achilles, and a thousand other heroes of the great Past were marching in ghostly procession through our fancies? What were sunsets to us, who were about to live and breathe and walk in actual Athens; yea, and go far down into the dead centuries and bid in person for the slaves, Diogenes and Plato, in the public marketplace, or gossip with the neighbors about the siege of Troy or the splendid deeds of Marathon? We scorned to consider sunsets.

We arrived, and entered the ancient harbor of the Piraeus

at last. We dropped anchor within half a mile of the village. Away off, across the undulating plain of Attica, could be seen a little square-topped hill with a something on it, which our glasses soon discovered to be the ruined edifices of the citadel of the Athenians, and most prominent among them loomed the venerable Parthenon. So exquisitely clear and pure is this wonderful atmosphere that every column of the noble structure was discernible through the telescope, and even the smaller ruins about it assumed some semblance of shape. This at a distance of five or six miles. In the valley, near the Acropolis (the square-topped hill before spoken of), Athens itself could be vaguely made out with an ordinary lorgnette. Everybody was anxious to get ashore and visit these classic localities as quickly as possible. No land we had yet seen had aroused such universal interest among the passengers.

But bad news came. The commandant of the Piraeus came in his boat and said we must either depart or else get outside the harbor and remain imprisoned in our ship, under rigid quarantine, for eleven days! So we took up the anchor and moved outside, to lie a dozen hours or so taking in supplies and then sail for Constantinople. It was the bitterest disappointment we had yet experienced. To lie a whole day in sight of the Acropolis and yet be obliged to go away without visiting Athens! Disappointment was hardly a strong enough word to describe the circumstances.

All hands were on deck all the afternoon, with books and maps and glasses, trying to determine which "narrow rocky ridge" was the Areopagus, which sloping hill the Pnyx, which elevation the Museum Hill, and so on. And we got things confused. Discussion became heated, and party spirit ran high. Church members were gazing with emotion upon a hill which they said was the one St. Paul preached from, and another faction claimed that that hill was Hymettus, and another that it was Pentelikon! After all the trouble, we could be certain of only one thing—the square-topped hill was the Acropolis and the grand ruin that crowned it was the Parthenon, whose picture we knew in infancy in the school books.

We inquired of everybody who came near the ship whether there were guards in the Piraeus, whether they were strict, what the chances were of capture should any of us slip ashore, and in case any of us made the venture and were caught, what would be probably done to us? The answers were discouraging: There was a strong guard or police force; the Piraeus was a small town, and any stranger seen in it would surely attract attention—capture would be certain. The commandant said the punishment would be "heavy"; when asked, "How heavy?" he said it would be "very severe" —that was all we could get out of him.

At eleven o'clock at night, when most of the ship's company were abed, four of us stole softly ashore in a small boat, a clouded moon favoring the enterprise, and started two and two, and far apart, over a low hill, intending to go clear around the Piraeus, out of the range of its police. Picking our way so stealthily over that rocky, nettle-grown eminence made me feel a good deal as if I were on my way somewhere to steal something. My immediate comrade and I talked in an undertone about quarantine laws and their penalties, but we found nothing cheering in the subject. I was posted. Only a few days before, I was talking with our captain, and he mentioned the case of a man who swam ashore from a quarantined ship somewhere, and got imprisoned six months for it; and when he was in Genoa a few years ago, a captain of a quarantined ship went in his boat to a departing ship, which was already outside of the harbor, and put a letter on board to be taken to his family, and the authorities imprisoned him three months for it, and then conducted him and his ship fairly to sea and warned him never to show himself in that port again while he lived. This kind of conversation did no good further than to give a sort of dismal interest to our quarantine-breaking expedition, and so we dropped it. We made the entire circuit of the town without seeing anybody but one man, who stared at us curiously but said nothing, and a dozen persons asleep on the ground before their doors, whom we walked among and never woke, but we woke up dogs enough, in all conscience—we always had one or two barking at our heels, and several times we had as many as ten and twelve at once. They made such a preposterous din that persons aboard our ship said they could tell how we were progressing for a long time and where we were by the barking of the dogs. The clouded moon still favored us. When we had made the whole circuit, and were passing among the houses on the further side of the town, the moon came out splendidly, but we no longer feared the light. As we approached a well near a house, to get a drink, the owner merely glanced at us and went within. He left the quiet, slumbering town at our mercy. I record it here proudly that we didn't do anything to it.

Seeing no road, we took a tall hill to the left of the distant Acropolis for a mark and steered straight for it over all obstructions, and over a little rougher piece of country than exists anywhere else outside of the state of Nevada, perhaps. Part of the way it was covered with small, loose stones—we trod on six at a time and they all rolled. Another part of it was dry, loose, newly plowed ground. Still another part of it was a long stretch of low grapevines, which were tanglesome and troublesome, and which we took to be brambles. The Attic Plain, barring the grapevines, was a barren, desolate, unpoetical waste—I wonder what it was in Greece's Age of Glory, five hundred years before Christ.

In the neighborhood of one o'clock in the morning, when we were heated with fast walking and parched with thirst, Denny exclaimed, "Why, these weeds are grapevines!" And in five minutes we had a score of bunches of large, white, delicious grapes, and were reaching down for more when a dark shape rose mysteriously up out of the shadows beside us and said, "Ho!" And so we left.

In ten minutes more we struck into a beautiful road, and unlike some others we had stumbled upon at intervals, it led in the right direction. We followed it. It was broad and smooth and white, handsome and in perfect repair, and shaded on both sides for a mile or so with single ranks of trees and also with luxuriant vineyards. Twice we entered and stole grapes, and the second time somebody shouted at us from some invisible place. Whereupon we left again. We speculated in grapes no more on that side of Athens.

Shortly we came upon an ancient stone aqueduct built upon arches, and from that time forth we had ruins all about us—we were approaching our journey's end. We could not see the Acropolis now or the high hill, either, and I wanted to follow the road till we were abreast of them, but the others overruled me, and we toiled laboriously up the stony hill immediately in our front—and from its summit saw another—climbed it and saw another! It was an hour of exhausting work. Soon we came upon a row of open graves cut in the solid rock (for a while one of them served Socrates for a prison); we passed around the shoulder of the hill, and the citadel, in all its ruined magnificence, burst upon us! We hurried across the ravine and up a winding road and stood on the

old Acropolis, with the prodigious walls of the citadel towering above our heads. We did not stop to inspect their massive blocks of marble or measure their height or guess at
their extraordinary thickness, but passed at once through a
great arched passage like a railway tunnel and went straight
to the gate that leads to the ancient temples. It was locked!
So, after all, it seemed that we were not to see the great
Parthenon face to face. We sat down and held a council of
war. Result: the gate was only a flimsy structure of wood—
we would break it down. It seemed like desecration, but then
we had traveled far, and our necessities were urgent. We
could not hunt up guides and keepers—we must be on the
ship before daylight. So we argued. This was all very fine,
but when we came to break the gate, we could not do it. We
moved around an angle of the wall and found a low bastion:
eight feet high without, ten or twelve within. Denny prepared
to scale it, and we got ready to follow. By dint of hard scram-
bling he finally straddled the top, but some loose stones crumbled away and fell with a crash into the court within. There
was instantly a banging of doors and a shout. Denny dropped
from the wall in a twinkling, and we retreated in disorder to
the gate. Xerxes took that mighty citadel four hundred and
eighty years before Christ, when his five millions of soldiers
and camp followers followed him to Greece, and if we four
Americans could have remained unmolested five minutes
longer, we would have taken it too.

The garrison had turned out—four Greeks. We clamored
at the gate, and they admitted us. [Bribery and corruption.]

We crossed a large court, entered a great door, and stood
upon a pavement of purest white marble, deeply worn by
footprints. Before us in the flooding moonlight rose the
noblest ruins we had ever looked upon—the Propylae; a
small Temple of Minerva; the Temple of Hercules; and the
grand Parthenon. [We got these names from the Greek
guide, who didn't seem to know more than seven men ought
to know.] These edifices were all built of the whitest Pen-
telik marble, but have a pinkish stain upon them now. Where
any part is broken, however, the fracture looks like fine loaf
sugar. Six caryatids, or marble women, clad in flowing robes,
support the portico of the Temple of Hercules, but the
porticoes and colonnades of the other structures are formed
of massive Doric and Ionic pillars, whose flutings and capitals

are still measurably perfect, notwithstanding the centuries
that have gone over them and the sieges they have suffered.
The Parthenon originally was two hundred and twenty-six
feet long, one hundred wide, and seventy high, and had two
rows of great columns, eight in each, at either end, and single
rows of seventeen each down the sides, and was one of the
most graceful and beautiful edifices ever erected.

Most of the Parthenon's imposing columns are still standing, but the roof is gone. It was a perfect building two hundred and fifty years ago, when a shell dropped into the Venetian magazine stored here, and the explosion which followed
wrecked and unroofed it. I remember but little about the
Parthenon, and I have put in one or two facts and figures for
the use of other people with short memories. Got them from
the guidebook.

As we wandered thoughtfully down the marble-paved
length of this stately temple the scene about us was strangely
impressive. Here and there in lavish profusion were gleaming
white statues of men and women, propped against blocks of
marble, some of them armless, some without legs, others
headless—but all looking mournful in the moonlight and
startlingly human! They rose up and confronted the midnight intruder on every side—they stared at him with stony
eyes from unlooked-for nooks and recesses; they peered at
him over fragmentary heaps far down the desolate corridors;
they barred his way in the midst of the broad forum and solemnly pointed with handless arms the way from the sacred
fane; and through the roofless temple the moon looked down
and banded the floor and darkened the scattered fragments
and broken statues with the slanting shadows of the columns.

What a world of ruined sculpture was about us! Set up in
rows—stacked up in piles—scattered broadcast over the wide
area of the Acropolis—were hundreds of crippled statues of
all sizes and of the most exquisite workmanship; and vast
fragments of marble that once belonged to the entablatures,
covered with bas-reliefs representing battles and sieges, ships
of war with three and four tiers of oars, pageants and processions—everything one could think of. History says that the
temples of the Acropolis were filled with the noblest works of
Praxiteles and Phidias and of many a great master in sculpture besides—and surely these elegant fragments attest it.

We walked out into the grass-grown, fragment-strewn court
beyond the Parthenon. It startled us every now and then to

see a stony white face stare suddenly up at us out of the grass with its dead eyes. The place seemed alive with ghosts. I half expected to see the Athenian heroes of twenty centuries ago glide out of the shadows and steal into the old temple they knew so well and regarded with such boundless pride.

The full moon was riding high in the cloudless heavens now. We sauntered carelessly and unthinkingly to the edge of the lofty battlements of the citadel and looked down—a vision! And such a vision! Athens by moonlight! The prophet that thought the splendors of the New Jerusalem were revealed to him surely saw this instead! It lay in the level plain right under our feet—all spread abroad like a picture—and we looked down upon it as we might have looked from a balloon. We saw no semblance of a street, but every house, every window, every clinging vine, every projection, was as distinct and sharply marked as if the time were noonday; and yet there was no glare, no glitter, nothing harsh or repulsive—the noiseless city was flooded with the mellowest light that ever streamed from the moon, and seemed like some living creature wrapped in peaceful slumber. On its further side was a little temple, whose delicate pillars and ornate front glowed with a rich luster that chained the eye like a spell; and nearer by, the palace of the king reared its creamy walls out of the midst of a great garden of shrubbery that was flecked all over with a random shower of amber lights—a spray of golden sparks that lost their brightness in the glory of the moon and glinted softly upon the sea of dark foliage like the pallid stars of the Milky Way. Overhead the stately columns, majestic still in their ruin—under foot the dreaming city—in the distance the silver sea—not on the broad earth is there another picture half so beautiful!

As we turned and moved again through the temple I wished that the illustrious men who had sat in it in the remote ages could visit it again and reveal themselves to our curious eyes —Plato, Aristotle, Demosthenes, Socrates, Phocion, Pythagoras, Euclid, Pindar, Xenophon, Herodotus, Praxiteles and Phidias, Zeuxis the painter. What a constellation of celebrated names! But more than all, I wished that old Diogenes, groping so patiently with his lantern, searching so zealously for one solitary honest man in all the world, might meander along and stumble on our party. I ought not to say it, maybe, but still I suppose he would have put out his light.

We left the Parthenon to keep its watch over old Athens, as it had kept it for twenty-three hundred years, and went and stood outside the walls of the citadel. In the distance was the ancient but still almost perfect Temple of Theseus, and close by, looking to the west, was the Bema, from whence Demosthenes thundered his philippics and fired the wavering patriotism of his countrymen. To the right was Mars Hill, where the Areopagus sat in ancient times and where St. Paul defined his position, and below was the marketplace where he "disputed daily" with the gossip-loving Athenians. We climbed the stone steps St. Paul ascended, and stood in the square-cut place he stood in, and tried to recollect the Bible account of the matter—but for certain reasons I could not recall the words, I have found them since:

Now while Paul waited for them at Athens, his spirit was stirred in him, when he saw the city wholly given up to idolatry.

Therefore disputed he in the synagogue with the Jews, and with the devout persons, and in the market daily with them that met with him. .

And they took him and brought him unto Areopagus, saying, May we know what this new doctrine whereof thou speakest is? . . .

Then Paul stood in the midst of Mars Hill, and said, Ye men of Athens, I perceive that in all things ye are too superstitious;

For as I passed by and beheld your devotions, I found an altar with this inscription: To THE UNKNOWN GOD. Whom, therefore, ye ignorantly worship, him declare I unto you.— Acts, Ch. xvii.

It occurred to us after a while that if we wanted to get home before daylight betrayed us, we had better be moving. So we hurried away. When far on our road, we had a parting view of the Parthenon with the moonlight streaming through its open colonnades and touching its capitals with silver. As it looked then—solemn, grand, and beautiful—it will always remain in our memories.

As we marched along we began to get over our fears and ceased to care much about quarantine scouts or anybody else. We grew bold and reckless; and once, in a sudden burst of courage, I even threw a stone at a dog. It was a pleasant reflection, though, that I did not hit him, because his master might just possibly have been a policeman. Inspired by this happy failure, my valor became utterly uncontrollable, and at intervals I absolutely whistled, though on a moderate key. But boldness breeds boldness, and shortly I plunged into a vineyard, in the full light of the moon, and captured a gallon of superb grapes, not even minding the presence of a peasant who rode by on a mule. Denny and Birch followed my example. Now I had grapes enough for a dozen, but then Jackson was all swollen up with courage, too, and he was obliged to enter a vineyard presently. The first bunch he seized brought trouble. A frowzy, bearded brigand sprang into the road with a shout and flourished a musket in the light of the moon! We sidled toward the Piraeus—not running, you understand, but only advancing with celerity. The brigand shouted again, but still we advanced. It was getting late, and we had no time to fool away on every ass that wanted to drivel Greek platitudes to us. We would just as soon have talked with him as not if we had not been in a hurry. Presently Denny said, "Those fellows are following us!"

We turned, and sure enough, there they were—three fantastic pirates armed with guns. We slackened our pace to let them come up, and in the meantime I got out my cargo of grapes and dropped them firmly but reluctantly into the shadows by the wayside. But I was not afraid. I only felt that it was not right to steal grapes. And all the more so when the owner was around—and not only around, but with his friends around also. The villains came up and searched a bundle Dr. Birch had in his hand and scowled upon him when they found it had nothing in it but some holy rocks from Mars Hill, and these were not contraband. They evidently suspected him of playing some wretched fraud upon them and seemed half inclined to scalp the party. But finally they dismissed us with a warning, couched in excellent Greek, I suppose, and dropped tranquilly in our wake. When they had gone three hundred yards they stopped, and we went on rejoiced. But behold, another armed rascal came out of the shadows and took their place and followed us two hundred yards. Then he delivered us over to another miscreant, who emerged from some mysterious place, and he in turn to another! For a mile and a half our rear was guarded all the while by armed men. I never traveled in so much state before in all my life.

It was a good while after that before we ventured to steal

any more grapes, and when we did we stirred up another troublesome brigand, and then we ceased all further speculation in that line. I suppose that fellow that rode by on the mule posted all the sentinels, from Athens to the Piraeus, about us.

Every field on that long route was watched by an armed sentinel, some of whom had fallen asleep, no doubt, but were on hand nevertheless. This shows what sort of a country modern Attica is—a community of questionable characters. These men were not there to guard their possessions against strangers, but against each other; for strangers seldom visit Athens and the Piraeus, and when they do, they go in daylight and can buy all the grapes they want for a trifle. The modern inhabitants are confiscators and falsifiers of high repute, if gossip speaks truly concerning them, and I freely believe it does.

Just as the earliest tinges of the dawn flushed the eastern sky and turned the pillared Parthenon to a broken harp hung in the pearly horizon, we closed our thirteenth mile of weary, roundabout marching and emerged upon the seashore abreast the ships, with our usual escort of fifteen hundred Piraean dogs howling at our heels. We hailed a boat that was two or three hundred yards from shore and discovered in a moment that it was a police boat on the lookout for any quarantine-breakers that might chance to be abroad. So we dodged— we were used to that by this time—and when the scouts reached the spot we had so lately occupied, we were absent. They cruised along the shore, but in the wrong direction, and shortly our own boat issued from the gloom and took us aboard. They had heard our signal on the ship. We rowed noiselessly away, and before the police boat came in sight again, we were safe at home once more.

Four more of our passengers were anxious to visit Athens, and started half an hour after we returned; but they had not been ashore five minutes till the police discovered and chased them so hotly that they barely escaped to their boat again, and that was all. They pursued the enterprise no further.

We set sail for Constantinople today, but some of us little care for that. We have seen all there was to see in the old city that had its birth sixteen hundred years before Christ was born, and was an old town before the foundations of

Troy were laid—and saw it in its most attractive aspect. Wherefore, why should *we* worry?

Two other passengers ran the blockade successfully last night. So we learned this morning. They slipped away so quietly that they were not missed from the ship for several hours. They had the hardihood to march into the Piraeus in the early dusk and hire a carriage. They ran some danger of adding two or three months' imprisonment to the other novelties of their Holy Land Pleasure Excursion. I admire "cheek." * But they went and came safely and never walked a step.

33

From Athens all through the islands of the Grecian archipelago we saw little but forbidding seawalls and barren hills, sometimes surmounted by three or four graceful columns of some ancient temple, lonely and deserted—a fitting symbol of the desolation that has come upon all Greece in these latter ages. We saw no plowed fields, very few villages, no trees or grass or vegetation of any kind scarcely, and hardly ever an isolated house. Greece is a bleak, unsmiling desert, without agriculture, manufactures, or commerce apparently. What supports its poverty-stricken people or its government is a mystery.

I suppose that ancient Greece and modern Greece compared furnish the most extravagant contrast to be found in history. George I, an infant of eighteen, and a scraggy nest of foreign office-holders, sit in the places of Themistocles, Pericles, and the illustrious scholars and generals of the Golden Age of Greece. The fleets that were the wonder of the world when the Parthenon was new are a beggarly handful of fishing smacks now, and the manly people that performed such miracles of valor at Marathon are only a tribe of unconsidered slaves today. The classic Illissus has gone dry, and so

* Quotation from the Pilgrims.

have all the sources of Grecian wealth and greatness. The nation numbers only eight hundred thousand souls, and there is poverty and misery and mendacity enough among them to furnish forty millions and be liberal about it. Under King Otho the revenues of the State were five millions of dollars—raised from a tax of *one-tenth* of all the agricultural products of the land (which tenth the farmer had to bring to the royal granaries on pack mules any distance not exceeding six leagues) and from extravagant taxes on trade and commerce. Out of that five millions the small tyrant tried to keep an army of ten thousand men, pay all the hundreds of useless Grand Equerries in Waiting, First Grooms of the Bedchamber, Lord High Chancellors of the Exploded Exchequer, and all the other absurdities which these puppy kingdoms indulge in, in imitation of the great monarchies; and in addition he set about building a white marble palace to cost about five millions itself. The result was, simply: ten into five goes no times and none over. All these things could not be done with five millions, and Otho fell into trouble.

The Greek throne, with its unpromising adjuncts of a ragged population of ingenious rascals who were out of employment eight months in the year because there was little for them to borrow and less to confiscate, and a waste of barren hills and weed-grown deserts, went begging for a good while. It was offered to one of Victoria's sons and afterwards to various other younger sons of royalty who had no thrones and were out of business, but they all had the charity to decline the dreary honor, and veneration enough for Greece's ancient greatness to refuse to mock her sorrowful rags and dirt with a tinsel throne in this day of her humiliation—till they came to this young Danish George, and he took it. He has finished the splendid palace I saw in the radiant moonlight the other night and is doing many other things for the salvation of Greece, they say.

We sailed through the barren archipelago and into the narrow channel they sometimes call the Dardanelles and sometimes the Hellespont. This part of the country is rich in historic reminiscences and poor as Sahara in everything else. For instance, as we approached the Dardanelles, we coasted along the plains of Troy and past the mouth of the Scamander; we saw where Troy had stood (in the distance), and where it does not stand now—a city that perished when the world was young. The poor Trojans are all dead now. They were born too late to see Noah's ark and died too soon to see our menagarie. We saw where Agamemnon's fleets rendezvoused, and away inland a mountain which the map said was Mount Ida. Within the Hellespont we saw where the original first shoddy contract mentioned in history was carried out, and the "parties of the second part" gently rebuked by Xerxes. I speak of the famous bridge of boats which Xerxes ordered to be built over the narrowest part of the Hellespont (where it is only two or three miles wide). A moderate gale destroyed the flimsy structure, and the King, thinking that to publicly rebuke the contractors might have a good effect on the next set, called them out before the army and had them beheaded. In the next ten minutes he let a new contract for the bridge. It has been observed by ancient writers that the second bridge was a very good bridge. Xerxes crossed his host of five millions of men on it, and if it had not been purposely destroyed, it would probably have been there yet. If our government would rebuke some of our shoddy contractors occasionally, it might work much good. In the Hellespont we saw where Leander and Lord Byron swam across, the one to see her upon whom his soul's affections were fixed with a devotion that only death could impair, and the other merely for a flyer, as Jack says. We had two noted tombs near us, too. On one shore slept Ajax and on the other Hecuba.

We had water batteries and forts on both sides of the Hellespont, flying the crimson flag of Turkey, with its white crescent, and occasionally a village, and sometimes a train of camels; we had all these to look at till we entered the broad Sea of Marmara, and then, the land soon fading from view, we resumed euchre and whist once more.

We dropped anchor in the mouth of the Golden Horn at daylight in the morning. Only three or four of us were up to see the great Ottoman capital. The passengers do not turn out at unseasonable hours, as they used to, to get the earliest possible glimpse of strange foreign cities. They are well over that. If we were lying in sight of the pyramids of Egypt, they would not come on deck until after breakfast nowadays.

The Golden Horn is a narrow arm of the sea, which branches from the Bosporus (a sort of broad river which connects the Marmara and Black seas) and, curving around, divides the city in the middle. Galata and Pera are on one side of the Bosporus, and the Golden Horn; Stamboul (ancient

Byzantium) is upon the other. On the other bank of the Bosporus is Scutari and other suburbs of Constantinople. This great city contains a million inhabitants, but so narrow are its streets, and so crowded together are its houses, that it does not cover much more than half as much ground as New York City. Seen from the anchorage or from a mile or so up the Bosporus, it is by far the handsomest city we have seen. Its dense array of houses swells upward from the water's edge and spreads over the domes of many hills; and the gardens that peep out here and there, the great globes of the mosques, and the countless minarets that meet the eye everywhere invest the metropolis with the quaint Oriental aspect one dreams of when he reads books of Eastern travel. Constantinople makes a noble picture.

But its attractiveness begins and ends with its picturesqueness. From the time one starts ashore till he gets back again, he execrates it. The boat he goes in is admirably miscalculated for the service it is built for. It is handsomely and neatly fitted up, but no man could handle it well in the turbulent currents that sweep down the Bosporus from the Black Sea, and few men could row it satisfactorily even in still water. It is a long, light canoe (caïque), large at one end and tapering to a knife blade at the other. They make that long sharp end the bow, and you can imagine how these boiling currents spin it about. It has two oars, and sometimes four, and no rudder. You start to go to a given point and you run in fifty different directions before you get there. First one oar is backing water and then the other; it is seldom that both are going ahead at once. This kind of boating is calculated to drive an impatient man mad in a week. The boatmen are the awkwardest, the stupidest, and the most unscientific on earth, without question.

Ashore it was—well, it was an eternal circus. People were thicker than bees in those narrow streets, and the men were dressed in all the outrageous, outlandish, idolatrous, extravagant, thunder-and-lightning costumes that ever a tailor with the delirium tremens and seven devils could conceive of. There was no freak in dress too crazy to be indulged in, no absurdity too absurd to be tolerated, no frenzy in ragged diabolism too fantastic to be attempted. No two men were dressed alike. It was a wild masquerade of all imaginable costumes—every struggling throng in every street was a dissolving view of stunning contrasts. Some patriarchs wore awful

turbans, but the grand mass of the infidel horde wore the
fiery red skullcap they call a fez. All the remainder of the
raiment they indulged in was utterly indescribable.

The shops here are mere coops, mere boxes, bathrooms,
closets—anything you please to call them—on the first floor.
The Turks sit cross-legged in them, and work and trade
and smoke long pipes, and smell like—like Turks. That covers
the ground. Crowding the narrow streets in front of them
are beggars, who beg forever, yet never collect anything;
and wonderful cripples, distorted out of all semblance of
humanity almost; vagabonds driving laden asses; porters carrying dry-goods boxes as large as cottages on their backs;
peddlers of grapes, hot corn, pumpkin seeds, and a hundred
other things yelling like fiends; and sleeping happily, comfortably, serenely, among the hurrying feet, are the famed
dogs of Constantinople; drifting noiselessly about are squads
of Turkish women, draped from chin to feet in flowing robes,
and with snowy veils bound about their heads that disclose
only the eyes and a vague, shadowy notion of their features.
Seen moving about, far away in the dim, arched aisles of
the Great Bazaar, they look as the shrouded dead must have
looked when they walked forth from their graves amid the
storms and thunders and earthquakes that burst upon Calvary
that awful night of the Crucifixion. A street in Constantinople
is a picture which one ought to see once—not oftener.

And then there was the goose-rancher—a fellow who drove
a hundred geese before him about the city and tried to sell
them. He had a pole ten feet long with a crook in the end of
it, and occasionally a goose would branch out from the flock
and make a lively break around the corner, with wings half
lifted and neck stretched to its utmost. Did the goose merchant get excited? No. He took his pole and reached after
that goose with unspeakable *sang froid,* took a hitch round
his neck, and "yanked" him back to his place in the flock
without an effort. He steered his geese with that stick as easily
as another man would steer a yawl. A few hours afterward
we saw him sitting on a stone at a corner, in the midst of the
turmoil, sound asleep in the sun, with his geese squatting
around him or dodging out of the way of asses and men. We
came by again within the hour, and he was taking account
of stock, to see whether any of his flock had strayed or been
stolen. The way he did it was unique. He put the end of his
stick within six or eight inches of a stone wall, and made the

geese march in single file between it and the wall. He counted
them as they went by. There was no dodging that arrangement.

If you want dwarfs—I mean just a few dwarfs for a curiosity—go to Genoa. If you wish to buy them by the gross
for retail, go to Milan. There are plenty of dwarfs all over
Italy, but it did seem to me that in Milan the crop was luxuriant. If you would see a fair average style of assorted cripples, go to Naples or travel through the Roman states. But
if you would see the very heart and home of cripples and
human monsters both, go straight to Constantinople. A beggar in Naples who can show a foot which has all run into one
horrible toe, with one shapeless nail on it, has a fortune—but
such an exhibition as that would not provoke any notice in
Constantinople. The man would starve. Who would pay
any attention to attractions like his among the rare monsters
that throng the bridges of the Golden Horn and display their
deformities in the gutters of Stamboul? O wretched impostor!
How could he stand against the three-legged woman and the
man with his eye in his cheek? How would he blush in
presence of the man with fingers on his elbow? Where would
he hide himself when the dwarf with seven fingers on each
hand, no upper lip, and his underjaw gone came down in his
majesty? Bismillah! The cripples of Europe are a delusion
and a fraud. The truly gifted flourish only in the byways of
Pera and Stamboul.

That three-legged woman lay on the bridge, with her stock
in trade so disposed as to command the most striking effect
—one natural leg and two long, slender, twisted ones with feet
on them like somebody else's forearm. Then there was a
man further along who had no eyes, and whose face was the
color of a fly-blown beefsteak and wrinkled and twisted like
a lava flow—and verily so tumbled and distorted were his
features that no man could tell the wart that served him
for a nose from his cheekbones. In Stamboul was a man
with a prodigious head, an uncommonly long body, legs eight
inches long, and feet like snowshoes. He traveled on those
feet and his hands, and was as swaybacked as if the Colossus
of Rhodes had been riding him. Ah, a beggar has to have
exceedingly good points to make a living in Constantinople.
A blue-faced man, who had nothing to offer except that he had
been blown up in a mine, would be regarded as a rank impostor, and a mere damaged soldier on crutches would never

make a cent. It would pay him to get a piece of his head
taken off and cultivate a wen like a carpet sack.

The mosque of St. Sophia is the chief lion of Constantinople. You must get a firman and hurry there the first thing.
We did that. We did not get a firman, but we took along
four or five francs apiece, which is much the same thing.

I do not think much of the mosque of St. Sophia. I suppose I lack appreciation. We will let it go at that. It is the
rustiest old barn in heathendom. I believe all the interest that
attaches to it comes from the fact that it was built for a
Christian church and then turned into a mosque, without
much alteration, by the Muhammadan conquerors of the
land. They made me take off my boots and walk into the
place in my stocking feet. I caught cold and got myself so
stuck up with a complication of gums, slime, and general
corruption that I wore out more than two thousand pair of
bootjacks getting my boots off that night, and even then some
Christian hide peeled off with them. I abate not a single boot-
jack.

St. Sophia is a colossal church, thirteen or fourteen hundred years old, and unsightly enough to be very, very much
older. Its immense dome is said to be more wonderful than
St. Peter's, but its dirt is much more wonderful than its dome,
though they never mention it. The church has a hundred and
seventy pillars in it, each a single piece, and all of costly
marbles of various kinds, but they came from ancient temples
at Baalbek, Heliopolis, Athens, and Ephesus, and are battered,
ugly, and repulsive. They were a thousand years old when this
church was new, and then the contrast must have been ghastly
—if Justinian's architects did not trim them any. The inside
of the dome is figured all over with a monstrous inscription in
Turkish characters, wrought in gold mosaic, that looks as
glaring as a circus bill; the pavements and the marble balustrades are all battered and dirty; the perspective is marred
everywhere by a web of ropes that depend from the dizzy
height of the dome and suspend countless dingy, coarse oil
lamps and ostrich eggs six or seven feet above the floor.
Squatting and sitting in groups, here and there and far and
near, were ragged Turks reading books, hearing sermons, or
receiving lessons like children, and in fifty places were more
of the same sort bowing and straightening up, bowing again
and getting down to kiss the earth, muttering prayers the

while, and keeping up their gymnastics till they ought to have been tired if they were not.

Everywhere was dirt and dust and dinginess and gloom; everywhere were signs of a hoary antiquity, but with nothing touching or beautiful about it; everywhere were those groups of fantastic pagans; overhead the gaudy mosaics and the web of lamp ropes—nowhere was there anything to win one's love or challenge his admiration.

The people who go into ecstasies over St. Sophia must surely get them out of the guidebook (where every church is spoken of as being "considered by good judges to be the most marvelous structure, in many respects, that the world has ever seen"). Or else they are those old connoisseurs from the wilds of New Jersey who laboriously learn the difference between a fresco and a fireplug and from that day forward feel privileged to void their critical bathos on painting, sculpture, and architecture forevermore.

We visited the dancing dervishes. There were twenty-one of them. They wore a long, light-colored, loose robe that hung to their heels. Each in his turn went up to the priest (they were all within a large circular railing) and bowed profoundly and then went spinning away deliriously and took his appointed place in the circle and continued to spin. When all had spun themselves to their places, they were about five or six feet apart—and so situated, the entire circle of spinning pagans spun itself three separate times around the room. It took twenty-five minutes to do it. They spun on the left foot, and kept themselves going by passing the right rapidly before it and digging it against the waxed floor. Some of them made incredible "time." Most of them spun around forty times in a minute, and one artist averaged about sixty-one times a minute and kept it up during the whole twenty-five. His robe filled with air and stood out all around him like a balloon.

They made no noise of any kind, and most of them tilted their heads back and closed their eyes, entranced with a sort of devotional ecstasy. There was a rude kind of music part of the time, but the musicians were not visible. None but spinners were allowed within the circle. A man had to either spin or stay outside. It was about as barbarous an exhibition as we have witnessed yet. Then sick persons came and lay down, and beside them women laid their sick children (one a babe at the breast), and the patriarch of the dervishes walked upon their bodies. He was supposed to cure their diseases by trampling upon their breasts or backs or standing on the back of their necks. This is well enough for a people who think all their affairs are made or marred by viewless spirits of the air—by giants, gnomes, and genii—and who still believe to this day all the wild tales in *The Arabian Nights*. Even so an intelligent missionary tells me.

We visited the Thousand and One Columns. I do not know what it was originally intended for, but they said it was built for a reservoir. It is situated in the center of Constantinople. You go down a flight of stone steps in the middle of a barren place, and there you are. You are forty feet underground and in the midst of a perfect wilderness of tall, slender, granite columns of Byzantine architecture. Stand where you would or change your position as often as you pleased, you were always a center from which radiated a dozen long archways and colonnades that lost themselves in distance and the somber twilight of the place. This old dried-up reservoir is occupied by a few ghostly silk-spinners now, and one of them showed me a cross cut high up in one of the pillars. I suppose he meant me to understand that the institution was there before the Turkish occupation, and I thought he made a remark to that effect; but he must have had an impediment in his speech, for I did not understand him.

We took off our shoes and went into the marble mausoleum of the Sultan Mahmud, the neatest piece of architecture, inside, that I have seen lately. Mahmud's tomb was covered with a black velvet pall, which was elaborately embroidered with silver; it stood within a fancy silver railing; at the sides and corners were silver candlesticks that would weigh more than a hundred pounds, and they supported candles as large as a man's leg; on the top of the sarcophagus was a fez with a handsome diamond ornament upon it, which an attendant said cost a hundred thousand pounds, and lied like a Turk when he said it. Mahmud's whole family were comfortably planted around him.

We went to the Great Bazaar in Stamboul, of course, and I shall not describe it further than to say it is a monstrous hive of little shops—thousands, I should say—all under one roof and cut up into innumerable little blocks by narrow streets which are arched overhead. One street is devoted to a particular kind of merchandise, another to another, and so on. When you wish to buy a pair of shoes you have the swing of the whole street—you do not have to walk yourself down hunting stores in different localities. It is the same with silks, antiquities, shawls, etc. The place is crowded with people all the time, and as the gay-colored Eastern fabrics are lavishly displayed before every shop, the Great Bazaar of Stamboul is one of the sights that are worth seeing. It is full of life and stir and business, dirt, beggars, asses, yelling peddlers, porters, dervishes, high-born Turkish female shoppers, Greeks, and weird-looking and weirdly dressed Muhammadans from the mountains and the far provinces—and the only solitary thing one does not smell when he is in the Great Bazaar is something which smells good.

34

Mosques are plenty, churches are plenty, graveyards are plenty, but morals and whiskey are scarce. The Koran does not permit Muhammadans to drink. Their natural instincts do not permit them to be moral. They say the Sultan has eight hundred wives. This almost amounts to bigamy. It makes our cheeks burn with shame to see such a thing permitted here in Turkey. We do not mind it so much in Salt Lake, however.

Circassian and Georgian girls are still sold in Constantinople by their parents, but not publicly. The great slave marts we have all read so much about—where tender young girls were stripped for inspection and criticized and discussed just as if they were horses at an agricultural fair—no longer exist. The exhibition and the sales are private now. Stocks are up just at present, partly because of a brisk demand created by the recent return of the Sultan's suite from the courts of Europe; partly on account of an unusual abundance of breadstuffs, which leaves holders untortured by hunger and enables them to hold back for high prices; and partly because buyers are too weak to bear the market while sellers are amply prepared to bull it. Under these circumstances, if the American metropolitan newspapers were published here in Constantinople, their next commercial report would read about as follows, I suppose:

SLAVE-GIRL MARKET REPORT

Best brands Circassians, crop of 1850, £200; 1852, £250; 1854, £300. Best brands Georgian, none in market; second quality, 1851, £180. Nineteen fair to middling Wallachian girls offered at £130 @150, but no takers; sixteen prime A 1 sold in small lots to close out—terms private.

Sales of one lot Circassians, prime to good, 1852 to 1854, at £240 @ 242½, buyer 30; one forty-niner—damaged—at £23, seller ten, no deposit. Several Georgians, fancy brands, 1852, changed hands to fill orders. The Georgians now on hand are mostly last year's crop, which was unusually poor. The new crop is a little backward, but will be coming in shortly. As regards its quantity and quality, the accounts are most encouraging. In this connection we can safely say, also, that the new crop of Circassians is looking extremely well. His Majesty the Sultan has already sent in large orders for his new harem, which will be finished within a fortnight, and this has naturally strengthened the market and given Circassian stock a strong upward tendency. Taking advantage of the inflated market, many of our shrewdest operators are selling short. There are hints of a "corner" on Wallachians.

There is nothing new in Nubians. Slow sale.

Eunuchs—none offering; however, large cargoes are expected from Egypt today.

I think the above would be about the style of the commercial report. Prices are pretty high now and holders firm; but two or three years ago parents in a starving condition brought their young daughters down here and sold them for even twenty and thirty dollars when they could do no better, simply to save themselves and the girls from dying of want. It is sad to think of so distressing a thing as this, and I for one am sincerely glad the prices are up again.

Commercial morals, especially, are bad. There is no gainsaying that. Greek, Turkish, and Armenian morals consist only in attending church regularly on the appointed Sabbaths and in breaking the Ten Commandments all the balance of the week. It comes natural to them to lie and cheat in the first place, and then they go on and improve on nature until they arrive at perfection. In recommending his son to a merchant as a valuable salesman, a father does not say he is a nice, moral, upright boy and goes to Sunday School and is honest, but he says, "This boy is worth his weight in broad pieces of a hundred—for behold, he will cheat whomsoever hath dealings with him, and from the Euxine to the waters of Marmara there abideth not so gifted a liar!" How is that for a recommendation? The missionaries tell me that they hear encomiums like that passed upon people every day. They say of a person they admire, "Ah, he is a charming swindler and a most exquisite liar!"

Everybody lies and cheats—everybody who is in business, at any rate. Even foreigners soon have to come down to the custom of the country, and they do not buy and sell long in Constantinople till they lie and cheat like a Greek. I say like a Greek, because the Greeks are called the worst transgressors in this line. Several Americans long resident in Constantinople contend that most Turks are pretty trustworthy, but few claim that the Greeks have any virtues that a man can discover—at least without a fire assay.

I am half willing to believe that the celebrated dogs of Constantinople have been misrepresented—slandered. I have always been led to suppose that they were so thick in the streets that they blocked the way; that they moved about in organized companies, platoons, and regiments and took what they wanted by determined and ferocious assault; and that at night they drowned all other sounds with their terrible howlings. The dogs I see here cannot be those I have read of.

I find them everywhere, but not in strong force. The most I have found together has been about ten or twenty. And night or day a fair proportion of them were sound asleep. Those that were not asleep always looked as if they wanted to be. I never saw such utterly wretched, starving, sad-visaged, brokenhearted looking curs in my life. It seemed a grim satire to accuse such brutes as these of taking things by force of arms. They hardly seemed to have strength enough or ambition enough to walk across the street—I do not know that I have seen one walk that far yet. They are mangy and bruised and mutilated, and often you see one with the hair singed off him in such wide and well-defined tracts that he looks like a map of the new territories. They are the sorriest beasts that breathe—the most abject—the most pitiful. In their faces is a settled expression of melancholy, an air of hopeless despondency. The hairless patches on a scalded dog are preferred by the fleas of Constantinople to a wider range on a healthier dog, and the exposed places suit the fleas exactly. I saw a dog of this kind start to nibble at a flea—a fly attracted his attention and he made a snatch at him; the flea called for him once more, and that forever unsettled him; he looked sadly at his flea pasture, then sadly looked at his bald spot. Then he heaved a sigh and dropped his head resignedly upon his paws. He was not equal to the situation.

The dogs sleep in the streets, all over the city. From one end of the street to the other, I suppose they will average about eight or ten to a block. Sometimes, of course, there are fifteen or twenty to a block. They do not belong to anybody, and they seem to have no close personal friendships among each other. But they district the city themselves, and the dogs of each district, whether it be half a block in extent or ten blocks, have to remain within its bounds. Woe to a dog if he crosses the line! His neighbors would snatch the balance of his hair off in a second. So it is said. But they don't look it.

They sleep in the streets these days. They are my compass—my guide. When I see the dogs sleep placidly on while men, sheep, geese, and all moving things turn out and go around them, I know I am not in the great street where the hotel is, and must go further. In the Grand Rue the dogs have a sort of air of being on the lookout—an air born of being obliged to get out of the way of many carriages every day—and that expression one recognizes in a moment. It does not exist upon the face of any dog without the confines of that street. All others sleep placidly and keep no watch. They would not move, though the Sultan himself passed by.

In one narrow street (but none of them are wide) I saw three dogs lying coiled up about a foot or two apart. End to end they lay, and so they just bridged the street neatly from gutter to gutter. A drove of a hundred sheep came along. They stepped right over the dogs, the rear crowding the front, impatient to get on. The dogs looked lazily up, flinched a little when the impatient feet of the sheep touched their raw backs—sighed and lay peacefully down again. No talk could be plainer than that. So some of the sheep jumped over them and others scrambled between, occasionally chipping a leg with their sharp hoofs, and when the whole flock had made the trip, the dogs sneezed a little in the cloud of dust, but never budged their bodies an inch. I thought I was lazy, but I am a steam engine compared to a Constantinople dog. But was not that a singular scene for a city of a million inhabitants?

These dogs are the scavengers of the city. That is their official position, and a hard one it is. However, it is their protection. But for their usefulness in partially cleansing these terrible streets, they would not be tolerated long. They eat anything and everything that comes in their way, from melon rinds and spoiled grapes up through all the grades and species of dirt and refuse to their own dead friends and relatives—and yet they are always lean, always hungry, always despondent. The people are loath to kill them—do not kill them, in fact. The Turks have an innate antipathy to taking the life of any dumb animal, it is said. But they do worse. They hang and kick and stone and scald these wretched creatures to the very verge of death, and then leave them to live and suffer.

Once a sultan proposed to kill off all the dogs here and did begin the work—but the populace raised such a howl of horror about it that the massacre was stayed. After a while he proposed to remove them all to an island in the Sea of Marmara. No objection was offered, and a shipload or so was taken away. But when it came to be known that somehow or other the dogs never got to the island, but always fell overboard in the night and perished, another howl was raised and the transportation scheme was dropped.

So the dogs remain in peaceable possession of the streets. I do not say that they do not howl at night, nor that they do not attack people who have not a red fez on their heads. I only say that it would be mean for *me* to accuse them of these unseemly things who have not seen them do them with my own eyes or heard them with my own ears.

I was a little surprised to see Turks and Greeks playing newsboy right here in the mysterious land where the giants and genii of *The Arabian Nights* once dwelt—where winged horses and hydra-headed dragons guarded enchanted castles —where princes and princesses flew through the air on carpets that obeyed a mystic talisman—where cities whose houses were made of precious stones sprang up in a night under the hand of the magician—and where busy marts were suddenly stricken with a spell and each citizen lay or sat or stood with weapon raised or foot advanced, just as he was, speechless and motionless, till time had told a hundred years!

It was curious to see newsboys selling papers in so dreamy a land as that. And, to say truly, it is comparatively a new thing here. The selling of newspapers had its birth in Constantinople about a year ago, and was a child of the Prussian and Austrian war.

There is one paper published here in the English language—the *Levant Herald*—and there are generally a number of Greek and a few French papers rising and falling, struggling up and falling again. Newspapers are not popular with the Sultan's government. They do not understand journalism. The proverb says, "The unknown is always great." To the court, the newspaper is a mysterious and rascally institution. They know what a pestilence is because they have one occasionally that thins the people out at the rate of two thousand a day, and they regard a newspaper as a mild form of pestilence. When it goes astray, they suppress it—pounce upon it without warning and throttle it. When it don't go astray for a long time, they get suspicious and throttle it anyhow, because they think it is hatching deviltry. Imagine the Grand Vizier in solemn council with the magnates of the realm, spelling his way through the hated newspaper, and finally delivering his profound decision: "This thing means mischief—it is too darkly, too suspiciously inoffensive—suppress it! Warn the publisher that we cannot have this sort of thing; put the editor in prison!"

The newspaper business has its inconveniences in Constantinople. Two Greek papers and one French one were suppressed here within a few days of each other. No victories of the Cretans are allowed to be printed. From time to time the Grand Vizier sends a notice to the various editors that the Cretan insurrection is entirely suppressed, and although that editor knows better, he still has to print the notice. The *Levant Herald* is too fond of speaking praisefully of Americans to be popular with the Sultan, who does not relish our sympathy with the Cretans, and therefore that paper has to be particularly circumspect in order to keep out of trouble. Once the editor, forgetting the official notice in his paper that the Cretans were crushed out, printed a letter of a very different tenor from the American consul in

Crete, and was fined two hundred and fifty dollars for it. Shortly he printed another from the same source, and was imprisoned three months for his pains. I think I could get the assistant editorship of the *Levant Herald,* but I am going to try to worry along without it.

To suppress a paper here involves the ruin of the publisher almost. But in Naples I think they speculate on misfortunes of that kind. Papers are suppressed there every day, and spring up the next day under a new name. During the ten days or a fortnight we stayed there one paper was murdered and resurrected twice. The newsboys are smart there, just as they are elsewhere. They take advantage of popular weaknesses. When they find they are not likely to sell out, they approach a citizen mysteriously and say in a low voice, "Last copy, sir; double price; paper just been suppressed!" The man buys it, of course, and finds nothing in it. They do say—I do not vouch for it, but they do say— that men sometimes print a vast edition of a paper, with a ferociously seditious article in it, distribute it quickly among the newsboys, and clear out till the government's indignation cools. It pays well. Confiscation don't amount to anything. The type and presses are not worth taking care of.

There is only one English newspaper in Naples. It has seventy subscribers. The publisher is getting rich very deliberately—very deliberately indeed.

I never shall want another Turkish lunch. The cooking apparatus was in the little lunchroom near the bazaar, and it was all open to the street. The cook was slovenly, and so was the table, and it had no cloth on it. The fellow took a mass of sausage meat and coated it round a wire and laid it on a charcoal fire to cook. When it was done, he laid it aside and a dog walked sadly in and nipped it. He smelled it first and probably recognized the remains of a friend. The cook took it away from him and laid it before us. Jack said, "I pass"—he plays euchre sometimes—and we all passed in turn. Then the cook baked a broad, flat, wheaten cake, greased it well with the sausage, and started toward us with it. It dropped in the dirt, and he picked it up and polished it on his breeches and laid it before us. Jack said, "I pass." We all passed. He put some eggs in a frying pan and stood pensively prying slabs of meat from between his teeth with a fork. Then he used the fork to turn the eggs with—and brought them along. Jack said, "Pass again." All followed suit. We did not know what to do, and so we ordered a new ration of sausage. The cook got out his wire, apportioned a proper amount of sausage meat, spat it on his hands, and fell to work! This time, with one accord, we all passed out. We paid and left. This is all I learned about Turkish lunches. A Turkish lunch is good, no doubt, but it has its little drawbacks.

When I think how I have been swindled by books of Oriental travel, I want a tourist for breakfast. For years and years I have dreamed of the wonders of the Turkish bath; for years and years I have promised myself that I would yet enjoy one. Many and many a time in fancy I have lain in the marble bath and breathed the slumbrous fragrance of Eastern spices that filled the air; then passed through a weird and complicated system of pulling and hauling, and drenching and scrubbing, by a gang of naked savages who loomed vast and vaguely through the steaming mists like demons; then rested for a while on a divan fit for a king; then passed through another complex ordeal, and one more fearful than the first; and finally, swathed in soft fabrics, been conveyed to a princely saloon and laid on a bed of eiderdown, where eunuchs, gorgeous of costume, fanned me while I drowsed and dreamed or contentedly gazed at the rich hangings of the apartment, the soft carpets, the sumptuous furniture, the pictures, and drank delicious coffee, smoked the soothing narghile, and dropped, at the last, into tranquil repose, lulled by sensuous odors from unseen censers, by the gentle influence of the narghile's Persian tobacco, and by the music of fountains that counterfeited the pattering of summer rain.

That was the picture just as I got it from incendiary books of travel. It was a poor, miserable imposture. The reality is no more like it than the Five Points are like the Garden of Eden. They received me in a great court, paved with marble slabs; around it were broad galleries, one above another, carpeted with seedy matting, railed with unpainted balustrades, and furnished with huge rickety chairs, cushioned with rusty old mattresses, indented with impressions left by the forms of nine successive generations of men who had reposed upon them. The place was vast, naked, dreary; its court a barn, its galleries stalls for human horses. The cadaverous, half-nude varlets that served in the establishment had nothing of poetry in their appearance, nothing of romance, nothing of Oriental splendor. They shed no entrancing odors—just the contrary. Their hungry eyes and their lank forms continually suggested one glaring, unsentimental fact—they wanted what they term in California "a square meal."

I went into one of the racks and undressed. An unclean starveling wrapped a gaudy tablecloth about his loins and hung a white rag over my shoulders. If I had had a tub then, it would have come natural to me to take in washing. I was then conducted downstairs into the wet, slippery court, and the first things that attracted my attention were my heels. My fall excited no comment. They expected it, no doubt. It belonged in the list of softening, sensuous influences peculiar to this home of Eastern luxury. It was softening enough, certainly, but its application was not happy. They now gave me a pair of wooden clogs—benches in miniature with leather straps over them to confine my feet (which they would have done, only I do not wear No. 13s). These things dangled uncomfortably by the straps when I lifted up my feet, and came down in awkward and unexpected places when I put them on the floor again, and sometimes turned sideways and wrenched my ankles out of joint. However, it was all Oriental luxury, and I did what I could to enjoy it.

They put me in another part of the barn and laid me on a stuffy sort of pallet, which was not made of cloth of gold or Persian shawls, but was merely the unpretending sort of thing I have seen in the Negro quarters of Arkansas. There was nothing whatever in this dim marble prison but five more of these biers. It was a very solemn place. I expected that the spiced odors of Araby were going to steal over my senses now, but they did not. A copper-colored skeleton, with a rag around him, brought me a glass decanter of water, with a lighted tobacco pipe in the top of it, and a pliant stem a yard long with a brass mouthpiece to it.

It was the famous "narghile" of the East—the thing the Grand Turk smokes in the pictures. This began to look like luxury. I took one blast at it, and it was sufficient; the smoke went in a great volume down into my stomach, my lungs, even into the uttermost parts of my frame. I exploded one mighty cough, and it was as if Vesuvius had let go. For the next five minutes I smoked at every pore, like a frame house that is on fire on the inside. Not any more narghile for me. The smoke had a vile taste, and the taste of a thousand infidel tongues that remained on that brass mouthpiece was viler still. I was getting discouraged. Whenever hereafter I see the cross-legged Grand Turk smoking his narghile, in pretended bliss, on the outside of a paper of Connecticut tobacco, I shall know him for the shameless humbug he is.

This prison was filled with hot air. When I had got warmed up sufficiently to prepare me for a still warmer temperature, they took me where it was—into a marble room, wet, slippery, and steamy, and laid me out on a raised platform in the center. It was very warm. Presently my man sat me down by a tank of hot water, drenched me well, gloved his hand with a coarse mitten, and began to polish me all over with it. I began to smell disagreeably. The more he polished, the worse I smelled. It was alarming. I said to him:

"I perceive that I am pretty far gone. It is plain that I ought to be buried without any unnecessary delay. Perhaps you had better go after my friends at once, because the weather is warm and I cannot 'keep' long."

He went on scrubbing and paid no attention. I soon saw that he was reducing my size. He bore hard on his mitten, and from under it rolled little cylinders, like maccaroni. It could not be dirt, for it was too white. He pared me down in this way for a long time. Finally I said:

"It is a tedious process. It will take hours to trim me to the size you want me; I will wait; go and borrow a jack plane."

He paid no attention at all.

After a while he brought a basin, some soap, and something that seemed to be the tail of a horse. He made up a prodigious quantity of soapsuds, deluged me with them from head to foot, without warning me to shut my eyes, and then swabbed me viciously with the horsetail. Then he left me there, a snowy statue of lather, and went away. When I got tired of waiting I went and hunted him up. He was propped against the wall, in another room, asleep. I woke him. He was not disconcerted. He took me back and flooded me with hot water, then turbaned my head, swathed me with dry tablecloths, and conducted me to a latticed chicken coop in one of the galleries, and pointed to one of those Arkansas beds. I mounted it and vaguely expected the odors of Araby again. They did not come.

The blank, unornamented coop had nothing about it of that Oriental voluptuousness one reads of so much. It was more suggestive of the county hospital than anything else.

The skinny servitor brought a narghile, and I got him to take it out again without wasting any time about it. Then he brought the world-renowned Turkish coffee that poets have sung so rapturously for many generations, and I seized upon it as the last hope that was left of my old dreams of Eastern luxury. It was another fraud. Of all the unchristian beverages that ever passed my lips, Turkish coffee is the worst. The cup is small, it is smeared with grounds; the coffee is black, thick, unsavory of smell, and execrable in taste. The bottom of the cup has a muddy sediment in it half an inch deep. This goes down your throat, and portions of it lodge by the way and produce a tickling aggravation that keeps you barking and coughing for an hour.

Here endeth my experience of the celebrated Turkish bath, and here also endeth my dream of the bliss the mortal revels in who passes through it. It is a malignant swindle. The man who enjoys it is qualified to enjoy anything that is repulsive to sight or sense, and he that can invest it with a charm of poetry is able to do the same with anything else in the world that is tedious, and wretched, and dismal, and nasty.

35

We left a dozen passengers in Constantinople and sailed through the beautiful Bosporus and far up into the Black Sea. We left them in the clutches of the celebrated Turkish guide "FARAWAY MOSES," who will seduce them into buying a ship-load of attar of roses, splendid Turkish vestments, and all manner of curious things they can never have any use for. Murray's invaluable guidebooks have mentioned Faraway Moses' name, and he is a made man. He rejoices daily in the fact that he is a recognized celebrity. However, we cannot alter our established customs to please the whims of guides; we cannot show partialities this late in the day. Therefore, ignoring this fellow's brilliant fame, and ignoring the fanciful name he takes such pride in, we called him Ferguson, just as we had done with all other guides. It has kept him in a state of smothered exasperation all the time. Yet we meant him no harm. After he has gotten himself up, regardless of expense, in showy, baggy trousers, yellow, pointed slippers, fiery fez, silken jacket of blue, voluminous waist sash of fancy Persian stuff filled with a battery of silver-mounted horse pistols, and has strapped on his terrible scimitar, he considers it an unspeakable humiliation to be called Ferguson. It cannot be helped. All guides are Fergusons to us. We cannot master their dreadful foreign names.

Sevastopol is probably the worst battered town in Russia or anywhere else. But we ought to be pleased with it nevertheless, for we have been in no country yet where we have been so kindly received and where we felt that to be Americans was a sufficient visa for our passports. The moment the anchor was down, the governor of the town immediately dispatched an officer on board to inquire if he could be of any assistance to us, and to invite us to make ourselves at home in Sevastopol! If you know Russia, you know that this was a wild stretch of hospitality. They are usually so suspicious of strangers that they worry them excessively with the delays and aggravations incident to a complicated passport system. Had we come from any other country, we could not have had permission to enter Sevastopol and leave again under three days—but as it was, we were at liberty to go and come when and where we pleased. Everybody in Constantinople warned us to be very careful about our passports, see that they were strictly *en regle*, and never to mislay them for a moment; and they told us of numerous instances of Englishmen and others who were delayed days, weeks, and even months in Sevastopol, on account of trifling informalities in their passports and for which they were not to blame. I had lost my passport and was traveling under my roommate's, who stayed behind in Constantinople to await our return. To read the description of him in that passport and then look at me, any man could see that I was no more like him than I am like Hercules. So I went into the harbor of Sevastopol with fear and trembling—full of a vague, horrible apprehension that I was going to be found out and hanged. But all that time my true passport had been floating gallantly overhead—and behold it was only our flag. They never asked us for any other.

We have had a great many Russian and English gentlemen and ladies on board today, and the time has passed cheer-

fully away. They were all happy-spirited people, and I never
heard our mother tongue sound so pleasantly as it did when
it fell from those English lips in this far-off land. I talked to
the Russians a good deal, just to be friendly, and they talked
to me from the same motive; I am sure that both enjoyed the
conversation, but never a word of it either of us understood.
I did most of my talking to those English people, though, and
I am sorry we cannot carry some of them along with us.

We have gone whithersoever we chose today and have met
with nothing but the kindest attentions. Nobody inquired
whether we had any passports or not.

Several of the officers of the government have suggested
that we take the ship to a little watering place thirty miles
from here, and pay the Emperor of Russia a visit. He is
rusticating there. These officers said they would take it upon
themselves to ensure us a cordial reception. They said if we
would go, they would not only telegraph the Emperor, but
send a special courier overland to announce our coming. Our
time is so short, though, and more especially our coal is so
nearly out, that we judged it best to forgo the rare pleasure
of holding social intercourse with an emperor.

Ruined Pompeii is in good condition compared to Sevastopol. Here you may look in whatsoever direction you please,
and your eye encounters scarcely anything but ruin, ruin,
ruin! Fragments of houses, crumbled walls, torn and ragged
hills, devastation everywhere! It is as if a mighty earthquake
had spent all its terrible forces upon this one little spot. For
eighteen long months the storms of war beat upon the helpless town and left it at last the saddest wreck that ever the
sun has looked upon. Not one solitary house escaped unscathed—not one remained habitable, even. Such utter and
complete ruin one could hardly conceive of. The houses had
all been solid, dressed stone structures; most of them were
plowed through and through by cannon balls—unroofed and
sliced down from eaves to foundation—and now a row of
them, half a mile long, looks merely like an endless procession of battered chimneys. No semblance of a house remains
in such as these. Some of the larger buildings had corners
knocked off, pillars cut in two, cornices smashed, holes driven
straight through the walls. Many of these holes are as round
and as cleanly cut as if they had been made with an auger.
Others are half pierced through, and the clean impression is
there in the rock, as smooth and as shapely as if it were

done in putty. Here and there a ball still sticks in a wall, and from it iron tears trickle down and discolor the stone.

The battlefields were pretty close together. The Malakoff tower is on a hill which is right in the edge of the town. The Redan was within rifle shot of the Malakoff, Inkerman was a mile away, and Balaklava removed but an hour's ride. The French trenches, by which they approached and invested the Malakoff, were carried so close under its sloping sides that one might have stood by the Russian guns and tossed a stone into them. Repeatedly, during three terrible days, they swarmed up the little Malakoff hill, and were beaten back with terrible slaughter. Finally they captured the place and drove the Russians out, who then tried to retreat into the town, but the English had taken the Redan and shut them off with a wall of flame; there was nothing for them to do but go back and retake the Malakoff or die under its guns. They did go back; they took the Malakoff and retook it two or three times, but their desperate valor could not avail, and they had to give up at last.

These fearful fields, where such tempests of death used to rage, are peaceful enough now; no sound is heard, hardly a living thing moves about them, they are lonely and silent— their desolation is complete.

There was nothing else to do, and so everybody went to hunting relics. They have stocked the ship with them. They brought them from the Malakoff, from the Redan, Inkerman, Balaklava—everywhere. They have brought cannon balls, broken ramrods, fragments of shell—iron enough to freight a sloop. Some have even brought bones—brought them laboriously from great distances—and were grieved to hear the surgeon pronounce them only bones of mules and oxen. I knew Blucher would not lose an opportunity like this. He brought a sackful on board and was going for another. I prevailed upon him not to go. He has already turned his stateroom into a museum of worthless trumpery, which he has gathered up in his travels. He is labeling his trophies now. I picked up one a while ago and found it marked "Fragment of a Russian General." I carried it out to get a better light upon it—it was nothing but a couple of teeth and part of the jawbone of a horse. I said with some asperity:

"Fragment of a Russian General! This is absurd. Are you never going to learn any sense?"

He only said: "Go slow—the old woman won't know any different." [His aunt.]

This person gathers mementos with a perfect recklessness nowadays, mixes them all up together, and then serenely labels them without any regard to truth, propriety, or even plausibility. I have found him breaking a stone in two and labeling half of it "Chunk busted from the pulpit of Demosthenes" and the other half "Darnick from the Tomb of Abelard and Héloïse." I have known him to gather up a handful of pebbles by the roadside, and bring them on board ship and label them as coming from twenty celebrated localities five hundred miles apart. I remonstrate against these outrages upon reason and truth, of course, but it does no good. I get the same tranquil, unanswerable reply every time:

"It don't signify—the old woman won't know any different."

Ever since we three or four fortunate ones made the midnight trip to Athens, it has afforded him genuine satisfaction to give everybody in the ship a pebble from the Mars Hill where St. Paul preached. He got all those pebbles on the seashore abreast the ship, but professes to have gathered them from one of our party. However, it is not of any use for me to expose the deception—it affords him pleasure and does no harm to anybody. He says he never expects to run out of mementos of St. Paul as long as he is in reach of a sandbank. Well, he is no worse than others. I notice that all travelers supply deficiencies in their collections in the same way. I shall never have any confidence in such things again while I live.

36

We have got so far east now—a hundred and fifty-five degrees of longitude from San Francisco—that my watch cannot "keep the hang" of the time anymore. It has grown discouraged and stopped. I think it did a wise thing. The difference in time between Sevastopol and the Pacific coast is enormous. When it is six o'clock in the morning here, it is somewhere about week before last in California. We are excusable for getting a little tangled as to time. These distractions and distresses about the time have worried me so much that I was afraid my mind was so much affected that I never would have any appreciation of time again; but when I noticed how handy I was yet about comprehending when it was dinnertime, a blessed tranquillity settled down upon me, and I am tortured with doubts and fears no more.

Odessa is about twenty hours' run from Sevastopol and is the most northerly port in the Black Sea. We came here to get coal principally. The city has a population of one hundred and thirty-three thousand, and is growing faster than any other small city out of America. It is a free port and is the great grain mart of this particular part of the world. Its roadstead is full of ships. Engineers are at work now turning the open roadstead into a spacious artificial harbor. It is to be almost enclosed by massive stone piers, one of which will extend into the sea over three thousand feet in a straight line.

I have not felt so much at home for a long time as I did when I "raised the hill" and stood in Odessa for the first time. It looked just like an American city: fine, broad streets and straight as well; low houses (two or three stories), wide, neat, and free from any quaintness of architectural ornamentation; locust trees bordering the sidewalks (they call them acacias); a stirring, business look about the streets and the stores; fast walkers; a familiar *new* look about the houses and everything; yea, and a driving and smothering cloud of dust that was so like a message from our own dear native land that we could hardly refrain from shedding a few grateful tears and execrations in the old time-honored American way. Look up the street or down the street, this way or that way, we saw only America! There was not one thing to remind us that we were in Russia. We walked for some little distance, reveling in this home vision, and then we came upon a church and a hack driver, and presto! the illusion vanished! The church had a slender-spired dome that rounded inward at its base and looked like a turnip turned upside down, and the hackman seemed to be dressed in a long petticoat without any hoops. These things were essentially foreign, and so were the carriages—but everybody knows about these things and there is no occasion for my describing them.

We were only to stay here a day and a night and take in coal; we consulted the guidebooks and were rejoiced to know that there were no sights in Odessa to see; and so we had one good, untrammeled holiday on our hands, with nothing to do but idle about the city and enjoy ourselves. We sauntered through the markets and criticized the fearful and wonderful costumes from the back country, examined the populace as far as eyes could do it, and closed the entertainment with an ice-cream debauch. We do not get ice cream everywhere, and so when we do we are apt to dissipate to excess. We never cared anything about ice cream at home, but we look upon it with a sort of idolatry now that it is so scarce in these red-hot climates of the East.

We only found two pieces of statuary, and this was another blessing. One was a bronze image of the Duc de Richelieu, grand-nephew of the splendid cardinal. It stood in a spacious, handsome promenade overlooking the sea, and from its base a vast flight of stone steps led down to the harbor—two hundred of them, fifty feet long, and a wide landing at the bottom of every twenty. It is a noble staircase, and from a distance the people toiling up it looked like insects. I mention this statue and this stairway because they have their story. Richelieu founded Odessa—watched over it with paternal care—labored with a fertile brain and a wise understanding for its best interests—spent his fortune freely to the same end—endowed it with a sound prosperity and one which will yet make it one of the great cities of the Old World—built this noble stairway with money from his own private purse —and— Well, the people for whom he had done so much let him walk down these same steps one day, unattended, old, poor, without a second coat to his back; and when, years afterwards, he died in Sevastopol in poverty and neglect, they called a meeting, subscribed liberally, and immediately erected this tasteful monument to his memory and named a great street after him. It reminds me of what Robert Burns' mother said when they erected a stately monument to his memory: "Ah, Robbie, ye asked them for bread and they hae gi'en ye a stane."

The people of Odessa have warmly recommended us to go and call on the Emperor, as did the Sevastopolians. They have telegraphed His Majesty, and he has signified his willingness to grant us an audience. So we are getting up the an-

chors and preparing to sail to his watering place. What a
scratching around there will be now! What a holding of important meetings and appointing of solemn committees! And
what a furbishing up of claw-hammer coats and white silk
neckties! As this fearful ordeal we are about to pass through
pictures itself to my fancy in all its dread sublimity, I begin
to feel my fierce desire to converse with a genuine emperor
cooling down and passing away. What am I to do with my
hands? What am I to do with my feet? What in the world
am I to do with myself?

37

We anchored here at Yalta, Russia, two or three days ago.
To me the place was a vision of the Sierras. The tall, gray
mountains that back it, their sides bristling with pines—
cloven with ravines—here and there a hoary rock towering
into view—long, straight streaks sweeping down from the
summit to the sea, marking the passage of some avalanche
of former times—all these were as like what one sees in the
Sierras as if the one were a portrait of the other. The little
village of Yalta nestles at the foot of an amphitheater which
slopes backward and upward to the wall of hills, and looks as
if it might have sunk quietly down to its present position from
a higher elevation. This depression is covered with the great
parks and gardens of noblemen, and through the mass of
green foliage the bright colors of their palaces bud out here
and there like flowers. It is a beautiful spot.

We had the United States Consul on board—the Odessa
Consul. We assembled in the cabin and commanded him to
tell us what we must do to be saved, and tell us quickly. He
made a speech. The first thing he said fell like a blight on
every hopeful spirit: he had never seen a court reception.
(Three groans for the Consul.) But he said he had seen recep-

tions at the Governor-General's in Odessa, and had often listened to people's experiences of receptions at the Russian and other courts, and believed he knew very well what sort of ordeal we were about to essay. (Hope budded again.) He said we were many; the summer palace was small—a mere mansion; doubtless we should be received in summer fashion —in the garden; we would stand in a row, all the gentlemen in swallowtail coats, white kids, and white neckties, and the ladies in light-colored silks or something of that kind; at the proper moment—12 meridian—the Emperor, attended by his suite arrayed in splendid uniforms, would appear and walk slowly along the line, bowing to some and saying two or three words to others. At the moment His Majesty appeared, a universal, delighted, enthusiastic smile ought to break out like a rash among the passengers—a smile of love, of gratification, of admiration—and with one accord, the party must begin to bow—not obsequiously, but respectfully, and with dignity; at the end of fifteen minutes the Emperor would go in the house, and we could run along home again. We felt immensely relieved. It seemed, in a manner, easy. There was not a man in the party but believed that with a little practice he could stand in a row, especially if there were others along; there was not a man but believed he could bow without tripping on his coattail and breaking his neck; in a word, we came to believe we were equal to any item in the performance except that complicated smile. The Consul also said we ought to draft a little address to the Emperor and present it to one of his aides-de-camp, who would forward it to him at the proper time. Therefore five gentlemen were appointed to prepare the document, and the fifty others went sadly smiling about the ship—practicing. During the next twelve hours we had the general appearance somehow of being at a funeral where everybody was sorry the death had occurred, but glad it was over—where everybody was smiling and yet brokenhearted.

A committee went ashore to wait on His Excellency the Governor-General and learn our fate. At the end of three hours of boding suspense they came back and said the Emperor would receive us at noon the next day—would send carriages for us—would hear the address in person. The Grand Duke Michael had sent to invite us to his palace also. Any man could see that there was an intention here to show that Russia's friendship for America was so genuine as to render even her private citizens objects worthy of kindly attentions.

At the appointed hour we drove out three miles and assembled in the handsome garden in front of the Emperor's palace.

We formed a circle under the trees before the door, for there was no one room in the house able to accommodate our threescore persons comfortably, and in a few minutes the imperial family came out, bowing and smiling, and stood in our midst. A number of great dignitaries of the empire, in undress uniforms, came with them. With every bow His Majesty said a word of welcome. I copy these speeches. There is character in them—Russian character—which is politeness itself, and the genuine article. The French are polite, but it is often mere ceremonious politeness. A Russian imbues his polite things with a heartiness, both of phrase and expression, that compels belief in their sincerity. As I was saying, the Czar punctuated his speeches with bows:

"Good morning—I am glad to see you—I am gratified—I am delighted—I am happy to receive you!"

All took off their hats, and the Consul inflicted the address on him. He bore it with unflinching fortitude, then took the rusty-looking document and handed it to some great officer or other, to be filed away among the archives of Russia—in the stove. He thanked us for the address and said he was very much pleased to see us, especially as such friendly relations existed between Russia and the United States. The Empress said the Americans were favorites in Russia, and she hoped the Russians were similarly regarded in America. These were all the speeches that were made, and I recommend them to parties who present policemen with gold watches as models of brevity and point. After this the Empress went and talked sociably (for an empress) with various ladies around the circle; several gentlemen entered into a disjointed general conversation with the Emperor; the dukes and princes, admirals and maids of honor, dropped into free-and-easy chat with first one and then another of our party, and whoever chose stepped forward and spoke with the modest little Grand Duchess Marie, the Czar's daughter. She is fourteen years old, light-haired, blue-eyed, unassuming, and pretty. Everybody talks English.

The Emperor wore a cap, frock coat, and pantaloons, all of some kind of plain white drilling—cotton or linen—and sported no jewelry or any insignia whatever of rank. No costume could be less ostentatious. He is very tall and spare, and a determined-looking man, though a very pleasant-looking one, nevertheless. It is easy to see that he is kind and affectionate. There is something very noble in his expression when his cap is off. There is none of that cunning in his eye that all of us noticed in Louis Napoleon's.

The Empress and the little Grand Duchess wore simple suits of foulard (or foulard silk, I don't know which is proper) with a small blue spot in it; the dresses were trimmed with blue; both ladies wore broad blue sashes about their waists, linen collars and clerical ties of muslin, low-crowned straw hats trimmed with blue velvet, parasols and flesh-colored gloves. The Grand Duchess had no heels on her shoes. I do not know this of my own knowledge, but one of our ladies told me so. I was not looking at her shoes. I was glad to observe that she wore her own hair, plaited in thick braids against the back of her head, instead of the uncomely thing they call a waterfall, which is about as much like a waterfall as a canvas-covered ham is like a cataract. Taking the kind expression that is in the Emperor's face and the gentleness that is in his young daughter's into consideration, I wondered if it would not tax the Czar's firmness to the utmost to condemn a supplicating wretch to misery in the wastes of Siberia if she pleaded for him. Every time their eyes met I saw more and more what a tremendous power that weak, diffident schoolgirl could wield if she chose to do it. Many and many a time she might rule the autocrat of Russia, whose lightest word is law to seventy millions of human beings! She was only a girl, and she looked like a thousand others I have seen, but never a girl provoked such a novel and peculiar interest in me before. A strange, new sensation is a rare thing in this humdrum life, and I had it here. There was nothing stale or worn out about the thoughts and feelings the situation and the circumstances created. It seemed strange—stranger than I can tell—to think that the central figure in the cluster of men and women, chatting here under the trees like the most ordinary individual in the land, was a man who could open his lips and ships would fly through the waves, locomotives would speed over the plains, couriers would hurry from village to village, a hundred telegraphs would flash the word to the four corners of an empire that stretches its vast proportions over a seventh part of the habitable globe, and a countless multitude of men would spring to do his bidding. I had a sort of vague desire to examine his hands and see if they were of flesh and blood, like other men's. Here was a man who could do this wonderful thing, and yet if I chose I could knock him down. The case was plain, but it seemed preposterous nevertheless—as preposterous as trying to knock down a mountain or wipe out a continent. If this man sprained his ankle, a million miles of telegraph would carry the news over mountains—valleys—uninhabited deserts—under the trackless sea—and ten thousand newspapers would prate of it; if he were grievously ill, all the nations would know it before the sun rose again; if he dropped lifeless where he stood, his fall might shake the thrones of half a world! If I could have stolen his coat, I would have done it. When I meet a man like that, I want something to remember him by.

As a general thing, we have been shown through palaces by some plush-legged filagreed flunky or other, who charged a franc for it; but after talking with the company half an hour, the Emperor of Russia and his family conducted us all through their mansion themselves. They made no charge. They seemed to take a real pleasure in it.

We spent half an hour idling through the palace, admiring the cozy apartments and the rich but eminently homelike appointments of the place, and then the imperial family bade our party a kind good-bye and proceeded to count the spoons.

An invitation was extended to us to visit the palace of the eldest son, the Crown Prince of Russia, which was near at hand. The young man was absent, but the dukes and countesses and princes went over the premises with us as leisurely as was the case at the Emperor's, and conversation continued as lively as ever.

It was a little after one o'clock now. We drove to the Grand Duke Michael's, a mile away, in response to his invitation previously given.

We arrived in twenty minutes from the Emperor's. It is a lovely place. The beautiful palace nestles among the grand old groves of the park, the park sits in the lap of the picturesque crags and hills, and both look out upon the breezy ocean. In the park are rustic seats, here and there, in secluded nooks that are dark with shade; there are rivulets of crystal water; there are lakelets, with inviting, grassy banks; there are glimpses of sparkling cascades through openings in the wilderness of foliage; there are streams of clear water gushing from mimic knots on the trunks of forest trees; there are miniature marble temples perched upon gray old crags; there are airy lookouts whence one may gaze upon a broad expanse of landscape and ocean. The palace is modeled after the choicest forms of Grecian architecture, and its wide colonnades surround a central court that is banked with rare flowers that fill the place with their fragrance, and in their midst springs a fountain that cools the summer air and may possibly breed mosquitoes, but I do not think it does.

The Grand Duke and his Duchess came out, and the presentation ceremonies were as simple as they had been at the Emperor's. In a few minutes conversation was under way, as before. The Empress appeared in the veranda, and the little Grand Duchess came out into the crowd. They had beaten us there. In a few minutes the Emperor came himself on horseback. It was very pleasant. You can appreciate it if you have ever visited royalty and felt occasionally that possibly you might be wearing out your welcome—though as a general thing, I believe, royalty is not scrupulous about discharging you when it is done with you.

The Grand Duke is the third brother of the Emperor, is about thirty-seven years old perhaps, and is the princeliest figure in Russia. He is even taller than the Czar, as straight as an Indian, and bears himself like one of those gorgeous knights we read about in romances of the Crusades. He looks like a great-hearted fellow who would pitch an enemy into the river in a moment and then jump in and risk his life fishing him out again. The stories they tell of him show him to be of a brave and generous nature. He must have been desirous of proving that Americans were welcome guests in the imperial palaces of Russia, because he rode all the way to Yalta and escorted our procession to the Emperor's himself, and kept his aids scurrying about clearing the road and offering assistance wherever it could be needed. We were rather familiar with him then because we did not know who he was. We recognized him now and appreciated the friendly spirit that prompted him to do us a favor that any other grand duke in the world would have doubtless declined to do. He had plenty of servitors whom he could have sent, but he chose to attend to the matter himself.

The Grand Duke was dressed in the handsome and showy uniform of a cossack officer. The Grand Duchess had on a white alpaca robe, with the seams and gores trimmed with black barb lace, and a little gray hat with a feather of the same color. She is young, rather pretty, modest, and unpretending, and full of winning politeness.

Our party walked all through the house, and then the nobility escorted them all over the grounds and finally brought them back to the palace about half-past two o'clock to breakfast. They called it breakfast, but we would have called it luncheon. It consisted of two kinds of wine; tea, bread, cheese, and cold meats, and was served on the center tables in the reception room and the verandas—anywhere that was convenient; there was no ceremony. It was a sort of picnic. I had heard before that we were to breakfast there, but Blucher said he believed Baker's boy had suggested it to His Imperial Highness. I think not—though it would be like him. Baker's boy is the famine-breeder of the ship. He is always hungry. They say he goes about the staterooms when the passengers are out and eats up all the soap. And they say he eats oakum. They say he will eat anything he can get between meals, but he prefers oakum. He does not like oakum for dinner, but he likes it for a lunch, at odd hours, or anything that way. It makes him very disagreeable, because it makes his breath bad and keeps his teeth all stuck up with tar. Baker's boy may have suggested the breakfast, but I hope he did not. It went off well anyhow. The illustrious host moved about from place to place and helped to destroy the provisions and keep the conversation lively, and the Grand Duchess talked with the veranda parties and such as had satisfied their appetites and straggled out from the reception room.

The Grand Duke's tea was delicious. They give one a lemon to squeeze into it or iced milk if he prefers it. The former is best. This tea is brought overland from China. It injures the article to transport it by sea.

When it was time to go, we bade our distinguished hosts good-bye, and they retired happy and contented to their apartments to count *their* spoons.

We had spent the best part of half a day in the home of royalty and had been as cheerful and comfortable all the time as we could have been in the ship. I would as soon have thought of being cheerful in Abraham's bosom as in the palace of an emperor. I supposed that emperors were terrible people. I thought they never did anything but wear magnificent crowns and red velvet dressing gowns with dabs of wool sewed on them in spots, and sit on thrones and scowl at the flunkies and the people in the parquet, and order dukes and duchesses off to execution. I find, however, that when one is so fortunate as to get behind the scenes and see them at home and in the privacy of their firesides, they are strangely like common mortals. They are pleasanter to look upon then than they are in their theatrical aspect. It seems to come as natural to them to dress and act like other people as it is to put a friend's cedar pencil in your pocket when you are done using it. But I can never have any confidence in the tinsel kings of the theater after this. It will be a great loss. I used to take such a thrilling pleasure in them. But hereafter I will turn me sadly away and say:

"This does not answer—this isn't the style of king that *I* am acquainted with."

When they swagger around the stage in jeweled crowns and splendid robes, I shall feel bound to observe that all the emperors that ever *I* was personally acquainted with wore the commonest sort of clothes and did not swagger. And when they come on the stage attended by a vast bodyguard of supes in helmets and tin breastplates, it will be my duty as well as my pleasure to inform the ignorant that no crowned head of my acquaintance has a soldier anywhere about his house or his person.

Possibly it may be thought that our party tarried too long or did other improper things, but such was not the case. The company felt that they were occupying an unusually responsible position—they were representing the people of America, not the government—and therefore they were careful to do their best to perform their high mission with credit.

On the other hand, the imperial families, no doubt, considered that in entertaining us they were more especially entertaining the people of America than they could by showering attentions on a whole platoon of ministers plenipotentiary; and therefore they gave to the event its fullest significance, as an expression of goodwill and friendly feeling toward the entire country. We took the kindnesses we received as attentions thus directed, of course, and not to ourselves as a party. That we felt a personal pride in being received as the representatives of a nation we do not deny; that we felt a national pride in the warm cordiality of that reception cannot be doubted.

Our poet has been rigidly suppressed, from the time we let go the anchor. When it was announced that we were going to

visit the Emperor of Russia, the fountains of his great deep
were broken up, and he rained ineffable bosh for four-and-
twenty hours. Our original anxiety as to what we were going
to do with ourselves was suddenly transformed into anxiety
about what we were going to do with our poet. The problem
was solved at last. Two alternatives were offered him—he
must either swear a dreadful oath that he would not issue a
line of his poetry while he was in the Czar's dominions or
else remain under guard on board the ship until we were
safe at Constantinople again. He fought the dilemma long,
but yielded at last. It was a great deliverance. Perhaps the
savage reader would like a specimen of his style. I do not
mean this term to be offensive. I only use it because "the gentle reader" has been used so often that any change from it
cannot but be refreshing.

> Save us and sanctify us, and finally, then,
> See good provisions we enjoy while we journey
>   to Jerusalem.
> For so man proposes, which it is most true,
> And time will wait for none, nor for us too.

The sea has been unusually rough all day. However, we
have had a lively time of it anyhow. We have had quite a run
of visitors. The Governor-General came, and we received
him with a salute of nine guns. He brought his family with
him. I observed that carpets were spread from the pierhead
to his carriage for him to walk on, though I have seen him
walk there without any carpet when he was not on business.
I thought maybe he had what the accidental-insurance people
might call an extrahazardous polish ("policy"—joke, but not
above mediocrity) on his boots, and wished to protect them,
but I examined and could not see that they were blacked any
better than usual. It may have been that he had forgotten his
carpet before, but he did not have it with him anyhow. He
was an exceedingly pleasant old gentleman; we all liked him,
especially Blucher. When he went away, Blucher invited him
to come again and fetch his carpet along.

Prince Dolgorouki and a grand admiral or two, whom we
had seen yesterday at the reception, came on board also. I
was a little distant with these parties at first, because when I
have been visiting emperors I do not like to be too familiar
with people I only know by reputation, and whose moral characters and standing in society I cannot be thoroughly ac-

quainted with. I judged it best to be a little offish at first. I said to myself, "Princes and counts and grand admirals are very well, but they are not emperors, and one cannot be too particular about who he associates with."

Baron Wrangel came also. He used to be Russian ambassador at Washington. I told him I had an uncle who fell down a shaft and broke himself in two as much as a year before that. That was a falsehood, but then I was not going to let any man eclipse me on surprising adventures merely for the want of a little invention. The baron is a fine man, and is said to stand high in the Emperor's confidence and esteem.

Baron Ungern-Sternberg, a boisterous, whole-souled old nobleman, came with the rest. He is a man of progress and enterprise—a representative man of the age. He is the chief director of the railway system of Russia—a sort of railroad king. In his line he is making things move along in this country. He has traveled extensively in America. He says he has tried convict labor on his railroads and with perfect success. He says the convicts work well and are quiet and peaceable. He observed that he employs nearly ten thousand of them now. This appeared to be another call on my resources. I was equal to the emergency. I said we had eighty thousand convicts employed on the railways in America—all of them under sentence of death for murder in the first degree. That closed *him* out.

We had General Todtleben (the famous defender of Sevastopol during the siege) and many inferior army and also navy officers, and a number of unofficial Russian ladies and gentlemen. Naturally a champagne luncheon was in order, and was accomplished without loss of life. Toasts and jokes were discharged freely, but no speeches were made save one thanking the Emperor and the Grand Duke, through the Governor-General, for our hospitable reception, and one by the Governor-General in reply, in which he returned the Emperor's thanks for the speech, etc., etc.

38

We returned to Constantinople, and after a day or two spent in exhausting marches about the city and voyages up the Golden Horn in caïques, we steamed away again. We passed through the Sea of Marmara and the Dardanelles, and steered for a new land—a new one to us at least—Asia. We had as yet only acquired a bowing acquaintance with it, through pleasure excursions to Scutari and the regions round about.

We passed between Lemnos and Mytilene, and saw them as we had seen Elba and the Balearic Isles—mere bulky shapes with the softening mists of distance upon them—whales in a fog, as it were. Then we held our course southward and began to "read up" celebrated Smyrna.

At all hours of the day and night the sailors in the forecastle amused themselves and aggravated us by burlesquing our visit to royalty. The opening paragraph of our address to the Emperor was framed as follows:

We are a handful of private citizens of America, traveling simply for recreation—and unostentatiously, as becomes our unofficial state—and, therefore, we have no excuse to tender for presenting ourselves before Your Majesty save the desire of offering our grateful acknowledgments to the lord of a realm which, through good and through evil report, has been the steadfast friend of the land we love so well.

The third cook, crowned with a resplendent tin basin and wrapped royally in a tablecloth mottled with grease spots and coffee stains, and bearing a scepter that looked strangely like a belaying pin, walked upon a dilapidated carpet and perched himself on the capstan, careless of the flying spray; his tarred and weather-beaten chamberlains, dukes, and lord high admirals surrounded him, arrayed in all the pomp that spare tarpaulins and remnants of old sails could furnish. Then the visiting "watch below," transformed into graceless ladies and uncouth pilgrims, by rude travesties upon waterfalls, hoop-skirts, white kid gloves, and swallowtail coats, moved solemnly up the companionway and, bowing low, began a system of complicated and extraordinary smiling which few monarchs could look upon and live. Then the mock consul, a slush-plastered deck sweep, drew out a soiled fragment of paper and proceeded to read, laboriously:

" 'To His Imperial Majesty, Alexander II, Emperor of Russia:

" 'We are a handful of private citizens of America, traveling simply for recreation—and unostentatiously, as becomes our unofficial state—and, therefore, we have no excuse to tender for presenting ourselves before your Majesty——' "

The Emperor: "Then what the devil did you come for?"

" '——Save the desire of offering our grateful acknowledgments to the lord of a realm which——' "

The Emperor: "Oh, d—n the address! Read it to the police. Chamberlain, take these people over to my brother, the Grand Duke's, and give them a square meal. Adieu! I am happy—I am gratified—I am delighted—I am bored. Adieu, adieu—vamos the ranch! The First Groom of the Palace will proceed to count the portable articles of value belonging to the premises."

The farce then closed, to be repeated again with every change of the watches, and embellished with new and still more extravagant inventions of pomp and conversation.

At all times of the day and night the phraseology of that tiresome address fell upon our ears. Grimy sailors came down out of the foretop placidly announcing themselves as "a handful of private citizens of America, *traveling simply for recreation* and unostentatiously," etc.; the coal passers moved to their duties in the profound depths of the ship, explaining the blackness of their faces and their uncouthness of dress with the reminder that *they* were "a handful of private citizens . . . traveling simply for recreation," etc., and when the cry rang through the vessel at midnight: "EIGHT BELLS! LARBOARD WATCH, TURN OUT!" the larboard watch came gaping and stretching out of their den with the everlasting formula: "Aye, aye, sir! We are a handful of private citizens of America, traveling simply for recreation—and unostentatiously, as becomes our unofficial state!"

As I was a member of the committee and helped to frame the address, these sarcasms came home to me. I never heard a sailor proclaiming himself as a handful of American citizens traveling for recreation but I wished he might trip and fall overboard, and so reduce his handful by one individual, at least. I never was so tired of any one phrase as the sailors made me of the opening sentence of the address to the Emperor of Russia.

This seaport of Smyrna, our first notable acquaintance in Asia, is a closely packed city of one hundred and thirty thousand inhabitants, and, like Constantinople, it has no outskirts. It is as closely packed at its outer edges as it is in the center, and then the habitations leave suddenly off and the plain beyond seems houseless. It is just like any other Oriental city. That is to say, its Muslim houses are heavy and dark and as comfortless as so many tombs; its streets are crooked, rudely and roughly paved, and as narrow as an ordinary staircase; the streets uniformly carry a man to any other place than the one he wants to go to and surprise him by landing him in the most unexpected localities; business is chiefly carried on in great covered bazaars, celled like a honeycomb with innumerable shops no larger than a common closet, and the whole hive cut up into a maze of alleys about wide enough to accommodate a laden camel, and well calculated to confuse a stranger and eventually lose him; everywhere there is dirt, everywhere there are fleas, everywhere there are lean, brokenhearted dogs; every alley is thronged with people; wherever you look, your eye rests upon a wild masquerade of extravagant costumes; the workshops are all open to the streets and the workmen visible; all manner of sounds assail the ear, and over them all rings out the muezzin's cry from some tall minaret, calling the faithful vagabonds to prayer; and superior to the call to prayer, the noises in the streets, the interest of the costumes—superior to everything, and claiming the bulk of attention first, last, and all the time—is a combination of Muhammadan stenches to which the smell of even a Chinese quarter would be as pleasant as the roasting odors of the fatted calf to the nostrils of the returning Prodigal. Such is Oriental luxury—such is Oriental splendor! We read about it all our days, but we comprehend it not until we see it. Smyrna is a very old city. Its name occurs several times in the Bible, one or two of the disciples of Christ visited it, and here was located one of the original seven apocalyptic churches spoken of in Revelations. These churches were symbolized in the Scriptures as candlesticks, and on certain conditions there was a sort of implied promise that Smyrna should be endowed with a "crown of life." She was to "be faithful unto death"—those were the terms. She has not kept up her faith straight along, but the pilgrims that wander hither consider that she has come near enough to it to save her, and so they point to the fact that Smyrna today wears her crown of life, and is a great city with a great commerce and full of energy, while the cities wherein were located the other six churches, and to which no crown of life was promised, have vanished from the earth. So Smyrna really still possesses her crown of life, in a business point of view. Her career for eighteen centuries has been a checkered one, and she has been under the rule of princes of many creeds, yet there has been no season during all that time, as far as we know (and during such seasons as she was inhabited at all), that she has been without her little community of Christians "faithful unto death." Hers was the only church against which no threats were implied in the Revelations, and the only one which survived.

With Ephesus, forty miles from here, where was located another of the seven churches, the case was different. The "candlestick" has been removed from Ephesus. Her light has been put out. Pilgrims, always prone to find prophecies in the Bible, and often where none exist, speak cheerfully and complacently of poor, ruined Ephesus as the victim of prophecy. And yet there is no sentence that promises, without due qualification, the destruction of the city. The words are:

Remember, therefore, from whence thou art fallen, and repent, and do the first works; or else I will come unto thee quickly, and will remove thy candlestick out of this place, except thou repent.

That is all; the other verses are singularly *complimentary* to Ephesus. The threat is qualified. There is no history to show that she did not repent. But the cruelest habit the modern prophecy-savants have is that one of coolly and arbitrarily fitting the prophetic shirt onto the wrong man. They do it without regard to rhyme or reason. Both the cases I have just mentioned are instances in point. Those "prophecies" are distinctly leveled at the "*churches* of Ephesus, Smyrna," etc., and yet the pilgrims invariably make them refer to the *cities* instead. No crown of life is promised to the town of Smyrna and its commerce, but to the handful of Christians who formed its "church." If *they* were "faithful unto death," they have their crown now—but no amount of faithfulness and legal shrewdness combined could legitimately drag the *city* into a participation in the promises of the prophecy. The stately language of the Bible refers to a crown of life whose luster will reflect the day beams of the endless ages of eternity, not the butterfly existence of a city built by men's hands, which must pass to dust with the builders and be forgotten even in the mere handful of centuries vouchsafed to the solid world itself between its cradle and its grave.

The fashion of delving out fulfillments of prophecy where that prophecy consists of mere "ifs" trenches upon the absurd. Suppose a thousand years from now a malarious swamp builds itself up in the shallow harbor of Smyrna, or something else kills the town; and suppose also that within that time the swamp that has filled the renowned harbor of Ephesus and rendered her ancient site deadly and uninhabitable today becomes hard and healthy ground; suppose the natural consequence ensues, to wit: that Smyrna becomes a melancholy ruin and Ephesus is rebuilt. What would the prophecy-savants say? They would coolly skip over our age of the world and say: "Smyrna was not faithful unto death, and so her crown of life was denied her; Ephesus repented, and lo! her candlestick was not removed. Behold these evidences! How wonderful is prophecy!"

Smyrna has been utterly destroyed six times. If her crown of life had been an insurance policy, she would have had an opportunity to collect on it the first time she fell. But she holds it on sufferance and by a complimentary construction of language which does not refer to her. Six different times, however, I suppose some infatuated prophecy-enthusiast blundered along and said, to the infinite disgust of Smyrna and the Smyrniotes: "In sooth, here is astounding fulfillment of prophecy! Smyrna hath not been faithful unto death, and behold her crown of life is vanished from her head. Verily, these things be astonishing!"

Such things have a bad influence. They provoke worldly men into using light conversation concerning sacred subjects. Thick-headed commentators upon the Bible, and stupid preachers and teachers, work more damage to religion than sensible, cool-brained clergymen can fight away again, toil as they may. It is not good judgment to fit a crown of life upon a city which has been destroyed six times. That other class

of wiseacres who twist prophecy in such a manner as to make
it promise the destruction and desolation of the same city
use judgment just as bad, since the city is in a very flourishing
condition now, unhappily for them. These things put arguments into the mouth of infidelity.

A portion of the city is pretty exclusively Turkish; the Jews
have a quarter to themselves; the Franks another quarter; so
also with the Armenians. The Armenians, of course, are Christians. Their houses are large, clean, airy, handsomely paved
with black and white squares of marble, and in the center
of many of them is a square court, which has in it a luxuriant
flower garden and a sparkling fountain; the doors of all the
rooms open on this. A very wide hall leads to the street door,
and in this the women sit the most of the day. In the cool
of the evening they dress up in their best raiment and show
themselves at the door. They are all comely of countenance
and exceedingly neat and cleanly; they look as if they were
just out of a bandbox. Some of the young ladies—many of
them, I may say—are even very beautiful; they average a
shade better than American girls—which treasonable words I
pray may be forgiven me. They are very sociable and will
smile back when a stranger smiles at them, bow back when he
bows, and talk back if he speaks to them. No introduction is
required. An hour's chat at the door with a pretty girl one
never saw before is easily obtained and is very pleasant. I have
tried it. I could not talk anything but English, and the girl
knew nothing but Greek or Armenian or some such barbarous
tongue, but we got along very well. I find that in cases like
these the fact that you cannot comprehend each other isn't
much of a drawback. In that Russian town of Yalta I danced
an astonishing sort of dance an hour long, and one I had not
heard of before, with a very pretty girl, and we talked incessantly and laughed exhaustingly, and neither one ever
knew what the other was driving at. But it was splendid. There
were twenty people in the set, and the dance was very lively
and complicated. It was complicated enough without me—
with me it was more so. I threw in a figure now and then that
surprised those Russians. But I have never ceased to think of
that girl. I have written to her, but I cannot direct the epistle
because her name is one of those nine-jointed Russian affairs,
and there are not letters enough in our alphabet to hold out.
I am not reckless enough to try to pronounce it when I am
awake, but I make a stagger at it in my dreams, and get up

with the lockjaw in the morning. I am fading. I do not take my meals now with any sort of regularity. Her dear name haunts me still in my dreams. It is awful on teeth. It never comes out of my mouth but it fetches an old snag along with it. And then the lockjaw closes down and nips off a couple of the last syllables—but they taste good.

Coming through the Dardanelles, we saw camel trains on-shore with the glasses, but we were never close to one till we got to Smyrna. These camels are very much larger than the scrawny specimens one sees in the menagerie. They stride along these streets in single file, a dozen in a train, with heavy loads on their backs, and a fancy-looking Negro in Turkish costume or an Arab preceding them on a little donkey, and completely overshadowed and rendered insignificant by the huge beasts. To see a camel train laden with the spices of Arabia and the rare fabrics of Persia come marching through the narrow alleys of the bazaar, among porters with their burdens, money-changers, lamp merchants, Alnaschars in the glassware business, portly cross-legged Turks smoking the famous narghile, and the crowds drifting to and fro in the fanciful costumes of the East, is a genuine revelation of the Orient. The picture lacks nothing. It casts you back at once into your forgotten boyhood, and again you dream over the wonders of *The Arabian Nights*; again your companions are princes, your lord is the Caliph Haroun Al Raschid, and your servants are terrific giants and genii that come with smoke and lightning and thunder, and go as a storm goes when they depart!

39

We inquired and learned that the lions of Smyrna consisted of the ruins of the ancient citadel, whose broken and prodigious battlements frown upon the city from a lofty hill just in the edge of the town—the Mount Pagus of Scripture, they call it; the site of that one of the Seven Apocalyptic

Churches of Asia which was located here in the first century of the Christian era; and the grave and the place of martyrdom of the venerable Polycarp, who suffered in Smyrna for his religion some eighteen hundred years ago.

We took little donkeys and started. We saw Polycarp's tomb and then hurried on.

The "Seven Churches"—thus they abbreviate it—came next on the list. We rode there—about a mile and a half in the sweltering sun—and visited a little Greek church which they said was built upon the ancient site; and we paid a small fee, and the holy attendant gave each of us a little wax candle as a remembrancer of the place, and I put mine in my hat and the sun melted it and the grease all ran down the back of my neck; and so now I have not anything left but the wick, and it is a sorry and a wilted-looking wick at that.

Several of us argued as well as we could that the "church" mentioned in the Bible meant a party of Christians, and not a building; that the Bible spoke of them as being very poor— so poor, I thought, and so subject to persecution (as per Polycarp's martyrdom) that in the first place they probably could not have afforded a church edifice, and in the second would not have dared to build it in the open light of day if they could; and finally that if they had had the privilege of building it, common judgment would have suggested that they build it somewhere near the town. But the elders of the ship's family ruled us down and scouted our evidences. However, retribution came to them afterward. They found that they had been led astray and had gone to the wrong place; they discovered that the accepted site is in the city.

Riding through the town, we could see marks of the six Smyrnas that have existed here and been burned up by fire or knocked down by earthquakes. The hills and the rocks are rent asunder in places, excavations expose great blocks of building stone that have lain buried for ages, and all the mean houses and walls of modern Smyrna along the way are spotted white with broken pillars, capitals, and fragments of sculptured marble that once adorned the lordly palaces that were the glory of the city in the olden time.

The ascent of the hill of the citadel is very steep, and we proceeded rather slowly. But there were matters of interest about us. In one place, five hundred feet above the sea, the perpendicular bank on the upper side of the road was ten or fifteen feet high, and the cut exposed three veins of oyster

shells, just as we have seen quartz veins exposed in the cutting
of a road in Nevada or Montana. The veins were about eighteen inches thick and two or three feet apart, and they slant-
ed along downward for a distance of thirty feet or more and
then disappeared where the cut joined the road. Heaven only
knows how far a man might trace them by "stripping." They
were clean, nice oyster shells, large, and just like any other
oyster shells. They were thickly massed together, and none
were scattered above or below the veins. Each one was a well-
defined lead by itself, and without a spur. My first instinct
was to set up the usual

NOTICE:

We, the undersigned, claim five claims of two hundred feet
each (and one for discovery) on this ledge or lode of oyster
shells, with all its dips, spurs, angles, variations, and sinuosi-
ties, and fifty feet on each side of the same, to work it, etc.,
etc., according to the mining laws of Smyrna.

They were such perfectly natural-looking leads that I could
hardly keep from "taking them up." Among the oyster shells
were mixed many fragments of ancient, broken crockeryware.
Now how did those masses of oyster shells get there? I cannot determine. Broken crockery and oyster shells are suggestive of restaurants—but then they could have had no such
places away up there on that mountainside in our time, because nobody has lived up there. A restaurant would not pay
in such a stony, forbidding, desolate place. And besides, there
were no champagne corks among the shells. If there ever was
a restaurant there, it must have been in Smyrna's palmy days,
when the hills were covered with palaces. I could believe in
one restaurant on those terms, but then how about the three?
Did they have restaurants there at three different periods of
the world? Because there are two or three feet of solid earth
between the oyster leads. Evidently the restaurant solution
will not answer.

The hill might have been the bottom of the sea once, and
been lifted up, with its oyster beds, by an earthquake—but,
then, how about the crockery? And moreover, how about
three oyster beds, one above another, and thick strata of good
honest earth between?

That theory will not do. It is just possible that this hill is
Mount Ararat, and that Noah's Ark rested here, and he ate

oysters and threw the shells overboard. But that will not do, either. There are the three layers again and the solid earth between—and besides, there were only eight in Noah's family, and they could not have eaten all these oysters in the two or three months they stayed on top of that mountain. The beasts —however, it is simply absurd to suppose he did not know any more than to feed the beasts on oyster suppers.

It is painful—it is even humiliating—but I am reduced at last to one slender theory: that the oysters climbed up there of their own accord. But what object could they have had in view? What did they want up there? What could any oyster want to climb a hill for? To climb a hill must necessarily be fatiguing and annoying exercise for an oyster. The most natural conclusion would be that the oysters climbed up there to look at the scenery. Yet when one comes to reflect upon the nature of an oyster, it seems plain that he does not care for scenery. An oyster has no taste for such things; he cares nothing for the beautiful. An oyster is of a retiring disposition and not lively—not even cheerful above the average and never enterprising. But above all, an oyster does not take any interest in scenery—he scorns it. What have I arrived at now? Simply at the point I started from, namely, *those oyster shells are there*, in regular layers, five hundred feet above the sea, and no man knows how they got there. I have hunted up the guidebooks, and the gist of what they say is this: "They are there, but how they got there is a mystery."

Twenty-five years ago a multitude of people in America put on their ascension robes, took a tearful leave of their friends, and made ready to fly up into heaven at the first blast of the trumpet. But the angel did not blow it. Miller's resurrection day was a failure. The Millerites were disgusted. I did not suspect that there were Millers in Asia Minor, but a gentleman tells me that they had it all set for the world to come to an end in Smyrna one day about three years ago. There was much buzzing and preparation for a long time previously, and it culminated in a wild excitement at the appointed time. A vast number of the populace ascended the citadel hill early in the morning to get out of the way of the general destruction, and many of the infatuated closed up their shops and retired from all earthly business. But the strange part of it was that about three in the afternoon, while this gentleman and his friends were at dinner in the hotel, a terrific storm of rain, accompanied by thunder and lightning, broke forth and continued with dire fury for two or three hours. It was a thing unprecedented in Smyrna at that time of the year. and scared some of the most skeptical. The streets ran rivers and the hotel floor was flooded with water. The dinner had to be suspended. When the storm finished and left everybody drenched through and through, and melancholy and half drowned, the ascensionists came down from the mountain as dry as so many charity sermons! They had been looking down upon the fearful storm going on below, and really believed that their proposed destruction of the world was proving a grand success.

A railway here in Asia—in the dreamy realm of the Orient—in the fabled land of *The Arabian Nights*—is a strange thing to think of. And yet they have one already and are building another. The present one is well built and well conducted by an English company, but is not doing an immense amount of business. The first year it carried a good many passengers, but its freight list only comprised eight hundred pounds of figs!

It runs almost to the very gates of Ephesus—a town great in all ages of the world—a city familiar to readers of the Bible, and one which was as old as the very hills when the disciples of Christ preached in its streets. It dates back to the shadowy ages of tradition, and was the birthplace of gods renowned in Grecian mythology. The idea of a locomotive tearing through such a place as this, and waking the phantoms of its old days of romance out of their dreams of dead and gone centuries, is curious enough.

We journey thither tomorrow to see the celebrated ruins.

40

This has been a stirring day. The superintendent of the railway put a train at our disposal and did us the further kindness of accompanying us to Ephesus and giving to us his watchful care. We brought sixty scarcely perceptible donkeys in the freight cars, for we had much ground to go over. We have seen some of the most grotesque costumes, along the line of the railroad, that can be imagined. I am glad that no possible combination of words could describe them, for I might then be foolish enough to attempt it.

At ancient Ayassalook, in the midst of a forbidding desert, we came upon long lines of ruined aqueducts, and other remnants of architectural grandeur that told us plainly enough we were nearing what had been a metropolis once. We left the train and mounted the donkeys, along with our invited guests—pleasant young gentlemen from the officers' list of an American man-of-war.

The little donkeys had saddles upon them which were made very high in order that the rider's feet might not drag the ground. The preventative did not work well in the cases of our tallest pilgrims, however. There were no bridles—nothing but a single rope tied to the bit. It was purely ornamental, for the donkey cared nothing for it. If he were drifting to starboard, you might put your helm down hard the other way, if it were any satisfaction to you to do it, but he would continue to drift to starboard all the same. There was only one process which could be depended on, and that was to get down and lift his rear around until his head pointed in the right direction, or take him under your arm and carry him to a part of the road which he could not get out of without climbing. The sun flamed down as hot as a furnace, and neckscarfs, veils, and umbrellas seemed hardly any protection; they served only to make the long procession look more than ever fantastic—for be it known, the ladies were all riding astride because they could not stay on the shapeless saddles sidewise, the men were perspiring and out of temper, their feet were banging against the rocks, the donkeys were capering in every direction but the right one and being belabored with clubs for it, and every now and then a broad umbrella would suddenly go down out of the cavalcade, announcing to all that one more pilgrim had bitten the dust. It was a wilder picture than those solitudes had seen for many a day. No donkeys ever existed that were as hard to navigate as these, I think, or that had so many vile, exasperating instincts. Occasionally we grew so tired and breathless with fighting them that we had to desist—and immediately the donkey would come down to a deliberate walk. This, with the fatigue and the sun, would put a man asleep; and as

soon as the man was asleep, the donkey would lie down.
My donkey shall never see his boyhood's home again. He
has lain down once too often. He must die.

We all stood in the vast theater of ancient Ephesus—the
stone-benched amphitheater, I mean—and had our picture
taken. We looked as proper there as we would look anywhere, I suppose. We do not embellish the general desolation
of a desert much. We add what dignity we can to a stately
ruin with our green umbrellas and jackasses, but it is little.
However, we mean well.

I wish to say a brief word of the aspect of Ephesus.

On a high, steep hill, toward the sea, is a gray ruin of
ponderous blocks of marble, wherein, tradition says, St. Paul
was imprisoned eighteen centuries ago. From these old walls
you have the finest view of the desolate scene where once
stood Ephesus, the proudest city of ancient times, and whose
Temple of Diana was so noble in design and so exquisite
of workmanship that it ranked high in the list of the Seven
Wonders of the World.

Behind you is the sea; in front is a level green valley (a
marsh, in fact) extending far away among the mountains;
to the right of the front view is the old citadel of Ayassalook,
on a high hill; the ruined Mosque of the Sultan Selim stands
near it in the plain (this is built over the grave of St. John,
and was formerly a Christian Church); further toward you is
the hill of Pion, around whose front is clustered all that remains of the ruins of Ephesus that still stand; divided from
it by a narrow valley is the long, rocky, rugged mountain of
Coressus. The scene is a pretty one, and yet desolate—for
in that wide plain no man can live, and in it is no human
habitation. But for the crumbling arches and monstrous piers
and broken walls that rise from the foot of the hill of Pion,
one could not believe that in this place once stood a city
whose renown is older than tradition itself. It is incredible
to reflect that things as familiar all over the world today as
household words belong in the history and in the shadowy
legends of this silent, mournful solitude. We speak of Apollo
and of Diana—they were born here; of the metamorphosis of
Syrinx into a reed—it was done here; of the great god Pan—
he dwelt in the caves of this hill of Coressus; of the Amazons
—this was their best prized home; of Bacchus and Hercules
—both fought the warlike women here; of the Cyclops—
they laid the ponderous marble blocks of some of the ruins

yonder; of Homer—this was one of his many birthplaces; of Cimon of Athens; of Alcibiades, Lysander, Agesilaus—they visited here; so did Alexander the Great; so did Hannibal and Antiochus, Scipio, Lucullus, and Sylla; Brutus, Cassius, Pompey, Cicero, and Augustus; Antony was a judge in this place, and left his seat in the open court, while the advocates were speaking, to run after Cleopatra, who passed the door; from this city these two sailed on pleasure excursions, in galleys with silver oars and perfumed sails, and with companies of beautiful girls to serve them and actors and musicians to amuse them; in days that seem almost modern, so remote are they from the early history of this city, Paul the Apostle preached the new religion here, and so did John, and here it is supposed the former was pitted against wild beasts, for in 1 Corinthians, xv. 32, he says:

"If after the manner of men I have fought with beasts at Ephesus," etc.,

when many men still lived who had seen the Christ; here Mary Magdalen died, and here the Virgin Mary ended her days with John, albeit Rome has since judged it best to locate her grave elsewhere; six or seven hundred years ago—almost yesterday, as it were—troops of mail-clad Crusaders thronged the streets; and to come down to trifles, we speak of meandering streams and find a new interest in a common word when we discover that the crooked river Meander, in yonder valley, gave it to our dictionary. It makes me feel as old as these dreary hills to look down upon these moss-hung ruins, this historic desolation. One may read the Scriptures and believe, but he cannot go and stand yonder in the ruined theater and in imagination people it again with the vanished multitudes who mobbed Paul's comrades there and shouted, with one voice, "Great is Diana of the Ephesians!" The idea of a shout in such a solitude as this almost makes one shudder.

It was a wonderful city, this Ephesus. Go where you will about these broad plains, you find the most exquisitely sculptured marble fragments scattered thick among the dust and weeds; and protruding from the ground or lying prone upon it are beautiful fluted columns of porphyry and all precious marbles; and at every step you find elegantly carved capitals and massive bases and polished tablets engraved with Greek inscriptions. It is a world of precious relics, a wilderness of marred and mutilated gems. And yet what are these things to the wonders that lie buried here under the ground? At Constantinople, at Pisa, in the cities of Spain, are great mosques and cathedrals whose grandest columns came from the temples and palaces of Ephesus, and yet one has only to scratch the ground here to match them. We shall never know what magnificence is until this imperial city is laid bare to the sun.

The finest piece of sculpture we have yet seen and the one that impressed us most (for we do not know much about art and cannot easily work up ourselves into ecstasies over it) is one that lies in this old theater of Ephesus, which St. Paul's riot has made so celebrated. It is only the headless body of a man, clad in a coat of mail, with a Medusa head upon the breastplate, but we feel persuaded that such dignity and such majesty were never thrown into a form of stone before.

What builders they were, these men of antiquity! The massive arches of some of these ruins rest upon piers that are fifteen feet square and built entirely of solid blocks of marble, some of which are as large as a Saratoga trunk and some the size of a boardinghouse sofa. They are not shells or shafts of stone filled inside with rubbish, but the whole pier is a mass of solid masonry. Vast arches that may have been the gates of the city are built in the same way. They have braved the storms and sieges of three thousand years, and have been shaken by many an earthquake, but still they stand. When they dig alongside of them, they find ranges of ponderous masonry that are as perfect in every detail as they were the day those old Cyclopian giants finished them. An English company is going to excavate Ephesus—and then!

And now am I reminded of:

THE LEGEND OF THE SEVEN SLEEPERS

In the Mount of Pion, yonder, is the Cave of the Seven Sleepers. Once upon a time, about fifteen hundred years ago, seven young men lived near each other in Ephesus, who belonged to the despised sect of the Christians. It came to pass that the good King Maximilianus (I am telling this story for nice little boys and girls), it came to pass, I say, that the good King Maximilianus fell to persecuting the Christians, and as time rolled on he made it very warm for them. So the seven young men said one to the other, "Let us get up and travel." And they got up and traveled. They tarried not to bid their fathers and mothers good-bye or any friend they knew. They only took certain moneys which their parents had and garments that belonged unto their friends, whereby they might remember them when far away; and they took also the dog Ketmehr, which was the property of their neighbor Malchus, because the beast did run his head into a noose which one of the young men was carrying carelessly, and they had not time to release him; and they took also certain chickens that seemed lonely in the neighboring coops, and likewise some bottles of curious liquors that stood near the grocer's window; and then they departed from the city. By and by they came to a marvelous cave in the Hill of Pion and entered into it and feasted, and presently they hurried on again. But they forgot the bottles of curious liquors and left them behind. They traveled in many lands and had many strange adventures. They were virtuous young men and lost no opportunity that fell in their way to make their livelihood. Their motto was in these words, namely, "Procrastination is the thief of time." And so, whenever they did come upon a man who was alone, they said, "Behold, this person hath the wherewithal—let us go through him." And they went through him. At the end of five years they had waxed tired of travel and adventure and longed to revisit their old home again and hear the voices and see the faces that were dear unto their youth. Therefore they went through such parties as fell in their way where they sojourned at that time, and journeyed back toward Ephesus again. For the good King Maximilianus was become converted unto the new faith, and the Christians rejoiced because they were no longer persecuted. One day as the sun went down, they came to the cave in the Mount of Pion, and they said, each to his fellow, "Let us sleep here, and go and feast and make merry with our friends when the morning cometh." And each of the seven lifted up his voice and said, "It is a whiz." So they went in, and lo, where they had put them, there lay the bottles of strange liquors, and they judged that age had not impaired their excellence. Wherein the wanderers were right, and the heads of the same were level. So each of the young men drank six bottles, and behold they felt very tired then and lay down and slept soundly.

When they awoke, one of them, Johannes—surnamed Smithianus—said, "We are naked." And it was so. Their raiment was all gone, and the money which they had gotten from a stranger whom they had proceeded through as they approached the city was lying upon the ground, corroded and rusted and defaced. Likewise the dog Ketmehr was gone, and nothing save the brass that was upon his collar remained. They wondered much at these things. But they took the money, and they wrapped about their bodies some leaves and came up to the top of the hill. Then were they perplexed. The wonderful Temple of Diana was gone; many grand edifices they had never seen before stood in the city; men in strange garbs moved about the streets, and everything was changed.

Johannes said, "It hardly seems like Ephesus. Yet here is the great gymnasium; here is the mighty theater, wherein I have seen seventy thousand men assembled; here is the Agora; there is the font where the sainted John the Baptist immersed the converts; yonder is the prison of the good St. Paul, where we all did use to go to touch the ancient chains that bound him and be cured of our distempers; I see the tomb of the disciple Luke, and afar off is the church wherein repose the ashes of the holy John, where the Christians of Ephesus go twice a year to gather the dust from the tomb, which is able to make bodies whole again that are corrupted by disease, and cleanse the soul from sin; but see how the wharves encroach upon the sea and what multitudes of ships are anchored in the bay; see also how the city hath stretched abroad, far over the valley behind Pion, and even unto the walls of Ayassalook; and lo, all the hills are white with palaces and ribbed with colonnades of marble. How mighty is Ephesus become!"

And wondering at what their eyes had seen, they went down into the city and purchased garments and clothed themselves. And when they would have passed on, the merchant bit the coins which they had given him with his teeth, and turned them about and looked curiously upon them, and cast them upon his counter, and listened if they rang; and then he said, "These be bogus." And they said, "Depart thou to Hades," and went their way. When they were come to their houses, they recognized them, albeit they seemed old and mean; and they rejoiced and were glad. They ran to the doors and knocked, and strangers opened and looked inquiringly upon them. And they said, with great excitement, while their hearts beat high and the color in their faces came and went, "Where is my father? Where is my mother? Where are Dionysius and Serapion, and Pericles and Decius?" And the strangers that opened said, "We know not these." The Seven said, "How, you know them not? How long have ye dwelt here, and whither are they gone that dwelt here before ye?" And the strangers said, "Ye play upon us with a jest, young men; we and our fathers have sojourned under these roofs these six generations; the names ye utter rot upon the tombs, and they that bore them have run their brief race, have laughed and sung, have borne the sorrows and the weariness that were allotted them, and are at rest; for ninescore years the summers have come and gone, and the autumn leaves have fallen, since the roses faded out of their cheeks and they laid them to sleep with the dead."

Then the seven young men turned them away from their homes, and the strangers shut the doors upon them. The wanderers marveled greatly and looked into the faces of all they met, as hoping to find one that they knew; but all were strange, and passed them by and spake no friendly word. They were sore distressed and sad. Presently they spake unto a citizen and said, "Who is king in Ephesus?" And the citizen answered and said, "Whence come ye that ye know not that great Laertius reigns in Ephesus?" They looked one at the other, greatly perplexed, and presently asked again, "Where, then, is the good King Maximilianus?" The citizen moved him apart, as one who is afraid, and said, "Verily these men be mad, and dream dreams, else would they know that the king whereof they speak is dead above two hundred years agone."

Then the scales fell from the eyes of the Seven, and one said, "Alas, that we drank of the curious liquors. They have made us weary, and in dreamless sleep these two long centuries have we lain. Our homes are desolate, our friends are dead. Behold, the jig is up—let us die." And that same day went they forth and laid them down and died. And in that selfsame day, likewise, the Seven-up did cease in Ephesus, for that the Seven that were up were down again, and departed and dead withal. And the names that be upon their tombs, even unto this time are Johannes Smithianus, Trumps, Gift, High, and Low, Jack, and the Game. And with the sleepers lie also the bottles wherein were once the curious

liquors; and upon them is writ, in ancient letters, such words
as these—names of heathen gods of olden time, perchance
—Rumpunch, Jinsling, Egnog.

Such is the story of the Seven Sleepers (with slight variations), and I know it is true, because I have seen the cave
myself.

Really, so firm a faith had the ancients in this legend
that as late as eight or nine hundred years ago learned
travelers held it in superstitious fear. Two of them record
that they ventured into it, but ran quickly out again, not
daring to tarry lest they should fall asleep and outlive their
great-grandchildren a century or so. Even at this day the
ignorant denizens of the neighboring country prefer not to
sleep in it.

41

When I last made a memorandum we were at Ephesus.
We are in Syria now, encamped in the mountains of Lebanon. The interregnum has been long, both as to time
and distance. We brought not a relic from Ephesus! After
gathering up fragments of sculptured marbles and breaking
ornaments from the interior work of the mosques, and after
bringing them at a cost of infinite trouble and fatigue, five
miles on muleback to the railway depot, a government officer
compelled all who had such things to disgorge! He had an
order from Constantinople to *look out for our party* and
see that we carried nothing off. It was a wise, a just, and a
well-deserved rebuke, but it created a sensation. I never resist
a temptation to plunder a stranger's premises without feeling
insufferably vain about it. This time I felt proud beyond expression. I was serene in the midst of the scoldings that
were heaped upon the Ottoman government for its affront
offered to a pleasuring party of entirely respectable gentlemen and ladies. I said, "We that have free souls, it touches
us not." The shoe not only pinched our party, but it pinched

hard; a principal sufferer discovered that the imperial order was enclosed in an envelope bearing the seal of the British Embassy at Constantinople, and therefore must have been inspired by the representative of the Queen. This was bad— very bad. Coming solely from the Ottomans, it might have signified only Ottoman hatred of Christians and a vulgar ignorance as to genteel methods of expressing it; but coming from the Christianized, educated, politic British legation, it simply intimated that we were a sort of gentlemen and ladies who would bear watching! So the party regarded it, and were incensed accordingly. The truth doubtless was that the same precautions would have been taken against *any* travelers, because the English company who have acquired the right to excavate Ephesus, and have paid a great sum for that right, need to be protected and deserve to be. They cannot afford to run the risk of having their hospitality abused by travelers, especially since travelers are such notorious scorners of honest behavior.

We sailed from Smyrna in the wildest spirit of expectancy, for the chief feature, the grand goal of the expedition, was near at hand—we were approaching the Holy Land! Such a burrowing into the hold for trunks that had lain buried for weeks, yes, for months; such a hurrying to and fro above decks and below; such a riotous system of packing and un-packing; such a littering up of the cabins with shirts and skirts and indescribable and unclassable odds and ends; such a making up of bundles and setting apart of umbrellas, green spectacles, and thick veils; such a critical inspection of saddles and bridles that had never yet touched horses; such a cleaning and loading of revolvers and examining of bowie knives; such a half-soling of the seats of pantaloons with serviceable buckskin; then such a poring over ancient maps; such a reading up of Bibles and Palestine travels; such a marking out of routes; such exasperating efforts to divide up the company into little bands of congenial spirits who might make the long and arduous journey without quar-reling; and morning, noon, and night, such mass meetings in the cabins, such speech-making, such sage suggesting, such worrying and quarreling, and such a general raising of the very mischief was never seen in the ship before!

But it is all over now. We are cut up into parties of six or eight and by this time are scattered far and wide. Ours is the only one, however, that is venturing on what is called

"the long trip"—that is, out into Syria, by Baalbek to Da
mascus, and thence down through the full length of Palestine
It would be a tedious and also a too risky journey at this ho
season of the year for any but strong, healthy men, accus
tomed somewhat to fatigue and rough life in the open air
The other parties will take shorter journeys.

For the last two months we have been in a worry abou
one portion of this Holy Land pilgrimage. I refer to transpor
tation service. We knew very well that Palestine was a country
which did not do a large passenger business, and every mar
we came across who knew anything about it gave us to
understand that not half of our party would be able to ge
dragomen and animals. At Constantinople everybody fell to
telegraphing the American Consuls at Alexandria and Beirut
to give notice that we wanted dragomen and transportation.
We were desperate, would take horses, jackasses, camelopards,
kangaroos—anything. At Smyrna more telegraphing was done,
to the same end. Also, fearing for the worst, we telegraphed
for a large number of seats in the diligence for Damascus
and horses for the ruins of Baalbek.

As might have been expected, a notion got abroad in
Syria and Egypt that the whole population of the province of
America (the Turks consider us a trifling little province in
some unvisited corner of the world) were coming to the
Holy Land—and so, when we got to Beirut yesterday, we
found the place full of dragomen and their outfits. We had
all intended to go by diligence to Damascus, and switch off
to Baalbek as we went along—because we expected to rejoin the ship, go to Mount Carmel, and take to the woods
from there. However, when our own private party of eight
found that it was possible, and proper enough, to make the
"long trip," we adopted that program. We have never been
much trouble to a consul before, but we have been a fearful
nuisance to our consul at Beirut. I mention this because I
cannot help admiring his patience, his industry, and his
accommodating spirit. I mention it also because I think some
of our ship's company did not give him as full credit for
his excellent services as he deserved.

Well, out of our eight, three were selected to attend to
all business connected with the expedition. The rest of us
had nothing to do but look at the beautiful city of Beirut,
with its bright, new houses nestled among a wilderness of
green shrubbery spread abroad over an upland that sloped

ently down to the sea; and also at the mountains of Leb-
non, that environ it; and likewise to bathe in the transparent
lue water that rolled its billows about the ship (we did
ot know there were sharks there). We had also to range
p and down through the town and look at the costumes.
These are picturesque and fanciful, but not so varied as at
Constantinople and Smyrna; the women of Beirut add an
agony: in the two former cities the sex wear a thin veil
which one can see through (and they often expose their
ankles), but at Beirut they cover their entire faces with dark-
colored or black veils, so that they look like mummies,
and then expose their breasts to the public. A young gentleman (I believe he was a Greek) volunteered to show us
around the city and said it would afford him great pleasure,
because he was studying English and wanted practice in that
language. When we had finished the rounds, however, he
called for remuneration—said he hoped the gentlemen would
give him a trifle in the way of a few piasters (equivalent
to a few five-cent pieces). We did so. The Consul was surprised when he heard it, and said he knew the young fellow's
family very well and that they were an old and highly respectable family and worth a hundred and fifty thousand
dollars! Some people, so situated, would have been ashamed
of the berth he had with us and his manner of crawling
into it.

At the appointed time our business committee reported
and said all things were in readiness—that we were to start
today, with horses, pack animals, and tents, and go to
Baalbek, Damascus, the Sea of Tiberias, and thence southward by the way of the scene of Jacob's Dream and other
notable Bible localities to Jerusalem—from thence probably
to the Dead Sea, but possibly not—and then strike for the
ocean and rejoin the ship three or four weeks hence at Joppa;
terms, five dollars a day apiece, in gold, and everything to
be furnished by the dragoman. They said we would live
as well as at a hotel. I had read something like that before,
and did not shame my judgment by believing a word of it.
I said nothing, however, but packed up a blanket and a
shawl to sleep in, pipes and tobacco, two or three woolen
shirts, a portfolio, a guidebook, and a Bible. I also took
along a towel and a cake of soap, to inspire respect in the
Arabs, who would take me for a king in disguise.

We were to select our horses at 3 P.M. At that hour

Abraham, the dragoman, marshaled them before us. With all solemnity I set it down here that those horses were the hardest lot I ever did come across, and their accouterments were in exquisite keeping with their style. One brute had an eye out; another had his tail sawed off close, like a rabbit, and was proud of it; another had a bony ridge running from his neck to his tail, like one of those ruined aqueducts one sees about Rome, and had a neck on him like a bowsprit; they all limped and had sore backs, and likewise raw places and old scales scattered about their persons like brass nails in a hair trunk; their gaits were marvelous to contemplate and replete with variety—under way the procession looked like a fleet in a storm. It was fearful. Blucher shook his head and said:

"That dragon is going to get himself into trouble fetching these old crates out of the hospital the way they are, unless he has got a permit."

I said nothing. The display was exactly according to the guidebook, and were we not traveling by the guidebook? I selected a certain horse because I thought I saw him shy, and I thought that a horse that had spirit enough to shy was not to be despised.

At 6 o'clock P.M. we came to a halt here on the breezy summit of a shapely mountain overlooking the sea, and the handsome valley where dwelt some of those enterprising Phoenicians of ancient times we read so much about; all around us are what were once the dominions of Hiram, King of Tyre, who furnished timber from the cedars of these Lebanon hills to build portions of King Solomon's Temple with.

Shortly after six our pack train arrived. I had not seen it before, and a good right I had to be astonished. We had nineteen serving men and twenty-six pack mules! It was a perfect caravan. It looked like one, too, as it wound among the rocks. I wondered what in the very mischief we wanted with such a vast turnout as that, for eight men. I wondered awhile, but soon I began to long for a tin plate and some bacon and beans. I had camped out many and many a time before and knew just what was coming. I went off, without waiting for serving men, and unsaddled my horse, and washed such portions of his ribs and his spine as projected through his hide, and when I came back, behold, five stately circus tents were up—tents that were brilliant within with blue and gold and crimson and all manner of splendid adornment! I was speechless. Then they brought eight little iron bedsteads and set them up in the tents; they put a soft mattress and pillows and good blankets and two snow-white sheets on each bed. Next they rigged a table about the center pole and on it placed pewter pitchers, basins, soap, and the whitest of towels—one set for each man; they pointed to pockets in the tent and said we could put our small trifles in them for convenience, and if we needed pins or such things, they were sticking everywhere. Then came the finishing touch—they spread carpets on the floor! I simply said, "If you call this camping out, all right—but it isn't the style *I* am used to; my little baggage that I brought along is at a discount."

It grew dark, and they put candles on the tables—candles set in bright, new, brazen candlesticks. And soon the bell—a genuine, simon-pure bell—rang, and we were invited to "the saloon." I had thought before that we had a tent or so too many, but now here was one, at least, provided for; it was to be used for nothing but an eating saloon. Like the others, it was high enough for a family of giraffes to live in, and was very handsome and clean and bright-colored within. It was a gem of a place. A table for eight and eight canvas chairs; a tablecloth and napkins whose whiteness and whose fineness laughed to scorn the things we were used to in the great excursion steamer; knives and forks, soup plates, dinner plates—everything in the handsomest kind of style. It was wonderful! And they call *this* camping out. Those stately fellows in baggy trousers and turbaned fezzes brought in a dinner which consisted of roast mutton, roast chicken, roast goose, potatoes, bread, tea, pudding, apples, and delicious grapes; the viands were better cooked than any we had eaten for weeks, and the table made a finer appearance, with its large German silver candlesticks and other finery, than any table we had sat down to for a good while, and yet that polite dragoman, Abraham, came bowing in and apologizing for the whole affair, on account of the unavoidable confusion of getting under way for a very long trip, and promising to do a great deal better in future!

It is midnight now, and we break camp at six in the morning.

They call this camping out. At this rate it is a glorious privilege to be a pilgrim to the Holy Land.

42

We are camped near Temnin el Foka—a name which the boys have simplified a good deal for the sake of convenience in spelling. They call it Jacksonville. It sounds a little strangely, here in the valley of Lebanon, but it has the merit of being easier to remember than the Arabic name.

COME LIKE SPIRITS, SO DEPART

The night shall be filled with music,
And the cares that infest the day
Shall fold their tents like the Arabs,
And as silently steal away.

I slept very soundly last night, yet when the dragoman's bell rang at half-past five this morning and the cry went abroad of "Ten minutes to dress for breakfast!" I heard both. It surprised me, because I have not heard the breakfast gong in the ship for a month, and whenever we have had occasion to fire a salute at daylight, I have only found it out in the course of conversation afterward. However, camping out, even though it be in a gorgeous tent, makes one fresh and lively in the morning—especially if the air you are breathing is the cool, fresh air of the mountains.

I was dressed within the ten minutes and came out. The saloon tent had been stripped of its sides and had nothing left but its roof; so when we sat down to table we could look out over a noble panorama of mountain, sea, and hazy valley. And sitting thus, the sun rose slowly up and suffused the picture with a world of rich coloring.

Hot mutton chops, fried chicken, omelets, fried potatoes, and coffee—all excellent. This was the bill of fare. It was sauced with a savage appetite purchased by hard riding the day before and refreshing sleep in a pure atmosphere. As I called for a second cup of coffee I glanced over my shoulder, and behold, our white village was gone—the splendid tents had vanished like magic! It was wonderful how quickly those Arabs had "folded their tents"; and it was wonderful also how quickly they had gathered the thousand odds and ends of the camp together and disappeared with them.

By half-past six we were under way, and all the Syrian world seemed to be under way also. The road was filled with mule trains and long processions of camels. This reminds me that we have been trying for some time to think what a camel looks like, and now we have made it out. When he is down on all his knees, flat on his breast to receive his load, he looks something like a goose swimming, and when he is upright he looks like an ostrich with an extra set of legs. Camels are not beautiful, and their long underlip gives them an exceedingly "gallus" * expression. They have immense, flat, forked cushions of feet, that make a track in the dust like a pie with a slice cut out of it. They are not particular about their diet. They would eat a tombstone if they could bite it. A thistle grows about here which has needles on it that would pierce through leather, I think; if one touches you, you can find relief in nothing but profanity. The camels eat these. They show by their actions that they enjoy them. I suppose it would be a real treat to a camel to have a keg of nails for supper.

While I am speaking of animals I will mention that I have a horse now by the name of "Jericho." He is a mare. I have seen remarkable horses before, but none so remarkable as this. I wanted a horse that could shy, and this one fills the bill. I had an idea that shying indicated spirit. If I was correct, I have got the most spirited horse on earth. He shies at everything he comes across, with the utmost impartiality. He appears to have a mortal dread of telegraph poles especially; and it is fortunate that these are on both sides of the road, because as it is now, I never fall off twice in succession on the same side. If I fell on the same side always, it would get to be monotonous after a while. This creature has scared at everything he has seen today except a haystack. He walked up to that with an intrepidity and a recklessness that were astonishing. And it would fill anyone with admiration to see how he preserves his self-possession in the presence of a barley sack. This daredevil bravery will be the death of this horse someday.

* Excuse the slang—no other word will describe it.

He is not particularly fast, but I think he will get me through the Holy Land. He has only one fault. His tail has been chopped off, or else he has sat down on it too hard some time or other, and he has to fight the flies with his heels. This is all very well, but when he tries to kick a fly off the top of his head with his hindfoot, it is too much variety. He is going to get himself into trouble that way someday. He reaches around and bites my legs too. I do not care particularly about that, only I do not like to see a horse too sociable.

I think the owner of this prize had a wrong opinion about him. He had an idea that he was one of those fiery, untamed steeds, but he is not of that character. I know the Arab had this idea, because when he brought the horse out for inspection in Beirut, he kept jerking at the bridle and shouting in Arabic, "Ho! Will you? Do you want to run away, you ferocious beast, and break your neck?" when all the time the horse was not doing anything in the world, and only looked like he wanted to lean up against something and think. Whenever he is not shying at things or reaching after a fly, he wants to do that yet. How it would surprise his owner to know this.

We have been in a historical section of country all day. At noon we camped three hours and took luncheon at Mekseh, near the junction of the Lebanon Mountains and the Jebel el Kuneiyiseh, and looked down into the immense, level, garden-like valley of Lebanon. Tonight we are camping near the same valley and have a very wide sweep of it in view. We can see the long, whale-backed ridge of Mount Hermon projecting above the eastern hills. The "dews of Hermon" are falling upon us now, and the tents are almost soaked with them.

Over the way from us, and higher up the valley, we can discern through the glasses the faint outlines of the wonderful ruins of Baalbek, the supposed Baal-Gad of Scripture. Joshua and another person were the two spies who were sent into this land of Canaan by the children of Israel to report upon its character—I mean they were the spies who reported favorably. They took back with them some specimens of the grapes of this country, and in the children's picture books they are always represented as bearing one monstrous bunch swung to a pole between them, a respectable load for a pack train. The Sunday-school books exaggerated it a little. The grapes are most excellent to this day, but the bunches are not as large as those in the pictures. I was surprised and hurt when I saw them, because those colossal bunches of grapes were one of my most cherished juvenile traditions.

Joshua reported favorably, and the children of Israel journeyed on, with Moses at the head of the general government and Joshua in command of the army of six hundred thousand fighting men. Of women and children and civilians, there was a countless swarm. Of all that mighty host, none but the two faithful spies ever lived to set their feet in the Promised Land. They and their descendants wandered forty years in the desert, and then Moses, the gifted warrior, poet, statesman, and philosopher, went up into Pisgah and met his mysterious fate. Where he was buried no man knows—for

> . . . no man dug that sepulchre,
>   And no man saw it e'er—
>   For the Sons of God upturned the sod
>   And laid the dead man there!

Then Joshua began his terrible raid, and from Jericho clear to this Baal-Gad, he swept the land like the Genius of Destruction. He slaughtered the people, laid waste their soil, and razed their cities to the ground. He wasted thirty-one kings also. One may call it that, though really it can hardly be called wasting them, because there were always plenty of kings in those days and to spare. At any rate, he destroyed thirty-one kings and divided up their realms among his Israelites. He divided up this valley stretched out here before us, and so it was once Jewish territory. The Jews have long since disappeared from it, however.

Back yonder, an hour's journey from here, we passed through an Arab village of stone dry-goods boxes (they look like that) where Noah's tomb lies under lock and key. [Noah built the ark.] Over these old hills and valleys the ark that contained all that was left of a vanished world once floated.

I make no apology for detailing the above information. It will be news to some of my readers, at any rate.

Noah's tomb is built of stone and is covered with a long stone building. Bucksheesh let us in. The building had to be long, because the grave of the honored old navigator is two hundred and ten feet long itself! It is only about four feet high, though. He must have cast a shadow like a lightning rod. The proof that this is the genuine spot where Noah was buried can only be doubted by uncommonly incredulous people. The evidence is pretty straight. Shem, the son of Noah, was present at the burial, and showed the place to his descendants, who transmitted the knowledge to their descendants, and the lineal descendants of these introduced themselves to us today. It was pleasant to make the acquaintance of members of so respectable a family. It was a thing to be proud of. It was the next thing to being acquainted with Noah himself.

Noah's memorable voyage will always possess a living interest for me henceforward.

If ever an oppressed race existed, it is this one we see fettered around us under the inhuman tyranny of the Ottoman empire. I wish Europe would let Russia annihilate Turkey a little—not much, but enough to make it difficult to find the place again without a divining rod or a diving bell. The Syrians are very poor, and yet they are ground down by a system of taxation that would drive any other nation frantic. Last year their taxes were heavy enough, in all conscience—but this year they have been increased by the addition of taxes that were forgiven them in times of famine in former years. On top of this, the government has levied a tax of *one-tenth* of the whole proceeds of the land. This is only half the story. The pasha of a pashalic does not trouble himself with appointing tax collectors. He figures up what all these taxes ought to amount to in a certain district. Then he farms the collection out. He calls the rich men together, the highest bidder gets the speculation, pays the pasha on the spot, and then sells out to smaller fry, who sell in turn to a piratical horde of still smaller fry. These latter compel the peasant to bring his little trifle of grain to the village at his own cost. It must be weighed, the various taxes set apart, and the remainder returned to the producer. But the collector delays this duty day after day, while the producer's family are perishing for bread; at last the poor wretch, who cannot but understand the game, says, "Take a quarter— take half—take two-thirds if you will, and let me go!" It is a most outrageous state of things.

These people are naturally goodhearted and intelligent, and with education and liberty would be a happy and contented race. They often appeal to the stranger to know if the great world will not someday come to their relief and save them.

The Sultan has been lavishing money like water in England and Paris, but his subjects are suffering for it now.

This fashion of camping out bewilders me. We have boot-jacks and a bathtub now, and yet all the mysteries the pack mules carry are not revealed. What next?

43

We had a tedious ride of about five hours, in the sun, across the valley of Lebanon. It proved to be not quite so much of a garden as it had seemed from the hillsides. It was a desert, weed-grown waste, littered thickly with stones the size of a man's fist. Here and there the natives had scratched the ground and reared a sickly crop of grain, but for the most part the valley was given up to a handful of shepherds, whose flocks were doing what they honestly could to get a living, but the chances were against them. We saw rude piles of stones standing near the roadside at intervals, and recognized the custom of marking boundaries which obtained in Jacob's time. There were no walls, no fences, no hedges—nothing to secure a man's possessions but these random heaps of stones. The Israelites held them sacred in the old patriarchal times, and these other Arabs, their lineal descendants, do so likewise. An American of ordinary intelligence would soon widely extend his property, at an outlay of mere manual labor, performed at night, under so loose a system of fencing as this.

The plows these people use are simply a sharpened stick, such as Abraham plowed with, and they still winnow their wheat as he did—they pile it on the housetop and then toss it by shovelfuls into the air until the wind has blown all the chaff away. They never invent anything, never learn anything.

We had a fine race, of a mile, with an Arab perched on a camel. Some of the horses were fast and made very good time, but the camel scampered by them without any very great effort. The yelling and shouting, and whipping and galloping, of all parties interested made it an exhilarating, exciting, and particularly boisterous race.

At eleven o'clock our eyes fell upon the walls and columns of Baalbek, a noble ruin whose history is a sealed book. It has stood there for thousands of years, the wonder and admiration of travelers; but who built it or when it was built are questions that may never be answered. One thing is very sure, though. Such grandeur of design and such grace of execution as one sees in the temples of Baalbek have not been equaled or even approached in any work of men's hands that has been built within twenty centuries past.

The great Temple of the Sun, the Temple of Jupiter, and several smaller temples are clustered together in the midst of one of these miserable Syrian villages, and look strangely enough in such plebeian company. These temples are built upon massive substructions that might support a world almost; the materials used are blocks of stone as large as an omnibus—very few, if any of them, are smaller than a carpenter's tool chest—and these substructions are traversed by tunnels of masonry through which a train of cars might pass. With such foundations as these, it is little wonder that Baalbek has lasted so long. The Temple of the Sun is nearly three hundred feet long and one hundred and sixty feet wide. It had fifty-four columns around it, but only six are standing now—the others lie broken at its base, a confused and picturesque heap. The six columns are perfect, as also are their bases, Corinthian capitals and entablature—and six more shapely columns do not exist. The columns and the entablature together are ninety feet high—a prodigious altitude for shafts of stone to reach, truly—and yet one only thinks of their beauty and symmetry when looking at them; the pillars look slender and delicate; the entablature, with its elaborate sculpture, looks like rich stuccowork. But when you have gazed aloft till your eyes are weary, you glance at the great fragments of pillars among which you are standing and find that they are eight feet through; and with them lie beautiful capitals apparently as large as a small cottage, and also single slabs of stone, superbly sculptured, that are four or five feet thick and would completely cover the floor of any ordinary parlor. You wonder where these monstrous things came from, and it takes some little time to satisfy yourself that the airy and graceful fabric that towers above your head is made up of their mates. It seems too preposterous.

The Temple of Jupiter is a smaller ruin than the one I have been speaking of, and yet is immense. It is in a tolerable state of preservation. One row of nine columns stands almost uninjured. They are sixty-five feet high and support a sort of porch or roof, which connects them with the roof of the building. This porch roof is composed of tremendous slabs of stone, which are so finely sculptured on the underside that the work looks like a fresco from below. One or two of these slabs had fallen, and again I wondered if the gigantic masses of carved stone that lay about me were no larger than those above my head. Within the temple the ornamentation was elaborate and colossal. What a wonder of architectural beauty and grandeur this edifice must have been when it was new! And what a noble picture it and its statelier companion, with the chaos of mighty fragments scattered about them, yet makes in the moonlight!

I cannot conceive how those immense blocks of stone were ever hauled from the quarries or how they were ever raised to the dizzy heights they occupy in the temples. And yet these sculptured blocks are trifles in size compared with the rough-hewn blocks that form the wide veranda, or platform, which surrounds the great temple. One stretch of that platform, two hundred feet long, is composed of blocks of stone as large, and some of them larger, than a streetcar. They surmount a wall about ten or twelve feet high. I thought those were large rocks, but they sank into insignificance compared with those which formed another section of the platform. These were three in number, and I thought that each of them was about as long as three streetcars placed end to end, though of course they are a third wider and a third higher than a streetcar. Perhaps two railway freight cars of the largest pattern, placed end to end, might better represent their size. In combined length these three stones stretch nearly two hundred feet; they are thirteen feet square; two of them are sixty-four feet long each, and the third is sixty-nine. They are built into the massive wall some twenty feet above the ground. They are there, but how they got there is the question. I have seen the hull of a steamboat that was smaller than one of those stones. All these great walls are as exact and shapely as the flimsy things we build of bricks in these days. A race of gods or of giants must have inhabited

Baalbek many a century ago. Men like the men of our day could hardly rear such temples as these.

We went to the quarry from whence the stones of Baalbek were taken. It was about a quarter of a mile off and downhill. In a great pit lay the mate of the largest stone in the ruins. It lay there just as the giants of that old forgotten time had left it when they called hence—just as they had left it, to remain for thousands of years, an eloquent rebuke unto such as are prone to think slightingly of the men who lived before them. This enormous block lies there, squared and ready for the builders' hands—a solid mass fourteen feet by seventeen and but a few inches less than seventy feet long! Two buggies could be driven abreast of each other, on its surface, from one end of it to the other, and leave room enough for a man or two to walk on either side.

One might swear that all the John Smiths and George Wilkinsons, and all the other pitiful nobodies between Kingdom Come and Baalbek, would inscribe their poor little names upon the walls of Baalbek's magnificent ruins, and would add the town, the country, and the state they came from—and swearing thus, be infallibly correct. It is a pity some great ruin does not fall in and flatten out some of these reptiles, and scare their kind out of ever giving their names to fame upon any walls or monuments again forever.

Properly, with the sorry relics we bestrode, it was a three days' journey to Damascus. It was necessary that we should do it in less than two. It was necessary because our three pilgrims would not travel on the Sabbath day. We were all perfectly willing to keep the Sabbath day, but there are times when to keep the *letter* of a sacred law whose spirit is righteous becomes a sin, and this was a case in point. We pleaded for the tired, ill-treated horses, and tried to show that their faithful service deserved kindness in return and their hard lot compassion. But when did ever self-righteousness know the sentiment of pity? What were a few long hours added to the hardships of some overtaxed brutes when weighed against the peril of those human souls? It was not the most promising party to travel with and hope to gain a higher veneration for religion through the example of its devotees. We said the Saviour, who pitied dumb beasts and taught that the ox must be rescued from the mire even on the Sabbath day, would not have counseled a forced march like this. We said the "long trip" was exhausting and therefore dangerous in the blistering heats of summer, even when the ordinary day's stages were traversed, and if we persisted in this hard march, some of us might be stricken down with the fevers of the country in consequence of it. Nothing could move the pilgrims. They *must* press on. Men might die, horses might die, but they must enter upon holy soil next week with no Sabbath-breaking stain upon them. Thus they were willing to commit a sin against the spirit of religious law in order that they might preserve the letter of it. It was not worthwhile to tell them "the letter kills." I am talking now about personal friends, men whom I like, men who are good citizens, who are honorable, upright, conscientious, but whose idea of the Saviour's religion seems to me distorted. They lecture our shortcomings unsparingly, and every night they call us together and read to us chapters from the Testament that are full of gentleness, of charity, and of tender mercy; and then all the next day they stick to their saddles clear up to the summits of these rugged mountains and clear down again. Apply the Testament's gentleness and charity and tender mercy to a toiling, worn and weary horse? Nonsense—these are for God's human creatures, not his dumb ones. What the pilgrims choose to do, respect for their almost sacred character demands that I should allow to pass—but I would so like to catch any other member of the party riding his horse up one of these exhausting hills once!

We have given the pilgrims a good many examples that might benefit them, but it is virtue thrown away. They have never heard a cross word out of our lips toward each other —but *they* have quarreled once or twice. We love to hear them at it after they have been lecturing us. The very first thing they did, coming ashore at Beirut, was to quarrel in the boat. I have said I like them, and I do like them—but every time they read me a scorcher of a lecture I mean to talk back in print.

Not content with doubling the legitimate stages, they switched off the main road and went away out of the way to visit an absurd fountain called Figia, because Baalam's ass had drank there once. So we journeyed on, through the terrible hills and deserts and the roasting sun, and then far into the night, seeking the honored pool of Baalam's ass, the patron saint of all pilgrims like us. I find no entry but this in my notebook:

Rode today all together thirteen hours, through deserts
partly, and partly over barren, unsightly hills, and latterly
through wild, rocky scenery, and camped at about eleven
o'clock at night on the banks of a limpid stream, near a
Syrian village. Do not know its name—do not wish to know
it—want to go to bed. Two horses lame (mine and Jack's) and
the others worn out. Jack and I walked three or four miles
over the hills and led the horses. Fun—but of a mild type.

Twelve or thirteen hours in the saddle, even in a Christian
land and a Christian climate, and on a good horse, is a tiresome journey; but in an oven like Syria, in a ragged spoon
of a saddle that slips fore and aft, and "thort-ships," and
every way, and on a horse that is tired and lame and yet
must be whipped and spurred with hardly a moment's ces-
sation all day long, till the blood comes from his side, and
your conscience hurts every time you strike if you are
half a man—it is a journey to be remembered in bit-
terness of spirit and execrated with emphasis for a liberal division of a man's lifetime.

44

The next day was an outrage upon men and horses both.
It was another thirteen-hour stretch (including an hour's
"nooning"). It was over the barrenest chalk hills and through
the baldest canyons that even Syria can show. The heat
quivered in the air everywhere. In the canyons we almost
smothered in the baking atmosphere. On high ground the
reflection from the chalk hills was blinding. It was cruel to
urge the crippled horses, but it had to be done in order to
make Damascus Saturday night. We saw ancient tombs and
temples of fanciful architecture carved out of the solid
rock high up in the face of precipices above our heads, but
we had neither time nor strength to climb up there and examine them. The terse language of my notebook will answer for the rest of this day's experiences:

Broke camp at 7 A.M. and made a ghastly trip through the Zeb Dana Valley and the rough mountains—horses limping and that Arab screech owl that does most of the singing and carries the waterskins, always a thousand miles ahead, of course, and no water to drink—will he *never* die? Beautiful stream in a chasm, lined thick with pomegranate, fig, olive and quince orchards, and nooned an hour at the celebrated Baalam's Ass Fountain of Figia, second in size in Syria, and the coldest water out of Siberia—guidebooks do not say Baalam's ass ever drank there—somebody been imposing on the pilgrims maybe. Bathed in it—Jack and I. Only a second —ice water. It is the principal source of the Abana River— only one-half mile down to where it joins. Beautiful place— giant trees all around—*so* shady and cool, if one could keep awake—vast stream gushes straight out from under the mountain in a torrent. Over it is a very ancient ruin, with no known history—supposed to have been for the worship of the deity of the fountain or Baalam's ass or somebody. Wretched nest of human vermin about the fountain—rags, dirt, sunken cheeks, pallor of sickness, sores, projecting bones, dull, aching misery in their eyes and ravenous hunger speaking from every eloquent fiber and muscle from head to foot. How they sprang upon a bone, how they crunched the bread we gave them! Such as these to swarm about one and watch every bite he takes, with greedy looks, and swallow unconsciously every time he swallows, as if they half fancied the precious morsel went down their own throats—hurry up the caravan!—I never shall enjoy a meal in this distressful country. To think of eating three times every day under *such* circumstances for three weeks yet—it is worse punishment than riding all day in the sun. There are sixteen starving babies from one to six years old in the party, and their legs are no larger than broom handles. Left the fountain at 1 P.M. (the fountain took us at least two hours out of our way) and reached Muhammad's lookout perch, over Damascus, in time to get a good long look before it was necessary to move on. Tired? Ask of the winds that far away with fragments strewed the sea.

As the glare of day mellowed into twilight we looked down upon a picture which is celebrated all over the world. I think I have read about four hundred times that when Muhammad was a simple camel driver he reached this point and looked down upon Damascus for the first time, and then made a certain renowned remark. He said man could enter only one paradise; he preferred to go to the one above. So he sat down there and feasted his eyes upon the earthly paradise of Damascus and then went away without entering its gates. They have erected a tower on the hill to mark the spot where he stood.

Damascus *is* beautiful from the mountain. It is beautiful even to foreigners accustomed to luxuriant vegetation, and I can easily understand how unspeakably beautiful it must be to eyes that are only used to the God-forsaken barrenness and desolation of Syria. I should think a Syrian would go wild with ecstasy when such a picture bursts upon him for the first time.

From his high perch one sees before him and below him a wall of dreary mountains, shorn of vegetation, glaring fiercely in the sun; it fences in a level desert of yellow sand, smooth as velvet and threaded far away with fine lines that stand for roads, and dotted with creeping mites we know are camel trains and journeying men; right in the midst of the desert is spread a billowy expanse of green foliage; and nestling in its heart sits the great white city, like an island of pearls and opals gleaming out of a sea of emeralds. This is the picture you see spread far below you, with distance to soften it, the sun to glorify it, strong contrasts to heighten the effects, and over it and about it a drowsing air of repose to spiritualize it and make it seem rather a beautiful estray from the mysterious worlds we visit in dreams than a substantial tenant of our coarse, dull globe. And when you think of the leagues of blighted, blasted, sandy, rocky, sunburned, ugly, dreary, infamous country you have ridden over to get here, you think it is the most beautiful, beautiful picture that ever human eyes rested upon in all the broad universe! If I were to go to Damascus again, I would camp on Muhammad's hill about a week and then go away. There is no need to go inside the walls. The prophet was wise without knowing it when he decided not to go down into the paradise of Damascus.

There is an honored old tradition that the immense garden which Damascus stands in was the Garden of Eden, and modern writers have gathered up many chapters of evidence tending to show that it really was the Garden of Eden, and that the rivers Pharpar and Abana are the "two rivers" that watered Adam's Paradise. It may be so, but it is not paradise now, and one would be as happy outside of it as he would be likely to be within. It is so crooked and cramped and dirty that one cannot realize that he is in the splendid city he saw from the hilltop. The gardens are hidden by high mud walls, and the paradise is become a very sink of pollution and uncomeliness. Damascus has plenty of clear, pure water in it, though, and this is enough, of itself, to make an Arab think it beautiful and blessed. Water is scarce in blistered Syria. We run railways by our large cities in America; in Syria they curve the roads so as to make them run by the meager little puddles they call "fountains," and which are not found oftener on a journey than every four hours. But the "rivers" of Pharpar and Abana of Scripture (mere creeks) run through Damascus, and so every house and every garden have their sparkling fountains and rivulets of water. With her forest of foliage and her abundance of water, Damascus must be a wonder of wonders to the Bedouin from the deserts. Damascus is simply an oasis—that is what it is. For four thousand years its waters have not gone dry or its fertility failed. Now we can understand why the city has existed so long. It could not die. So long as its waters remain to it away out there in the midst of that howling desert, so long will Damascus live to bless the sight of the tired and thirsty wayfarer.

Though old as history itself, thou art fresh as the breath of spring, blooming as thine own rose-bud, and fragrant as thine own orange flower, O Damascus, pearl of the East!

Damascus dates back anterior to the days of Abraham, and is the oldest city in the world. It was founded by Uz, the grandson of Noah. "The early history of Damascus is shrouded in the mists of a hoary antiquity." Leave the matters written of in the first eleven chapters of the Old Testament out, and no recorded event has occurred in the world but Damascus was in existence to receive the news of it. Go back as far as you will into the vague past, there was always a Damascus. In the writings of every century for more than four thousand years, its name has been mentioned and its praises sung. To Damascus years are only moments, decades are only flitting trifles of time. She measures time not by days and months and years, but by the empires she has seen rise and prosper and crumble to ruin. She is a type of immortality. She saw the foundations of Baalbek and Thebes and Ephesus laid; she saw these villages grow into mighty cities and amaze the world with their grandeur—and she has lived to see them desolate, deserted, and given over to the owls and the bats. She saw the Israelitish empire exalted, and she saw it annihilated. She saw Greece rise and flourish two thousand years and die. In her old age she saw Rome built;

she saw it overshadow the world with its power; she saw it perish. The few hundreds of years of Genoese and Venetian might and splendor were, to grave old Damascus, only a trifling scintillation hardly worth remembering. Damascus has seen all that has ever occurred on earth, and still she lives. She has looked upon the dry bones of a thousand empires, and will see the tombs of a thousand more before she dies. Though another claims the name, old Damascus is by right the Eternal City.

We reached the city gates just at sundown. They do say that one can get into any walled city of Syria after night, for baksheesh, except Damascus. But Damascus, with its four thousand years of respectability in the world, has many old-fogy notions. There are no street lamps there, and the law compels all who go abroad at night to carry lanterns, just as was the case in old days, when heroes and heroines of *The Arabian Nights* walked the streets of Damascus or flew away toward Baghdad on enchanted carpets.

It was fairly dark a few minutes after we got within the wall, and we rode long distances through wonderfully crooked streets, eight to ten feet wide and shut in on either side by the high mud walls of the gardens. At last we got to where lanterns could be seen flitting about here and there, and knew we were in the midst of the curious old city. In a little narrow street crowded with our pack mules and with a swarm of uncouth Arabs, we alighted and through a kind of a hole in the wall entered the hotel. We stood in a great flagged court, with flowers and citron trees about us, and a huge tank in the center that was receiving the waters of many pipes. We crossed the court and entered the rooms prepared to receive four of us. In a large marble-paved recess between the two rooms was a tank of clear, cool water, which was kept running over all the time by the streams that were pouring into it from half a dozen pipes. Nothing in this scorching, desolate land could look so refreshing as this pure water flashing in the lamplight; nothing could look so beautiful, nothing could sound so delicious, as this mimic rain to ears long unaccustomed to sounds of such a nature. Our rooms were large, comfortably furnished, and even had their floors clothed with soft, cheerful-tinted carpets. It was a pleasant thing to see a carpet again, for if there is anything drearier than the tomblike, stone-paved parlors and bedrooms of Europe and Asia, I do not know what it is. They make one think of the grave all the time. A very broad, gaily caparisoned divan, some twelve or fourteen feet long, extended across one side of each room, and opposite were single beds with spring mattresses. There were great looking-glasses and marble-top tables. All this luxury was as grateful to systems and senses worn out with an exhausting day's travel as it was unexpected—for one cannot tell what to expect in a Turkish city of even a quarter of a million inhabitants.

I do not know, but I think they used that tank between the rooms to draw drinking water from; that did not occur to me, however, until I had dipped my baking head far down into its cool depths. I thought of it then, and superb as the bath was, I was sorry I had taken it, and was about to go and explain to the landlord. But a finely curled and scented poodle dog frisked up and nipped the calf of my leg just then, and before I had time to think, I had soused him to the bottom of the tank, and when I saw a servant coming with a pitcher I went off and left the pup trying to climb out and not succeeding very well. Satisfied revenge was all I needed to make me perfectly happy, and when I walked in to supper that first night in Damascus I was in that condition. We lay on those divans a long time after supper, smoking narghiles and long-stemmed chibouks, and talking about the dreadful ride of the day, and I knew then what I had sometimes known before—that it is worthwhile to get tired out because one so enjoys resting afterward.

In the morning we sent for donkeys. It is worthy of note that we had to *send* for these things. I said Damascus was an old fossil, and she is. Anywhere else we would have been assailed by a clamorous army of donkey drivers, guides, peddlers, and beggars—but in Damascus they so hate the very sight of a foreign Christian that they want no intercourse whatever with him; only a year or two ago his person was not always safe in Damascus streets. It is the most fanatical Muhammadan purgatory out of Arabia. Where you see one green turban of a hadji elsewhere (the honored sign that my lord has made the pilgrimage to Mecca), I think you will see a dozen in Damascus. The Damascenes are the ugliest, wickedest-looking villains we have seen. All the veiled women we had seen yet, nearly, left their eyes exposed, but numbers of these in Damascus completely hid the face under a close-drawn black veil that made the woman look like a mummy. If ever we caught an eye exposed, it was quickly hidden from our contaminating Christian vision; the beggars actually passed us by without demanding baksheesh; the merchants in the bazaars did not hold up their goods and cry out eagerly, "Hey, John!" or "Look this, Howajji!" On the contrary, they only scowled at us and said never a word.

The narrow streets swarmed like a hive with men and women in strange Oriental costumes, and our small donkeys knocked them right and left as we plowed through them, urged on by the merciless donkey boys. These persecutors run after the animals, shouting and goading them for hours together; they keep the donkey in a gallop always, yet never get tired themselves or fall behind. The donkeys fell down and spilled us over their heads occasionally, but there was nothing for it but to mount and hurry on again. We were banged against sharp corners, loaded porters, camels, and citizens generally; and we were so taken up with looking out for collisions and casualties that we had no chance to look about us at all. We rode half through the city and through the famous "street which is called Straight" without seeing anything hardly. Our bones were nearly knocked out of joint, we were wild with excitement, and our sides ached with the jolting we had suffered. I do not like riding in the Damascus streetcars.

We were on our way to the reputed houses of Judas and Ananias. About eighteen or nineteen hundred years ago Saul, a native of Tarsus, was particularly bitter against the new sect called Christians, and he left Jerusalem and started across the country on a furious crusade against them. He went forth "breathing threatenings and slaughter against the disciples of the Lord."

And as he journeyed, he came near Damascus, and suddenly there shined round about him a light from heaven:

And he fell to the earth and heard a voice saying unto him, "Saul, Saul, why persecutest thou me?"

And when he knew that it was Jesus that spoke to him he trembled, and was astonished, and said, "Lord, what wilt thou have me to do?"

He was told to arise and go into the ancient city and one would tell him what to do. In the meantime his soldiers stood speechless and awestricken, for they heard the mysterious voice but saw no man. Saul rose up and found that that fierce supernatural light had destroyed his sight, and he was blind, so "they led him by the hand and brought him to Damascus." He was converted.

Paul lay three days blind in the house of Judas, and during that time he neither ate nor drank.

There came a voice to a citizen of Damascus, named Ananias, saying, "Arise, and go into the street which is called Straight, and inquire at the house of Judas, for one called Saul, of Tarsus; for behold, he prayeth."

Ananias did not wish to go at first, for he had heard of Saul before, and he had his doubts about that style of a "chosen vessel" to preach the gospel of peace. However, in obedience to orders, he went into the "street called Straight" (how he ever found his way into it and, after he did, how he ever found his way out of it again are mysteries only to be accounted for by the fact that he was acting under divine inspiration). He found Paul and restored him, and ordained him a preacher; and from this old house we had hunted up in the street which is miscalled Straight, he had started out on that bold missionary career which he prosecuted till his death. It was not the house of the disciple who sold the Master for thirty pieces of silver. I make this explanation in justice to Judas, who was a far different sort of man from the person just referred to. A very different style of man, and lived in a very good house. It is a pity we do not know more about him.

I have given, in the above paragraphs, some more information for people who will not read Bible history until they are defrauded into it by some such method as this. I hope that no friend of progress and education will obstruct or interfere with my peculiar mission.

The street called Straight is straighter than a corkscrew, but not as straight as a rainbow. St. Luke is careful not to commit himself; he does not say it is the street which *is* straight, but the "street which is *called* Straight." It is a fine piece of irony; it is the only facetious remark in the Bible, I believe. We traversed the street called Straight a good way, and then turned off and called at the reputed house of Ananias. There is small question that a part of the original house is there still; it is an old room twelve or fifteen feet underground, and its masonry is evidently ancient. If Ananias did not live there in St. Paul's time, somebody else did, which is just as well. I took a drink out of Ananias' well, and singularly enough, the water was just as fresh as if the well had been dug yesterday.

We went out toward the north end of the city to see the place where the disciples let Paul down over the Damascus wall at dead of night—for he preached Christ so fearlessly in Damascus that the people sought to kill him, just as they would today for the same offense, and he had to escape and flee to Jerusalem.

Then we called at the tomb of Muhammad's children and at a tomb which purported to be that of St. George, who killed the dragon, and so on out to the hollow place under a rock where Paul hid during his flight till his pursuers gave him up, and to the mausoleum of the five thousand Christians who were massacred in Damascus in 1861 by the Turks. They say those narrow streets ran blood for several days, and that men, women, and children were butchered indiscriminately and left to rot by hundreds all through the Christian quarter; they say, further, that the stench was dreadful. All the Christians who could get away fled from the city, and the Muhammadans would not defile their hands by burying the "infidel dogs." The thirst for blood extended to the highlands of Hermon and Anti-Lebanon, and in a short time twenty-five thousand more Christians were massacred and their possessions laid waste. How they hate a Christian in Damascus!—and pretty much all over Turkeydom as well. And how they will pay for it when Russia turns her guns upon them again!

It is soothing to the heart to abuse England and France for interposing to save the Ottoman empire from the destruction it has so richly deserved for a thousand years. It hurts my vanity to see these pagans refuse to eat of food that has been cooked for us, or to eat from a dish we have eaten from, or to drink from a goatskin which we have polluted with our Christian lips except by filtering the water through a rag which they put over the mouth of it or through a sponge! I never disliked a Chinaman as I do these degraded Turks and Arabs, and when Russia is ready to war with them again, I hope England and France will not find it good breeding or good judgment to interfere.

In Damascus they think there are no such rivers in all the world as their little Abana and Pharpar. The Damascenes have always thought that way. In 2 Kings, chapter v, Naaman boasts extravagantly about them. That was three thousand years ago. He says: "Are not Abana and Pharpar, rivers of Damascus, better than all the waters of Israel? May I not wash in them and be clean?" But some of my readers have forgotten who Naaman was, long ago. Naaman was the commander of the Syrian armies. He was the favorite of the king and lived in great state. "He was a mighty man of valor, but he was a leper." Strangely enough, the house they point out to you now as his has been turned into a leper hospital, and the inmates expose their horrid deformities and hold up their hands and beg for baksheesh when a stranger enters.

One cannot appreciate the horror of this disease until he looks upon it in all its ghastliness, in Naaman's ancient dwelling in Damascus. Bones all twisted out of shape, great knots protruding from face and body, joints decaying and dropping away—horrible!

45

The last twenty-four hours we stayed in Damascus I lay prostrate with a violent attack of cholera or cholera morbus, and therefore had a good chance and a good excuse to lie there on that wide divan and take an honest rest. I had nothing to do but listen to the pattering of the fountains and take medicine and throw it up again. It was dangerous recreation, but it was pleasanter than traveling in Syria. I had plenty of snow from Mount Hermon, and as it would not stay on my stomach, there was nothing to interfere with my eating it—there was always room for more. I enjoyed myself very well. Syrian travel has its interesting features, like travel in any other part of the world, and yet to break your leg or have the cholera adds a welcome variety to it.

We left Damascus at noon and rode across the plain a couple of hours, and then the party stopped awhile in the shade of some fig trees to give me a chance to rest. It was the hottest day we had seen yet—the sun flames shot down like the shafts of fire that stream out before a blowpipe; the rays seemed to fall in a steady deluge on the head and pass downward like rain from a roof. I imagined I could distinguish between the floods of rays—I thought I could tell when each flood struck my head, when it reached my shoulders, and when the next one came. It was terrible. All the desert glared so fiercely that my eyes were swimming in tears all the time. The boys had white umbrellas heavily lined with dark green. They were a priceless blessing. I thanked fortune that I had one, too, notwithstanding it was packed up with the baggage and was ten miles ahead. It is madness to travel in Syria without an umbrella. They told me in Beirut (these people who always gorge you with advice) that it was madness to travel in Syria without an umbrella. It was on this account that I got one.

But, honestly, I think an umbrella is a nuisance anywhere when its business is to keep the sun off. No Arab wears a brim to his fez or uses an umbrella or anything to shade his eyes or his face, and he always looks comfortable and proper in the sun. But of all the ridiculous sights I ever have seen, our party of eight is the most so—they do cut such an outlandish figure. They travel single file; they all wear the endless white rag of Constantinople wrapped round and round their hats and dangling down their backs; they all wear thick green spectacles, with side glasses to them; they all hold white umbrellas, lined with green, over their heads; without exception their stirrups are too short—they are the very worst gang of horsemen on earth; their animals to a horse trot fearfully hard—and when they get strung out one after the other; glaring straight ahead and breathless; bouncing high and out of turn, all along the line; knees well up and stiff, elbows flapping like a rooster's that is going to crow, and the long file of umbrellas popping convulsively up and down —when one sees this outrageous picture exposed to the light of day, he is amazed that the gods don't get out their thunderbolts and destroy them off the face of the earth! I do—I wonder at it. I wouldn't let any such caravan go through a country of mine.

And when the sun drops below the horizon and the boys close their umbrellas and put them under their arms, it is only a variation of the picture, not a modification of its absurdity.

But maybe you cannot see the wild extravagance of my panorama. You could if you were here. Here you feel all the time just as if you were living about the year 1200 before Christ—or back to the patriarchs—or forward to the New Era. The scenery of the Bible is about you—the customs of the patriarchs are around you—the same people, in the same flowing robes and in sandals, cross your path—the same long trains of stately camels go and come—the same impressive religious solemnity and silence rest upon the desert and the mountains that were upon them in the remote ages of antiquity, and behold, intruding upon a scene like this, comes this fantastic mob of green-spectacled Yanks, with their flapping elbows and bobbing umbrellas! It is Daniel in the lion's den, with a green cotton umbrella under his arm, all over again.

My umbrella is with the baggage, and so are my green spectacles—and there they shall stay. I will not use them. I will show some respect for the eternal fitness of things. It will be bad enough to get sunstruck without looking ridiculous into the bargain. If I fall, let me fall bearing about me the semblance of a Christian at least.

Three or four hours out from Damascus we passed the spot where Saul was so abruptly converted, and from this place we looked back over the scorching desert and had our last glimpse of beautiful Damascus, decked in its robes of shining green. After nightfall we reached our tents, just outside of the nasty Arab village of Jonesborough. Of course the real name of the place is El something or other, but the boys still refuse to recognize the Arab names or try to pronounce them. When I say that that village is of the usual style, I mean to insinuate that all Syrian villages within fifty miles of Damascus are alike—so much alike that it would require more than human intelligence to tell wherein one differed from another. A Syrian village is a hive of huts one story high (the height of a man), and as square as a dry-goods box; it is mud-plastered all over, flat roof and all, and generally whitewashed after a fashion. The same roof often extends over half the town, covering many of the *streets,* which are generally about a yard wide. When you ride through one of these villages at noonday, you first meet a melancholy dog that looks up at you and silently begs that you won't run over him, but he does not offer to get out of the way; next you meet a young boy without any clothes on, and he holds out his hand and says, "Baksheesh!"—he don't really expect a cent, but then he learned to say that before he learned to say mother, and now he cannot break himself of it; next you meet a woman with a black veil drawn closely over her face, and her bust exposed; finally, you come to several sore-eyed children and children in all stages of mutilation and decay; and sitting humbly in the dust, and all fringed with filthy rags, is a poor devil whose arms and legs are gnarled and twisted like grapevines. These are all the people you are likely to see. The balance of the population are asleep within doors or abroad tending goats in the plains and on the hillsides. The village is built on some consumptive little watercourse, and about it is a little fresh-looking vegetation. Beyond this charmed circle, for miles on every side, stretches a weary desert of sand and gravel, which produces a gray bunchy shrub like sagebrush. A Syrian village is the sorriest sight in the world, and its surroundings are eminently in keeping with it.

I would not have gone into this dissertation upon Syrian villages but for the fact that Nimrod, the Mighty Hunter of Scriptural notoriety, is buried in Jonesborough, and I wished the public to know about how he is located. Like Homer, he is said to be buried in many other places, but this is the only true and genuine place his ashes inhabit.

When the original tribes were dispersed, more than four thousand years ago, Nimrod and a large party traveled three or four hundred miles and settled where the great city of Babylon afterwards stood. Nimrod built that city. He also began to build the famous Tower of Babel, but circumstances over which he had no control put it out of his power to finish it. He ran it up eight stories high, however, and two of them still stand at this day—a colossal mass of brickwork, rent down the center by earthquakes, and seared and vitrified by the lightnings of an angry God. But the vast ruin will still stand for ages, to shame the puny labors of these modern generations of men. Its huge compartments are tenanted by owls and lions, and old Nimrod lies neglected in this wretched village, far from the scene of his grand enterprise.

We left Jonesborough very early in the morning and rode forever and forever and forever, it seemed to me, over parched deserts and rocky hills, hungry and with no water to drink. We had drained the goatskins dry in a little while. At noon we halted before the wretched Arab town of El Yuba

Dam, perched on the side of a mountain, but the dragoman said if we applied there for water we would be attacked by the whole tribe, for they did not love Christians. We had to journey on. Two hours later we reached the foot of a tall isolated mountain, which is crowned by the crumbling castle of Baniyas, the stateliest ruin of that kind on earth, no doubt. It is a thousand feet long and two hundred wide, all of the most symmetrical and at the same time the most ponderous masonry. The massive towers and bastions are more than thirty feet high, and have been sixty. From the mountain's peak its broken turrets rise above the groves of ancient oaks and olives and look wonderfully picturesque. It is of such high antiquity that no man knows who built it or when it was built. It is utterly inaccessible except in one place, where a bridle path winds upward among the solid rocks to the old portcullis. The horses' hoofs have bored holes in these rocks to the depth of six inches during the hundreds and hundreds of years that the castle was garrisoned. We wandered for three hours among the chambers and crypts and dungeons of the fortress, and trod where the mailed heels of many a knightly Crusader had rang and where Phoenician heroes had walked ages before them.

We wondered how such a solid mass of masonry could be affected even by an earthquake, and could not understand what agency had made Baniyas a ruin; but we found the destroyer after a while, and then our wonder was increased tenfold. Seeds had fallen in crevices in the vast walls; the seeds had sprouted; the tender, insignificant sprouts had hardened; they grew larger and larger, and by a steady, imperceptible pressure forced the great stones apart, and now are bringing sure destruction upon a giant work that has even mocked the earthquakes to scorn! Gnarled and twisted trees spring from the old walls everywhere, and beautify and overshadow the gray battlements with a wild luxuriance of foliage.

From these old towers we looked down upon a broad, far-reaching green plain, glittering with the pools and rivulets which are the sources of the sacred River Jordan. It was a grateful vision after so much desert.

And as the evening drew near we clambered down the mountain, through groves of the Biblical oaks of Bashan (for we were just stepping over the border and entering the long-sought Holy Land), and at its extreme foot, toward the wide valley, we entered this little execrable village of Baniyas and camped in a great grove of olive trees near a torrent of sparkling water whose banks are arrayed in fig trees, pomegranates, and oleanders in full leaf. Barring the proximity of the village, it is a sort of paradise.

The very first thing one feels like doing when he gets into camp, all burning up and dusty, is to hunt up a bath. We followed the stream up to where it gushes out of the mountainside, three hundred yards from the tents, and took a bath that was so icy that if I did not know this was the main source of the sacred river, I would expect harm to come of it. It was bathing at noonday in the chilly source of the Abana, "River of Damascus," that gave me the cholera, so Dr. B. said. However, it generally does give me the cholera to take a bath.

The incorrigible pilgrims have come in with their pockets full of specimens broken from the ruins. I wish this vandalism could be stopped. They broke off fragments from Noah's tomb; from the exquisite sculptures of the temples of Baalbek; from the houses of Judas and Ananias, in Damascus; from the tomb of Nimrod the Mighty Hunter in Jonesborough; from the worn Greek and Roman inscriptions set in the hoary walls of the castle of Baniyas; and now they have been hacking and chipping these old arches here that Jesus looked upon in the flesh. Heaven protect the Sepulchre when this tribe invades Jerusalem!

The ruins here are not very interesting. There are the massive walls of a great square building that was once the citadel; there are many ponderous old arches that are so smothered with debris that they barely project above the ground; there are heavy-walled sewers through which the crystal brook of which Jordan is born still runs; in the hillside are the substructions of a costly marble temple that Herod the Great built here—patches of its handsome mosaic floors still remain; there is a quaint old stone bridge that was here before Herod's time maybe; scattered everywhere, in the paths and in the woods, are Corinthian capitals, broken porphyry pillars, and little fragments of sculpture; and up yonder, in the precipice where the fountain gushes out, are well-worn Greek inscriptions over niches in the rock where in ancient times the Greeks and, after them, the Romans worshiped the sylvan god Pan. But trees and bushes grow above many of these ruins now; the miserable huts of a little crew of filthy Arabs are perched upon the broken masonry of antiquity, the whole place has a sleepy, stupid, rural look about it, and one can hardly bring himself to believe that a busy, substantially built city once existed here, even two thousand years ago. The place was nevertheless the scene of an event whose effects have added page after page and volume after volume to the world's history. For in this place Christ stood when he said to Peter:

"Thou art Peter; and upon this rock will I build my church, and the gates of hell shall not prevail against it. And I will give unto thee the keys of the Kingdom of Heaven; and whatsoever thou shalt bind on earth shall be bound in heaven, and whatsoever thou shalt loose on earth shall be loosed in heaven."

On those little sentences have been built up the mighty edifice of the Church of Rome; in them lie the authority for the imperial power of the popes over temporal affairs and their godlike power to curse a soul or wash it white from sin. To sustain the position of "the only true Church," which Rome claims was thus conferred upon her, she has fought and labored and struggled for many a century, and will continue to keep herself busy in the same work to the end of time. The memorable words I have quoted give to this ruined city about all the interest it possesses to people of the present day.

It seems curious enough to us to be standing on ground that was once actually pressed by the feet of the Saviour. The situation is suggestive of a reality and a tangibility that seem at variance with the vagueness and mystery and ghostliness that one naturally attaches to the character of a god. I cannot comprehend yet that I am sitting where a god has stood, and looking upon the brook and the mountains which that god looked upon, and am surrounded by dusky men and women whose ancestors saw him, and even talked with him, face to face, and carelessly, just as they would have done with any other stranger. I cannot comprehend this; the gods of my understanding have been always hidden in clouds and very far away.

This morning, during breakfast, the usual assemblage of squalid humanity sat patiently without the charmed circle of the camp and waited for such crumbs as pity might bestow upon their misery. There were old and young, brown-skinned and yellow. Some of the men were tall and stalwart (for one hardly sees anywhere such splendid-looking men as here in the East), but all the women and children looked worn and sad and distressed with hunger. They reminded me much of Indians, did these people. They had but little clothing, but such as they had was fanciful in character and fantastic in its arrangement. Any little absurd gewgaw or gimcrack they had they disposed in such a way as to make it attract attention most readily. They sat in silence, and with tireless patience watched our every motion with that vile, uncomplaining impoliteness which is so truly Indian, and which makes a white man so nervous and uncomfortable and savage that he wants to exterminate the whole tribe.

These people about us had other peculiarities which I have noticed in the noble red man, too: they were infested with vermin, and the dirt had caked on them till it amounted to bark.

The little children were in a pitiable condition—they all had sore eyes, and were otherwise afflicted in various ways. They say that hardly a native child in all the East is free from sore eyes, and that thousands of them go blind of one eye or both every year. I think this must be so, for I see plenty of blind people every day, and I do not remember seeing any children that hadn't sore eyes. And would you suppose that an American mother could sit for an hour, with her child in her arms, and let a hundred flies roost upon its eyes all that time undisturbed? I see that every day. It makes my flesh creep. Yesterday we met a woman riding on a little jackass, and she had a little child in her arms; honestly, I thought the child had goggles on as we approached, and I wondered how its mother could afford so much style. But when we drew near, we saw that the goggles were nothing but a camp meeting of flies assembled around each of the child's eyes, and at the same time there was a detachment prospecting its nose. The flies were happy, the child was contented, and so the mother did not interfere.

As soon as the tribe found out that we had a doctor in our party, they began to flock in from all quarters. Dr. B., in the charity of his nature, had taken a child from a woman who sat nearby and put some sort of a wash upon its diseased eyes. That woman went off and started the whole nation, and it was a sight to see them swarm! The lame, the halt, the blind, the leprous—all the distempers that are bred of indolence, dirt, and iniquity—were represented in the Congress in ten minutes, and still they came! Every woman that had a sick baby brought it along, and every woman that hadn't, borrowed one. What reverent and what worshiping looks they bent upon that dread, mysterious power, the Doctor! They watched him take his phials out; they watched him measure the particles of white powder; they watched him add drops of one precious liquid and drops of another; they lost not the slightest movement; their eyes were riveted upon him with a fascination that nothing could distract. I believe they thought he was gifted like a god. When each individual got his portion of medicine, his eyes were radiant with joy—notwithstanding by nature they are a thankless and impassive race—and upon his face was written the unquestioning faith that nothing on earth could prevent the patient from getting well now.

Christ knew how to preach to these simple, superstitious, disease-tortured creatures: He healed the sick. They flocked to our poor human doctor this morning when the fame of what he had done to the sick child went abroad in the land, and they worshiped him with their eyes while they did not know as yet whether there was virtue in his simples or not. The ancestors of these—people precisely like them in color, dress, manners, customs, simplicity—flocked in vast multitudes after Christ, and when they saw him make the afflicted whole with a word, it is no wonder they worshiped him. No wonder his deeds were the talk of the nation. No wonder the multitude that followed him was so great that at one time —thirty miles from here—they had to let a sick man down through the roof because no approach could be made to the door; no wonder his audiences were so great at Galilee that he had to preach from a ship removed a little distance from the shore; no wonder that even in the desert places about Bethsaida, five thousand invaded his solitude, and he had to feed them by a miracle or else see them suffer for their confiding faith and devotion; no wonder when there was a great commotion in a city in those days, one neighbor explained it to another in words to this effect: "They say that Jesus of Nazareth is come!"

Well, as I was saying, the doctor distributed medicine as long as he had any to distribute, and his reputation is mighty in Galilee this day. Among his patients was the child of the Sheikh's daughter—for even this poor, ragged handful of sores and sin has its royal sheikh—a poor old mummy that looked as if he would be more at home in a poorhouse than in the chief magistracy of this tribe of hopeless, shirtless savages. The princess—I mean the Sheikh's daughter—was only thirteen or fourteen years old, and had a very sweet face and a pretty one. She was the only Syrian female we have seen yet who was not so sinfully ugly that she couldn't smile after ten o'clock Saturday night without breaking the Sabbath. Her child was a hard specimen, though—there wasn't enough of it to make a pie—and the poor little thing looked so pleadingly up at all who came near it (as if it had an idea that now was its chance or never) that we were filled with compassion which was genuine and not put on.

But this last new horse I have got is trying to break his neck over the tent ropes, and I shall have to go out and anchor him. Jericho and I have parted company. The new horse is not much to boast of, I think. One of his hindlegs bends the wrong way, and the other one is as straight and stiff as a tent pole. Most of his teeth are gone, and he is as blind as a bat. His nose has been broken at some time or other and is arched like a culvert now. His underlip hangs down like a camel's, and his ears are chopped off close to his head. I had some trouble at first to find a name for him, but I finally concluded to call him Baalbek, because he is such a magnificent ruin. I cannot keep from talking about my horses, because I have a very long and tedious journey before me, and they naturally occupy my thoughts about as much as matters of apparently much greater importance.

We satisfied our pilgrims by making those hard rides from Baalbek to Damascus, but Dan's horse and Jack's were so crippled we had to leave them behind and get fresh animals for them. The dragoman says Jack's horse died. I swapped horses with Muhammad, the kingly-looking Egyptian who is our Ferguson's lieutenant. By Ferguson I mean our dragoman Abraham, of course. I did not take this horse on account of his personal appearance, but because I have not seen his back. I do not wish to see it. I have seen the backs of all the other horses and found most of them covered with dreadful saddle boils which I know have not been washed or doctored for years. The idea of riding all day long over such ghastly inquisitions of torture is sickening. My horse must be like the others, but I have at least the consolation of not knowing it to be so.

I hope that in future I may be spared any more sentimental

praises of the Arab's idolatry of his horse. In boyhood I longed to be an Arab of the desert and have a beautiful mare, and call her Selim or Benjamin or Muhammad, and feed her with my own hands, and let her come into the tent, and teach her to caress me and look fondly upon me with her great tender eyes; and I wished that a stranger might come at such a time and offer me a hundred thousand dollars for her, so that I could do like the other Arabs—hesitate, yearn for the money, but, overcome by my love for my mare, at last say, "Part with thee, my beautiful one! Never with my life! Away, tempter, I scorn thy gold!" and then bound into the saddle and speed over the desert like the wind!

But I recall those aspirations. If these Arabs be like the other Arabs, their love for their beautiful mares is a fraud. These of my acquaintance have no love for their horses, no sentiment of pity for them, and no knowledge of how to treat them or care for them. The Syrian saddle blanket is a quilted mattress two or three inches thick. It is never removed from the horse, day or night. It gets full of dirt and hair, and becomes soaked with sweat. It is bound to breed sores. These pirates never think of washing a horse's back. They do not shelter the horses in the tents, either; they must stay out and take the weather as it comes. Look at poor cropped and dilapidated "Baalbek," and weep for the sentiment that has been wasted upon the Selims of romance!

46

About an hour's ride over a rough, rocky road, half flooded with water, and through a forest of oaks of Bashan, brought us to Dan.

From a little mound here in the plain issues a broad stream of limpid water and forms a large shallow pool, and then rushes furiously onward, augmented in volume. This puddle is an important source of the Jordan. Its banks and those of the brook are respectably adorned with blooming oleanders, but the unutterable beauty of the spot will not throw a well-balanced man into convulsions, as the Syrian books of travel would lead one to suppose.

From the spot I am speaking of, a cannonball would carry beyond the confines of Holy Land and light upon profane ground three miles away. We were only one little hour's travel within the borders of Holy Land—we had hardly begun to appreciate yet that we were standing upon any different sort of earth than that we had always been used to—and yet see how the historic names began already to cluster! Dan—Bashan—Lake Hule—the sources of Jordan—the Sea of Galilee. They were all in sight but the last, and it was not far away. The little township of Bashan was once the kingdom so famous in Scripture for its bulls and its oaks. Lake Hule is the Biblical "Waters of Merom." Dan was the northern and Beersheba the southern limit of Palestine—hence the expression "from Dan to Beersheba." It is equivalent to our phrases "from Maine to Texas," "from Baltimore to San Francisco." Our expression and that of the Israelites both mean the same—great distance. With their slow camels and asses it was about a seven days' journey from Dan to Beersheba—say a hundred and fifty or sixty miles—it was the entire length of their country, and was not to be undertaken without great preparation and much ceremony. When the Prodigal traveled to "a far country," it is not likely that he went more than eighty or ninety miles. Palestine is only from forty to sixty miles wide. The state of Missouri could be split into three Palestines and there would then be enough material left for part of another—possibly a whole one. From Baltimore to San Francisco is several thousand miles, but it will be only a seven days' journey in the cars when I am two or three years older.* If I live I shall necessarily have to go across the continent every now and then in those cars, but one journey from Dan to Beersheba will be sufficient, no doubt. It must be the most trying of the two. Therefore if we chance to discover that from Dan to Beersheba seemed a mighty stretch of country to the Israelites, let us not be airy with them, but reflect that it *was* and *is* a mighty stretch when one cannot traverse it by rail.

The small mound I have mentioned awhile ago was once occupied by the Phoenician city of Laish. A party of filibus-

* The railroad has been completed since the above was written.

ters from Zorah and Eschol captured the place and lived there in a free and easy way, worshiping gods of their own manufacture and stealing idols from their neighbors whenever they wore their own out. Jeroboam set up a golden calf here to fascinate his people and keep them from making dangerous trips to Jerusalem to worship, which might result in a return to their rightful allegiance. With all respect for those ancient Israelites, I cannot overlook the fact that they were not always virtuous enough to withstand the seductions of a golden calf. Human nature has not changed much since then.

Some forty centuries ago the city of Sodom was pillaged by the Arab princes of Mesopotamia, and among other prisoners they seized upon the patriarch Lot and brought him here on their way to their own possessions. They brought him to Dan, and father Abraham, who was pursuing them, crept softly in at dead of night, among the whispering oleanders and under the shadows of the stately oaks, and fell upon the slumbering victors and startled them from their dreams with the clash of steel. He recaptured Lot and all the other plunder.

We moved on. We were now in a green valley five or six miles wide and fifteen long. The streams which are called the sources of the Jordan flow through it to Lake Hule, a shallow pond three miles in diameter, and from the southern extremity of the lake the concentrated Jordan flows out. The lake is surrounded by a broad marsh grown with reeds. Between the marsh and the mountains which wall the valley is a respectable strip of fertile land; at the end of the valley, toward Dan, as much as half the land is solid and fertile, and watered by Jordan's sources. There is enough of it to make a farm. It almost warrants the enthusiasm of the spies of that rabble of adventurers who captured Dan. They said: "We have seen the land, and behold it is very good. . . . A place where there is no want of anything that is in the earth."

Their enthusiasm was at least warranted by the fact that they had never seen a country as good as this. There was enough of it for the ample support of their six hundred men and their families, too.

When we got fairly down on the level part of the Danite farm, we came to places where we could actually run our horses. It was a notable circumstance.

We had been painfully clambering over interminable hills

and rocks for days together, and when we suddenly came upon this astonishing piece of rockless plain, every man drove the spurs into his horse and sped away with a velocity he could surely enjoy to the utmost, but could never hope to comprehend in Syria.

Here were evidences of cultivation—a rare sight in this country—an acre or two of rich soil studded with last season's dead cornstalks of the thickness of your thumb and very wide apart. But in such a land it was a thrilling spectacle. Close to it was a stream, and on its banks a great herd of curious-looking Syrian goats and sheep were gratefully eating gravel. I do not state this as a petrified fact—I only *suppose* they were eating gravel, because there did not appear to be anything else for them to eat. The shepherds that tended them were the very pictures of Joseph and his brethren, I have no doubt in the world. They were tall, muscular, and very dark-skinned Bedouins, with inky black beards. They had firm lips, unquailing eyes, and a kingly stateliness of bearing. They wore the particolored half bonnet, half hood, with fringed ends falling upon their shoulders, and the full, flowing robe barred with broad black stripes—the dress one sees in all pictures of the swarthy sons of the desert. These chaps would sell their younger brothers if they had a chance, I think. They have the manners, the customs, the dress, the occupation, and the loose principles of the ancient stock. [They attacked our camp last night, and I bear them no goodwill.] They had with them the pygmy jackasses one sees all over Syria and remembers in all pictures of the "Flight into Egypt," where Mary and the Young Child are riding and Joseph is walking alongside, towering high above the little donkey's shoulders.

But really, here the man rides and carries the child, as a general thing, and the woman walks. The customs have not changed since Joseph's time. We would not have in our houses a picture representing Joseph riding and Mary walking; we would see profanation in it, but a Syrian Christian would not. I know that hereafter the picture I first spoke of will look odd to me.

We could not stop to rest two or three hours out from our camp, of course, albeit the brook was beside us. So we went on an hour longer. We saw water then, but nowhere in all the waste around was there a foot of shade, and we were scorching to death. "Like unto the shadow of a great rock in a weary land." Nothing in the Bible is more beautiful than that, and surely there is no place we have wandered to that is able to give it such touching expression as this blistering, naked, treeless land.

Here you do not stop just when you please, but when you can. We found water, but no shade. We traveled on and found a tree at last, but no water. We rested and lunched, and came on to this place, Ain Mellahah (the boys call it Baldwinsville). It was a very short day's run, but the drago-man does not want to go further, and has invented a plausible lie about the country beyond this being infested by ferocious Arabs, who would make sleeping in their midst a dangerous pastime. Well, they ought to be dangerous. They carry a rusty old weather-beaten flintlock gun, with a barrel that is longer than themselves; it has no sights on it; it will not carry farther than a brickbat, and is not half so certain. And the great sash they wear in many a fold around their waists has two or three absurd old horse pistols in it that are rusty from eternal disuse—weapons that would hang fire just about long enough for you to walk out of range, and then burst and blow the Arab's head off. Exceedingly dangerous these sons of the desert are.

It used to make my blood run cold to read Wm. C. Grimes's hairbreadth escapes from Bedouins, but I think I could read them now without a tremor. He never said he was attacked by Bedouins, I believe, or was ever treated uncivilly, but then in about every other chapter he discovered them approaching anyhow, and he had a blood-curdling fashion of working up the peril; and of wondering how his relations far away would feel could they see their poor wandering boy, with his weary feet and his dim eyes, in such fearful danger; and of thinking for the last time of the old homestead, and the dear old church, and the cow, and those things; and of finally straightening his form to its utmost height in the saddle, drawing his trusty revolver, and then dashing the spurs into "Muhammad" and sweeping down upon the ferocious enemy determined to sell his life as dearly as possible. True the Bedouins never did anything to him when he arrived, and never had any intention of doing anything to him in the first place, and wondered what in the mischief he was making all that to-do about; but still I could not divest myself of the idea somehow that a frightful peril had been escaped through that man's daredevil bravery, and so I never could read about Wm. C. Grimes's Bedouins and sleep comfortably afterward. But I believe the Bedouins to be a fraud now. I have seen the monster, and I can outrun him. I shall never be afraid of his daring to stand behind his own gun and discharge it.

About fifteen hundred years before Christ, this campground of ours by the Waters of Merom was the scene of one of Joshua's exterminating battles. Jabin, King of Hazor (up yonder above Dan), called all the sheikhs about him together, with their hosts, to make ready for Israel's terrible general who was approaching.

"And when all these Kings were met together, they came and pitched together by the Waters of Merom, to fight against Israel.

"And they went out, they and all their hosts with them, much people, even as the sand that is upon the sea-shore for multitude," etc.

But Joshua fell upon them and utterly destroyed them, root and branch. That was his usual policy in war. He never left any chance for newspaper controversies about who won the battle. He made this valley, so quiet now, a reeking slaughter pen.

Somewhere in this part of the country—I do not know exactly where—Israel fought another bloody battle a hundred years later. Deborah, the prophetess, told Barak to take ten thousand men and sally forth against another King Jabin, who had been doing something. Barak came down from Mount Tabor, twenty or twenty-five miles from here, and gave battle to Jabin's forces, who were in command of Sisera. Barak won the fight, and while he was making the victory complete, by the usual method of exterminating the remnant of the defeated host, Sisera fled away on foot, and when he was nearly exhausted by fatigue and thirst, one Jael, a woman he seems to have been acquainted with, invited him to come into her tent and rest himself. The weary soldier acceded readily enough, and Jael put him to bed. He said he was very thirsty and asked his generous preserver to get him a cup of water. She brought him some milk, and he drank of it gratefully and lay down again, to forget in pleasant dreams his lost battle and his humbled pride. Presently when he was asleep she came softly in with a hammer and drove a hideous tent pin down through his brain!

"For he was fast asleep and weary. So he died." Such is the touching language of the Bible. "The Song of Deborah and Barak" praises Jael for the memorable service she had rendered, in an exultant strain:

Blessed above women shall Jael the wife of Heber the Kenite be, blessed shall she be above women in the tent.

He asked for water, and she gave him milk; she brought forth butter in a lordly dish.

She put her hand to the nail, and her right hand to the workman's hammer; and with the hammer she smote Sisera, she smote off his head when she had pierced and stricken through his temples.

At her feet he bowed, he fell, he lay down: at her feet he bowed, he fell: where he bowed, there he fell down dead.

Stirring scenes like these occur in this valley no more. There is not a solitary village throughout its whole extent —not for thirty miles in either direction. There are two or three small clusters of Bedouin tents, but not a single permanent habitation. One may ride ten miles hereabouts and not see ten human beings.

To this region one of the prophecies is applied:

I will bring the land into desolation; and your enemies which dwell therein shall be astonished at it. And I will scatter you among the heathen, and I will draw out a sword after you; and your land shall be desolate and your cities waste.

No man can stand here by deserted Ain Mellahah and say the prophecy has not been fulfilled.

In a verse from the Bible which I have quoted above occurs the phrase "all these kings." It attracted my attention in a moment, because it carries to my mind such a vastly different significance from what it always did at home. I can see easily enough that if I wish to profit by this tour and come to a correct understanding of the matters of interest connected with it, I must studiously and faithfully unlearn a great many things I have somehow absorbed concerning Palestine. I must begin a system of reduction. Like my grapes which the spies bore out of the Promised Land, I have got everything in Palestine on too large a scale. Some of my ideas were wild enough. The word "Palestine" always brought to my mind a vague suggestion of a country as large as the United States. I do not know why, but such was the case. I suppose it was because I could not conceive of a small country having so large a history. I think I was a little surprised to find that the grand Sultan of Turkey was a man of only ordinary size. I must try to reduce my ideas of Palestine to a more reasonable shape. One gets large impressions in boyhood sometimes, which he has to fight against all his life. "All these kings." When I used to read that in Sunday school, it suggested to me the several kings of such countries as England, France, Spain, Germany, Russia, etc., arrayed in splendid robes ablaze with jewels, marching in grave procession, with scepters of gold in their hands and flashing crowns upon their heads. But here in Ain Mellahah, after coming through Syria, and after giving serious study to the character and customs of the country, the phrase "all these kings" loses its grandeur. It suggests only a parcel of petty chiefs—ill-clad and ill-conditioned savages much like our Indians, who lived in full sight of each other and whose "kingdoms" were large when they were five miles square and contained two thousand souls. The combined monarchies of the thirty "kings" destroyed by Joshua on one of his famous campaigns only covered an area about equal to four of our counties of ordinary size. The poor old sheikh we saw at Caesarea Philippi, with his ragged band of a hundred followers, would have been called a "king" in those ancient times.

It is seven in the morning, and as we are in the country, the grass ought to be sparkling with dew, the flowers enriching the air with their fragrance, and the birds singing in the trees. But alas, there is no dew here, nor flowers, nor birds, nor trees. There is a plain and an unshaded lake, and beyond them some barren mountains. The tents are tumbling, the Arabs are quarreling like dogs and cats, as usual, the campground is strewn with packages and bundles, the labor of packing them upon the backs of the mules is progressing with great activity, the horses are saddled, the umbrellas are out, and in ten minutes we shall mount and the long procession will move again. The white city of the Mellahah, resurrected for a moment out of the dead centuries, will have disappeared again and left no sign.

47

We traversed some miles of desolate country whose soil is
rich enough, but is given over wholly to weeds; a silent,
mournful expanse, wherein we saw only three persons—
Arabs with nothing on but a long coarse shirt like the "tow-
linen" shirts which used to form the only summer garment of
little Negro boys on Southern plantations. Shepherds they
were, and they charmed their flocks with the traditional shepherd's pipe—a reed instrument that made music as exquisitely
infernal as these same Arabs create when they sing.

In their pipes lingered no echo of the wonderful music the
shepherd forefathers heard in the plains of Bethlehem that
time the angels sang, "Peace on earth, good will to men."

Part of the ground we came over was not ground at all, but
rocks—cream-colored rocks, worn smooth, as if by water;
with seldom an edge or a corner on them, but scooped out,
honeycombed, bored out with eyeholes, and thus wrought
into all manner of quaint shapes, among which the uncouth
imitation of skulls was frequent. Over this part of the route
were occasional remains of an old Roman road like the
Appian Way, whose paving stones still clung to their places
with Roman tenacity.

Gray lizards, those heirs of ruin, of sepulchers and desolation, glided in and out among the rocks or lay still and
sunned themselves. Where prosperity has reigned, and fallen;
where glory has flamed, and gone out; where beauty has
dwelt, and passed away; where gladness was, and sorrow is;
where the pomp of life has been, and silence and death brood
in its high places—there this reptile makes his home and
mocks at human vanity. His coat is the color of ashes: and
ashes are the symbol of hopes that have perished, of aspirations that came to naught, of loves that are buried. If he
could speak, he would say, Build temples: I will lord it in
their ruins; build palaces: I will inhabit them; erect empires:

351

I will inherit them; bury your beautiful: I will watch the worms at their work; and you, who stand here and moralize over me: I will crawl over *your* corpse at the last.

A few ants were in this desert place, but merely to spend the summer. They brought their provisions from Ain Mellahah—eleven miles.

Jack is not very well today, it is easy to see; but boy as he is, he is too much of a man to speak of it. He exposed himself to the sun too much yesterday, but since it came of his earnest desire to learn and to make this journey as useful as the opportunities will allow, no one seeks to discourage him by faultfinding. We missed him an hour from the camp and then found him some distance away, by the edge of a brook, and with no umbrella to protect him from the fierce sun. If he had been used to going without his umbrella, it would have been well enough, of course; but he was not. He was just in the act of throwing a clod at a mud turtle which was sunning itself on a small log in the brook. We said:

"Don't do that, Jack. What do you want to harm him for? What has he done?"

"Well, then, I won't kill him, but I ought to, because he is a fraud."

We asked him why, but he said it was no matter. We asked him why once or twice as we walked back to the camp, but he still said it was no matter. But late at night, when he was sitting in a thoughtful mood on the bed, we asked him again and he said:

"Well, it don't matter; I don't mind it now, but I did not like it today, you know, because *I* don't tell anything that isn't so, and I don't think the Colonel ought to, either. But he did; he told us at prayers in the pilgrims' tent last night, and he seemed as if he was reading it out of the Bible, too, about this country flowing with milk and honey and about the voice of the turtle being heard in the land. I thought that was drawing it a little strong, about the turtles anyhow, but I asked Mr. Church if it was so, and he said it was, and what Mr. Church tells me, I believe. But I sat there and watched that turtle nearly an hour today, and I almost burned up in the sun; but I never heard him sing. I believe I sweated a double handful of sweat—I *know* I did, because it got in my eyes and it was running down over my nose all the time; and you know my pants are tighter than anybody else's— Paris foolishness—and the buckskin seat of them got wet with sweat, and then got dry again and began to draw up and pinch and tear loose—it was awful—but I never heard him sing. Finally I said, 'This is a fraud—that is what it is, it is a fraud—and if I had had any sense I might have known a cursed mud turtle couldn't sing.' And then I said, 'I don't wish to be hard on this fellow, and I will just give him ten minutes to commence; ten minutes—and then if he don't, down goes his building.' But he *didn't* commence, you know. I had stayed there all that time, thinking maybe he might pretty soon, because he kept on raising his head up and letting it down, and drawing the skin over his eyes for a minute and then opening them out again, as if he was trying to study up something to sing, but just as the ten minutes were up and I was all beat out and blistered, he laid his blamed head down on a knot and went fast asleep."

"It *was* a little hard, after you had waited so long."

"I should think so. I said, 'Well, if you won't sing, you shan't sleep anyway'; and if you fellows had let me alone I would have made him shin out of Galilee quicker than any turtle ever did yet. But it isn't any matter now—let it go. The skin is all off the back of my neck."

About ten in the morning we halted at Joseph's Pit. This is a ruined khan of the Middle Ages, in one of whose side courts is a great walled and arched pit with water in it, and this pit, one tradition says, is the one Joseph's brethren cast him into. A more authentic tradition, aided by the geography of the country, places the pit in Dothan, some two days' journey from here. However, since there are many who believe in this present pit as the true one, it has its interest.

It is hard to make a choice of the most beautiful passage in a book which is so gemmed with beautiful passages as the Bible; but it is certain that not many things within its lids may take rank above the exquisite story of Joseph. Who taught those ancient writers their simplicity of language, their felicity of expression, their pathos, and above all, their faculty of sinking themselves entirely out of sight of the reader and making the narrative stand out alone and seem to tell itself? Shakespeare is always present when one reads his book; Macaulay is present when we follow the march of his stately sentences; but the Old Testament writers are hidden from view.

If the pit I have been speaking of is the right one, a scene transpired there, long ages ago, which is familiar to us all in pictures. The sons of Jacob had been pasturing their flocks near there. Their father grew uneasy at their long absence and sent Joseph, his favorite, to see if anything had gone wrong with them. He traveled six or seven days' journey; he was only seventeen years old and, boylike, he toiled through that long stretch of the vilest, rockiest, dustiest country in Asia, arrayed in the pride of his heart, his beautiful clawhammer coat of many colors. Joseph was the favorite, and that was one crime in the eyes of his brethren; he had dreamed dreams and interpreted them to foreshadow his elevation far above all his family in the far future, and that was another; he was dressed well and had doubtless displayed the harmless vanity of youth in keeping the fact prominently before his brothers. These were crimes his elders fretted over among themselves and proposed to punish when the opportunity should offer. When they saw him coming up from the Sea of Galilee, they recognized him and were glad. They said, "Lo, here is this dreamer—let us kill him." But Reuben pleaded for his life, and they spared it. But they seized the boy and stripped the hated coat from his back and pushed him into the pit. *They* intended to let him die there, but Reuben intended to liberate him secretly. However, while Reuben was away for a little while the brethren sold Joseph to some Ishmaelitish merchants who were journeying toward Egypt. Such is the history of the pit. And the selfsame pit is there in that place even to this day; and there it will remain until the next detachment of image-breakers and tombdesecraters arrives from the *Quaker City* excursion, and they will infallibly dig it up and carry it away with them. For behold, in them is no reverence for the solemn monuments of the past, and whithersoever they go they destroy and spare not.

Joseph became rich, distinguished, powerful—as the Bible expresses it, "lord over all the land of Egypt." Joseph was the real king, the strength, the brain of the monarchy, though Pharaoh held the title. Joseph is one of the truly great men of the Old Testament. And he was the noblest and the manliest save Esau. Why shall we not say a good word for the princely Bedouin? The only crime that can be brought against him is that he was unfortunate. Why must everybody praise Joseph's great-hearted generosity to his cruel brethren, without stint of fervent language, and fling only a reluctant bone of praise to Esau for his still sublimer generosity to the brother who had wronged him? Jacob took advantage of Esau's consuming hunger to rob him of his birthright and the great honor and consideration that belonged to the position; by treachery and falsehood he robbed him of his father's blessing; he made of him a stranger in his home and a wanderer. Yet after twenty years had passed away and Jacob met Esau and fell at his feet, quaking with fear and begging piteously to be spared the punishment he knew he deserved, what did that magnificent savage do? He fell upon his neck and embraced him! When Jacob—who was incapable of comprehending nobility of character—still doubting, still fearing, insisted upon "finding grace with my lord" by the bribe of a present of cattle, what did the gorgeous son of the desert say?

"Nay, I have enough, my brother; keep that thou hast unto thyself"!

Esau found Jacob rich, beloved by wives and children, and traveling in state, with servants, herds of cattle, and trains of camels—but he himself was still the uncourted outcast this brother had made him. After thirteen years of romantic mystery, the brethren who had wronged Joseph came, strangers in a strange land, hungry and humble, to buy "a little food"; and being summoned to a palace, charged with crime, they beheld in its owner their wronged brother; they were trembling beggars—he, the lord of a mighty empire! What Joseph that ever lived would have thrown away such a chance to "show off"? Who stands first—outcast Esau forgiving Jacob in prosperity or Joseph on a king's throne forgiving the ragged tremblers whose happy rascality placed him there?

Just before we came to Joseph's Pit, we had "raised" a hill, and there, a few miles before us, with not a tree or a shrub to interrupt the view, lay a vision which millions of worshipers in the far lands of the earth would give half their possessions to see—the sacred Sea of Galilee!

Therefore we tarried only a short time at the pit. We rested the horses and ourselves, and felt for a few minutes the blessed shade of the ancient buildings. We were out of water, but the two or three scowling Arabs, with their long guns, who were idling about the place, said they had none and that there was none in the vicinity. They knew there was a little brackish water in the pit, but they venerated a place made sacred by their ancestor's imprisonment too much to be willing to see Christian dogs drink from it. But Ferguson tied rags and handkerchiefs together till he made a rope long enough to lower a vessel to the bottom, and we drank and then rode on; and in a short time we dismounted on those shores which the feet of the Saviour have made holy ground.

At noon we took a swim in the Sea of Galilee—a blessed privilege in this roasting climate—and then lunched under a neglected old fig tree at the fountain they call Ain et Tin, a hundred yards from ruined Capernaum. Every rivulet that gurgles out of the rocks and sands of this part of the world is dubbed with the title of "fountain," and people familiar with the Hudson, the Great Lakes, and the Mississippi fall into transports of admiration over them and exhaust their powers of composition in writing their praises. If all the poetry and nonsense that have been discharged upon the fountains and the bland scenery of this region were collected in a book, it would make a most valuable volume to burn.

During luncheon, the pilgrim enthusiasts of our party, who had been so lighthearted and happy ever since they touched holy ground that they did little but mutter incoherent rhapsodies, could scarcely eat, so anxious were they to "take shipping" and sail in very person upon the waters that had borne the vessels of the Apostles. Their anxiety grew and their excitement augmented with every fleeting moment, until my fears were aroused and I began to have misgivings that in their present condition they might break recklessly loose from all considerations of prudence and buy a whole fleet of ships to sail in instead of hiring a single one for an hour, as quiet folk are wont to do. I trembled to think of the ruined purses this day's performances might result in. I could not help reflecting bodingly upon the intemperate zeal with which middle-aged men are apt to surfeit themselves upon a seductive folly which they have tasted for the first time. And yet I did not feel that I had a right to be surprised at the state of things which was giving me so much concern. These men had been taught from infancy to revere, almost to worship, the holy places whereon their happy eyes were resting now. For many and many a year this very picture had visited their thoughts by day and floated through their dreams by night. To stand before it in the flesh—to see it as they saw it now—to sail upon the hallowed sea and kiss the holy soil that compassed it about: these were aspirations they had cherished while a generation dragged its lagging seasons by and left its furrows in their faces and its frosts upon their hair. To look upon this picture and sail upon this sea they had forsaken home and its idols and journeyed thousands and thousands of miles, in weariness and tribulation. What wonder that the sordid lights of workday prudence should pale before the glory of a hope like theirs in the full splendor of its fruition? Let them squander millions! I said—who speaks of money at a time like this?

In this frame of mind I followed, as fast as I could, the eager footsteps of the pilgrims, and stood upon the shore of the lake, and swelled, with hat and voice, the frantic hail they sent after the "ship" that was speeding by. It was a success. The toilers of the sea ran in and beached their barque. Joy sat upon every countenance.

"How much? Ask him how much, Ferguson! How much to take us all—eight of us and you—to Bethsaida yonder and to the mouth of Jordan, and to the place where the swine ran down into the sea—quick!—and we want to coast around everywhere—everywhere!—all day long!—*I* could sail a year in these waters!—and tell him we'll stop at Magdala and finish at Tiberias!—ask him how much—anything—anything whatever!—tell him we don't care what the expense is!" [I said to myself, I knew how it would be.]

Ferguson (interpreting): "He says two napoleons—eight dollars."

One or two countenances fell. Then a pause.

"Too much! We'll give him one!"

I never shall know how it was—I shudder yet when I think how the place is given to miracles—but in a single instant of time, as it seemed to me, that ship was twenty paces from the shore and speeding away like a frightened thing! Eight crestfallen creatures stood upon the shore, and oh, to think of it! This—this—after all that overmastering ecstasy! Oh, shameful, shameful ending, after such unseemly boasting! It was too much like "Ho! Let me at him!" followed by a prudent "Two of you hold him—one can hold me!"

Instantly there was wailing and gnashing of teeth in the camp. The two napoleons were offered—more if necessary— and pilgrims and dragoman shouted themselves hoarse with pleadings to the retreating boatmen to come back. But they sailed serenely away and paid no further heed to pilgrims who had dreamed all their lives of some day skimming over the sacred waters of Galilee and listening to its hallowed story in the whisperings of its waves, and had journeyed countless leagues to do it, and—and then concluded that the fare was too high. Impertinent Muhammadan Arabs, to think such things of gentlemen of another faith!

Well, there was nothing to do but just submit and forgo the privilege of voyaging on Gennesaret, after coming half around the globe to taste that pleasure. There was a time, when the Saviour taught here, that boats were plenty among the fishermen of the coasts—but boats and fishermen both are gone now; and old Josephus had a fleet of men-of-war in these waters eighteen centuries ago—a hundred and thirty bold canoes—but they also have passed away and left no sign. They battle here no more by sea, and the commercial marine of Galilee numbers only two small ships, just of a pattern with the little skiffs the disciples knew. One was lost to us for good—the other was miles away and far out of hail. So we mounted the horses and rode grimly on toward Magdala, cantering along in the edge of the water for want of the means of passing over it.

How the pilgrims abused each other! Each said it was the other's fault, and each in turn denied it. No word was spoken by the sinners—even the mildest sarcasm might have been dangerous at such a time. Sinners that have been kept down and had examples held up to them, and suffered frequent lectures, and been so put upon in a moral way and in the matter of going slow and being serious and bottling up slang, and so crowded in regard to the matter of being proper and always and forever behaving that their lives have become a burden to them, would not lag behind pilgrims at such a time as this, and wink furtively, and be joyful, and commit other such crimes—because it would not occur to them to do it. Otherwise they would. But they did do it, though—and it did them a world of good to hear the pilgrims abuse each other, too. We took an unworthy satisfaction in seeing them fall out now and then, because it showed that they were only poor human people like us after all.

So we all rode down to Magdala while the gnashing of teeth waxed and waned by turns, and harsh words troubled the holy calm of Galilee.

Lest any man think I mean to be ill-natured when I talk about our pilgrims as I have been talking, I wish to say in all

sincerity that I do not. I would not listen to lectures from
men I did not like and could not respect; and none of these
can say I ever took their lectures unkindly, or was restive under the infliction, or failed to try to profit by what they said
to me. They are better men than I am; I can say that
honestly; they are good friends of mine, too—and besides,
if they did not wish to be stirred up occasionally in print,
why in the mischief did they travel with me? They knew
me. They knew my liberal way—that I like to give and take
—when it is for me to give and other people to take. When
one of them threatened to leave me in Damascus when I had
the cholera, he had no real idea of doing it—I knew his passionate nature and the good impulses that underlie it. And
did I not overhear Church, another pilgrim, say he did not
care who went or who stayed, *he* would stand by me till I
walked out of Damascus on my own feet or was carried out
in a coffin if it was a year? And do I not include Church
every time I abuse the pilgrims—and would I be likely to
speak ill-naturedly of him? I wish to stir them up and make
them healthy; that is all.

We had left Capernaum behind us. It was only a shapeless
ruin. It bore no semblance to a town and had nothing about
it to suggest that it had ever been a town. But all desolate
and unpeopled as it was, it was illustrious ground. From it
sprang that tree of Christianity whose broad arms overshadow so many distant lands today. After Christ was
tempted of the devil in the desert, he came here and began
his teachings; and during the three or four years he lived
afterward, this place was his home almost altogether. He began to heal the sick, and his fame soon spread so widely
that sufferers came from Syria and beyond Jordan, and
even from Jerusalem, several days' journey away, to be cured
of their diseases. Here he healed the centurion's servant
and Peter's mother-in-law, and multitudes of the lame and
the blind and persons possessed of devils; and here also
he raised Jairus' daughter from the dead. He went into a
ship with his disciples, and when they roused him from sleep
in the midst of a storm, he quieted the winds and lulled
the troubled sea to rest with his voice. He passed over to
the other side, a few miles away, and relieved two men of
devils, which passed into some swine. After his return he
called Matthew from the receipt of customs, performed some
cures, and created scandal by eating with publicans and sin-

ners. Then he went healing and teaching through Galilee, and even journeyed to Tyre and Sidon. He chose the twelve disciples, and sent them abroad to preach the new gospel. He worked miracles in Bethsaida and Chorazin—villages two or three miles from Capernaum. It was near one of them that the miraculous draft of fishes is supposed to have been taken, and it was in the desert places near the other that he fed the thousands by the miracles of the loaves and fishes. He cursed them both, and Capernaum also, for not repenting, after all the great works he had done in their midst, and prophesied against them. They are all in ruins now— which is gratifying to the pilgrims, for, as usual, they fit the eternal words of gods to the evanescent things of this earth; Christ, it is more probable, referred to the *people*, not their shabby villages of wigwams: he said it would be sad for them at "the day of judgment"—and what business have mud hovels at the Day of Judgment? It would not affect the prophecy in the least—it would neither prove it or disprove it—if these towns were splendid cities now instead of the almost vanished ruins they are. Christ visited Magdala, which is nearby Capernaum, and he also visited Caesarea Philippi. He went up to his old home at Nazareth and saw his brothers, Joses and Judas and James and Simon —those persons who, being own brothers to Jesus Christ, one would expect to hear mentioned sometimes, yet who ever saw their names in a newspaper or heard them from a pulpit? Who ever inquires what manner of youths they were; and whether they slept with Jesus, played with him and romped about him; quarreled with him concerning toys and trifles; struck him in anger, not suspecting what he was? Who ever wonders what they thought when they saw him come back to Nazareth a celebrity, and looked long at his unfamiliar face to make sure and then said, "It *is* Jesus?" Who wonders what passed in their minds when they saw this brother (who was *only* a brother to them, however much he might be to others a mysterious stranger who was a god and had stood face to face with God above the clouds) doing strange miracles with crowds of astonished people for witnesses? Who wonders if the brothers of Jesus asked him to come home with them, and said his mother and his sisters were grieved at his long absence, and would be wild with delight to see his face again? Who ever gives a thought to the sisters of Jesus at all? Yet he had sisters; and memories of them must have stolen into his mind often when he was ill-treated among strangers; when he was homeless and said he had not where to lay his head; when all deserted him, even Peter, and he stood alone among his enemies.

Christ did few miracles in Nazareth and stayed but a little while. The people said, "*This* the Son of God! Why, his father is nothing but a carpenter. We know the family. We see them every day. Are not his brothers named so and so, and his sisters so and so, and is not his mother the person they call Mary? This is absurd." He did not curse his home, but he shook its dust from his feet and went away.

Capernaum lies close to the edge of the little sea, in a small plain some five miles long and a mile or two wide, which is mildly adorned with oleanders which look all the better contrasted with the bald hills and the howling deserts which surround them, but they are not as deliriously beautiful as the books paint them. If one be calm and resolute he can look upon their comeliness and live.

One of the most astonishing things that have yet fallen under our observation is the exceedingly small portion of the earth from which sprang the now flourishing plant of Christianity. The longest journey our Saviour ever performed was from here to Jerusalem—about one hundred to one hundred and twenty miles. The next longest was from here to Sidon, —say about sixty or seventy miles. Instead of being wide apart—as American appreciation of distances would naturally suggest—the places made most particularly celebrated by the presence of Christ are nearly all right here in full view, and within cannon-shot of Capernaum. Leaving out two or three short journeys of the Saviour, he spent his life, preached his gospel, and performed his miracles within a compass no larger than an ordinary county in the United States. It is as much as I can do to comprehend this stupefying fact. How it wears a man out to have to read up a hundred pages of history every two or three miles—for verily the celebrated localities of Palestine occur that close together. How wearily, how bewilderingly they swarm about your path!

In due time we reached the ancient village of Magdala.

48

Magdala is not a beautiful place. It is thoroughly Syrian, and that is to say that it is thoroughly ugly and cramped, squalid, uncomfortable and filthy—just the style of cities that have adorned the country since Adam's time, as all writers have labored hard to prove and have succeeded. The streets of Magdala are anywhere from three to six feet wide and reeking with uncleanliness. The houses are from five to seven feet high and all built upon one arbitrary plan —the ungraceful form of a dry-goods box. The sides are daubed with a smooth white plaster and tastefully frescoed aloft and alow with disks of camel dung placed there to dry. This gives the edifice the romantic appearance of having been riddled with cannonballs and imparts to it a very warlike aspect. When the artist has arranged his materials with an eye to just proportion—the small and the large flakes in alternate rows, and separated by carefully considered intervals—I know of nothing more cheerful to look upon than a spirited Syrian fresco. The flat, plastered roof is garnished by picturesque stacks of fresco materials, which, having become thoroughly dried and cured, are placed there where it will be convenient. It is used for fuel. There is no timber of any consequence in Palestine—none at all to waste upon fires—and neither are there any mines of coal. If my description has been intelligible, you will perceive now that a square, flat-roofed hovel, neatly frescoed, with its wall tops gallantly bastioned and turreted with dried camel refuse, gives to a landscape a feature that is exceedingly festive and picturesque, especially if one is careful to remember to stick in a cat wherever, about the premises, there is room for a cat to sit. There are no windows to a Syrian hut and no chimneys. When I used to read that they let a bedridden man down through the roof of a house in Capernaum to get him into the presence of the Saviour, I generally had a three-story brick in my mind, and marveled that they did not break his neck with the strange experiment. I perceive now, however, that they might have taken him by the heels and thrown him clear over the house without discommoding him very much. Palestine is not changed any since those days, in manners, customs, architecture, or people.

As we rode into Magdala not a soul was visible. But the ring of the horses' hoofs roused the stupid population, and they all came trooping out—old men and old women, boys and girls, the blind, the crazy, and the crippled, all in ragged, soiled, and scanty raiment, and all abject beggars by nature, instinct, and education. How the vermin-tortured vagabonds did swarm! How they showed their scars and sores, and piteously pointed to their maimed and crooked limbs, and begged with their pleading eyes for charity! We had invoked a spirit we could not lay. They hung to the horses' tails, clung to their manes and the stirrups, closed in on every side in scorn of dangerous hoofs—and out of their infidel throats, with one accord, burst an agonizing and most infernal chorus: "Howajji, baksheesh! Howajji, baksheesh! Howajji, baksheesh! Baksheesh! Baksheesh!" I never was in a storm like that before.

As we paid the baksheesh out to sore-eyed children and brown, buxom girls with repulsively tattooed lips and chins, we filed through the town and by many an exquisite fresco, till we came to a bramble-infested enclosure and a Roman-looking ruin which had been the veritable dwelling of St. Mary Magdalene, the friend and follower of Jesus. The guide believed it, and so did I. I could not well do otherwise, with the house right there before my eyes as plain as day. The pilgrims took down portions of the front wall for specimens, as is their honored custom, and then we departed.

We are camped in this place now, just within the city walls of Tiberias. We went into the town before nightfall and looked at its people—we cared nothing about its houses. Its people are best examined at a distance. They are particularly uncomely Jews, Arabs, and Negroes. Squalor and poverty are the pride of Tiberias. The young women wear their dower strung upon a strong wire that curves downward from the top of the head to the jaw—Turkish silver coins which they have raked together or inherited. Most of these maidens were not wealthy, but some few had been very kindly dealt with by fortune. I saw heiresses there worth, in their own right—worth, well, I suppose I might venture to say, as much as nine dollars and a half. But such cases are rare. When you come across one of these, she naturally puts on airs. She will not ask for baksheesh. She will not even permit of undue familiarity. She assumes a crushing dignity and goes on serenely practicing with her fine-tooth comb and quoting poetry just the same as if you were not present at all. Some people cannot stand prosperity.

They say that the long-nosed, lanky, dyspeptic-looking body-snatchers, with the indescribable hats on and a long curl dangling down in front of each ear, are the old, familiar, self-righteous Pharisees we read of in the Scriptures. Verily, they look it. Judging merely by their general style, and without other evidence, one might easily suspect that self-righteousness was their specialty.

From various authorities I have culled information concerning Tiberias. It was built by Herod Antipas, the murderer of John the Baptist, and named after the Emperor Tiberius. It is believed that it stands upon the site of what must have been, ages ago, a city of considerable architectural pretensions, judging by the fine porphyry pillars that are scattered through Tiberias and down the lake shore southward. These were fluted once, and yet, although the stone is about as hard as iron, the flutings are almost worn away. These pillars are small, and doubtless the edifices they adorned were distinguished more for elegance than grandeur. This modern town—Tiberias—is only mentioned in the New Testament; never in the Old.

The Sanhedrin met here last, and for three hundred years Tiberias was the metropolis of the Jews in Palestine. It is one of the four holy cities of the Israelites, and is to them what Mecca is to the Muhammadan and Jerusalem to the Christian. It has been the abiding place of many learned and famous Jewish rabbis. They lie buried here, and near them lie also twenty-five thousand of their faith who traveled far to be near them while they lived and lie with them when they died. The great Rabbi Ben Israel spent three years here in the early part of the third century. He is dead now.

The celebrated Sea of Galilee is not so large a sea as Lake

Tahoe * by a good deal—it is just about two-thirds as large. And when we come to speak of beauty, this sea is no more to be compared to Tahoe than a meridian of longitude is to a rainbow. The dim waters of this pool cannot suggest the limpid brilliancy of Tahoe; these low, shaven, yellow hillocks of rocks and sand, so devoid of perspective, cannot suggest the grand peaks that compass Tahoe like a wall, and whose ribbed and chasmed fronts are clad with stately pines that seem to grow small and smaller as they climb, till one might fancy them reduced to weeds and shrubs far upward, where they join the everlasting snows. Silence and solitude brood over Tahoe; and silence and solitude brood also over this lake of Gennesaret. But the solitude of the one is as cheerful and fascinating as the solitude of the other is dismal and repellent.

In the early morning one watches the silent battle of dawn and darkness upon the waters of Tahoe with a placid interest; but when the shadows sulk away and one by one the hidden beauties of the shore unfold themselves in the full splendor of noon; when the still surface is belted like a rainbow with broad bars of blue and green and white, half the distance from circumference to center; when, in the lazy summer afternoon, he lies in a boat, far out to where the dead blue of the deep water begins, and smokes the pipe of peace and idly winks at the distant crags and patches of snow from under his cap brim; when the boat drifts shoreward to the white water, and he lolls over the gunwale and gazes by the hour down through the crystal depths and notes the colors of the pebbles and reviews the finny armies gliding in procession a hundred feet below; when at night he sees moon and stars, mountain ridges feathered with pines, jutting white capes, bold promontories, grand sweeps of rugged scenery topped with bald, glimmering peaks, all magnificently pictured in the polished mirror of the lake in richest, softest detail, the tranquil interest that was born with the morning deepens and deepens, by sure degrees, till it culminates at last in resistless fascination!

It is solitude, for birds and squirrels on the shore and

---

* I measure all lakes by Tahoe, partly because I am far more familiar with it than with any other, and partly because I have such a high admiration for it and such a world of pleasant recollections of it that it is very nearly impossible for me to speak of lakes and not mention it.

fishes in the water are all the creatures that are near to make it otherwise, but it is not the sort of solitude to make one dreary. Come to Galilee for that. If these unpeopled deserts, these rusty mounds of barrenness, that never, never, never do shake the glare from their harsh outlines, and fade and faint into vague perspective; that melancholy ruin of Capernaum; this stupid village of Tiberias, slumbering under its six funereal plumes of palms; yonder desolate declivity where the swine of the miracle ran down into the sea, and doubtless thought it was better to swallow a devil or two and get drowned into the bargain than have to live longer in such a place; this cloudless, blistering sky; this solemn, sailless, tintless lake, reposing within its rim of yellow hills and low, steep banks, and looking just as expressionless and unpoetical (when we leave its sublime history out of the question) as any metropolitan reservoir in Christendom—if these things are not food for "Rock Me to Sleep, Mother," none exist, I think.

But I should not offer the evidence for the prosecution and leave the defense unheard. Wm. C. Grimes deposes as follows:

We had taken ship to go over to the other side. The sea was not more than six miles wide. Of the beauty of the scene, however, I cannot say enough, nor can I imagine where those travelers carried their eyes who have described the scenery of the lake as tame or uninteresting. The first great characteristic of it is the deep basin in which it lies. This is from three to four hundred feet deep on all sides except at the lower end, and the sharp slope of the banks, which are all of the richest green, is broken and diversified by the wâdys and watercourses which work their way down through the sides of the basin, forming dark chasms or light sunny valleys. Near Tiberias these banks are rocky, and ancient sepulchres open in them, with their doors toward the water. They selected grand spots, as did the Egyptians of old, for burial places, as if they designed that when the voice of God should reach the sleepers, they should walk forth and open their eyes on scenes of glorious beauty. On the east, the wild and desolate mountains contrast finely with the deep blue lake; and toward the north, sublime and majestic, Hermon looks down on the sea, lifting his white crown to heaven with the pride of a hill that has seen the departing footsteps of a hundred generations. On the north-east shore of the sea was a single tree, and this is the only tree of any size visible from the water of the lake, except a few lonely palms in the city of Tiberias, and by its solitary position attracts more attention than would a forest. The whole appearance of the scene is precisely what we would expect and desire the scenery of Gennesaret to be, grand beauty, but quiet calm. The very mountains are calm.

It is an ingeniously written description and well calculated to deceive. But if the paint and the ribbons and the flowers be stripped from it, a skeleton will be found beneath.

So stripped, there remains a lake six miles wide and neutral in color; with steep green banks unrelieved by shrubbery; at one end bare, unsightly rocks, with (almost invisible) holes in them of no consequence to the picture; eastward, "wild and desolate mountains" (low, desolate hills, he should have said); in the north a mountain called Hermon, with snow on it; peculiarity of the picture, "calmness"; its prominent feature, one tree.

No ingenuity could make such a picture beautiful—to one's actual vision.

I claim the right to correct misstatements, and have so corrected the color of the water in the above recapitulation. The waters of Gennesaret are of an exceedingly mild blue, even from a high elevation and a distance of five miles. Close at hand (the witness was sailing on the lake), it is hardly proper to call them blue at all, much less "deep" blue. I wish to state also, not as a correction but as matter of opinion, that Mount Hermon is not a striking or picturesque mountain by any means, being too near the height of its immediate neighbors to be so. That is all. I do not object to the witness dragging a mountain forty-five miles to help the scenery under consideration, because it is entirely proper to do it, and besides, the picture needs it.

"C.W.E." (of *Life in the Holy Land*) deposes as follows:

A beautiful sea lies unbosomed among the Galilean hills, in the midst of that land once possessed by Zebulon and Naphtali, Asher and Dan. The azure of the sky penetrates the depths of the lake, and the waters are sweet and cool. On the west, stretch broad fertile plains; on the north the rocky shores rise step by step until in the far distance tower the snowy heights of Hermon; on the east through a misty veil are seen the high plains of Perea, which stretch away in rugged mountains leading the mind by varied paths toward Jerusalem the Holy. Flowers bloom in this terrestrial paradise, once beautiful and verdant with waving trees; singing birds enchant the ear; the turtle-dove soothes with its soft note; the crested lark sends up its song toward heaven, and the grave and stately stork inspires the mind with thought, and leads it on to meditation and repose. Life here was once idyllic, charming; here were once no rich, no poor, no high, no low. It was a world of ease, simplicity, and beauty; now it is a scene of desolation and misery.

This is not an ingenious picture. It is the worst I ever saw. It describes in elaborate detail what it terms a "terrestrial paradise," and closes with the startling information that this paradise is "a scene of *desolation and misery*."

I have given two fair, average specimens of the character of the testimony offered by the majority of the writers who visit this region. One says, "Of the beauty of the scene I cannot say enough," and then proceeds to cover up with a woof of glittering sentences a thing which, when stripped for inspection, proves to be only an unobtrusive basin of water, some mountainous desolation, and one tree. The other, after a conscientious effort to build a terrestrial paradise out of the same materials, with the addition of a "grave and stately stork," spoils it all by blundering upon the ghastly truth at the last.

Nearly every book concerning Galilee and its lake describes the scenery as beautiful. No—not always so straightforward as that. Sometimes the *impression* intentionally conveyed is that it is beautiful, at the same time that the author is careful not to *say* that it is in plain Saxon. But a careful analysis of these descriptions will show that the materials of which they are formed are not individually beautiful and cannot be wrought into combinations that are beautiful. The veneration and the affection which some of these men felt for the scenes they were speaking of heated their fancies and biased their judgment; but the pleasant falsities they wrote were full of honest sincerity, at any rate. Others wrote as they did because they feared it would be unpopular to write otherwise. Others were hypocrites and deliberately meant to deceive. Any of them would say in a moment, if asked, that it was *always* right and always *best* to tell the truth. They would say that, at any rate, if they did not perceive the drift of the question.

But why should not the truth be spoken of this region? Is the truth harmful? Has it ever needed to hide its face? God made the Sea of Galilee and its surroundings as they are. Is it the province of Mr. Grimes to improve upon the work?

I am sure, from the tenor of books I have read, that many who have visited this land in years gone by were Presbyterians, and came seeking evidences in support of their particular creed; they found a Presbyterian Palestine, and they had already made up their minds to find no other, though possibly they did not know it, being blinded by their zeal. Others were Baptists, seeking Baptist evidences and a Baptist Palestine. Others were Catholics, Methodists, Episcopalians, seeking evidences endorsing their several creeds and a Catholic, a Methodist, an Episcopalian Palestine. Honest as these men's intentions may have been, they were full of partialities and prejudices, they entered the country with their verdicts already prepared, and they could no more write dispassionately and impartially about it than they could about their own wives and children. Our pilgrims have brought *their* verdicts with them. They have shown it in their conversation ever since we left Beirut. I can almost tell, in set phrase, what they will say when they see Tabor, Nazareth, Jericho, and Jerusalem—*because I have the books they will "smouch" their ideas from.* These authors write pictures and frame rhapsodies, and lesser men follow and see with the author's eyes instead of their own, and speak with his tongue. What the pilgrims said at Caesarea Philippi surprised me with its wisdom. I found it afterwards in Robinson. What they said when Gennesaret burst upon their vision charmed me with its grace. I find it in Mr. Thompson's *Land and the Book.* They have spoken often, in happily worded language which never varied, of how they mean to lay their weary heads upon a stone at Bethel, as Jacob did, and close their dim eyes, and dream, perchance, of angels descending out of heaven on a ladder. It was very pretty. But I have recognized the weary head and the dim eyes finally. They borrowed the idea—and the words—and the construction—and the punctuation—from Grimes. The pilgrims will tell of Palestine, when they get home, not as it appeared to *them,* but as it appeared to Thompson and Robinson and Grimes—with the tints varied to suit each pilgrim's creed.

Pilgrims, sinners, and Arabs are all abed now, and the camp is still. Labor in loneliness is irksome. Since I made my last few notes, I have been sitting outside the tent for half an hour. Night is the time to see Galilee. Gennesaret under these lustrous stars has nothing repulsive about it. Gennesaret with the glittering reflections of the constellations flecking its surface almost makes me regret that I ever saw the rude glare of the day upon it. Its history and its associations are its chiefest charm in any eyes, and the spells they weave are feeble in the searching light of the sun. *Then* we scarcely feel the fetters. Our thoughts wander constantly to the practical concerns of life and refuse to dwell upon things that seem vague and unreal. But when the day is done, even the most unimpressible must yield to the dreamy influences of this tranquil starlight. The old traditions of the place steal upon his memory and haunt his reveries, and then his fancy clothes all sights and sounds with the supernatural. In the lapping of the waves upon the beach he hears the dip of ghostly oars; in the secret noises of the night he hears spirit voices; in the soft sweep of the breeze, the rush of invisible wings. Phantom ships are on the sea, the dead of twenty centuries come forth from the tombs, and in the dirges of the night wind the songs of old forgotten ages find utterance again.

In the starlight Galilee has no boundaries but the broad compass of the heavens, and is a theater meet for great events, meet for the birth of a religion able to save a world, and meet for the stately Figure appointed to stand upon its stage and proclaim its high decrees. But in the sunlight one says: Is it for the deeds which were done and the words which were spoken in this little acre of rocks and sand eighteen centuries gone that the bells are ringing today in the remote islands of the sea and far and wide over continents that clasp the circumference of the huge globe?

One can comprehend it only when night has hidden all incongruities and created a theater proper for so grand a drama.

49

We took another swim in the Sea of Galilee at twilight yesterday and another at sunrise this morning. We have not sailed, but three swims are equal to a sail, are they not? There were plenty of fish visible in the water, but we have no outside aids in this pilgrimage but *Tent Life in the Holy Land, The Land and the Book,* and other literature of like description—no fishing tackle. There were no fish to be had in the village of Tiberias. True, we saw two or three vagabonds mending their nets, but never trying to catch anything with them.

We did not go to the ancient warm baths two miles below Tiberias. I had no desire in the world to go there. This seemed a little strange, and prompted me to try to discover what the cause of this unreasonable indifference was. It turned out to be simply because Pliny mentions them. I have conceived a sort of unwarrantable unfriendliness toward Pliny and St. Paul, because it seems as if I can never ferret out a place that I can have to myself. It always and eternally transpires that St. Paul has been to that place and Pliny has "mentioned" it.

In the early morning we mounted and started. And then a weird apparition marched forth at the head of the procession —a pirate, I thought, if ever a pirate dwelt upon land. It was a tall Arab, as swarthy as an Indian, young—say thirty years of age. On his head he had closely bound a gorgeous yellow and red striped silk scarf, whose ends, lavishly fringed with tassels, hung down between his shoulders and dallied with the wind. From his neck to his knees, in ample folds, a robe swept down that was a very star-spangled banner of curved and sinuous bars of black and white. Out of his back, somewhere, apparently, the long stem of a chibouk projected and reached far above his right shoulder. Athwart his back, diagonally, and extending high above his left shoulder, was an Arab gun of Saladin's time, that was splendid with silver plating from stock clear up to the end of its measureless stretch of barrel. About his waist was bound many and many a yard of elaborately figured but sadly tarnished stuff that came from sumptuous Persia, and among the baggy folds in front, the sunbeams glinted from a formidable battery of old brass-mounted horse pistols and the gilded hilts of bloodthirsty knives. There were holsters for more pistols appended to the wonderful stack of long-haired goatskins and Persian carpets, which the man had been taught to regard in the light of a saddle; and down among the pendulous rank of vast tassels that swung from that saddle, and clanging against the iron shovel of a stirrup that propped the warrior's knees up toward his chin, was a crooked, silver-clad scimitar of such awful dimensions and such implacable expression that no man might hope to look upon it and not shudder. The fringed and bedizened prince whose privilege it is to ride the pony and lead the elephant into a country village is poor and naked compared to this chaos of paraphernalia, and the happy vanity of the one is the very poverty of satisfaction compared to the majestic serenity, the overwhelming complacency, of the other.

"*Who* is this? *What* is this?" That was the trembling inquiry all down the line.

"Our guard! From Galilee to the birthplace of the Saviour, the country is infested with fierce Bedouins, whose sole happiness it is, in this life, to cut and stab and mangle and murder unoffending Christians. Allah be with us!"

"Then hire a regiment! Would you send us out among these desperate hordes with no salvation in our utmost need but this old turret?"

The dragoman laughed—not at the facetiousness of the simile, for verily that guide or that courier or that dragoman never yet lived upon earth who had in him the faintest appreciation of a joke, even though that joke were so broad and so ponderous that if it fell on him it would flatten him out like a postage stamp—the dragoman laughed and then, emboldened by some thought that was in his brain, no doubt, proceeded to extremities and winked.

In straits like these, when a man laughs, it is encouraging; when he winks, it is positively reassuring. He finally intimated that one guard would be sufficient to protect us, but that that one was an absolute necessity. It was because of the moral weight his awful panoply would have with the Bedouins. Then I said we didn't want any guard at all. If one fantastic vagabond could protect eight armed Christians and a pack of Arab servants from all harm, surely that detachment could protect themselves. He shook his head doubtfully. Then I said, just think of how it looks—think of how it would read, —to self-reliant Americans that we went sneaking through this deserted wilderness under the protection of this masquerading Arab, who would break his neck getting out of the country if a man that *was* a man ever started after him. It was a mean, low, degrading position. Why were we ever told to bring navy revolvers with us if we had to be protected at last by this infamous star-spangled scum of the desert? These appeals were vain—the dragoman only smiled and shook his head.

I rode to the front and struck up an acquaintance with King Solomon-in-all-his-glory and got him to show me his linger-

ng eternity of a gun. It had a rusty flintlock; it was ringed
nd barred and plated with silver from end to end, but it was
is desperately out of the perpendicular as are the billiard cues
f '49 that one finds yet in service in the ancient mining
camps of California. The muzzle was eaten by the rust of
centuries into a ragged filagreework, like the end of a burnt-
out stovepipe. I shut one eye and peered within—it was
flaked with iron rust like an old steamboat boiler. I borrowed
he ponderous pistols and snapped them. They were rusty inside, too—had not been loaded for a generation. I went back,
full of encouragement, and reported to the guide and asked
him to discharge this dismantled fortress. It came out then.
This fellow was a retainer of the Sheikh of Tiberias. He was
a source of government revenue. He was to the empire of
Tiberias what the customs are to America. The Sheikh imposed guards upon travelers and charged them for it. It is a
lucrative source of emolument and sometimes brings into the
national treasury as much as thirty-five or forty dollars a
year.

I knew the warrior's secret now; I knew the hollow vanity
of his rusty trumpery and despised his asinine complacency.
I told on him, and with reckless daring the cavalcade rode
straight ahead into the perilous solitudes of the desert and
scorned his frantic warnings of the mutilation and death that
hovered about them on every side.

Arrived at an elevation of twelve hundred feet above the
lake (I ought to mention that the lake lies six hundred feet
below the level of the Mediterranean—no traveler ever neglects
to flourish that fragment of news in his letters), as bald and
unthrilling a panorama as any land can afford, perhaps, was
spread out before us. Yet it was so crowded with historical
interest that if all the pages that have been written about it
were spread upon its surface, they would flag it from horizon
to horizon like a pavement. Among the localities comprised
in this view were Mount Hermon; the hills that border Caesarea Philippi, Dan, the sources of the Jordan, and the Waters
of Merom; Tiberias; the Sea of Galilee; Joseph's Pit; Capernaum; Bethsaida; the supposed scenes of the Sermon on the
Mount, the feeding of the multitudes and the miraculous
draft of fishes; the declivity down which the swine ran to
the sea; the entrance and the exit of the Jordan; Safed, "the
city set upon a hill," one of the four holy cities of the Jews,
and the place where they believe the real Messiah will appear

when he comes to redeem the world; part of the battlefield
of Hattin, where the knightly Crusaders fought their last
fight and in a blaze of glory passed from the stage and ended
their splendid career forever; Mount Tabor, the traditional
scene of the Lord's Transfiguration. And down toward the
southeast lay a landscape that suggested to my mind a quotation (imperfectly remembered, no doubt):

The Ephraimites, not being called upon to share in the
rich spoils of the Ammonitish war, assembled a mighty host
to fight against Jeptha, Judge of Israel; who, being apprised of
their approach, gathered together the men of Israel and gave
them battle and put them to flight. To make his victory the
more secure, he stationed guards at the different fords and
passages of the Jordan, with instructions to let none pass who
could not say Shibboleth. The Ephraimites, being of a different tribe, could not frame to pronounce the word aright,
but called it Sibboleth, which proved them enemies and cost
them their lives; wherefore, forty and two thousand fell at
the different fords and passages of the Jordan that day.

We jogged along peacefully over the great caravan route
from Damascus to Jerusalem and Egypt, past Lubia and other
Syrian hamlets, perched, in the unvarying style, upon the summit of steep mounds and hills and fenced round about with
giant cactuses (the sign of worthless land) with prickly pears
upon them like hams, and came at last to the battlefield of
Hattin.

It is a grand, irregular plateau and looks as if it might have
been created for a battlefield. Here the peerless Saladin met
the Christian host some seven hundred years ago and broke
their power in Palestine for all time to come. There had long
been a truce between the opposing forces, but according to the
guidebook, Raynauld of Chatillon, Lord of Kerak, broke it
by plundering a Damascus caravan and refusing to give up
either the merchants or their goods when Saladin demanded
them. This conduct of an insolent petty chieftain stung the
Sultan to the quick, and he swore that he would slaughter
Raynauld with his own hand, no matter how or when or
where he found him. Both armies prepared for war. Under
the weak King of Jerusalem was the very flower of the Christian chivalry. He foolishly compelled them to undergo a long,
exhausting march, in the scorching sun and then, without
water or other refreshment, ordered them to encamp in this
open plain. The splendidly mounted masses of Muslim soldiers

swept round the north end of Gennesaret, burning and destroying as they came, and pitched their camp in front of the opposing lines. At dawn the terrific fight began. Surrounded on all sides by the Sultan's swarming battalions, the Christian knights fought on without a hope for their lives. They fought with desperate valor, but to no purpose; the odds of heat and numbers and consuming thirst were too great against them. Toward the middle of the day the bravest of their band cut their way through the Muslim ranks and gained the summit of a little hill, and there, hour after hour, they closed around the banner of the Cross and beat back the charging squadrons of the enemy.

But the doom of the Christian power was sealed. Sunset found Saladin lord of Palestine, the Christian chivalry strewn in heaps upon the field, and the King of Jerusalem, the Grand Master of the Templars, and Raynauld of Chatillon captives in the Sultan's tent. Saladin treated two of the prisoners with princely courtesy and ordered refreshments to be set before them. When the King handed an iced sherbet to Chatillon, the Sultan said, "It is thou that givest it to him, not I." He remembered his oath and slaughtered the hapless knight of Chatillon with his own hand.

It was hard to realize that this silent plain had once resounded with martial music and trembled to the tramp of armed men. It was hard to people this solitude with rushing columns of cavalry, and stir its torpid pulses with the shouts of victors, the shrieks of the wounded, and the flash of banner and steel above the surging billows of war. A desolation is here that not even imagination can grace with the pomp of life and action.

We reached Tabor safely and considerably in advance of that old iron-clad swindle of a guard. We never saw a human being on the whole route, much less lawless hordes of Bedouins. Tabor stands solitary and alone, a giant sentinel above the Plain of Esdraelon. It rises some fourteen hundred feet above the surrounding level, a green, wooden cone, symmetrical and full of grace—a prominent landmark and one that is exceedingly pleasant to eyes surfeited with the repulsive monotony of desert Syria. We climbed the steep path to its summit, through breezy glades of thorn and oak. The view presented from its highest peak was almost beautiful. Below was the broad, level Plain of Esdraelon, checkered with fields like a chessboard, and full as smooth and level seemingly, dotted about its borders with white, compact villages, and faintly penciled, far and near, with the curving lines of roads and trails. When it is robed in the fresh verdure of spring, it must form a charming picture, even by itself. Skirting its southern border rises "Little Hermon," over whose summit a glimpse of Gilboa is caught. Nain, famous for the raising of the widow's son, and Endor, as famous for the performances of her witch, are in view. To the eastward lies the valley of the Jordan and beyond it the mountains of Gilead. Westward is Mount Carmel. Hermon in the north—the tablelands of Bashan—Safed, the holy city, gleaming white upon a tall spur of the mountains of Lebanon—a steel-blue corner of the Sea of Galilee—saddle-peaked Hattin, traditional "Mount of Beatitudes" and mute witness of the last brave fight of the Crusading host for Holy Cross—these fill up the picture.

To glance at the salient features of this landscape through the picturesque framework of a ragged and ruined stone window arch of the time of Christ, thus hiding from sight all that is unattractive, is to secure to yourself a pleasure worth climbing the mountain to enjoy. One must stand on his head to get the best effect in a fine sunset, and set a landscape in a bold, strong framework that is very close at hand, to bring out all its beauty. One learns this latter truth never more to forget it, in that mimic land of enchantment, the wonderful garden of my lord the Count Pallavicini, near Genoa. You go wandering for hours among hills and wooded glens, artfully contrived to leave the impression that Nature shaped them and not man; following winding paths and coming suddenly upon leaping cascades and rustic bridges; finding sylvan lakes where you expected them not; loitering through battered mediaeval castles in miniature that seem hoary with age and yet were built a dozen years ago; meditating over ancient crumbling tombs, whose marble columns were marred and broken purposely by the modern artist that made them; stumbling unawares upon toy palaces, wrought of rare and costly materials, and again upon a peasant's hut, whose dilapidated furniture would never suggest that it was made so to order; sweeping round and round in the midst of a forest on an enchanted wooden horse that is moved by some invisible agency; traversing Roman roads and passing under majestic triumphal arches; resting in quaint bowers where unseen spirits discharge jets of water on you from every possible direction, and where even the flowers you touch assail you with a shower; boating on a subterranean lake among caverns and arches royally draped with clustering stalactites, and passing out into open day upon another lake, which is bordered with sloping banks of grass and gay with patrician barges that swim at anchor in the shadow of a miniature marble temple that rises out of the clear water and glasses its white statues, its rich capitals, and fluted columns in the tranquil depths. So, from marvel to marvel you have drifted on, thinking all the time that the one last seen must be the chiefest. And, verily, the chiefest wonder *is* reserved until the last, but you do not see it until you step ashore, and passing through a wilderness of rare flowers, collected from every corner of the earth, you stand at the door of one more mimic temple. Right in this place the artist taxed his genius to the utmost and fairly opened the gates of fairyland. You look through an unpretending pane of glass, stained yellow; the first thing you see is a mass of quivering foliage, ten short steps before you, in the midst of which is a ragged opening like a gateway—a thing that is common enough in nature, and not apt to excite suspicions of a deep human design—and above the bottom of the gateway, project, in the most careless way, a few broad tropic leaves and brilliant flowers. All of a sudden, through this bright, bold gateway, you catch a glimpse of the faintest, softest, richest picture that ever graced the dream of a dying saint, since John saw the New Jerusalem glimmering above the clouds of heaven. A broad sweep of sea, flecked with careening sails; a sharp, jutting cape, and a lofty lighthouse on it; a sloping lawn behind it; beyond, a portion of the old "city of palaces," with its parks and hills and stately mansions; beyond these a prodigious mountain, with its strong outlines sharply cut against ocean and sky; and over all, vagrant shreds and flakes of cloud, floating in a sea of gold. The ocean is gold, the city is gold, the meadow, the mountain, the sky—everything is golden—rich and mellow and dreamy as a vision of paradise. No artist could put upon canvas its entrancing beauty, and yet, without the yellow glass and the carefully contrived accident of a framework that cast it into enchanted distance and shut out from it all unattractive features, it was not a picture to fall into ecstasies over. Such is life, and the trail of the serpent is over us all.

There is nothing for it now but to come back to old Tabor, though the subject is tiresome enough, and I cannot stick to

it for wandering off to scenes that are pleasanter to remember.
I think I will skip anyhow. There is nothing about Tabor
(except we concede that it was the scene of the Transfiguration) but some gray old ruins, stacked up there in all ages of
the world from the days of stout Gideon and parties that
flourished thirty centuries ago to the fresh yesterday of Crusading times. It has its Greek convent, and the coffee there
is good, but never a splinter of the true Cross or bone of a
hallowed saint to arrest the idle thoughts of worldlings and
turn them into graver channels. A Catholic church is nothing
to me that has no relics.

The Plain of Esdraelon—"the battlefield of the nations"—
only sets one to dreaming of Joshua and Benhadad and Saul
and Gideon; Tamerlane, Tancred, Coeur de Lion, and Saladin; the warrior kings of Persia, Egypt's heroes, and Napoleon
—for they all fought here. If the magic of the moonlight could
summon from the graves of forgotten centuries and many
lands the countless myriads that have battled on this wide,
far-reaching floor, and array them in the thousand strange
costumes of their hundred nationalities, and send the vast
host sweeping down the plain, splendid with plumes and banners and glittering lances, I could stay here an age to see the
phantom pageant. But the magic of the moonlight is a vanity
and a fraud, and whoso putteth his trust in it shall suffer
sorrow and disappointment.

Down at the foot of Tabor, and just at the edge of the storied Plain of Esdraelon, is the insignificant village of Deburieh, where Deborah, prophetess of Israel, lived. It is just like
Magdala.

50

We descended from Mount Tabor, crossed a deep ravine, and
followed a hilly, rocky road to Nazareth—distant two hours.
All distances in the East are measured by hours, not miles.
A good horse will walk three miles an hour over nearly any
kind of a road; therefore an hour here always stands for three
miles. This method of computation is bothersome and annoy-

ing; and until one gets thoroughly accustomed to it, it carries no intelligence to his mind until he has stopped and translated the pagan hours into Christian miles, just as people do with the spoken words of a foreign language they are acquainted with but not familiarly enough to catch the meaning in a moment. Distances traveled by human feet are also estimated by hours and minutes, though I do not know what the base of the calculation is. In Constantinople you ask, "How far is it to the Consulate?" and they answer, "About ten minutes." "How far is it to the Lloyds' Agency?" "Quarter of an hour." "How far is it to the lower bridge?" "Four minutes." I cannot be positive about it, but I think that there, when a man orders a pair of pantaloons, he says he wants them a quarter of a minute in the legs and nine seconds around the waist.

Two hours from Tabor to Nazareth—and as it was an uncommonly narrow, crooked trail, we necessarily met all the camel trains and jackass caravans between Jericho and Jacksonville in that particular place and nowhere else. The donkeys do not matter so much, because they are so small that you can jump your horse over them if he is an animal of spirit, but a camel is not jumpable. A camel is as tall as any ordinary dwelling house in Syria—which is to say a camel is from one to two and sometimes nearly three feet taller than a good-sized man. In this part of the country his load is oftenest in the shape of colossal sacks—one on each side. He and his cargo take up as much room as a carriage. Think of meeting this style of obstruction in a narrow trail. The camel would not turn out for a king. He stalks serenely along, bringing his cushioned stilts forward with the long, regular swing of a pendulum, and whatever is in the way must get out of the way peaceably or be wiped out forcibly by the bulky sacks. It was a tiresome ride to us and perfectly exhausting to the horses. We were compelled to jump over upwards of eighteen hundred donkeys, and only one person in the party was unseated less than sixty times by the camels. This seems like a powerful statement, but the poet has said, "Things are not what they seem." I cannot think of anything now more certain to make one shudder than to have a soft-footed camel sneak up behind him and touch him on the ear with its cold, flabby underlip. A camel did this for one of the boys, who was drooping over his saddle in a brown study. He glanced up and saw the majestic apparition hovering above him and made frantic efforts to get out of the way, but the camel reached out and bit him on the shoulder before he accomplished it. This was the only pleasant incident of the journey.

At Nazareth we camped in an olive grove near the Virgin Mary's fountain, and that wonderful Arab "guard" came to collect some baksheesh for his "services" in following us from Tiberias and warding off invisible dangers with the terrors of his armament. The dragoman had paid his master, but that counted as nothing—if you hire a man to sneeze for you here, and another man chooses to help him, you have got to pay both. They do nothing whatever without pay. How it must have surprised these people to hear the way of salvation offered to them *"without money and without price."* If the manners, the people, or the customs of this country have changed since the Saviour's time, the figures and metaphors of the Bible are not the evidences to prove it by.

We entered the great Latin convent which is built over the traditional dwelling place of the Holy Family. We went down a flight of fifteen steps below the ground level and stood in a small chapel tricked out with tapestry hangings, silver lamps, and oil paintings. A spot marked by a cross in the marble floor, under the altar, was exhibited as the place made forever holy by the feet of the Virgin when she stood up to receive the message of the angel. So simple, so unpretending a locality to be the scene of so mighty an event! The very scene of the Annunciation—an event which has been commemorated by splendid shrines and august temples all over the civilized world, and one which the princes of art have made it their loftiest ambition to picture worthily on their canvas; a spot whose history is familiar to the very children of every house and city and obscure hamlet of the furthest lands of Christendom; a spot which myriads of men would toil across the breadth of a world to see, would consider it a priceless privilege to look upon. It was easy to think these thoughts. But it was not easy to bring myself up to the magnitude of the situation. I could sit off several thousand miles and imagine the angel appearing, with shadowy wings and lustrous countenance, and note the glory that streamed downward upon the Virgin's head while the message from the Throne of God fell upon her ears—anyone can do that beyond the ocean, but few can do it here. I saw the little recess from which the angel stepped, but could not fill its void. The angels that I know are creatures of unstable fancy —they will not fit in niches of substantial stone. Imagination labors best in distant fields. I doubt if any man can stand in the grotto of the Annunciation and people with the phantom images of his mind its too tangible walls of stone.

They showed us a broken granite pillar, depending from the roof, which they said was hacked in two by the Muslim conquerors of Nazareth in the vain hope of pulling down the sanctuary. But the pillar remained miraculously suspended in the air and, unsupported itself, supported then and still supports the roof. By dividing this statement up among eight, it was found not difficult to believe it.

These gifted Latin monks never do anything by halves. If they were to show you the Brazen Serpent that was elevated in the wilderness, you could depend upon it that they had on hand the pole it was elevated on also, and even the hole it stood in. They have got the "grotto" of the Annunciation here; and just as convenient to it as one's throat is to his mouth, they have also the Virgin's kitchen, and even her sitting room, where she and Joseph watched the infant Saviour play with Hebrew toys eighteen hundred years ago. All under one roof, and all clean, spacious, comfortable "grottoes." It seems curious that personages intimately connected with the Holy Family always lived in grottoes—in Nazareth, in Bethlehem, in imperial Ephesus—and yet nobody else in their day and generation thought of doing anything of the kind. If they ever did, their grottoes are all gone, and I suppose we ought to wonder at the peculiar marvel of the preservation of these I speak of. When the Virgin fled from Herod's wrath, she hid in a grotto in Bethlehem, and the same is there to this day. The slaughter of the innocents in Bethlehem was done in a grotto; the Saviour was born in a grotto—both are shown to pilgrims yet. It is exceedingly strange that these tremendous events all happened in grottoes—and exceedingly fortunate likewise, because the strongest houses must crumble to ruin in time, but a grotto in the living rock will last forever. It is an imposture—this grotto stuff—but it is one that all men ought to thank the Catholics for. Wherever they ferret out a lost locality made holy by some Scriptural event, they straightway build a massive—almost imperishable— church there and preserve the memory of that locality for the gratification of future generations. If it had been left to Protestants to do this most worthy work, we would not even know where Jerusalem is today, and the man who could go and put his finger on Nazareth would be too wise for this world. The world owes the Catholics its goodwill even for the happy rascality of hewing out these bogus grottoes in the rock; for it is infinitely more satisfactory to look at a grotto where people have faithfully believed for centuries that the Virgin once lived than to have to imagine a dwelling place for her somewhere, anywhere, nowhere, loose and at large all over this town of Nazareth. There is too large a scope of country. The imagination cannot work. There is no one particular spot to chain your eye, rivet your interest, and make you think. The memory of the Pilgrims cannot perish while Plymouth Rock remains to us. The old monks are wise. They know how to drive a stake through a pleasant tradition that will hold it to its place forever.

We visited the places where Jesus worked for fifteen years as a carpenter and where he attempted to teach in the synagogue, and was driven out by a mob. Catholic chapels stand upon these sites and protect the little fragments of the ancient walls which remain. Our pilgrims broke off specimens. We visited also a new chapel, in the midst of the town, which is built around a boulder some twelve feet long by four feet thick; the priests discovered a few years ago that the disciples had sat upon this rock to rest once when they had walked up from Capernaum. They hastened to preserve the relic. Relics are very good property. Travelers are expected to pay for seeing them, and they do it cheerfully. We like the idea. One's conscience can never be the worse for the knowledge that he has paid his way like a man. Our pilgrims would have liked very well to get out their lampblack and stencil plates and paint their names on that rock, together with the names of the villages they hail from in America, but the priests permit nothing of that kind. To speak the strict truth, however, our party seldom offend in that way, though we have men in the ship who never lose an opportunity to do it. Our pilgrims' chief sin is their lust for "specimens." I suppose that by this time they know the dimensions of that rock to an inch and its weight to a ton, and I do not hesitate to charge that they will go back there tonight and try to carry it off.

This "Fountain of the Virgin" is the one which tradition says Mary used to get water from twenty times a day, when she was a girl, and bear it away in a jar upon her head. The water streams through faucets in the face of a wall of ancient masonry which stands removed from the houses of the village. The young girls of Nazareth still collect about it by the dozen and keep up a riotous laughter and skylarking. The Nazarene girls are homely. Some of them have large, lustrous eyes, but none of them have pretty faces. These girls wear a single garment usually, and it is loose, shapeless, of undecided color; it is generally out of repair, too. They wear, from crown to jaw, curious strings of old coins, after the manner of the belles of Tiberias, and brass jewelry upon their wrists and in their ears. They wear no shoes and stockings. They are the most human girls we have found in the country yet, and the best-natured. But there is no question that these picturesque maidens sadly lack comeliness.

A pilgrim—the "Enthusiast"—said: "See that tall, graceful girl! Look at the Madonna-like beauty of her countenance!"

Another pilgrim came along presently and said: "Observe that tall, graceful girl; what queenly, Madonna-like gracefulness of beauty is in her countenance."

I said: "She is not tall, she is short; she is not beautiful, she is homely; she is graceful enough, I grant, but she is rather boisterous."

The third and last pilgrim moved by before long, and he said: "Ah, what a tall, graceful girl! What Madonna-like gracefulness of queenly beauty!"

The verdicts were all in. It was time to look up the authorities for all these opinions. I found this paragraph, which follows. Written by whom? Wm. C. Grimes:

After we were in the saddle, we rode down to the spring to have a last look at the women of Nazareth, who were, as a class, much the prettiest that we had seen in the East. As we approached the crowd a tall girl of nineteen advanced toward Miriam and offered her a cup of water. Her movement was graceful and queenly. We exclaimed on the spot at the Madonna-like beauty of her countenance. Whitely was suddenly thirsty, and begged for water, and drank it slowly, with his eyes over the top of the cup, fixed on her large black eyes, which gazed on him quite as curiously as he on her. Then Moreright wanted water. She gave it to him and he managed to spill it so as to ask for another cup, and by the time she came to me she saw through the operation; her eyes were full of fun as she looked at me. I laughed outright, and she joined me in as gay a shout as ever country maiden in old Orange county. I wished for a picture of her. A Madonna, whose face was a portrait of that beautiful Nazareth girl, would be a "thing of beauty" and "a joy forever."

That is the kind of gruel which has been served out from Palestine for ages. Commend me to Fenimore Cooper to find beauty in the Indians, and to Grimes to find it in the Arabs. Arab men are often fine-looking, but Arab women are not. We can all believe that the Virgin Mary was beautiful; it is not natural to think otherwise; but does it follow that it is our duty to find beauty in these present women of Nazareth?

I love to quote from Grimes, because he is so dramatic. And because he is so romantic. And because he seems to care but little whether he tells the truth or not, so he scares the reader or excites his envy or his admiration.

He went through this peaceful land with one hand forever on his revolver and the other on his pocket handkerchief. Always, when he was not on the point of crying over a holy place, he was on the point of killing an Arab. More surprising things happened to him in Palestine than ever happened to any traveler here or elsewhere since Munchausen died.

At Beit Jin, where nobody had interfered with him, he crept out of his tent at dead of night and shot at what he took to be an Arab lying on a rock, some distance away, planning evil. The ball killed a wolf. Just before he fired, he makes a dramatic picture of himself—as usual to scare the reader:

Was it imagination, or did I see a moving object on the surface of the rock? If it were a man, why did he not now drop me? He had a beautiful shot as I stood out in my black burnoose against the white tent. I had the sensation of an entering bullet in my throat, breast, brain.

Reckless creature!

Riding toward Gennesaret, they saw two Bedouins, and "we looked to our pistols and loosened them quietly in our shawls," etc. Always cool.

In Samaria he charged up a hill in the face of a volley of stones; he fired into the crowd of men who threw them. He says:

I never lost an opportunity of impressing the Arabs with the perfection of American and English weapons, and the danger of attacking any one of the armed Franks. I think the lesson of that ball not lost.

At Beitin he gave his whole band of Arab muleteers a piece of his mind, and then:

I contented myself with a solemn assurance that if there occurred another instance of disobedience to orders, I would thrash the responsible party as he never dreamed of being thrashed, and if I could not find who was responsible, I would whip them all, from first to last, whether there was a governor at hand to do it or I had to do it myself.

Perfectly fearless, this man.

He rode down the perpendicular path in the rocks, from the castle of Baniyas to the oak grove, at a flying gallop, his horse striding "thirty feet" at every bound. I stand prepared to bring thirty reliable witnesses to prove that Putnam's famous feat at Horseneck was insignificant compared to this.

Behold him—always theatrical—looking at Jerusalem—this time, by an oversight, with his hand off his pistol for once.

I stood in the road, my hand on my horse's neck, and with my dim eyes sought to trace the outlines of the holy places which I had long before fixed in my mind, but the fast-flowing tears forbade my succeeding. There were our Mohammedan servants, a Latin monk, two Armenians and a Jew in our cortege, and all alike gazed with overflowing eyes.

If Latin monks and Arabs cried, I know to a moral certainty that the horses cried also, and so the picture is complete.

But when necessity demanded, he could be firm as adamant. In the Lebanon Valley an Arab youth—a Christian; he is particular to explain that Muhammadans do not steal—robbed him of a paltry ten dollars' worth of powder and shot. He convicted him before a sheikh and looked on while he was punished by the terrible bastinado. Hear him:

He [Mousa] was on his back in a twinkling, howling, shouting, screaming, but he was carried out to the piazza before the door, where we could see the operation, and laid face down. One man sat on his back and one on his legs, the latter holding up his feet, while a third laid on the bare soles a rhinoceros-hide koorbash * that whizzed through the air at

* "A Koorbash is Arabic for cowhide, the cow being a rhinoceros. It is the most cruel whip known to fame. Heavy as lead, and flexible as India rubber, usually about forty inches long and tapering gradually from an inch in diameter to a point, it administers a blow which *leaves its mark for time*."—*Scow Life in Egypt*, by the same author.

every stroke. Poor Moreright was in agony, and Nama and Nama the Second [mother and sister of Mousa] were on their faces begging and wailing, now embracing my knees and now Whitely's, while the brother, outside, made the air ring with cries louder than Mousa's. Even Yusef came and asked me on his knees to relent, and last of all, Betuni—the rascal had lost a feed-bag in their house and had been loudest in his denunciations that morning—besought the Howajji to have mercy on the fellow.

But not he! The punishment was "suspended" at the *fifteenth blow,* to hear the confession. Then Grimes and his party rode away and left the entire Christian family to be fined and as severely punished as the *Muhammadan sheikh* should deem proper.

As I mounted, Yusef once more begged me to interfere and have mercy on them, but I looked around at the dark faces of the crowd, and I couldn't find one drop of pity in my heart for them.

He closes his picture with a rollicking burst of humor which contrasts finely with the grief of the mother and her children.

One more paragraph:

Then once more I bowed my head. It is no shame to have wept in Palestine. I wept, when I saw Jerusalem, I wept when I lay in the starlight at Bethlehem, I wept on the blessed shores of Galilee. My hand was no less firm on the rein, my finger did not tremble on the trigger of my pistol when I rode with it in my right hand along the shore of the blue sea [weeping]. My eye was not dimmed by those tears nor my heart in aught weakened. Let him who would sneer at my emotion close this volume here, for he will find little to his taste in my journeyings through Holy Land.

He never bored but he struck water.

I am aware that this is a pretty voluminous notice of Mr. Grime's book. However, it is proper and legitimate to speak of it, for *Nomadic Life in Palestine* is a representative book —the representative of a *class* of Palestine books—and a criticism upon it will serve for a criticism upon them all. And since I am treating it in the comprehensive capacity of a representative book, I have taken the liberty of giving to both book and author fictitious names. Perhaps it is in better taste anyhow to do this.

51

Nazareth is wonderfully interesting because the town has an air about it of being precisely as Jesus left it, and one finds himself saying all the time, "The boy Jesus has stood in this doorway—has played in that street—has touched these stones with his hands—has rambled over these chalky hills." Whoever shall write the boyhood of Jesus ingeniously will make a book which will possess a vivid interest for young and old alike. I judge so from the greater interest we found in Nazareth than any of our speculations upon Capernaum and the Sea of Galilee gave rise to. It was not possible, standing by the Sea of Galilee, to frame more than a vague, faraway idea of the majestic Personage who walked upon the crested waves as if they had been solid earth, and who touched the dead and they rose up and spoke. I read among my notes now, with a new interest, some sentences from an edition of 1621 of the Apocryphal New Testament. [Extract.]

Christ, kissed by a bride made dumb by sorcerers, cures her. A leprous girl cured by the water in which the infant Christ was washed, and becomes the servant of Joseph and Mary. The leprous son of a Prince cured in like manner.

A young man who had been bewitched and turned into a mule, miraculously cured by the infant Saviour being put on his back, and is married to the girl who had been cured of leprosy. Whereupon the bystanders praise God.

Chapter 16. Christ miraculously widens or contracts gates, milk-pails, sieves or boxes, not properly made by Joseph, he not being skillful at his carpenter's trade. The King of Jerusalem gives Joseph an order for a throne. Joseph works on it for two years and makes it two spans too short. The King being angry with him, Jesus comforts him—commands him to pull one side of the throne while he pulls the other, and brings it to its proper dimensions.

Chapter 19. Jesus, charged with throwing a boy from the roof of a house, miraculously causes the dead boy to speak and acquit him; fetches water for his mother, breaks the pitcher and miraculously gathers the water in his mantle and brings it home.

Sent to a schoolmaster, refuses to tell his letters, and the schoolmaster going to whip him, his hand withers.

Further on in this quaint volume of rejected gospels is an epistle of St. Clement to the Corinthians, which was used in the churches and considered genuine fourteen or fifteen hundred years ago. In it this account of the fabled phoenix occurs:

1. Let us consider that wonderful type of the resurrection, which is seen in the Eastern countries, that is to say, in Arabia.

2. There is a certain bird called a phoenix. Of this there is never but one at a time, and that lives five hundred years. And when the time of its dissolution draws near, that it must die, it makes itself a nest of frankincense, and myrrh, and other spices, into which, when its time is fulfilled, it enters and dies.

3. But its flesh, putrefying, breeds a certain worm, which, being nourished by the juice of the dead bird, brings forth feathers; and when it is grown to a perfect state, it takes up the nest in which the bones of its parent lie, and carries it from Arabia into Egypt, to a city called Heliopolis:

4. And flying in open day in the sight of all men, lays it upon the altar of the sun, and so returns from whence it came.

5. The priests then search into the records of the time, and find that it returned precisely at the end of five hundred years.

Business is business, and there is nothing like punctuality, especially in a phoenix.

The few chapters relating to the infancy of the Saviour contain many things which seem frivolous and not worth preserving. A large part of the remaining portions of the book read like good Scripture, however. There is one verse that ought not to have been rejected, because it so evidently prophetically refers to the general run of Congresses of the United States:

199. They carry themselves high, and as prudent men; and though they are fools, yet would seem to be teachers.

I have set these extracts down as I found them. Everywhere among the cathedrals of France and Italy one finds traditions of personages that do not figure in the Bible and of miracles that are not mentioned in its pages. But they are all in this Apocryphal New Testament, and though they have been ruled out of our modern Bible, it is claimed that they were accepted gospel twelve or fifteen centuries ago, and ranked as high in credit as any. One needs to read this book before he visits those venerable cathedrals, with their treasures of tabooed and forgotten tradition.

They imposed another pirate upon us at Nazareth—another invincible Arab guard. We took our last look at the city, clinging like a whitewashed wasp's nest to the hillside, and at eight o'clock in the morning departed. We dismounted and drove the horses down a bridle path which I think was fully as crooked as a corkscrew, which I know to be as steep as the downward sweep of a rainbow, and which I believe to be the worst piece of road in the geography except one in the Sandwich Islands, which I remember painfully, and possibly one or two mountain trails in the Sierra Nevadas. Often, in this narrow path, the horse had to poise himself nicely on a rude stone step and then drop his forefeet over the edge and down something more than half his own height. This brought his nose near the ground while his tail pointed up toward the sky somewhere, and gave him the appearance of preparing to stand on his head. A horse cannot look dignified in this position. We accomplished the long descent at last and trotted across the great Plain of Esdraelon.

Some of us will be shot before we finish this pilgrimage. The pilgrims read *Nomadic Life* and keep themselves in a constant state of quixotic heroism. They have their hands on their pistols all the time, and every now and then, when you least expect it, they snatch them out and take aim at Bedouins who are not visible, and draw their knives and make savage passes at other Bedouins who do not exist. I am in deadly peril always, for these spasms are sudden and irregular, and of course I cannot tell when to be getting out of the way. If I am accidentally murdered sometime during one of these romantic frenzies of the pilgrims, Mr. Grimes must be rigidly held to answer as an accessory before the fact. If the pilgrims would take deliberate aim and shoot at a man, it would be all right and proper—because that man would not be in any danger; but these random assaults are what I object to. I do not wish to see any more places like Esdraelon, where the ground is level and people can gallop. It puts melodramatic nonsense into the pilgrims' heads. All at once, when one is jogging along stupidly in the sun and thinking about something ever so far away, here they come, at a stormy gallop, spurring and whooping at those ridgy old sore-backed plugs till their heels fly higher than their heads, and as they whiz by out comes a little potato gun of a revolver, there is a startling little pop, and a small pellet goes singing through the air. Now that I have begun this pilgrimage, I intend to go through with it, though, sooth to say, nothing but the most desperate valor has kept me to my purpose up to the present time. I do not mind Bedouins—I am not afraid of them; because neither Bedouins nor ordinary Arabs have shown any disposition to harm us—but I *do* feel afraid of my own comrades.

Arriving at the furthest verge of the plain, we rode a little way up a hill and found ourselves at Endor, famous for its witch. Her descendants are there yet. They were the wildest horde of half-naked savages we have found thus far. They swarmed out of mud beehives; out of hovels of the dry-goods-box pattern; out of gaping caves under shelving rocks; out of crevices in the earth. In five minutes the dead solitude and silence of the place were no more, and a begging, screeching, shouting mob were struggling about the horses' feet and blocking the way. "Baksheesh! Baksheesh! Baksheesh! Howjji, baksheesh!" It was Magdala over again, only here the glare from the infidel eyes was fierce and full of hate. The population numbers two hundred and fifty, and more than half the citizens live in caves in the rock. Dirt, degradation, and savagery are Endor's specialty. We say no more about Magdala and Deburieh now. Endor heads the list. It is worse than any Indian *campoody*. The hill is barren, rocky, and forbidding. No sprig of grass is visible, and only one tree. This is a fig tree, which maintains a precarious footing among the rocks at the mouth of the dismal cavern once occupied by the veritable Witch of Endor. In this cavern, tradition says, Saul, the king, sat at midnight and stared and trembled while the earth shook, the thunders crashed among the hills, and out of the midst of fire and smoke the spirit of the dead prophet rose up and confronted him. Saul had crept to this place in the darkness while his army slept, to learn what fate awaited him in the morrow's battle. He went away a sad man, to meet disgrace and death.

A spring trickles out of the rock in the gloomy recesses of

the cavern, and we were thirsty. The citizens of Endor objected to our going in there. They do not mind dirt; they do not mind rags; they do not mind vermin; they do not mind barbarous ignorance and savagery; they do not mind a reasonable degree of starvation, but they *do* like to be pure and holy before their god, whoever he may be, and therefore they shudder and grow almost pale at the idea of Christian lips polluting a spring whose waters must descend into their sanctified gullets. We had no wanton desire to wound even *their* feelings or trample upon their prejudices, but we were out of water thus early in the day, and were burning up with thirst. It was at this time and under these circumstances that I framed an aphorism which has already become celebrated. I said: "Necessity knows no law." We went in and drank.

We got away from the noisy wretches finally, dropping them in squads and couples as we filed over the hills—the aged first, the infants next, the young girls further on; the strong men ran beside us a mile, and only left when they had secured the last possible piaster in the way of baksheesh.

In an hour we reached Nain, where Christ raised the widow's son to life. Nain is Magdala on a small scale. It has no population of any consequence. Within a hundred yards of it is the original graveyard, for aught I know; the tombstones lie flat on the ground, which is Jewish fashion in Syria. I believe the Muslims do not allow them to have upright tombstones. A Muslim grave is usually roughly plastered over and whitewashed, and has at one end an upright projection which is shaped into exceedingly rude attempts at ornamentation. In the cities there is often no appearance of a grave at all; a tall, slender, marble tombstone, elaborately lettered, gilded, and painted, marks the burial place, and this is surmounted by a turban so carved and shaped as to signify the dead man's rank in life.

They showed a fragment of ancient wall which they said was one side of the gate out of which the widow's dead son was being brought so many centuries ago when Jesus met the procession:

Now when he came nigh to the gate of the city, behold there was a dead man carried out, the only son of his mother, and she was a widow: and much people of the city was with her.

And when the Lord saw her, he had compassion on her, and said, Weep not.

And he came and touched the bier: and they that bare him stood still. And he said, Young man, I say unto thee, arise.

And he that was dead sat up, and began to speak. And he delivered him to his mother.

And there came a fear on all. And they glorified God, saying, That a great prophet is risen up among us; and That God hath visited his people.

A little mosque stands upon the spot which tradition says was occupied by the widow's dwelling. Two or three aged Arabs sat about its door. We entered and the pilgrims broke specimens from the foundation walls, though they had to touch and even step upon the "praying carpets" to do it. It was almost the same as breaking pieces from the hearts of those old Arabs. To step rudely upon the sacred praying mats with booted feet—a thing not done by any Arab—was to inflict pain upon men who had not offended us in any way. Suppose a party of armed foreigners were to enter a village church in America and break ornaments from the altar railings for curiosities, and climb up and walk upon the Bible and the pulpit cushions? However, the cases are different. One is the profanation of a temple of our faith—the other only the profanation of a pagan one.

We descended to the plain again and halted a moment at a well—of Abraham's time, no doubt. It was in a desert place. It was walled three feet aboveground with squared and heavy blocks of stone, after the manner of Bible pictures. Around it some camels stood, and others knelt. There was a group of sober little donkeys with naked, dusky children clambering about them or sitting astride their rumps or pulling their tails. Tawny, black-eyed, barefooted maids, arrayed in rags and adorned with brazen armlets and pinchbeck earrings, were poising water jars upon their heads or drawing water from the well. A flock of sheep stood by, waiting for the shepherds to fill the hollowed stones with water so that they might drink—stones which, like those that walled the well, were worn smooth and deeply creased by the chafing chins of a hundred generations of thirsty animals. Picturesque Arabs sat upon the ground in groups and solemnly smoked their long-stemmed chibouks. Other Arabs were filling black hogskins with water—skins which, well filled and distended with water till the short legs projected painfully out of the proper line, looked like the corpses of hogs bloated by drowning. Here was a grand Oriental picture which I had worshiped a thousand times in soft, rich steel engravings! But in the engraving there was no desolation; no dirt; no rags; no fleas; no ugly features; no sore eyes; no feasting flies; no besotted ignorance in the countenances; no raw places on the donkeys' backs; no disagreeable jabbering in unknown tongues; no stench of camels; no suggestion that a couple of tons of powder placed under the party and touched off would heighten the effect and give to the scene a genuine interest and a charm which it would always be pleasant to recall, even though a man lived a thousand years.

Oriental scenes look best in steel engravings. I cannot be imposed upon anymore by that picture of the Queen of Sheba visiting Solomon. I shall say to myself, "You look fine, madam, but your feet are not clean, and you smell like a camel."

Presently a wild Arab in charge of a camel train recognized an old friend in Ferguson, and they ran and fell upon each other's necks and kissed each other's grimy, bearded faces upon both cheeks. It explained instantly a something which had always seemed to me only a far-fetched Oriental figure of speech. I refer to the circumstance of Christ's rebuking a Pharisee or some such character, and reminding him that from him he had received no "kiss of welcome." It did not seem reasonable to me that men should kiss each other, but I am aware now that they did. There was reason in it, too. The custom was natural and proper; because people must kiss, and a man would not be likely to kiss one of the women of this country of his own free will and accord. One must travel to learn. Every day now old Scriptural phrases that never possessed any significance for me before take to themselves a meaning.

We journeyed around the base of the mountain—"Little Hermon"—past the old Crusaders' castle of El Fuleh, and arrived at Shunem. This was another Magdala, to a fraction, frescoes and all. Here, tradition says, the prophet Samuel was born, and here the Shunemite woman built a little house upon the city wall for the accommodation of the prophet Elisha. Elisha asked her what she expected in return. It was a perfectly natural question, for these people are and were in the habit of proffering favors and services and then expecting and begging for pay. Elisha knew them well. He could not comprehend that anybody should build for him that humble little chamber for the mere sake of old friendship, and with no selfish motive whatever. It used to seem a very impolite, not to say a rude, question for Elisha to ask the woman, but it does not seem so to me now. The woman said she expected nothing. Then for her goodness and her unselfishness, he rejoiced her heart with the news that she should bear a son. It was a high reward, but she would not have thanked him for a daughter—daughters have always been unpopular here. The son was born, grew, waxed strong, died. Elisha restored him to life in Shunem.

We found here a grove of lemon trees—cool, shady, hung with fruit. One is apt to overestimate beauty when it is rare, but to me this grove seemed very beautiful. It *was* beautiful. I do not overestimate it. I must always remember Shunem gratefully, as a place which gave to us this leafy shelter after our long, hot ride. We lunched, rested, chatted, smoked our pipes an hour, and then mounted and moved on.

As we trotted across the Plain of Jezreel we met half a dozen Digger Indians (Bedouins) with very long spears in their hands, cavorting around on old crowbait horses and spearing imaginary enemies; whooping and fluttering their rags in the wind and carrying on in every respect like a pack of hopeless lunatics. At last, here were the "wild, free sons of the desert, speeding over the plain like the wind, on their beautiful Arabian mares" we had read so much about and longed so much to see! Here were the "picturesque costumes"! This was the "gallant spectacle"! Tatterdemalion vagrants—cheap braggadocio—"Arabian mares" spined and necked like the ichthyosaurus in the museum and humped and cornered like a dromedary! To glance at the genuine son of the desert is to take the romance out of him forever—to behold his steed is to long in charity to strip his harness off and let him fall to pieces.

Presently we came to a ruinous old town on a hill, the same being the ancient Jezreel.

Ahab, King of Samaria (this was a very vast kingdom, for those days, and was very nearly half as large as Rhode Island), dwelt in the city of Jezreel, which was his capital. Near him lived a man by the name of Naboth, who had a vineyard. The King asked him for it, and when he would not give it, offered to buy it. But Naboth refused to sell it. In those days it was considered a sort of crime to part with one's inheritance at any price—and even if a man did part with it, it reverted to himself or his heirs again at the next jubilee year. So this spoiled child of a king went and lay down on the bed with his face to the wall and grieved sorely. The Queen, a notorious character in those days, and whose name is a by-word and a reproach even in these, came in and asked him wherefore he sorrowed, and he told her. Jezebel said she could secure the vineyard; and she went forth and forged letters to the nobles and wise men, in the King's name, and ordered them to proclaim a fast and set Naboth on high before the people and suborn two witnesses to swear that he had blasphemed. They did it, and the people stoned the accused by the city wall, and he died. Then Jezebel came and told the King and said, "Behold, Naboth is no more—rise up and seize the vineyard." So Ahab seized the vineyard and went into it to possess it. But the Prophet Elijah came to him there and read his fate to him, and the fate of Jezebel; and said that in the place where dogs licked the blood of Naboth, dogs should also lick his blood—and he said, likewise, the dogs should eat Jezebel by the wall of Jezreel. In the course of time the King was killed in battle, and when his chariot wheels were washed in the pool of Samaria, the dogs licked the blood. In after years, Jehu, who was King of Israel, marched down against Jezreel, by order of one of the prophets, and administered one of those convincing rebukes so common among the people of those days: he killed many kings and their subjects, and as he came along he saw Jezebel, painted and finely dressed, looking out of a window, and ordered that she be thrown down to him. A servant did it, and Jehu's horse trampled her under foot. Then Jehu went in and sat down to dinner; and presently he said, "Go and bury this cursed woman, for she is a King's daughter." The spirit of charity came upon him too late, however, for the prophecy had already been fulfilled—the dogs had eaten her, and they "found no more of her than the skull, and the feet, and the palms of her hands."

Ahab, the late king, had left a helpless family behind him, and Jehu killed seventy of the orphan sons. Then he killed all the relatives and teachers and servants and friends of the family, and rested from his labors, until he was come near to Samaria, where he met forty-two persons and asked them who they were; they said they were brothers of the King of Judah. He killed them. When he got to Samaria, he said he would show his zeal for the Lord; so he gathered all the

priests and people together that worshiped Baal, pretending
that he was going to adopt that worship and offer up a great
sacrifice, and when they were all shut up where they could
not defend themselves, he caused every person of them to be
killed. Then Jehu, the good missionary, rested from his
labors once more.

We went back to the valley, and rode to the Fountain of
Ain Jelud. They call it the Fountain of Jezreel usually. It
is a pond about one hundred feet square and four feet deep,
with a stream of water trickling into it from under an over-
hanging ledge of rocks. It is in the midst of a great solitude.
Here Gideon pitched his camp in the old times; behind Shunem lay the "Midianites, the Amalekites, and the Children
of the East," who were "as grasshoppers for multitude; both
they and their camels were without number, as the sand by
the sea-side for multitude." Which means that there were
one hundred and thirty-five thousand men, and that they had
transportation service accordingly.

Gideon, with only three hundred men, surprised them in
the night, and stood by and looked on while they butchered
each other until a hundred and twenty thousand lay dead on
the field.

We camped at Jenin before night, and got up and started
again at one o'clock in the morning. Somewhere toward
daylight we passed the locality where the best authenticated
tradition locates the pit into which Joseph's brethren threw
him, and about noon, after passing over a succession of
mountaintops, clad with groves of fig and olive trees, with
the Mediterranean in sight some forty miles away, and going
by many ancient Biblical cities whose inhabitants glowered
savagely upon our Christian procession, and were seemingly
inclined to practice on it with stones, we came to the singularly terraced and unlovely hills that betrayed that we were
out of Galilee and into Samaria at last.

We climbed a high hill to visit the city of Samaria, where
the woman may have hailed from who conversed with Christ
at Jacob's Well, and from whence, no doubt, came also the
celebrated Good Samaritan. Herod the Great is said to have
made a magnificent city of this place, and a great number of
coarse limestone columns, twenty feet high and two feet
through, that are almost guiltless of architectural grace of
shape and ornament, are pointed out by many authors as evi-

dence of the fact. They would not have been considered handsome in ancient Greece, however.

The inhabitants of this camp are particularly vicious and stoned two parties of our pilgrims a day or two ago who brought about the difficulty by showing their revolvers when they did not intend to use them—a thing which is deemed bad judgment in the Far West and ought certainly to be so considered anywhere. In the new territories, when a man puts his hand on a weapon, he knows that he must use it; he must use it instantly or expect to be shot down where he stands. Those pilgrims had been reading Grimes.

There was nothing for us to do in Samaria but buy handfuls of old Roman coins at a franc a dozen, and look at a dilapidated church of the Crusaders and a vault in it which once contained the body of John the Baptist. This relic was long ago carried away to Genoa.

Samaria stood a disastrous siege once, in the days of Elisha, at the hands of the King of Syria. Provisions reached such a figure that "an ass' head was sold for eighty pieces of silver and the fourth part of a cab of dove's dung for five pieces of silver."

An incident recorded of that heavy time will give one a very good idea of the distress that prevailed within these crumbling walls. As the King was walking upon the battlements one day, "a woman cried out, saying, Help, my lord, O King! And the King said, What aileth thee? and she answered, This woman said unto me, Give thy son, that we may eat him today, and we will eat my son tomorrow. So we boiled my son, and did eat him; and I said unto her on the next day, Give thy son that we may eat him; and she hath hid her son."

The prophet Elisha declared that within four-and-twenty hours the prices of food should go down to nothing almost, and it was so. The Syrian army broke camp and fled, for some cause or other, the famine was relieved from without, and many a shoddy speculator in dove's dung and ass's meat was ruined.

We were glad to leave this hot and dusty old village and hurry on. At two o'clock we stopped to lunch and rest at ancient Shechem, between the historic mounts of Gerizim and Ebal, where in the old times the books of the law, the curses and the blessings, were read from the heights to the Jewish multitudes below.

52

The narrow canyon in which Nablus, or Shechem, is situated is under high cultivation, and the soil is exceedingly black and fertile. It is well watered, and its affluent vegetation gains effect by contrast with the barren hills that tower on either side. One of these hills is the ancient Mount of Blessings and the other the Mount of Curses; and wise men who seek for fulfillments of prophecy think they find here a wonder of this kind—to wit, that the Mount of Blessings is strangely fertile and its mate as strangely unproductive. We could not see that there was really much difference between them in this respect, however.

Shechem is distinguished as one of the residences of the patriarch Jacob, and as the seat of those tribes that cut themselves loose from their brethren of Israel and propagated doctrines not in conformity with those of the original Jewish creed. For thousands of years this clan have dwelt in Shechem under strict taboo and having little commerce or fellowship with their fellow men of any religion or nationality. For generations they have not numbered more than one or two hundred, but they still adhere to their ancient faith and maintain their ancient rites and ceremonies. Talk of family and old descent! Princes and nobles pride themselves upon lineages they can trace back some hundreds of years. What is this trifle to this handful of old first families of Shechem, who can name their fathers straight back without a flaw for thousands—straight back to a period so remote that men reared in a country where the days of two hundred years ago are called "ancient" times grow dazed and bewildered when they try to comprehend it! Here is respectability for you—here is "family"—here is high descent worth talking about. This sad, proud remnant of a once mighty community still hold themselves aloof from all the world; they still live as their fathers lived, labor as their fathers labored, think as they did, feel as they did, worship in the same place, in sight of the same landmarks, and in the same quaint, patriarchal way their ancestors did more than thirty centuries ago. I found myself gazing at any straggling scion of this strange race with a riveted fascination, just as one would stare at a living mastodon or a megatherium that had moved in the gray dawn of creation and seen the wonders of that mysterious world that was before the flood.

Carefully preserved among the sacred archives of this curious community is a MS copy of the ancient Jewish law, which is said to be the oldest document on earth. It is written on vellum, and is some four or five thousand years old. Nothing but baksheesh can purchase a sight. Its fame is somewhat dimmed in these latter days because of the doubts so many authors of Palestine travels have felt themselves privileged to cast upon it. Speaking of this MS reminds me that I procured from the high priest of this ancient Samaritan community, at great expense, a secret document of still higher antiquity and far more extraordinary interest, which I propose to publish as soon as I have finished translating it.

Joshua gave his dying injunction to the children of Israel at Shechem and buried a valuable treasure secretly under an oak tree there about the same time. The superstitious Samaritans have always been afraid to hunt for it. They believe it is guarded by fierce spirits invisible to men.

About a mile and a half from Shechem we halted at the base of Mount Ebal, before a little square area, enclosed by a high stone wall, neatly whitewashed. Across one end of this enclosure is a tomb built after the manner of the Muslims. It is the tomb of Joseph. No truth is better authenticated than this.

When Joseph was dying he prophesied that exodus of the Israelites from Egypt which occurred four hundred years afterwards. At the same time he exacted of his people an oath that when they journeyed to the land of Canaan, they would bear his bones with them and bury them in the ancient inheritance of his fathers. The oath was kept.

And the bones of Joseph, which the children of Israel brought up out of Egypt, buried they in Shechem, in a parcel of ground which Jacob bought of the sons of Hamor the father of Shechem, for a hundred pieces of silver.

Few tombs on earth command the veneration of so many races and men of divers creeds as this of Joseph. "Samaritan and Jew, Moslem and Christian alike, revere it, and honor it with their visits. The tomb of Joseph, the dutiful son, the affectionate, forgiving brother, the virtuous man, the wise Prince and ruler. Egypt felt his influence—the world knows his history."

In this same "parcel of ground" which Jacob bought of the sons of Hamor for a hundred pieces of silver is Jacob's celebrated well. It is cut in the solid rock, and is nine feet square and ninety feet deep. The name of this unpretending hole in the ground, which one might pass by and take no notice of, is as familiar as household words to even the children and the peasants of many a far-off country. It is more famous than the Parthenon; it is older than the pyramids.

It was by this well that Jesus sat and talked with a woman of that strange, antiquated Samaritan community I have been speaking of, and told her of the mysterious water of life. As descendants of old English nobles still cherish in the traditions of their houses how that this king or that king tarried a day with some favored ancestor three hundred years ago, no doubt the descendants of the woman of Samaria, living there in Shechem, still refer with pardonable vanity to this conversation of their ancestor, held some little time gone by, with the Messiah of the Christians. It is not likely that they undervalue a distinction such as this. Samaritan nature is human nature, and human nature remembers contact with the illustrious always.

For an offense done to the family honor, the sons of Jacob exterminated all Shechem once.

We left Jacob's Well and traveled till eight in the evening, but rather slowly, for we had been in the saddle nineteen hours, and the horses were cruelly tired. We got so far ahead of the tents that we had to camp in an Arab village and sleep on the ground. We could have slept in the largest of the houses, but there were some little drawbacks: it was populous with vermin, it had a dirt floor, it was in no respect cleanly, and there was a family of goats in the only bedroom and two donkeys in the parlor. Outside there were no inconveniences, except that the dusky, ragged, earnest-eyed villagers of both sexes and all ages grouped themselves on their haunches all around us and discussed us and criticized us with noisy tongues till midnight. We did not mind the noise, being tired, but doubtless the reader is aware that it is almost an impossible thing to go to sleep when you know that people are looking at you. We went to bed at ten and got up again at two and started once more. Thus are people persecuted by dragomen, whose sole ambition in life is to get ahead of each other.

About daylight we passed Shiloh, where the Ark of the Covenant rested three hundred years, and at whose gates good old Eli fell down and "brake his neck" when the messenger, riding hard from the battle, told him of the defeat of his people, the death of his sons, and, more than all, the capture of Israel's pride, her hope, her refuge, the ancient Ark her forefathers brought with them out of Egypt. It is little wonder that under circumstances like these he fell down and brake his neck. But Shiloh had no charms for us. We were so cold that there was no comfort but in motion, and so drowsy we could hardly sit upon the horses.

After a while we came to a shapeless mass of ruins, which still bears the name of Beth-el. It was here that Jacob lay down and had that superb vision of angels flitting up and down a ladder that reached from the clouds to earth, and caught glimpses of their blessed home through the open gates of heaven.

The pilgrims took what was left of the hallowed ruin, and we pressed on toward the goal of our crusade, renowned Jerusalem.

The further we went, the hotter the sun got, and the more rocky and bare, repulsive and dreary the landscape became. There could not have been more fragments of stone strewn broadcast over this part of the world if every ten square feet of the land had been occupied by a separate and distinct stonecutter's establishment for an age. There was hardly a tree or a shrub anywhere. Even the olive and the cactus, those fast friends of a worthless soil, had almost deserted the country. No landscape exists that is more tiresome to the eye than that which bounds the approaches to Jerusalem. The only difference between the roads and the surrounding country, perhaps, is that there are rather more rocks in the roads than in the surrounding country.

We passed Ramah and Beroth, and on the right saw the tomb of the prophet Samuel, perched high upon a commanding eminence. Still no Jerusalem came in sight. We hurried on impatiently. We halted a moment at the ancient Fountain of Beira, but its stones, worn deeply by the chins of thirsty animals that are dead and gone centuries ago, had no interest for us—we longed to see Jerusalem. We spurred up hill after hill, and usually began to stretch our necks minutes before we got to the top—but disappointment always followed: more stupid hills beyond—more unsightly landscape—no Holy City.

At last, away in the middle of the day, ancient bits of wall and crumbling arches began to line the way—we toiled up one more hill, and every pilgrim and every sinner swung his hat on high! Jerusalem!

Perched on its eternal hills, white and domed and solid, massed together and hooped with high gray walls, the venerable city gleamed in the sun. So small! Why, it was no larger than an American village of four thousand inhabitants, and no larger than an ordinary Syrian city of thirty thousand. Jerusalem numbers only fourteen thousand people.

We dismounted and looked, without speaking a dozen sentences, across the wide intervening valley for an hour or more; and noted those prominent features of the city that pictures make familiar to all men from their school days till their death. We could recognize the Tower of Hippicus, the Mosque of Omar, the Damascus Gate, the Mount of Olives, the Valley of Jehoshaphat, the Tower of David, and the Garden of Gethsemane—and dating from these landmarks could tell very nearly the localities of many others we were not able to distinguish.

I record it here as a notable but not discreditable fact that not even our pilgrims wept. I think there was no individual in the party whose brain was not teeming with thoughts and images and memories invoked by the grand history of the venerable city that lay before us, but still among them all was no "voice of them that wept."

There was no call for tears. Tears would have been out of place. The thoughts Jerusalem suggests are full of poetry, sublimity, and, more than all, dignity. Such thoughts do not find their appropriate expression in the emotions of the nursery.

Just after noon we entered these narrow, crooked streets, by the ancient and the famed Damascus Gate, and now for several hours I have been trying to comprehend that I am actually in the illustrious old city where Solomon dwelt, where Abraham held converse with the Deity, and where walls still stand that witnessed the spectacle of the Crucifixion.

53

A fast walker could go outside the walls of Jerusalem and walk entirely around the city in an hour. I do not know how else to make one understand how small it is. The appearance of the city is peculiar. It is as knobby with countless little domes as a prison door is with bolt heads. Every house has from one to half a dozen of these white plastered domes of stone, broad and low, sitting in the center of or in a cluster upon the flat roof. Wherefore, when one looks down from an eminence upon the compact mass of houses (so closely crowded together, in fact, that there is no appearance of streets at all, and so the city looks solid), he sees the knobbiest town in the world, except Constantinople. It looks as if it might be roofed, from center to circumference, with inverted saucers. The monotony of the view is interrupted only by the great Mosque of Omar, the Tower of Hippicus, and one or two other buildings that rise into commanding prominence.

The houses are generally two stories high, built strongly of masonry, whitewashed or plastered outside, and have a cage of wooden latticework projecting in front of every window. To reproduce a Jerusalem street, it would only be necessary to up-end a chicken coop and hang it before each window in an alley of American houses.

The streets are roughly and badly paved with stone, and are tolerably crooked—enough so to make each street appear to close together constantly and come to an end about a hundred yards ahead of a pilgrim as long as he chooses to walk in it. Projecting from the top of the lower story of many of the houses is a very narrow porch roof, or shed, without supports from below; and I have several times seen cats jump across the street from one shed to the other when they were out calling. The cats could have jumped double the distance without extraordinary exertion. I mention these things to give an idea of how narrow the streets are. Since a cat can jump across them without the least inconvenience, it is hardly necessary to state that such streets are too narrow for carriages. These vehicles cannot navigate the Holy City.

The population of Jerusalem is composed of Muslims, Jews, Greeks, Latins, Armenians, Syrians, Copts, Abyssinians, Greek Catholics, and a handful of Protestants. One hundred of the latter sect are all that dwell now in this birthplace of Christianity. The nice shades of nationality comprised in the above list and the languages spoken by them are altogether too numerous to mention. It seems to me that all the races and colors and tongues of the earth must be represented among the fourteen thousand souls that dwell in Jerusalem. Rags, wretchedness, poverty, and dirt, those signs and symbols that indicate the presence of Muslim rule more surely than the crescent flag itself, abound. Lepers, cripples, the blind, and the idiotic assail you on every hand, and they know but one word of but one language apparently —the eternal "baksheesh." To see the numbers of maimed, malformed, and diseased humanity that throng the holy places and obstruct the gates, one might suppose that the ancient days had come again, and that the angel of the Lord was expected to descend at any moment to stir the waters of Bethesda. Jerusalem is mournful and dreary and lifeless. I would not desire to live here.

One naturally goes first to the Holy Sepulchre. It is right in the city, near the western gate; it and the place of the Crucifixion, and, in fact, every other place intimately connected with that tremendous event, are ingeniously massed together and covered by one roof—the dome of the Church of the Holy Sepulchre.

Entering the building, through the midst of the usual assemblage of beggars, one sees on his left a few Turkish guards —for Christians of different sects will not only quarrel, but fight, also, in this sacred place if allowed to do it. Before you is a marble slab, which covers the Stone of Unction, whereon the Saviour's body was laid to prepare it for burial. It was found necessary to conceal the real stone in this way in order to save it from destruction. Pilgrims were too much given to chipping off pieces of it to carry home. Nearby is a circular railing which marks the spot where the Virgin stood when the Lord's body was anointed.

Entering the great Rotunda, we stand before the most sacred locality in Christendom—the grave of Jesus. It is in the center of the church, and immediately under the great dome. It is enclosed in a sort of little temple of yellow and white stone, of fanciful design. Within the little temple is a portion of the very stone which was rolled away from the door of the Sepulchre, and on which the angel was sitting when Mary came thither "at early dawn." Stooping low, we enter the vault—the Sepulchre itself. It is only about six feet by seven, and the stone couch on which the dead Saviour lay extends from end to end of the apartment and occupies half its width. It is covered with a marble slab which has been much worn by the lips of pilgrims. This slab serves as an altar now. Over it hang some fifty gold and silver lamps, which are kept always burning, and the place is otherwise scandalized by trumpery, gewgaws, and tawdry ornamentation.

All sects of Christians (except Protestants) have chapels under the roof of the Church of the Holy Sepulchre, and each must keep to itself and not venture upon another's ground. It has been proven conclusively that they cannot worship together around the grave of the Saviour of the world in peace. The chapel of the Syrians is not handsome; that of the Copts is the humblest of them all. It is nothing but a dismal cavern, roughly hewn in the living rock of the Hill of Calvary. In one side of it two ancient tombs are hewn, which are claimed to be those in which Nicodemus and Joseph of Aramithea were buried.

As we moved among the great piers and pillars of another part of the church we came upon a party of black-robed, animal-looking Italian monks, with candles in their hands, who were chanting something in Latin and going through some kind of religious performance around a disk of white marble let into the floor. It was there that the risen Saviour appeared to Mary Magdalen in the likeness of a gardener. Nearby was a similar stone, shaped like a star—here the Magdalen herself stood at the same time. Monks were performing in this place also. They perform everywhere—all over the vast building and at all hours. Their candles are always flitting about in the gloom and making the dim old church more dismal than there is any necessity that it should be, even though it is a tomb.

We were shown the place where our Lord appeared to his

mother after the Resurrection. Here also a marble slab marks the place where St. Helena, the mother of the Emperor Constantine, found the crosses about three hundred years after the Crucifixion. According to the legend, this great discovery elicited extravagant demonstrations of joy. But they were of short duration. The question intruded itself: "Which bore the blessed Saviour, and which the thieves?" To be in doubt in so mighty a matter as this—to be uncertain which one to adore—was a grievous misfortune. It turned the public joy to sorrow. But when lived there a holy priest who could not set so simple a trouble as this at rest? One of these soon hit upon a plan that would be a certain test. A noble lady lay very ill in Jerusalem. The wise priests ordered that the three crosses be taken to her bedside one at a time. It was done. When her eyes fell upon the first one, she uttered a scream that was heard beyond the Damascus Gate, and even upon the Mount of Olives, it was said, and then fell back in a deadly swoon. They recovered her and brought the second cross. Instantly she went into fearful convulsions, and it was with the greatest difficulty that six strong men could hold her. They were afraid now to bring in the third cross. They began to fear that possibly they had fallen upon the wrong crosses, and that the true Cross was not with this number at all. However, as the woman seemed likely to die with the convulsions that were tearing her, they concluded that the third could do no more than put her out of her misery with a happy dispatch. So they brought it, and behold, a miracle! The woman sprang from her bed, smiling and joyful, and perfectly restored to health. When we listen to evidence like this, we cannot but believe. We would be ashamed to doubt, and properly, too. Even the very part of Jerusalem where this all occurred is there yet. So there is really no room for doubt.

The priests tried to show us, through a small screen, a fragment of the genuine Pillar of Flagellation, to which Christ was bound when they scourged him. But we could not see it because it was dark inside the screen. However, a baton is kept here, which the pilgrim thrusts through a hole in the screen, and then he no longer doubts that the true Pillar of Flagellation is in there. He cannot have any excuse to doubt it, for he can feel it with the stick. He can feel it as distinctly as he could feel anything.

Not far from here was a niche where they used to preserve

a piece of the true Cross, but it is gone now. This piece of the Cross was discovered in the sixteenth century. The Latin priests say it was stolen away, long ago, by priests of another sect. That seems like a hard statement to make, but we know very well that it *was* stolen, because we have seen it ourselves in several of the cathedrals of Italy and France.

But the relic that touched us most was the plain old sword of that stout Crusader Godfrey of Bouillon—King Godfrey of Jerusalem. No blade in Christendom wields such enchantment as this—no blade of all that rust in the ancestral halls of Europe is able to invoke such visions of romance in the brain of him who looks upon it—none that can prate of such chivalric deeds or tell such brave tales of the warrior days of old. It stirs within a man every memory of the Holy Wars that has been sleeping in his brain for years, and peoples his thoughts with mail-clad images, with marching armies, with battles, and with sieges. It speaks to him of Baldwin, and Tancred, the princely Saladin, and great Richard of the Lion Heart. It was with just such blades as these that these splendid heroes of romance used to segregate a man, so to speak, and leave the half of him to fall one way and the other half the other. This very sword has cloven hundreds of Saracen knights from crown to chin in those old times when Godfrey wielded it. It was enchanted then by a genius that was under the command of King Solomon. When danger approached its master's tent it always struck the shield and clanged out a fierce alarm upon the startled ear of night. In times of doubt, or in fog or darkness, if it were drawn from its sheath it would point instantly toward the foe, and thus reveal the way—and it would also attempt to start after them of its own accord. A Christian could not be so disguised that it would not know him and refuse to hurt him—nor a Muslim so disguised that it would not leap from its scabbard and take his life. These statements are all well authenticated in many legends that are among the most trustworthy legends the good old Catholic monks preserve. I can never forget old Godfrey's sword now. I tried it on a Muslim and clove him in twain like a doughnut. The spirit of Grimes was upon me, and if I had had a graveyard I would have destroyed all the infidels in Jerusalem. I wiped the blood off the old sword and handed it back to the priest—I did not want the fresh gore to obliterate those sacred spots that crimsoned its brightness one day six hundred years ago and thus gave Godfrey warning that before the sun went down his journey of life would end.

Still moving through the gloom of the Church of the Holy Sepulchre, we came to a small chapel, hewn out of the rock—a place which has been known as "The Prison of Our Lord" for many centuries. Tradition says that here the Saviour was confined just previously to the Crucifixion. Under an altar by the door was a pair of stone stocks for human legs. These things are called the "Bonds of Christ," and the use they were once put to has given them the name they now bear.

The Greek chapel is the most roomy, the richest and the showiest chapel in the Church of the Holy Sepulchre. Its altar, like that of all the Greek churches, is a lofty screen that extends clear across the chapel, and is gorgeous with gilding and pictures. The numerous lamps that hang before it are of gold and silver, and cost great sums.

But the feature of the place is a short column that rises from the middle of the marble pavement of the chapel and marks the exact *center of the earth*. The most reliable traditions tell us that this was known to be the earth's center, ages ago, and that when Christ was upon earth he set all doubts upon the subject at rest forever by stating with his own lips that the tradition was correct. Remember, he said that that particular column stood upon the center of the world. If the center of the world changes, the column changes its position accordingly. This column has moved three different times of its own accord. This is because, in great convulsions of nature, at three different times, masses of the earth—whole ranges of mountains, probably—have flown off into space, thus lessening the diameter of the earth and changing the exact locality of its center by a point or two. This is a very curious and interesting circumstance, and is a withering rebuke to those philosophers who would make us believe that it is not possible for any portion of the earth to fly off into space.

To satisfy himself that this spot was really the center of the earth, a skeptic once paid well for the privilege of ascending to the dome of the church to see if the sun gave him a shadow at noon. He came down perfectly convinced. The day was very cloudy and the sun threw no shadows at all; but the man was satisfied that if the sun had come out and made shadows it could not have made any for him.

Proofs like these are not to be set aside by the idle tongues of cavilers. To such as are not bigoted and are willing to be convinced, they carry a conviction that nothing can ever shake.

If even greater proofs than those I have mentioned are wanted, to satisfy the headstrong and the foolish that this is the genuine center of the earth, they are here. The greatest of them lies in the fact that from under this very column was taken the *dust from which Adam was made*. This can surely be regarded in the light of a settler. It is not likely that the original first man would have been made from an inferior quality of earth when it was entirely convenient to get first quality from the world's center. This will strike any reflecting mind forcibly. That Adam was formed of dirt procured in this very spot is amply proven by the fact that in six thousand years no man has ever been able to prove that the dirt was *not* procured here whereof he was made.

It is a singular circumstance that right under the roof of this same great church, and not far away from that illustrious column, Adam himself, the father of the human race, lies buried. There is no question that he is actually buried in the grave which is pointed out as his—there can be none—because it has never yet been proven that that grave is not the grave in which he is buried.

The tomb of Adam! How touching it was, here in a land of strangers, far away from home and friends and all who cared for me, thus to discover the grave of a blood relation. True, a distant one, but still a relation. The unerring instinct of nature thrilled its recognition. The fountain of my filial affection was stirred to its profoundest depths, and I gave way to tumultuous emotion. I leaned upon a pillar and burst into tears. I deem it no shame to have wept over the grave of my poor dead relative. Let him who would sneer at my emotion close this volume here, for he will find little to his taste in my journeyings through Holy Land. Noble old man —he did not live to see me—he did not live to see his child. And I—I—alas, I did not live to see *him*. Weighed down by sorrow and disappointment, he died before I was born—six thousand brief summers before I was born. But let us try to bear it with fortitude. Let us trust that he is better off where he is. Let us take comfort in the thought that his loss is our eternal gain.

The next place the guide took us to in the holy church was

an altar dedicated to the Roman soldier who was of the military guard that attended at the Crucifixion to keep order, and who—when the veil of the temple was rent in the awful darkness that followed; when the rock of Golgotha was split asunder by an earthquake; when the artillery of heaven thundered, and in the baleful glare of the lightnings the shrouded dead flitted about the streets of Jerusalem—shook with fear and said, "Surely this was the Son of God!" Where this altar stands now, that Roman soldier stood then, in full view of the crucified Saviour—in full sight and hearing of all the marvels that were transpiring far and wide about the circumference of the Hill of Calvary. And in this selfsame spot the priests of the temple beheaded him for those blasphemous words he had spoken.

In this altar they used to keep one of the most curious relics that human eyes ever looked upon—a thing that had power to fascinate the beholder in some mysterious way and keep him gazing for hours together. It was nothing less than the copper plate Pilate put upon the Saviour's cross, and upon which he wrote, "THIS IS THE KING OF THE JEWS." I think St. Helena, the mother of Constantine, found this wonderful memento when she was here in the third century. She traveled all over Palestine and was always fortunate. Whenever the good old enthusiast found a thing mentioned in her Bible, Old or New, she would go and search for that thing and never stop until she found it. If it was Adam, she would find Adam; if it was the Ark, she would find the Ark; if it was Goliath or Joshua, she would find *them*. She found the inscription here that I was speaking of, I think. She found it in this very spot, close to where the martyred Roman soldier stood. That copper plate is in one of the churches in Rome now. Anyone can see it there. The inscription is very distinct.

We passed along a few steps and saw the altar built over the very spot where the good Catholic priests say the soldiers divided the raiment of the Saviour.

Then we went down into a cavern which cavilers say was once a cistern. It is a chapel now, however—the Chapel of St. Helena. It is fifty-one feet long by forty-three wide. In it is a marble chair which Helena used to sit in while she superintended her workmen when they were digging and delving for the true Cross. In this place is an altar dedicated to St. Dimas, the penitent thief. A new bronze statue is here—a statue of St. Helena. It reminded us of poor Maximilian, so lately shot. He presented it to this chapel when he was about to leave for his throne in Mexico.

From the cistern we descended twelve steps into a large, roughly shaped grotto carved wholly out of the living rock. Helena blasted it out when she was searching for the true Cross. She had a laborious piece of work here, but it was richly rewarded. Out of this place she got the crown of thorns, the nails of the Cross, the true Cross itself, and the cross of the penitent thief. When she thought she had found everything and was about to stop, she was told in a dream to continue a day longer. It was very fortunate. She did so, and found the cross of the other thief.

The walls and roof of this grotto still weep bitter tears in memory of the event that transpired on Calvary, and devout pilgrims groan and sob when these sad tears fall upon them from the dripping rock. The monks call this apartment the "Chapel of the Invention of the Cross"—a name which is unfortunate, because it leads the ignorant to imagine that a tacit acknowledgment is thus made that the tradition that Helena found the true Cross here is a fiction—an invention. It is a happiness to know, however, that intelligent people do not doubt the story in any of its particulars.

Priests of any of the chapels and denominations in the Church of the Holy Sepulchre can visit this sacred grotto to weep and pray and worship the gentle Redeemer. Two different congregations are not allowed to enter at the same time, however, because they always fight.

Still marching through the venerable Church of the Holy Sepulchre—among chanting priests in coarse long robes and sandals; pilgrims of all colors and many nationalities, in all sorts of strange costumes; under dusky arches and by dingy piers and columns; through a somber cathedral gloom freighted with smoke and incense, and faintly starred with scores of candles that appeared suddenly and as suddenly disappeared, or drifted mysteriously hither and thither about the distant aisles like ghostly jack-o'-lanterns—we came at last to a small chapel which is called the "Chapel of the Mocking." Under the altar was a fragment of a marble column; this was the seat Christ sat on when he was reviled and mockingly made king, crowned with a crown of thorns, and sceptered with a reed. It was here that they blindfolded him and struck him and said in derision, "Prophesy who it is that smote thee." The tradition that this is the identical spot of the mocking is a very ancient one. The guide said that Saewulf was the first to mention it. I do not know Saewulf, but still, I cannot well refuse to receive his evidence—none of us can.

They showed us where the great Godfrey and his brother Baldwin, the first Christian kings of Jerusalem, once lay buried by that sacred sepulcher they had fought so long and so valiantly to wrest from the hands of the infidel. But the niches that had contained the ashes of these renowned Crusaders were empty. Even the coverings of their tombs were gone—destroyed by devout members of the Greek Church because Godfrey and Baldwin were Latin princes and had been reared in a Christian faith whose creed differed in some unimportant respects from theirs.

We passed on and halted before the tomb of Melchizedek! You will remember Melchizedek, no doubt; he was the king who came out and levied a tribute on Abraham the time that he pursued Lot's captors to Dan, and took all their property from them. That was about four thousand years ago, and Melchizedek died shortly afterward. However, his tomb is in a good state of preservation.

When one enters the Church of the Holy Sepulchre, the Sepulchre itself is the first thing he desires to see, and really is almost the first thing he does see. The next thing he has a strong yearning to see is the spot where the Saviour was crucified. But this they exhibit last. It is the crowning glory of the place. One is grave and thoughtful when he stands in the little Tomb of the Saviour—he could not well be otherwise in such a place—but he has not the slightest possible belief that ever the Lord lay there, and so the interest he feels in the spot is very, very greatly marred by that reflection. He looks at the place where Mary stood, in another part of the church, and where John stood and Mary Magdalen; where the mob derided the Lord; where the angel sat; where the crown of thorns was found and the true Cross; where the risen Saviour appeared—he looks at all these places with interest but with the same conviction he felt in the case of the Sepulchre, that there is nothing genuine about them and that they are imaginary holy places created by the monks. But the place of the Crucifixion affects him differently. He fully believes that he is looking upon the very spot where the Saviour gave up his life. He remembers

hat Christ was very celebrated long before he came to
erusalem; he knows that his fame was so great that crowds
ollowed him all the time; he is aware that his entry into
he city produced a stirring sensation, and that his recep-
ion was a kind of ovation; he cannot overlook the fact
hat when he was crucified there were very many in Jeru-
alem who believed that he was the true Son of God. To
ublicly execute such a personage was sufficient in itself to
make the locality of the execution a memorable place for
ges; added to this, the storm, the darkness, the earthquake,
he rending of the veil of the temple, and the untimely
waking of the dead were events calculated to fix the execu-
ion and the scene of it in the memory of even the most
houghtless witness. Fathers would tell their sons about the
trange affair and point out the spot; the sons would transmit
he story to their children, and thus a period of three hundred years would easily be spanned *—at which time Helena
came and built a church upon Calvary to commemorate
he death and burial of the Lord and preserve the sacred
place in the memories of men; since that time there has
always been a church there. It is not possible that there can
be any mistake about the locality of the Crucifixion. Not
half a dozen persons knew where they buried the Saviour
perhaps, and a burial is not a startling event anyhow; therefore we can be pardoned for unbelief in the Sèpulchre, but
not in the place of the Crucifixion. Five hundred years
hence there will be no vestige of Bunker Hill Monument
left, but America will still know where the battle was fought
and where Warren fell. The crucifixion of Christ was too
notable an event in Jerusalem, and the Hill of Calvary
made too celebrated by it, to be forgotten in the short space
of three hundred years. I climbed the stairway in the church
which brings one to the top of the small enclosed pinnacle
of rock, and looked upon the place where the true Cross
once stood, with a far more absorbing interest than I had
ever felt in anything earthly before. I could not believe that
the three holes in the top of the rock were the actual ones
the crosses stood in, but I felt satisfied that those crosses
had stood so near the place now occupied by them that the
few feet of possible difference were a matter of no consequence.

* The thought is Mr. Grime's, not mine, and is full of good
sense. I borrowed it from his *Tent Life*.—M.T.

When one stands where the Saviour was crucified, he finds it all he can do to keep it strictly before his mind that Christ was not crucified in a Catholic church. He must remind himself every now and then that the great event transpired in the open air, and not in a gloomy, candlelighted cell in a little corner of a vast church, upstairs—a small cell all bejeweled and bespangled with flashy ornamentation in execrable taste.

Under a marble altar like a table is a circular hole in the marble floor, corresponding with the one just under it in which the true Cross stood. The first thing everyone does is to kneel down and take a candle and examine this hole. He does this strange prospecting with an amount of gravity that can never be estimated or appreciated by a man who has not seen the operation. Then he holds his candle before a richly engraved picture of the Saviour, done on a massy slab of gold, and wonderfully rayed and starred with diamonds, which hangs above the hole within the altar, and his solemnity changes to lively admiration. He rises and faces the finely wrought figures of the Saviour and the malefactors uplifted upon their crosses behind the altar, and bright with a metallic luster of many colors. He turns next to the figures close to them of the Virgin and Mary Magdalen; next to the rift in the living rock made by the earthquake at the time of the Crucifixion, and an extension of which he had seen before in the wall of one of the grottoes below; he looks next at the showcase with a figure of the Virgin in it, and is amazed at the princely fortune in precious gems and jewelry that hangs so thickly about the form as to hide it like a garment almost. All about the apartment the gaudy trappings of the Greek Church offend the eye and keep the mind on the rack to remember that this is the place of the Crucifixion—Golgotha—the Mount of Calvary. And the last thing he looks at is that which was also the first—the place where the true Cross stood. That will chain him to the spot and compel him to look once more, and once again, after he has satisfied all curiosity and lost all interest concerning the other matters pertaining to the locality.

And so I close my chapter on the Church of the Holy Sepulchre—the most sacred locality on earth to millions and millions of men and women and children, the noble and the humble, bond and free. In its history from the first, and in its tremendous associations, it is the most illustrious edifice in Christendom. With all its claptrap sideshows and unseemly

impostures of every kind, it is still grand, reverend, venerable
—for a god died there; for fifteen hundred years its shrines
have been wet with the tears of pilgrims from the earth's remotest confines; for more than two hundred, the most gallant
knights that ever wielded sword wasted their lives away in a
struggle to seize it and hold it sacred from infidel pollution.
Even in our own day a war that cost millions of treasure
and rivers of blood was fought because two rival nations
claimed the sole right to put a new dome upon it. History is
full of this old Church of the Holy Sepulchre—full of blood
that was shed because of the respect and the veneration in
which men held the last resting place of the meek and
lowly, the mild and gentle, Prince of Peace!

54

We were standing in a narrow street, by the Tower of
Antonio. "On these stones that are crumbling away," the
guide said, "the Saviour sat and rested before taking up the
Cross. This is the beginning of the Sorrowful Way, or the
Way of Grief." The party took note of the sacred spot and
moved on. We passed under the "Ecce Homo Arch" and saw
the very window from which Pilate's wife warned her husband
to have nothing to do with the persecution of the Just Man.
This window is in an excellent state of preservation considering its great age. They showed us where Jesus rested the
second time, and where the mob refused to give him up,
and said, "Let his blood be upon our heads, and upon our
children's children forever." The French Catholics are building a church on this spot and, with their usual veneration for
historical relics, are incorporating into the new such scraps of
ancient walls as they have found there. Further on, we saw
the spot where the fainting Saviour fell under the weight of
his cross. A great granite column of some ancient temple lay
there at the time, and the heavy cross struck it such a blow

that it broke in two in the middle. Such was the guide's story when he halted us before the broken column.

We crossed a street and came presently to the former residence of St. Veronica. When the Saviour passed there, she came out, full of womanly compassion, and spoke pitying words to him, undaunted by the hootings and the threatenings of the mob, and wiped the perspiration from his face with her handkerchief. We had heard so much of St. Veronica and seen her picture by so many masters that it was like meeting an old friend unexpectedly to come upon her ancient home in Jerusalem. The strangest thing about the incident that has made her name so famous is that when she wiped the perspiration away, the print of the Saviour's face remained upon the handkerchief, a perfect portrait, and so remains unto this day. We knew this because we saw this handkerchief in a cathedral in Paris, in another in Spain, and in two others in Italy. In the Milan cathedral it costs five francs to see it, and at St. Peter's, at Rome, it is almost impossible to see it at any price. No tradition is so amply verified as this of St. Veronica and her handkerchief.

At the next corner we saw a deep indention in the hard stone masonry of the corner of a house, but might have gone heedlessly by it but that the guide said it was made by the elbow of the Saviour, who stumbled here and fell. Presently we came to just such another indention in a stone wall. The guide said the Saviour fell here also and made this depression with his elbow.

There were other places where the Lord fell, and others where he rested; but one of the most curious landmarks of ancient history we found, on this morning walk through the crooked lanes that lead toward Calvary, was a certain stone built into a house—a stone that was so seamed and scarred that it bore a sort of grotesque resemblance to the human face. The projections that answered for cheeks were worn smooth by the passionate kisses of generations of pilgrims from distant lands. We asked, "Why?" The guide said it was because this was one of "the very stones of Jerusalem" that Christ mentioned when he was reproved for permitting the people to cry "Hosannah!" when he made his memorable entry into the city upon an ass. One of the pilgrims said, "But there is no evidence that the stones *did* cry out— Christ said that if the people stopped from shouting Hosannah, the very stones *would* do it." The guide was perfectly serene. He said calmly, "This is one of the stones that *would* have cried out." It was of little use to try to shake this fellow's simple faith—it was easy to see that.

And so we came at last to another wonder, of deep and abiding interest—the veritable house where the unhappy wretch once lived who has been celebrated in song and story for more than eighteen hundred years as the Wandering Jew. On the memorable day of the Crucifixion he stood in this old doorway with his arms akimbo, looking out upon the struggling mob that was approaching, and when the weary Saviour would have sat down and rested him a moment, pushed him rudely away and said, "Move on!" The Lord said, "Move on, thou, likewise," and the command has never been revoked from that day to this. All men know how that the miscreant upon whose head that just curse fell has roamed up and down the wide world, for ages and ages, seeking rest and never finding it—courting death but always in vain— longing to stop, in city, in wilderness, in desert solitudes, yet hearing always that relentless warning to march—march on! They say—do these hoary traditions—that when Titus sacked Jerusalem and slaughtered eleven hundred thousand Jews in her streets and byways, the Wandering Jew was seen always in the thickest of the fight, and that when battle-axes gleamed in the air, he bowed his head beneath them; when swords flashed their deadly lightnings, he sprang in their way; he bared his breast to whizzing javelins, to hissing ar-rows, to any and to every weapon that promised death and forgetfulness and rest. But it was useless—he walked forth out of the carnage without a wound. And it is said that five hundred years afterward he followed Muhammad when he carried destruction to the cities of Arabia and then turned against him, hoping in this way to win the death of a traitor. His calculations were wrong again. No quarter was given to any living creature but one, and that was the only one of all the host that did not want it. He sought death five hundred years later, in the wars of the Crusades, and offered himself to famine and pestilence at Ascalon. He escaped again—he could not die. These repeated annoyances could have at last but one effect—they shook his con-fidence. Since then the Wandering Jew has carried on a kind of desultory toying with the most promising of the aids and implements of destruction, but with small hope, as a general thing. He has speculated some in cholera and railroads and has taken almost a lively interest in infernal machines and patent medicines. He is old now, and grave, as becomes an age like his; he indulges in no light amusements save that he goes sometimes to executions and is fond of funerals.

There is one thing he cannot avoid; go where he will about the world, he must never fail to report in Jerusalem every fiftieth year. Only a year or two ago he was here for the thirty-seventh time since Jesus was crucified on Calvary. They say that many old people who are here now saw him then, and had seen him before. He looks always the same—old and withered and hollow-eyed and listless, save that there is about him something which seems to suggest that he is looking for someone, expecting someone—the friends of his youth, perhaps. But the most of them are dead now. He always pokes about the old streets looking lonesome, making his mark on a wall here and there, and eyeing the oldest buildings with a sort of friendly half interest; and he sheds a few tears at the threshold of his ancient dwelling, and bitter, bitter tears they are. Then he collects his rent and leaves again. He has been seen standing near the Church of the Holy Sepulchre on many a starlight night, for he has cherished an idea for many centuries that if he could only enter there, he could rest. But when he approaches, the doors slam to with a crash, the earth trembles, and all the lights in Jerusalem burn a ghastly blue! He does this every fifty years just the same. It is hopeless, but then it is hard to break habits one has been eighteen hundred years accustomed to. The old tourist is far away on his wanderings now. How he must smile to see a pack of blockheads like us, galloping about the world and looking wise, and imagining we are finding out a good deal about it! He must have a consuming contempt for the ignorant, complacent asses that go scurrying about the world in these railroading days and call it traveling.

When the guide pointed out where the Wandering Jew had left his familiar mark upon a wall, I was filled with astonishment. It read:

S. T.—1860—X.

All I have revealed about the Wandering Jew can be amply proven by reference to our guide.

The mighty Mosque of Omar and the paved court around it occupy *a fourth part* of Jerusalem. They are upon Mount Moriah, where King Solomon's Temple stood. This mosque is the holiest place the Muhammadan knows outside of Mecca. Up to within a year or two past, no Christian could gain admission to it or its court for love or money. But the prohibition has been removed, and we entered freely for baksheesh.

I need not speak of the wonderful beauty and the exquisite grace and symmetry that have made this mosque so celebrated—because I did not see them. One cannot see such things at an instant glance—one frequently only finds out how really beautiful a really beautiful woman is after considerable acquaintance with her; and the rule applies to Niagara Falls, to majestic mountains, and to mosques—especially to mosques.

The great feature of the Mosque of Omar is the prodigious rock in the center of its rotunda. It was upon this rock that Abraham came so near offering up his son Isaac; this, at least, is authentic—it is very much more to be relied on than most of the traditions, at any rate. On this rock also the angel stood and threatened Jerusalem, and David persuaded him to spare the city. Muhammad was well acquainted with this stone. From it he ascended to heaven. The stone tried to follow him, and if the angel Gabriel had not happened by the merest good luck to be there to seize it, it would have done it. Very few people have a grip like Gabriel—the prints of his monstrous fingers, two inches deep, are to be seen in that rock today.

This rock, large as it is, is suspended in the air. It does not touch anything at all. The guide said so. This is very wonderful. In the place on it where Muhammad stood, he left his footprints in the solid stone. I should judge that he wore about eighteens. But what I was going to say, when I spoke of the rock being suspended, was that in the floor of the cavern under it they showed us a slab which they said covered a hole which was a thing of extraordinary interest to all Muhammadans, because that hole leads down to perdition, and every soul that is transferred from thence to heaven must pass up through this orifice. Muhammad stands there and lifts them out by the hair. All Muhammadans shave their heads, but they are careful to leave a lock of hair for the Prophet to take hold of. Our guide observed that a good

Muhammadan would consider himself doomed to stay with the damned forever if he were to lose his scalplock and die before it grew again. The most of them that I have seen ought to stay with the damned anyhow, without reference to how they were barbered.

For several ages no woman has been allowed to enter the cavern where that important hole is. The reason is that one of the sex was once caught there blabbing everything she knew about what was going on aboveground to the rapscallions in the infernal regions down below. She carried her gossiping to such an extreme that nothing could be kept private—nothing could be done or said on earth but everybody in perdition knew all about it before the sun went down. It was about time to suppress this woman's telegraph, and it was promptly done. Her breath subsided about the same time.

The inside of the great mosque is very showy, with variegated marble walls and with windows and inscriptions of elaborate mosaic. The Turks have their sacred relics like the Catholics. The guide showed us the veritable armor worn by the great son-in-law and successor of Muhammad, and also the buckler of Muhammad's uncle. The great iron railing which surrounds the rock was ornamented in one place with a thousand rags tied to its openwork. These are to remind Muhammad not to forget the worshipers who placed them there. It is considered the next best thing to tying threads around his finger by way of reminders.

Just outside the mosque is a miniature temple, which marks the spot where David and Goliath used to sit and judge the people.*

Everywhere about the Mosque of Omar are portions of pillars, curiously wrought altars, and fragments of elegantly carved marble—precious remains of Solomon's Temple. These have been dug from all depths in the soil and rubbish of Mount Moriah, and the Muslims have always shown a disposition to preserve them with the utmost care. At that portion of the ancient wall of Solomon's Temple which is called the Jew's Place of Wailing, and where the Hebrews assemble every Friday to kiss the venerated stones and weep over the fallen greatness of Zion, anyone can see a part

---

* A pilgrim informs me that it was not David and Goliath, but David and Saul. I stick to my own statement—the guide told me, and he ought to know.

of the unquestioned and undisputed Temple of Solomon, the same consisting of three or four stones lying one upon the other, each of which is about twice as long as a seven-octave piano and about as thick as such a piano is high. But, as I have remarked before, it is only a year or two ago that the ancient edict prohibiting Christian rubbish like ourselves to *enter* the Mosque of Omar and see the costly marbles that once adorned the inner temple was annulled. The designs wrought upon these fragments are all quaint and peculiar, and so the charm of novelty is added to the deep interest they naturally inspire. One meets with these venerable scraps at every turn, especially in the neighboring Mosque el Aksa, into whose inner walls a very large number of them are carefully built for preservation. These pieces of stone, stained and dusty with age, dimly hint at a grandeur we have all been taught to regard as the princeliest ever seen on earth; and they call up pictures of a pageant that is familiar to all imaginations—camels laden with spices and treasure—beautiful slaves, presents for Solomon's harem—a long cavalcade of richly caparisoned beasts and warriors—and Sheba's Queen in the van of this vision of "Oriental magnificence." These elegant fragments bear a richer interest than the solemn vastness of the stones the Jews kiss in the Place of Wailing can ever have for the heedless sinner.

Down in the hollow ground, underneath the olives and the orange trees that flourish in the court of the great mosque, is a wilderness of pillars—remains of the ancient temple; they supported it. There are ponderous archways down there also, over which the destroying "plough" of prophecy passed harmless. It is pleasant to know we are disappointed, in that we never dreamed we might see portions of the actual Temple of Solomon and yet experience no shadow of suspicion that they were a monkish humbug and a fraud.

We are surfeited with sights. Nothing has any fascination for us now but the Church of the Holy Sepulchre. We have been there every day and have not grown tired of it, but we are weary of everything else. The sights are too many. They swarm about you at every step; no single foot of ground in all Jerusalem or within its neighborhood seems to be without a stirring and important history of its own. It is a very relief to steal a walk of a hundred yards without a guide along to talk unceasingly about every stone you step upon and drag you back ages and ages to the day when it achieved celebrity.

It seems hardly real when I find myself leaning for a moment on a ruined wall and looking *listlessly* down into the historic pool of Bethesda. I did not think such things *could* be so crowded together as to diminish their interest. But in serious truth, we have been drifting about for several days, using our eyes and our ears more from a sense of duty than any higher and worthier reason. And too often we have been glad when it was time to go home and be distressed no more about illustrious localities.

Our pilgrims compress too much into one day. One can gorge sights to repletion as well as sweetmeats. Since we breakfasted this morning, we have seen enough to have furnished us food for a year's reflection if we could have seen the various objects in comfort and looked upon them deliberately. We visited the pool of Hezekiah, where David saw Uriah's wife coming from the bath and fell in love with her.

We went out of the city by the Jaffa Gate, and of course were told many things about its Tower of Hippicus.

We rode across the Valley of Hinnom, between two of the Pools of Gihon, and by an aqueduct built by Solomon, which still conveys water to the city. We ascended the Hill of Evil Counsel, where Judas received his thirty pieces of silver, and we also lingered a moment under the tree a venerable tradition says he hanged himself on.

We descended to the canyon again, and then the guide began to give name and history to every bank and boulder we came to: "This was the Field of Blood; these cuttings in the rocks were shrines and temples of Moloch; here they sacrificed children; yonder is the Zion Gate; the Tyropean Valley; the Hill of Ophel; here is the junction of the Valley of Jehoshaphat—on your right is the Well of Job." We turned up Jehoshaphat. The recital went on. "This is the Mount of Olives; this is the Hill of Offense; the nest of huts is the Village of Siloam; here yonder, everywhere, is the King's Garden; under this great tree Zacharias, the high priest, was murdered; yonder is Mount Moriah and the Temple wall; the tomb of Absalom; the tomb of St. James; the tomb of Zacharias; beyond are the Garden of Gethsemane and the tomb of the Virgin Mary; here is the Pool of Siloam and——"

We said we would dismount and quench our thirst and

rest. We were burning up with the heat. We were failing under the accumulated fatigue of days and days of ceaseless marching. All were willing.

The pool is a deep, walled ditch, through which a clear stream of water runs, that comes from under Jerusalem somewhere, and passing through the Fountain of the Virgin or being supplied from it, reaches this place by way of a tunnel of heavy masonry. The famous pool looked exactly as it looked in Solomon's time, no doubt, and the same dusky, Oriental women came down in their old Oriental way, and carried off jars of the water on their heads, just as they did three thousand years ago, and just as they will do fifty thousand years hence if any of them are still left on earth.

We went away from there and stopped at the Fountain of the Virgin. But the water was not good, and there was no comfort or peace anywhere, on account of the regiment of boys and girls and beggars that persecuted us all the time for baksheesh. The guide wanted us to give them some money, and we did it; but when he went on to say that they were starving to death, we could not but feel that we had done a great sin in throwing obstacles in the way of such a desirable consummation, and so we tried to collect it back, but it could not be done.

We entered the Garden of Gethsemane, and we visited the Tomb of the Virgin, both of which we had seen before. It is not meet that I should speak of them now. A more fitting time will come.

I cannot speak now of the Mount of Olives or its view of Jerusalem, the Dead Sea, and the mountains of Moab; nor of the Damascus Gate or the tree that was planted by King Godfrey of Jerusalem. One ought to feel pleasantly when he talks of these things. I cannot say anything about the stone column that projects over Jehoshaphat from the temple wall like a cannon except that the Muslins believe Muhammad will sit astride of it when he comes to judge the world. It is a pity he could not judge it from some roost of his own in Mecca, without trespassing on *our* holy ground. Close by is the Golden Gate, in the temple wall—a gate that was an elegant piece of sculpture in the time of the temple and is even so yet. From it, in ancient times, the Jewish high priest turned loose the scapegoat and let him flee to the wilderness and bear away his twelve-month load of the sins of the people. If they were to turn one loose now, he would not get as far as the Garden of Gethsemane till these miserable vagabonds here would gobble him up,* sins and all. *They* wouldn't care. Mutton chops and sin is good enough living for them. The Muslims watch the Golden Gate with a jealous eye, and an anxious one, for they have an honored tradition that when it falls, Islamism will fall, and with it the Ottoman empire. It did not grieve me any to notice that the old gate was getting a little shaky.

We are at home again. We are exhausted. The sun has roasted us almost.

We have full comfort in one reflection, however. Our experiences in Europe have taught us that in time this fatigue will be forgotten; the heat will be forgotten; the thirst, the tiresome volubility of the guide, the persecutions of the beggars—and then, all that will be left will be pleasant memories of Jerusalem, memories we shall call up with always-increasing interest as the years go by, memories which someday will become all beautiful when the last annoyance that encumbers them shall have faded out of our minds never again to return. Schoolboy days are no happier than the days of afterlife, but we look back upon them regretfully because we have forgotten our punishments at school and how we grieved when our marbles were lost and our kites destroyed— because we have forgotten all the sorrows and privations of that canonized epoch and remember only its orchard robberies, its wooden-sword pageants, and its fishing holidays. We are satisfied. We can wait. Our reward will come. To us Jerusalem and today's experiences will be an enchanted memory a year hence—a memory which money could not buy from us.

55

We cast up the account. It footed up pretty fairly. There was nothing more at Jerusalem to be seen except the tra-

---

* Favorite pilgrim expression.

ditional houses of Dives and Lazarus of the parable, the tombs of the Kings and those of the Judges; the spot where they stoned one of the disciples to death and beheaded another; the room and the table made celebrated by the Last Supper; the fig tree that Jesus withered; a number of historical places about Gethsemane and the Mount of Olives, and fifteen or twenty others in different portions of the city itself.

We were approaching the end. Human nature asserted itself now. Overwork and consequent exhaustion began to have their natural effect. They began to master the energies and dull the ardor of the party. Perfectly secure now against failing to accomplish any detail of the pilgrimage, they felt like drawing in advance upon the holiday soon to be placed to their credit. They grew a little lazy. They were late to breakfast and sat long at dinner. Thirty or forty pilgrims had arrived from the ship, by the short routes, and much swapping of gossip had to be indulged in. And in hot afternoons they showed a strong disposition to lie on the cool divans in the hotel and smoke and talk about pleasant experiences of a month or so gone by—for even thus early do episodes of travel which were sometimes annoying, sometimes exasperating, and full as often of no consequence at all when they transpired begin to rise above the dead level of monotonous reminiscences and become shapely landmarks in one's memory. The fog whistle, smothered among a million of trifling sounds, is not noticed a block away in the city, but the sailor hears it far at sea, whither none of those thousands of trifling sounds can reach. When one is in Rome, all the domes are alike; but when he has gone away twelve miles, the city fades utterly from sight and leaves St. Peter's swelling above the level plain like an anchored balloon. When one is traveling in Europe, the daily incidents seem all alike; but when he has placed them all two months and two thousand miles behind him, those that were worthy of being remembered are prominent and those that were really insignificant have vanished. This disposition to smoke and idle and talk was not well. It was plain that it must not be allowed to gain ground. A diversion must be tried or demoralization would ensue. The Jordan, Jericho, and the Dead Sea were suggested. The remainder of Jerusalem must be left unvisited for a little while. The journey was approved at once. New life stirred in every pulse. In the saddle—abroad on the plains—sleeping in beds bounded only by the horizon: fancy was at work with these things in a moment. It was painful to note how readily these town-bred men had taken to the free life of the camp and the desert. The nomadic instinct is a human instinct; it was born with Adam and transmitted through the patriarchs, and after thirty centuries of steady effort, civilization has not educated it entirely out of us yet. It has a charm which, once tasted, a man will yearn to taste again. The nomadic instinct cannot be educated out of an Indian at all.

The Jordan journey being approved, our dragoman was notified.

At nine in the morning the caravan was before the hotel door and we were at breakfast. There was a commotion about the place. Rumors of war and bloodshed were flying everywhere. The lawless Bedouins in the valley of the Jordan and the deserts down by the Dead Sea were up in arms and were going to destroy all comers. They had had a battle with a troop of Turkish cavalry and defeated them; several men killed. They had shut up the inhabitants of a village and a Turkish garrison in an old fort near Jericho and were besieging them. They had marched upon a camp of our excursionists by the Jordan, and the pilgrims only saved their lives by stealing away and flying to Jerusalem under whip and spur in the darkness of the night. Another of our parties had been fired on from an ambush and then attacked in the open day. Shots were fired on both sides. Fortunately there was no bloodshed. We spoke with the very pilgrim who had fired one of the shots and learned from his own lips how, in this imminent deadly peril, only the cool courage of the pilgrims, their strength of numbers, and imposing display of war material had saved them from utter destruction. It was reported that the Consul had requested that no more of our pilgrims should go to the Jordan while this state of things lasted; and further, that he was unwilling that any more should go, at least without an unusually strong military guard. Here was trouble. But with the horses at the door and everybody aware of what they were there for, what would *you* have done? Acknowledged that you were afraid and backed shamefully out? Hardly. It would not be human nature where there were so many women. You would have done as we did: said you were not afraid of a million Bedouins—and made your will and proposed quietly to yourself to take up an unostentatious position in the rear of the procession. I think we must all have determined upon the same line of tactics, for it did seem as if we never would get to Jericho. I had a notoriously slow horse, but somehow I could not keep him in the rear to save my neck. He was forever turning up in the lead. In such cases I trembled a little and got down to fix my saddle. But it was not of any use. The others all got down to fix their saddles, too. I never saw such a time with saddles. It was the first time any of them had got out of order in three weeks, and now they had all broken down at once. I tried walking, for exercise—I had not had enough in Jerusalem searching for holy places. But it was a failure. The whole mob were suffering for exercise, and it was not fifteen minutes till they were all on foot and I had the lead again. It was very discouraging.

This was all after we got beyond Bethany. We stopped at the village of Bethany, an hour out from Jerusalem. They showed us the tomb of Lazarus. I had rather live in it than in any house in the town. And they showed us also a large "Fountain of Lazarus," and in the center of the village the ancient dwelling of Lazarus. Lazarus appears to have been a man of property. The legends of the Sunday schools do him great injustice; they give one the impression that he was poor. It is because they get him confused with that Lazarus who had no merit but his virtue, and virtue never has been as respectable as money. The house of Lazarus is a three-story edifice of stone masonry, but the accumulated rubbish of ages has buried all of it but the upper story. We took candles and descended to the dismal cell-like chambers where Jesus sat at meat with Martha and Mary and conversed with them about their brother. We could not but look upon these old dingy apartments with a more than common interest.

We had had a glimpse, from a mountaintop, of the Dead Sea, lying like a blue shield in the plain of the Jordan, and now we were marching down a close, flaming, rugged, desolate defile, where no living creature could enjoy life except, perhaps, a salamander. It was such a dreary, repulsive, horrible solitude! It was the "wilderness" where John preached, with camel's hair about his loins—raiment enough—but he never could have got his locusts and wild honey here. We were moping along down through this dreadful place, every man in the rear. Our guards—two gorgeous young Arab sheikhs, with cargoes of swords, guns, pistols, and daggers on board—were loafing ahead.

"Bedouins!"

Every man shrunk up and disappeared in his clothes like a mud turtle. My first impulse was to dash forward and destroy the Bedouins. My second was to dash to the rear to see if there were any coming in that direction. I acted on the latter impulse. So did all the others. If any Bedouins had approached us then from that point of the compass, they would have paid dearly for their rashness. We all remarked that afterwards. There would have been scenes of riot and bloodshed there that no pen could describe. I know that because each man told what he would have done individually, and such a medley of strange and unheard-of inventions of cruelty you could not conceive of. One man said he had calmly made up his mind to perish where he stood if need be, but never yield an inch; he was going to wait, with deadly patience, till he could count the stripes upon the first Bedouin's jacket and then count them and let him have it. Another was going to sit still till the first lance reached within an inch of his breast and then dodge it and seize it. I forbear to tell what he was going to do to that Bedouin that owned it. It makes my blood run cold to think of it. Another was going to scalp such Bedouins as fell to his share and take his bald-headed sons of the desert home with him alive for trophies. But the wild-eyed pilgrim rhapsodist was silent. His orbs gleamed with a deadly light, but his lips moved not. Anxiety grew, and he was questioned. If he had got a Bedouin, what would he have done with him—shot him? He smiled a smile of grim contempt and shook his head. Would he have stabbed him? Another shake. Would he have quartered him—flayed him? More shakes. Oh, horror! What *would* he have done?

"Eat him!"

Such was the awful sentence that thundered from his lips. What was grammar to a desperado like that? I was glad in my heart that I had been spared these scenes of malignant carnage. No Bedouins attacked our terrible rear. And none attacked the front. The newcomers were only a reinforcement of cadaverous Arabs, in shirts and bare legs, sent far ahead of us to brandish rusty guns and shout and brag and carry on like lunatics, and thus scare away all bands of marauding Bedouins that might lurk about our path. What a shame it is that armed white Christians must travel under guard of vermin like this as a protection against the prowling vagabonds of the desert—those sanguinary outlaws who are always going to do something desperate, but never do it. I may as well mention here that on our whole trip we saw no Bedouins and had no more use for an Arab guard than we could have had for patent-leather boots and white kid gloves. The Bedouins that attacked the other parties of pilgrims so fiercely were provided for the occasion by the Arab guards of those parties and shipped from Jerusalem for temporary service as Bedouins. They met together in full view of the pilgrims, after the battle, and took lunch, divided the baksheesh extorted in the season of danger, and then accompanied the cavalcade home to the city! The nuisance of an Arab guard is one which is created by the sheikhs and the Bedouins together, for mutual profit, it is said, and no doubt there is a good deal of truth in it.

We visited the fountain the prophet Elisha sweetened (it is sweet yet), where he remained some time and was fed by the ravens.

Ancient Jericho is not very picturesque as a ruin. When Joshua marched around it seven times, some three thousand years ago, and blew it down with his trumpet, he did the work so well and so completely that he hardly left enough of the city to cast a shadow. The curse pronounced against the rebuilding of it has never been removed. One king, holding the curse in light estimation, made the attempt, but was stricken sorely for his presumption. Its site will always remain unoccupied, and yet it is one of the very best locations for a town we have seen in all Palestine.

At two in the morning they routed us out of bed—another piece of unwarranted cruelty—another stupid effort of our dragoman to get ahead of a rival. It was not two hours to the Jordan. However, we were dressed and under way before anyone thought of looking to see what time it was, and so we drowsed on through the chill night air and dreamed of campfires, warm beds, and other comfortable things.

There was no conversation. People do not talk when they are cold and wretched and sleepy. We nodded in the saddle at times, and woke up with a start to find that the procession had disappeared in the gloom. Then there was energy and attention to business until its dusky outlines came in sight again. Occasionally the order was passed in a low voice down the line: "Close up—close up! Bedouins lurk here every-where!" What an exquisite shudder it sent shivering along one's spine!

We reached the famous river before four o'clock, and the night was so black that we could have ridden into it without seeing it. Some of us were in an unhappy frame of mind. We waited and waited for daylight, but it did not come. Fi-nally we went away in the dark and slept an hour on the ground, in the bushes, and caught cold. It was a costly nap on that account, but otherwise it was a paying investment because it brought unconsciousness of the dreary minutes and put us in a somewhat fitter mood for a first glimpse of the sacred river.

With the first suspicion of dawn, every pilgrim took off his clothes and waded into the dark torrent, singing:

> "On Jordan's stormy banks I stand,
>   And cast a wistful eye
> To Canaan's fair and happy land,
>   Where my possessions lie."

But they did not sing long. The water was so fearfully cold that they were obliged to stop singing and scamper out again. Then they stood on the bank shivering, and so chagrined and so grieved that they merited honest compassion. Because an-other dream, another cherished hope, had failed. They had promised themselves all along that they would cross the Jor-dan where the Israelites crossed it when they entered Canaan from their long pilgrimage in the desert. They would cross where the twelve stones were placed in memory of that great event. While they did it they would picture to themselves that vast army of pilgrims marching through the cloven waters, bearing the hallowed Ark of the Covenant and shout-ing hosannahs and singing songs of thanksgiving and praise. Each had promised himself that he would be the first to cross. They were at the goal of their hopes at last, but the current was too swift, the water was too cold!

It was then that Jack did them a service. With that engag-ing recklessness of consequences which is natural to youth, and so proper and so seemly as well, he went and led the way across the Jordan, and all was happiness again. Every individual waded over then and stood upon the further bank. The water was not quite breast-deep anywhere. If it had been more, we could hardly have accomplished the feat, for the strong current would have swept us down the stream, and we would have been exhausted and drowned before reaching a place where we could make a landing. The main object compassed, the drooping, miserable party sat down to wait for the sun again, for all wanted to see the water as well as feel it. But it was too cold a pastime. Some cans were filled from the holy river, some canes cut from its banks, and then we mounted and rode reluctantly away to keep from freezing to death. So we saw the Jordan very dimly. The thickets of bushes that bordered its banks threw their shadows across its shallow, turbulent waters ("stormy," the hymn makes them, which is rather a complimentary stretch of fancy), and we could not judge of the width of the stream by the eye. We knew by our wading experience, however, that many streets in America are double as wide as the Jordan.

Daylight came, soon after we got under way, and in the course of an hour or two we reached the Dead Sea. Nothing grows in the flat, burning desert around it but weeds and the Dead Sea apple the poets say is beautiful to the eye, but crumbles to ashes and dust when you break it. Such as we found were not handsome, but they were bitter to the taste. They yielded no dust. It was because they were not ripe perhaps.

The desert and the barren hills gleam painfully in the sun around the Dead Sea, and there is no pleasant thing or living creature upon it or about its borders to cheer the eye. It is a scorching, arid, repulsive solitude. A silence broods over the scene that is depressing to the spirits. It makes one think of funerals and death.

The Dead Sea is small. Its waters are very clear, and it has a pebbly bottom and is shallow for some distance out from the shores. It yields quantities of asphaltum; fragments of it lie all about its banks; this stuff gives the place something of an unpleasant smell.

All our reading had taught us to expect that the first plunge into the Dead Sea would be attended with distressing results: our bodies would feel as if they were suddenly pierced by millions of red-hot needles; the dreadful smarting would continue for hours; we might even look to be blistered from head to foot and suffer miserably for many days. We were disappointed. Our eight sprang in at the same time that another party of pilgrims did, and nobody screamed once. None of them ever did complain of anything more than a slight pricking sensation in places where their skin was abraded, and then only for a short time. My face smarted for a couple of hours, but it was partly because I got it badly sunburned while I was bathing, and stayed in so long that it became plastered over with salt.

No, the water did not blister us; it did not cover us with a slimy ooze and confer upon us an atrocious fragrance; it was not very slimy; and I could not discover that we smelled really any worse than we have always smelled since we have been in Palestine. It was only a different kind of smell, but not conspicuous on that account, because we have a great deal of variety in that respect. We didn't smell, there on the Jordan, the same as we do in Jerusalem; and we don't smell in Jerusalem just as we did in Nazareth or Tiberias or Caesarea Philippi or any of those other ruinous ancient towns in Galilee. No, we change all the time, and generally for the worse. We do our own washing.

It was a funny bath. We could not sink. One could stretch himself at full length on his back, with his arms on his breast, and all of his body above a line drawn from the corner of his jaw past the middle of his side, the middle of his leg, and through his anklebone would remain out of water. He could lift his head clear out if he chose. No position can be retained long; you lose your balance and whirl over, first on your back and then on your face, and so on. You can lie comfortably on your back, with your head out and your legs out from your knees down, by steadying yourself with your hands. You can sit, with your knees drawn up to your chin and your arms clasped around them, but you are bound to turn over presently, because you are top-heavy in that position. You can stand up straight in water that is over your head, and from the middle of your breast upward you will not be wet. But you cannot remain so. The water will soon float your feet to the surface. You cannot swim on your back and make any progress of any consequence, because your feet stick away above the surface, and there is nothing to propel yourself with but your heels. If you swim on your face, you kick up the water like a sternwheel boat. You make no headway. A horse is so top-heavy that he can neither swim nor stand up in the Dead Sea. He turns over on his side at once. Some of us bathed for more than an hour and then came out coated with salt till we shone like icicles. We scrubbed it off with a coarse towel and rode off with a splendid brand-new smell, though it was one which was not any more disagreeable than those we have been for several weeks enjoying. It was the variegated villainy and novelty of it that charmed us. Salt crystals glitter in the sun about the shores of the lake. In places they coat the ground like a brilliant crust of ice.

When I was a boy I somehow got the impression that the River Jordan was four thousand miles long and thirty-five miles wide. It is only ninety miles long, and so crooked that a man does not know which side of it he is on half the time. In going ninety miles it does not get over more than fifty miles of ground. It is not any wider than Broadway in New York. There is the Sea of Galilee and this Dead Sea—neither of them twenty miles long or thirteen wide. And yet when I was in Sunday school I thought they were sixty thousand miles in diameter.

Travel and experience mar the grandest pictures and rob us of the most cherished traditions of our boyhood. Well, let them go. I have already seen the empire of King Solomon diminish to the size of the state of Pennsylvania; I suppose I can bear the reduction of the seas and the river.

We looked everywhere as we passed along, but never saw grain or crystal of Lot's wife. It was a great disappointment. For many and many a year we had known her sad story and taken that interest in her which misfortune always inspires. But she was gone. Her picturesque form no longer looms above the desert of the Dead Sea to remind the tourist of the doom that fell upon the lost cities.

I cannot describe the hideous afternoon's ride from the Dead Sea to Mars Saba. It oppresses me yet to think of it. The sun so pelted us that the tears ran down our cheeks once or twice. The ghastly, treeless, grassless, breathless canyons smothered us as if we had been in an oven. The sun had positive *weight* to it, I think. Not a man could sit erect under it. All drooped low in the saddles. John preached in this "Wilderness!" It must have been exhausting work. What a very heaven the massy towers and ramparts of vast Mars Saba looked to us when we caught a first glimpse of them!

We stayed at this great convent all night, guests of the hospitable priests. Mars Saba, perched upon a crag, a human nest stuck high up against a perpendicular mountain wall, is a world of grand masonry that rises, terrace upon terrace, away above your head, like the terraced and retreating colon-

nades one sees in fanciful pictures of Belshazzar's Feast and
the palaces of the ancient pharaohs. No other human dwelling
is near. It was founded many ages ago by a holy recluse who
lived at first in a cave in the rock—a cave which is enclosed
in the convent walls now and was reverently shown to us by
the priests. This recluse, by his rigorous torturing of his flesh,
his diet of bread and water, his utter withdrawal from all
society and from the vanities of the world, and his constant prayer and saintly contemplation of a skull, inspired
an emulation that brought about him many disciples. The
precipice on the opposite side of the canyon is well per-
forated with the small holes they dug in the rock to live
in. The present occupants of Mars Saba, about seventy in
number, are all hermits. They wear a coarse robe, an ugly,
brimless stovepipe of a hat, and go without shoes. They eat
nothing whatever but bread and salt; they drink nothing
but water. As long as they live they can never go outside
the walls or look upon a woman—for no woman is permitted to enter Mars Saba upon any pretext whatsoever.

Some of those men have been shut up there for thirty years.
In all that dreary time they have not heard the laughter of a
child or the blessed voice of a woman; they have seen no
human tears, no human smiles; they have known no human
joys, no wholesome human sorrows. In their hearts are no
memories of the past, in their brains no dreams of the future.
All that is lovable, beautiful, worthy, they have put far
away from them; against all things that are pleasant to look
upon and all sounds that are music to the ear, they have
barred their massive doors and reared their relentless walls
of stone forever. They have banished the tender grace of
life and left only the sapped and skinny mockery. Their lips
are lips that never kiss and never sing; their hearts are hearts
that never hate and never love; their breasts are breasts that
never swell with the sentiment "I have a country and a
flag." They are dead men who walk.

I set down these first thoughts because they are natural—
not because they are just or because it is right to set them
down. It is easy for book-makers to say, "I thought so and
so as I looked upon such and such a scene"—when the truth
is, they thought all those fine things afterwards. One's first
thought is not likely to be strictly accurate, yet it is no
crime to think it and none to write it down, subject to
modification by later experience. These hermits *are* dead men

in several respects, but not in all; and it is not proper that, thinking ill of them at first, I should go on doing so or, speaking ill of them, I should reiterate the words and stick to them. No, they treated us too kindly for that. There is something human about them somewhere. They knew we were foreigners and Protestants, and not likely to feel admiration or much friendliness toward them. But their large charity was above considering such things. They simply saw in us men who were hungry and thirsty and tired, and that was sufficient. They opened their doors and gave us welcome. They asked no questions, and they made no self-righteous display of their hospitality. They fished for no compliments. They moved quietly about, setting the table for us, making the beds, and bringing water to wash in, and paid no heed when we said it was wrong for them to do that when we had men whose business it was to perform such offices. We fared most comfortably and sat late at dinner. We walked all over the building with the hermits afterward, and then sat on the lofty battlements and smoked while we enjoyed the cool air, the wild scenery, and the sunset. One or two chose cozy bedrooms to sleep in, but the nomadic instinct prompted the rest to sleep on the broad divan that extended around the great hall, because it seemed like sleeping out of doors, and so was more cheery and inviting. It was a royal rest we had.

When we got up to breakfast in the morning, we were new men. For all this hospitality no strict charge was made. We could give something if we chose; we need give nothing if we were poor or if we were stingy. The pauper and the miser are as free as any in the Catholic convents of Palestine. I have been educated to enmity toward everything that is Catholic, and sometimes, in consequence of this, I find it much easier to discover Catholic faults than Catholic merits. But there is one thing I feel no disposition to overlook and no disposition to forget: and that is the honest gratitude I and all pilgrims owe to the convent Fathers in Palestine. Their doors are always open, and there is always a welcome for any worthy man who comes, whether he comes in rags or clad in purple. The Catholic convents are a priceless blessing to the poor. A pilgrim without money, whether he be a Protestant or a Catholic, can travel the length and breadth of Palestine, and in the midst of her desert wastes find wholesome food and a clean bed every night in these buildings. Pilgrims in better circumstances are often stricken down by the sun and the fevers of the country, and then their saving refuge is the convent. Without these hospitable retreats, travel in Palestine would be a pleasure which none but the strongest men could dare to undertake. Our party, pilgrims and all, will always be ready and always willing to touch glasses and drink health, prosperity, and long life to the convent Fathers of Palestine.

So, rested and refreshed, we fell into line and filed away over the barren mountains of Judea and along rocky ridges and through sterile gorges, where eternal silence and solitude reigned. Even the scattering groups of armed shepherds we met the afternoon before, tending their flocks of long-haired goats, were wanting here. We saw but two living creatures. They were gazelles, of "soft-eyed" notoriety. They looked like very young kids, but they annihilated distance like an express train. I have not seen animals that moved faster unless I might say it of the antelopes of our own Great Plains.

At nine or ten in the morning we reached the Plain of the Shepherds and stood in a walled garden of olives where the shepherds were watching their flocks by night, eighteen centuries ago, when the multitude of angels brought them the tidings that the Saviour was born. A quarter of a mile away was Bethlehem of Judea, and the pilgrims took some of the stone wall and hurried on.

The Plain of the Shepherds is a desert paved with loose stones, void of vegetation, glaring in the fierce sun. Only the music of the angels it knew once could charm its shrubs and flowers to life again and restore its vanished beauty. No less potent enchantment could avail to work this miracle.

In the huge Church of the Nativity, in Bethlehem, built fifteen hundred years ago by the inveterate St. Helena, they took us belowground and into a grotto cut in the living rock. This was the "manger" where Christ was born. A silver star set in the floor bears a Latin inscription to that effect. It is polished with the kisses of many generations of worshiping pilgrims. The grotto was tricked out in the usual tasteless style observable in all the holy places of Palestine. As in the Church of the Holy Sepulchre, envy and uncharitableness were apparent here. The priests and the members of the Greek and Latin churches cannot come by the same corridor to kneel in the sacred birthplace of the Redeemer, but are compelled to approach and retire by different avenues, lest they quarrel and fight on this holiest ground on earth.

I have no "meditations" suggested by this spot where the very first "Merry Christmas!" was uttered in all the world, and from whence the friend of my childhood, Santa Claus, departed on his first journey, to gladden and continue to gladden roaring firesides on wintry mornings in many a distant land forever and forever. I touch, with reverent finger, the actual spot where the infant Jesus lay, but I think— nothing.

You *cannot* think in this place any more than you can in any other in Palestine that would be likely to inspire reflection. Beggars, cripples, and monks compass you about and make you think only of baksheesh when you would rather think of something more in keeping with the character of the spot.

I was glad to get away, and glad when we had walked through the grottoes where Eusebius wrote, and Jerome fasted, and Joseph prepared for the flight into Egypt, and the dozen other distinguished grottoes, and knew we were done. The Church of the Nativity is almost as well packed with exceeding holy places as the Church of the Holy Sepulchre itself. They even have in it a grotto wherein twenty thousand children were slaughtered by Herod when he was seeking the life of the infant Saviour.

We went to the Milk Grotto of course—a cavern where Mary hid herself for a while before the flight into Egypt. Its walls were black before she entered, but in suckling the Child, a drop of her milk fell upon the floor and instantly changed the darkness of the walls to its own snowy hue. We took many little fragments of stone from here, because it is well known in all the East that a barren woman hath need only to touch her lips to one of these and her failing will depart from her. We took many specimens, to the end that we might confer happiness upon certain households that we wot of.

We got away from Bethlehem and its troops of beggars and relic-peddlers in the afternoon and, after spending some little time at Rachel's tomb, hurried to Jerusalem as fast as possible. I never was *so* glad to get home again before. I never have enjoyed rest as I have enjoyed it during these last few hours. The journey to the Dead Sea, the Jordan, and Bethlehem was short, but it was an exhausting one. Such roasting heat, such oppressive solitude, and such dismal desolation cannot surely exist elsewhere on earth. And *such* fatigue!

The commonest sagacity warns me that I ought to tell the customary pleasant lie and say I tore myself reluctantly away from every noted place in Palestine. Everybody tells that, but with as little ostentation as I may, I doubt the word of every he who tells it. I could take a dreadful oath that I have never heard any one of our forty pilgrims say anything of the sort, and they are as worthy and as sincerely devout as any that come here. They will say it when they get home, fast enough, but why should they not? They do not wish to array themselves against all the Lamartines and Grimeses in the world. It does not stand to reason that men are reluctant to leave places where the very life is almost badgered out of them by importunate swarms of beggars and peddlers who hang in strings to one's sleeves and coattails and shriek and shout in his ears and horrify his vision with the ghastly sores and malformations they exhibit. One is *glad* to get away. I have heard shameless people say they were glad to get away from ladies' festivals where they were importuned to buy by bevies of lovely young ladies. Transform those houris into dusky hags and ragged savages, and replace their rounded forms with shrunken and knotted distortions, their soft hands with scarred and hideous deformities, and the persuasive music of their voices with the discordant din of a hated language, and *then* see how much lingering reluctance to leave could be mustered. No, it is the neat thing to say you were reluctant and then append the profound thoughts that "struggled for utterance" in your brain; but it is the true thing to say you were not reluctant and found it impossible to think at all—though in good sooth it is not respectable to say it and not poetical, either.

We do not think, in the holy places; we think in bed, afterwards, when the glare and the noise and the confusion are gone, and in fancy we revisit alone the solemn monuments of the past and summon the phantom pageants of an age that has passed away.

56

We visited all the holy places about Jerusalem which we had left unvisited when we journeyed to the Jordan, and then, about three o'clock one afternoon, we fell into procession and marched out at the stately Damascus Gate, and the walls of Jerusalem shut us out forever. We paused on the summit of a distant hill and took a final look and made a final farewell to the venerable city which had been such a good home to us.

For about four hours we traveled downhill constantly. We followed a narrow bridle path which traversed the beds of the mountain gorges, and when we could we got out of the way of the long trains of laden camels and asses, and when we could not we suffered the misery of being mashed up against perpendicular walls of rock and having our legs bruised by the passing freight. Jack was caught two or three times, and Dan and Moult as often. One horse had a heavy fall on the slippery rocks, and the others had narrow escapes. However, this was as good a road as we had found in Palestine, and possibly even the best, and so there was not much grumbling.

Sometimes in the glens we came upon luxuriant orchards of figs, apricots, pomegranates, and such things, but oftener the scenery was rugged, mountainous, verdureless, and forbidding. Here and there towers were perched high up on acclivities which seemed almost inaccessible. This fashion is as old as Palestine itself and was adopted in ancient times for security against enemies.

We crossed the brook which furnished David the stone that killed Goliath, and no doubt we looked upon the very ground whereon that noted battle was fought. We passed by a picturesque old Gothic ruin whose stone pavements had rung to the armed heels of many a valorous Crusader, and we rode through a piece of country which we were told once knew Samson as a citizen.

439

We stayed all night with the good monks at the convent of Ramleh, and in the morning got up and galloped the horses a good part of the distance from there to Jaffa, or Joppa, for the plain was as level as a floor and free from stones, and besides, this was our last march in Holy Land. These two or three hours finished, we and the tired horses could have rest and sleep as long as we wanted it. This was the plain of which Joshua spoke when he said, "Sun, stand thou still on Gibeon, and thou moon in the valley of Ajalon." As we drew near to Jaffa the boys spurred up the horses and indulged in the excitement of an actual race—an experience we had hardly had since we raced on donkeys in the Azores islands.

We came finally to the noble grove of orange trees in which the Oriental city of Jaffa lies buried; we passed through the walls, and rode again down narrow streets and among swarms of animated rags, and saw other sights and had other experiences we had long been familiar with. We dismounted for the last time, and out in the offing, riding at anchor, we saw the ship! I put an exclamation point there because we felt one when we saw the vessel. The long pilgrimage was ended, and somehow we seemed to feel glad of it.

[For description of Jaffa, see *Universal Gazetteer*.] Simon the Tanner formerly lived here. We went to his house. All the pilgrims visit Simon the Tanner's house. Peter saw the vision of the beasts let down in a sheet when he lay upon the roof of Simon the Tanner's house. It was from Jaffa that Jonah sailed when he was told to go and prophesy against Nineveh, and no doubt it was not far from the town that the whale threw him up when he discovered that he had no ticket. Jonah was disobedient, and of a faultfinding, complaining disposition, and deserves to be lightly spoken of almost. The timbers used in the construction of Solomon's Temple were floated to Jaffa in rafts, and the narrow opening in the reef through which they passed to the shore is not an inch wider or a shade less dangerous to navigate than it was then. Such is the sleepy nature of the population Palestine's only good seaport has now and always had. Jaffa has a history and a stirring one. It will not be discovered anywhere in this book. If the reader will call at the circulating library and mention my name, he will be furnished with books which will afford him the fullest information concerning Jaffa.

So ends the pilgrimage. We ought to be glad that we did not make it for the purpose of feasting our eyes upon fascinating aspects of nature, for we should have been disappointed—at least at this season of the year. A writer in *Life in the Holy Land* observes:

Monotonous and uninviting as much of the Holy Land will appear to persons accustomed to the almost constant verdure of flowers, ample streams and varied surface of our own country, we must remember that its aspect to the Israelites after the weary march of forty years through the desert must have been very different.

Which all of us will freely grant. But it truly *is* "monotonous and uninviting," and there is no sufficient reason for describing it as being otherwise.

Of all the lands there are for dismal scenery, I think Palestine must be the prince. The hills are barren, they are dull of color, they are unpicturesque in shape. The valleys are unsightly deserts fringed with a feeble vegetation that has an expression about it of being sorrowful and despondent. The Dead Sea and the Sea of Galilee sleep in the midst of a vast stretch of hill and plain wherein the eye rests upon no pleasant tint, no striking object, no soft picture dreaming in a purple haze or mottled with the shadows of the clouds. Every outline is harsh, every feature is distinct, there is no perspective—distance works no enchantment here. It is a hopeless, dreary, heartbroken land.

Small shreds and patches of it must be very beautiful in the full flush of spring, however, and all the more beautiful by contrast with the far-reaching desolation that surrounds them on every side. I would like much to see the fringes of the Jordan in springtime, and Shechem, Esdraelon, Ajalon, and the borders of Galilee—but even then these spots would seem mere toy gardens set at wide intervals in the waste of a limitless desolation.

Palestine sits in sackcloth and ashes. Over it broods the spell of a curse that has withered its fields and fettered its energies. Where Sodom and Gomorrah reared their domes and towers, that solemn sea now floods the plain, in whose bitter waters no living thing exists—over whose waveless surface the blistering air hangs motionless and dead—about whose borders nothing grows but weeds, and scattering tufts of cane, and that treacherous fruit that promises refreshment to parching lips, but turns to ashes at the touch. Nazareth is forlorn; about that ford of Jordan where the hosts of Israel

entered the Promised Land with songs of rejoicing, one finds
only a squalid camp of fantastic Bedouins of the desert;
Jericho the accursed lies a moldering ruin today, even as
Joshua's miracle left it more than three thousand years ago;
Bethlehem and Bethany, in their poverty and their humiliation, have nothing about them now to remind one that they
once knew the high honor of the Saviour's presence; the hallowed spot where the shepherds watched their flocks by night,
and where the angels sang, "Peace on earth, good will to
men," is untenanted by any living creature and unblessed by
any feature that is pleasant to the eye. Renowned Jerusalem
itself, the stateliest name in history, has lost all its ancient
grandeur and is become a pauper village; the riches of
Solomon are no longer there to compel the admiration of
visiting Oriental queens; the wonderful temple which was the
pride and the glory of Israel is gone, and the Ottoman
crescent is lifted above the spot where, on that most memorable day in the annals of the world, they reared the Holy
Cross. The noted Sea of Galilee, where Roman fleets once
rode at anchor and the disciples of the Saviour sailed in
their ships, was long ago deserted by the devotees of war and
commerce, and its borders are a silent wilderness; Capernaum
is a shapeless ruin; Magdala is the home of beggared Arabs;
Bethsaida and Chorazin have vanished from the earth, and
the "desert places" round about them, where thousands of men
once listened to the Saviour's voice and ate the miraculous
bread, sleep in the hush of a solitude that is inhabited only
by birds of prey and skulking foxes.

Palestine is desolate and unlovely. And why should it be
otherwise? Can the *curse* of the Deity beautify a land?

Palestine is no more of this workday world. It is sacred
to poetry and tradition—it is dreamland.

57

It was worth a kingdom to be at sea again. It was a relief to
drop all anxiety whatsoever—all questions as to where we

should go; how long we should stay; whether it were worth-while to go or not; all anxieties about the condition of the horses; all such questions as "Shall we *ever* get to water?" "Shall we *ever* lunch?" "Ferguson, how many *more* million miles have we got to creep under this awful sun before we camp?" It was a relief to cast all these torturing little anxieties far away—ropes of steel they were, and every one with a separate and distinct strain on it—and feel the temporary contentment that is born of the banishment of all care and responsibility. We did not look at the compass: we did not care now where the ship went to, so that she went out of sight of land as quickly as possible. When I travel again, I wish to go in a pleasure ship. No amount of money could have purchased for us, in a strange vessel and among un-familiar faces, the perfect satisfaction and the sense of being *at home* again which we experienced when we stepped on board the *Quaker City*—our own ship—after this wearisome pilgrimage. It is a something we have felt always when we returned to her, and a something we had no desire to sell.

We took off our blue woolen shirts, our spurs and heavy boots, our sanguinary revolvers, and our buckskin-seated pantaloons, and got shaved and came out in Christian costume once more. All but Jack, who changed all other articles of his dress but clung to his traveling pantaloons. They still pre-served their ample buckskin seat intact; and so his short pea jacket and his long, thin legs assisted to make him a pic-turesque object whenever he stood on the forecastle looking abroad upon the ocean over the bows. At such times his father's last injunction suggested itself to me. He said:

"Jack, my boy, you are about to go among a brilliant com-pany of gentlemen and ladies, who are refined and cultivated and thoroughly accomplished in the manners and customs of good society. Listen to their conversation, study their habits of life, and learn. Be polite and obliging to all, and consider-ate toward everyone's opinions, failings, and prejudices. Com-mand the just respect of all your fellow voyagers, even though you fail to win their friendly regard. And Jack—don't you ever dare, while you live, appear in public on those decks in fair weather, in a costume unbecoming your mother's drawing room!"

It would have been worth any price if the father of this hopeful youth could have stepped on board sometime and seen him standing high on the forecastle—pea jacket, tasseled red fez, buckskin patch and all—placidly contemplating the ocean—a rare spectacle for anybody's drawing room.

After a pleasant voyage and a good rest we drew near to Egypt, and out of the mellowest of sunsets we saw the domes and minarets of Alexandria rise into view. As soon as the anchor was down Jack and I got a boat and went ashore. It was night by this time, and the other passengers were content to remain at home and visit ancient Egypt after breakfast. It was the way they did at Constantinople. They took a lively interest in new countries, but their schoolboy impatience had worn off, and they had learned that it was wisdom to take things easy and go along comfortably— these old countries do not go away in the night; they stay till after breakfast.

When we reached the pier we found an army of Egyptian boys with donkeys no larger than themselves, waiting for passengers—for donkeys are the omnibuses of Egypt. We preferred to walk, but we could not have our own way. The boys crowded about us, clamored around us, and slewed their donkeys exactly across our path, no matter which way we turned. They were good-natured rascals, and so were the donkeys. We mounted, and the boys ran behind us and kept the donkeys in a furious gallop, as is the fashion at Damascus. I believe I would rather ride a donkey than any beast in the world. He goes briskly, he puts on no airs, he is docile, though opinionated. Satan himself could not scare him, and he is convenient—very convenient. When you are tired riding you can rest your feet on the ground and let him gallop from under you.

We found the hotel and secured rooms, and were happy to know that the Prince of Wales had stopped there once. They had it everywhere on signs. No other princes had stopped there since, till Jack and I came. We went abroad through the town then and found it a city of huge commercial buildings and broad, handsome streets brilliant with gaslight. By night it was a sort of reminiscence of Paris. But finally Jack found an ice-cream saloon, and that closed investigations for that evening. The weather was very hot, it had been many a day since Jack had seen ice cream, and so it was useless to talk of leaving the saloon till it shut up.

In the morning the lost tribes of America came ashore and infested the hotels and took possession of all the donkeys and other open barouches that offered. They went in picturesque procession to the American Consul's; to the great gardens; to Cleopatra's Needles; to Pompey's Pillar; to the palace of the Viceroy of Egypt; to the Nile; to the superb groves of date palms. One of our most inveterate relic-hunters had his hammer with him and tried to break a fragment off the upright Needle and could not do it; he tried the prostrate one and failed; he borrowed a heavy sledge hammer from a mason and failed again. He tried Pompey's Pillar, and this baffled him. Scattered all about the mighty monolith were sphinxes of noble countenance, carved out of Egyptian granite as hard as blue steel, and whose shapely features the wear of five thousand years had failed to mark or mar. The relic-hunter battered at these persistently and sweated profusely over his work. He might as well have attempted to deface the moon. They regarded him serenely with the stately smile they had worn so long, and which seemed to say, "Peck away, poor insect; we were not made to fear such as you; in tenscore dragging ages we have seen more of your kind than there are sands at your feet—have they left a blemish upon us?"

But I am forgetting the Jaffa colonists. At Jaffa we had taken on board some forty members of a very celebrated community. They were male and female; babies, young boys, and young girls; young married people, and some who had passed a shade beyond the prime of life. I refer to the "Adams Jaffa colony." Others had deserted before. We left in Jaffa Mr. Adams, his wife, and fifteen unfortunates who not only had no money but did not know where to turn or whither to go. Such was the statement made to us. Our forty were miserable enough in the first place, and they lay about the decks seasick all the voyage, which about completed their misery, I take it. However, one or two young men remained upright, and by constant persecution we wormed out of them some little information. They gave it reluctantly and in a very fragmentary condition, for, having been shamefully humbugged by their prophet, they felt humiliated and un-happy. In such circumstances people do not like to talk.

The colony was a complete fiasco. I have already said that such as could get away did so from time to time. The prophet Adams—once an actor, then several other things, afterward a Mormon and a missionary, always an adventurer—remains at Jaffa with his handful of sorrowful subjects. The forty we brought away with us were chiefly destitute, though not all of them. They wished to get to Egypt. What might become of them then they did not know and probably did not care—anything to get away from hated Jaffa. They had little to hope for. Because after many appeals to the sympathies of New England, made by strangers of Boston, through the newspapers, and after the establishment of an office there for the reception of moneyed contributions for the Jaffa colonists, One Dollar was subscribed. The Consul General for Egypt showed me the newspaper paragraph which mentioned the circumstance and mentioned also the discontinuance of the effort and the closing of the office. It was evident that practical New England was not sorry to be rid of such visionaries and was not in the least inclined to hire anybody to bring them back to her. Still, to get to Egypt was something in the eyes of the unfortunate colonists, hopeless as the prospect seemed of ever getting further.

Thus circumstanced, they landed at Alexandria from our ship. One of our passengers, Mr. Moses S. Beach, of the New York *Sun*, inquired of the Consul General what it would cost to send these people to their home in Maine by the way of Liverpool, and he said fifteen hundred dollars in gold would do it. Mr. Beach gave his check for the money and so the troubles of the Jaffa colonists were at an end.*

Alexandria was too much like a European city to be novel, and we soon tired of it. We took the cars and came up here to ancient Cairo, which *is* an Oriental city and of the completest pattern. There is little about it to disabuse one's mind of the error if he should take it into his head that he was in the heart of Arabia. Stately camels and dromedaries, swarthy Egyptians, and likewise Turks and black Ethiopians, turbaned, sashed, and blazing in a rich variety of Oriental costumes of all shades of flashy colors, are what one sees on every hand crowding the narrow streets and the honeycombed bazaars. We are stopping at Shepherd's Hotel, which is the worst on earth except the one I stopped at once in a small town in the United States. It is pleasant to read this sketch in my notebook now and know that I can stand

---

* It was an unselfish act of benevolence; it was done without any ostentation and has never been mentioned in any newspaper, I think. Therefore it is refreshing to learn now, several months after the above narrative was written, that another man received all the credit of this rescue of the colonists. Such is life.

Shepherd's Hotel sure, because I have been in one just like it in America and survived:

I stopped at the Benton House. It used to be a good hotel, but that proves nothing—I used to be a good boy, for that matter. Both of us have lost character of late years. The Benton is not a good hotel. The Benton lacks a very great deal of being a good hotel. Perdition is full of better hotels than the Benton.

It was late at night when I got there, and I told the clerk I would like plenty of lights, because I wanted to read an hour or two. When I reached No. 15 with the porter (we came along a dim hall that was clad in ancient carpeting, faded, worn out in many places, and patched with old scraps of oil cloth—a hall that sank under one's feet and creaked dismally to every footstep), he struck a light—two inches of sallow, sorrowful, consumptive tallow candle, that burned blue and sputtered and got discouraged and went out. The porter lit it again, and I asked if that was all the light the clerk sent. He said, "Oh no, I've got another one here," and he produced another couple of inches of tallow candle. I said, "Light them both—I'll have to have one to see the other by." He did it, but the result was drearier than darkness itself. He was a cheery, accommodating rascal. He said he would go "somewheres" and steal a lamp. I abetted and encouraged him in his criminal design. I heard the landlord get after him in the hall ten minutes afterward.

"Where are you going with that lamp?"

"Fifteen wants it, sir."

"Fifteen! Why, he's got a double lot of candles—does the man want to illuminate the house? Does he want to get up a torchlight procession? What *is* he up to anyhow?"

"He don't like them candles—says he wants a lamp."

"Why, what in the nation does— Why, I never heard of such a thing. What on earth can he want with that lamp?"

"Well, he only wants to read—that's what he says."

"Wants to read, does he? Ain't satisfied with a thousand candles, but has to have a lamp! I do wonder what the devil that fellow wants that lamp for. Take him another candle, and then if——"

"But he wants the lamp—says he'll burn the d—d old house down if he don't get a lamp!" (A remark which I never made.)

"I'd like to see him at it once. Well, you take it along—but I swear it beats *my* time, though—and see if you can't find out what in the very nation he *wants* with that lamp."

And he went off growling to himself and still wondering and wondering over the unaccountable conduct of No. 15. The lamp was a good one, but it revealed some disagreeable things—a bed in the suburbs of a desert of room—a bed that had hills and valleys in it, and you'd have to accommodate your body to the impression left in it by the man that slept there last before you could lie comfortably; a carpet that had seen better days; a melancholy washstand in a remote corner, and a dejected pitcher on it sorrowing over a broken nose; a looking glass split across the center, which chopped your head off at the chin and made you look like some dreadful unfinished monster or other; the paper peeling in shreds from the walls.

I sighed and said: "This is charming; and now don't you think you could get me something to read?"

The porter said, "Oh, certain'y; the old man's got dead loads of books"; and he was gone before I could tell him what sort of literature I would rather have. And yet his countenance expressed the utmost confidence in his ability to execute the commission with credit to himself. The old man made a descent on him.

"What are you going to do with that pile of books?"

"Fifteen wants 'em, sir."

"Fifteen, is it? He'll want a warming pan next—he'll want a nurse! Take him everything there is in the house—take him the barkeeper—take him the baggage wagon—take him a chambermaid! Confound me, I never saw anything like it. What did he say he wants with those books?"

"Wants to read 'em, like enough; it ain't likely he wants to eat 'em, I don't reckon."

"Wants to read 'em—wants to read 'em this time of night —the infernal lunatic! Well, he can't have them."

"But he says he's mor'ly bound to have 'em; he says he'll just go a-rairin' and a-chargin' through this house and raise more— Well, there's no tellin' what he won't do if he don't get 'em; because he's drunk and crazy and desperate, and nothing'll soothe him down but them cussed books." [I had not made any threats and was not in the condition ascribed to me by the porter.]

"Well, go on; but I will be around when he goes to rairing and charging, and the first rair he makes I'll make him rair out of the window." And then the old gentleman went off, growling as before.

The genius of that porter was something wonderful. He put an armful of books on the bed and said "Good night" as confidently as if he knew perfectly well that those books were exactly my style of reading matter. And well he might. His selection covered the whole range of legitimate literature. It comprised *The Great Consummation*, by Rev. Dr. Cummings—theology; *Revised Statutes of the State of Missouri* —law; *The Complete Horse Doctor*—medicine; *The Toilers of the Sea*, by Victor Hugo—romance; *The Works of William Shakespeare*—poetry. I shall never cease to admire the tact and the intelligence of that gifted porter.

But all the donkeys in Christendom and most of the Egyptian boys, I think, are at the door, and there is some noise going on, not to put it in stronger language. We are about starting to the illustrious pyramids of Egypt, and the donkeys for the voyage are under inspection. I will go and select one before the choice animals are all taken.

58

The donkeys were all good, all handsome, all strong and in good condition, all fast and all willing to prove it. They were the best we had found anywhere, and the most recherché. I do not know what "recherché" is, but that is what these donkeys were anyhow. Some were of a soft mouse color, and the others were white, black, and varicolored. Some were close-shaven all over, except that a tuft like a paintbrush was left on the end of the tail. Others were so shaven in fanciful landscape garden patterns as to mark their bodies with curving lines, which were bounded on one side by hair and on the other by the close plush left by the shears. They had all been newly barbered and were exceedingly stylish. Several of the white ones were barred like zebras with rainbow stripes of blue and red and yellow paint. These were indescribably gorgeous. Dan and Jack selected from this lot because they brought back Italian reminiscences of the "old masters." The saddles were the high, stuffy, frog-shaped things we had known in Ephesus and Smyrna. The donkey boys were lively young Egyptian rascals who could follow a donkey and keep him in a canter half a day without tiring. We had plenty of spectators when we mounted, for the hotel was full of English people bound overland to India and officers getting ready for the African campaign against the Abyssinian King Theodorus. We were not a very large party, but as we charged through the streets of the great metropolis we made noise for five hundred and displayed activity and created excitement in proportion. Nobody can steer a donkey, and some collided with camels, dervishes, effendis, asses, beggars, and everything else that offered to the donkeys a reasonable chance for a collision. When we turned into the broad avenue that leads out of the city toward Old Cairo, there was plenty of room. The walls of stately date palms that fenced the gardens and bordered the way threw their shadows down and made the air cool and bracing. We rose to the spirit of the time and the race became a wild rout, a stampede, a terrific panic. I wish to live to enjoy it again.

Somewhere along this route we had a few startling exhibitions of Oriental simplicity. A girl apparently thirteen years of age came along the great thoroughfare dressed like Eve before the fall. We would have called her thirteen at home; but here girls who look thirteen are often not more than nine in reality. Occasionally we saw stark-naked men of superb build, bathing and making no attempt at concealment. However, an hour's acquaintance with this cheerful custom reconciled the pilgrims to it, and then it ceased to occasion remark. Thus easily do even the most startling novelties grow tame and spiritless to these sight-surfeited wanderers.

Arrived at Old Cairo, the camp followers took up the donkeys and tumbled them bodily aboard a small boat with a lateen sail, and we followed and got under way. The deck was closely packed with donkeys and men; the two sailors had to climb over and under and through the wedged mass to work the sails, and the steersman had to crowd four or five donkeys out of the way when he wished to swing his tiller and put his helm hard-down. But what were their troubles to us? We had nothing to do; nothing to do but enjoy the trip; nothing to do but shove the donkeys off our corns and look at the charming scenery of the Nile.

On the island at our right was the machine they call the Nilometer, a stone column whose business it is to mark the rise of the river and prophesy whether it will reach only thirty-two feet and produce a famine, or whether it will properly flood the land at forty and produce plenty, or whether it will rise to forty-three and bring death and destruction to flocks and crops—but how it does all this they could not explain to us so that we could understand. On the same island is still shown the spot where Pharaoh's daughter found Moses in the bulrushes. Near the spot we sailed from, the Holy Family dwelt when they sojourned in Egypt till

Herod should complete his slaughter of the innocents. The same tree they rested under when they first arrived was there a short time ago, but the Viceroy of Egypt sent it to the Empress Eugenie lately. He was just in time, otherwise our pilgrims would have had it.

The Nile at this point is muddy, swift, and turbid, and does not lack a great deal of being as wide as the Mississippi.

We scrambled up the steep bank at the shabby town of Ghizeh, mounted the donkeys again, and scampered away. For four or five miles the route lay along a high embankment which they say is to be the bed of a railway the Sultan means to build for no other reason than that when the Empress of the French comes to visit him she can go to the pyramids in comfort. This is true Oriental hospitality. I am very glad it is our privilege to have donkeys instead of cars.

At the distance of a few miles the pyramids rising above the palms looked very clean-cut, very grand and imposing, and very soft and filmy as well. They swam in a rich haze that took from them all suggestions of unfeeling stone and made them seem only the airy nothings of a dream—structures which might blossom into tiers of vague arches or ornate colonnades maybe, and change and change again into all graceful forms of architecture, while we looked, and then melt deliciously away and blend with the tremulous atmosphere.

At the end of the levee we left the mules and went in a sailboat across an arm of the Nile or an overflow, and landed where the sands of the great Sahara left their embankment, as straight as a wall, along the verge of the alluvial plain of the river. A laborious walk in the flaming sun brought us to the foot of the great pyramid of Cheops. It was a fairy vision no longer. It was a corrugated, unsightly mountain of stone. Each of its monstrous sides was a wide stairway which rose upward, step above step, narrowing as it went, till it tapered to a point far aloft in the air. Insect men and women—pilgrims from the *Quaker City*—were creeping about its dizzy perches, and one little black swarm were waving postage stamps from the airy summit—handkerchiefs will be understood.

Of course we were besieged by a rabble of muscular Egyptians and Arabs who wanted the contract of dragging us to the top—all tourists are. Of course you could not hear your own voice for the din that was around you. Of course the sheikhs said *they* were the only responsible parties, that all contracts must be made with them, all moneys paid over to them, and none exacted from us by any but themselves alone. Of course they contracted that the varlets who dragged us up should not mention baksheesh once. For such is the usual routine. Of course we contracted with them, paid them, were delivered into the hands of the draggers, dragged up the pyramids, and harried and bedeviled for baksheesh from the foundation clear to the summit. We paid it, too, for we were purposely spread very far apart over the vast side of the pyramid. There was no help near if we called, and the Herculeses who dragged us had a way of asking sweetly and flatteringly for baksheesh, which was seductive, and of looking fierce and threatening to throw us down the precipice, which was persuasive and convincing.

Each step being full as high as a dinner table; there being very, very many of the steps; an Arab having hold of each of our arms and springing upward from step to step and snatching us with them, forcing us to lift our feet as high as our breasts every time, and do it rapidly and keep it up till we were ready to faint—who shall say it is not lively, exhilarating, lacerating, muscle-straining, bone-wrenching and perfectly excruciating and exhausting pastime climbing the pyramids? I beseeched the varlets not to twist *all* my joints asunder; I iterated, reiterated, even *swore* to them that I did not wish to beat anybody to the top; did all I could to convince them that if I got there the last of all, I would feel blessed above men and grateful to them forever; I begged them, prayed them, pleaded with them to let me stop and rest a moment—only one little moment—and they only answered with some more frightful springs, and an unenlisted volunteer behind opened a bombardment of determined boosts with his head which threatened to batter my whole political economy to wreck and ruin.

Twice, for one minute, they let me rest while they extorted baksheesh, and then continued their maniac flight up the pyramid. They wished to beat the other parties. It was nothing to them that I, a stranger, must be sacrificed upon the altar of their unholy ambition. But in the midst of sorrow, joy blooms. Even in this dark hour I had a sweet consolation. For I knew that except these Muhammadans repented, they would go straight to perdition someday. And *they* never repent—they never forsake their paganism. This thought calmed me, cheered me, and I sank down, limp and exhausted, upon the summit, but happy, *so* happy and serene within.

On the one hand, a mighty sea of yellow sand stretched away toward the ends of the earth, solemn, silent, shorn of vegetation, its solitude uncheered by any forms of creature life; on the other, the Eden of Egypt was spread below us—a broad green floor, cloven by the sinuous river, dotted with villages, its vast distances measured and marked by the diminishing stature of receding clusters of palms. It lay asleep in an enchanted atmosphere. There was no sound, no motion. Above the date plumes in the middle distance swelled a domed and pinnacled mass, glimmering through a tinted, exquisite mist; away toward the horizon a dozen shapely pyramids watched over ruined Memphis; and at our feet the bland impassible sphinx looked out upon the picture from her throne in the sands as placidly and pensively as she had looked upon its like full fifty lagging centuries ago.

We suffered torture no pen can describe from the hungry appeals for baksheesh that gleamed from Arab eyes and poured incessantly from Arab lips. Why try to call up the traditions of vanished Egyptian grandeur; why try to fancy Egypt following dead Rameses to his tomb in the pyramid or the long multitude of Israel departing over the desert yonder? Why try to think at all? The thing was impossible. One must bring his meditations cut and dried, or else cut and dry them afterward.

The traditional Arab proposed, in the traditional way, to run down Cheops, cross the eighth of a mile of sand intervening between it and the tall pyramid of Cephron, ascend to Cephron's summit and return to us on the top of Cheops—all in nine minutes by the watch, and the whole service to be rendered for a single dollar. In the first flush of irritation I said let the Arab and his exploits go to the mischief. But stay. The upper third of Cephron was coated with dressed marble smooth as glass. A blessed thought entered my brain. He must infallibly break his neck. Close the contract with dispatch, I said, and let him go. He started. We watched. He went bounding down the vast broadside, spring after spring, like an ibex. He grew small and smaller till he became a bobbing pygmy, away down toward the bottom—then disappeared. We turned and peered over the other side—forty seconds—eighty seconds—a hundred—happiness, he is dead

already!—two minutes—and a quarter. "There he goes!" Too
true—it was too true. He was very small now. Gradually,
but surely, he overcame the level ground. He began to spring
and climb again. Up, up, up—at last he reached the smooth
coating—now for it. But he clung to it with toes and fingers,
like a fly. He crawled this way and that—away to the right,
slanting upward—away to the left, still slanting upward—
and stood at last, a black peg on the summit, and waved
his pygmy scarf! Then he crept downward to the raw steps
again, then picked up his agile heels and flew. We lost him
presently. But presently again we saw him under us, mount-
ing with undiminished energy. Shortly he bounded into our
midst with a gallant war whoop. Time: eight minutes, forty-
one seconds. He had won. His bones were intact. It was a
failure. I reflected. I said to myself, "He is tired and must
grow dizzy. I will risk another dollar on him."

He started again. Made the trip again. Slipped on the
smooth coating—I almost had him. But an infamous crevice
saved him. He was with us once more—perfectly sound.
Time: eight minutes, forty-six seconds.

I said to Dan, "Lend me a dollar—I can beat this game
yet."

Worse and worse. He won again. Time: eight minutes,
forty-eight seconds. I was out of all patience now. I was
desperate. Money was no longer of any consequence. I said,
"Sirrah, I will give you a hundred dollars to jump off this
pyramid head first. If you do not like the terms, name your
bet. I scorn to stand on expenses now. I will stay right here
and risk money on you as long as Dan has got a cent."

I was in a fair way to win now, for it was a dazzling
opportunity for an Arab. He pondered a moment, and would
have done it, I think, but his mother arrived then and interfered. Her tears moved me—I never can look upon the
tears of woman with indifference—and I said I would give
her a hundred to jump off, too.

But it was a failure. The Arabs are too high-priced in
Egypt. They put on airs unbecoming to such savages.

We descended, hot and out of humor. The dragoman lit
candles, and we all entered a hole near the base of the pyramid, attended by a crazy rabble of Arabs who thrust their
services upon us uninvited. They dragged us up a long inclined chute and dripped candle grease all over us. This
chute was not more than twice as wide and high as a Sara-

toga trunk, and was walled, roofed, and floored with solid blocks of Egyptian granite as wide as a wardrobe, twice as thick, and three times as long. We kept on climbing, through the oppressive gloom, till I thought we ought to be nearing the top of the pyramid again, and then came to the "Queen's Chamber" and shortly to the chamber of the King. These large apartments were tombs. The walls were built of monstrous masses of smoothed granite, neatly joined together. Some of them were nearly as large square as an ordinary parlor. A great stone sarcophagus like a bathtub stood in the center of the King's Chamber. Around it were gathered a picturesque group of Arab savages and soiled and tattered pilgrims, who held their candles aloft in the gloom while they chattered, and the winking blurs of light shed a dim glory down upon one of the irrepressible memento-seekers who was pecking at the venerable sarcophagus with his sacrilegious hammer.

We struggled out to the open air and the bright sunshine, and for the space of thirty minutes received ragged Arabs by couples, dozens, and platoons, and paid them baksheesh for services they swore and proved by each other that they had rendered, but which we had not been aware of before—and as each party was paid, they dropped into the rear of the procession and in due time arrived again with a newly invented delinquent list for liquidation.

We lunched in the shade of the pyramid, and in the midst of this encroaching and unwelcome company, and then Dan and Jack and I started away for a walk. A howling swarm of beggars followed us—surrounded us—almost headed us off. A sheikh, in flowing white burnoose and gaudy headgear, was with them. He wanted more baksheesh. But we had adopted a new code—it was millions for defense, but not a cent for baksheesh. I asked him if he could persuade the others to depart if we paid him. He said yes—for ten francs. We accepted the contract, and said:

"Now persuade your vassals to fall back."

He swung his long staff round his head and three Arabs bit the dust. He capered among the mob like a very maniac. His blows fell like hail, and wherever one fell a subject went down. We had to hurry to the rescue and tell him it was only necessary to damage them a little—he need not kill them. In two minutes we were alone with the sheikh, and remained so. The persuasive powers of this illiterate savage were remarkable.

Each side of the pyramid of Cheops is about as long as the Capitol at Washington or the Sultan's new palace on the Bosporus, and is longer than the greatest depth of St. Peter's at Rome—which is to say that each side of Cheops extends seven hundred and some-odd feet. It is about seventy-five feet higher than the cross on St. Peter's. The first time I ever went down the Mississippi, I thought the highest bluff on the river between St. Louis and New Orleans—it was near Selma, Missouri—was probably the highest mountain in the world. It is four hundred and thirteen feet high. It still looms in my memory with undiminished grandeur. I can still see the trees and bushes growing smaller and smaller as I followed them up its huge slant with my eye till they became a feathery fringe on the distant summit. This symmetrical pyramid of Cheops—this solid mountain of stone reared by the patient hands of men—this mighty tomb of a forgotten monarch—dwarfs my cherished mountain. For it is four hundred and eighty feet high. In still earlier years than those I have been recalling, Holliday's Hill, in our town, was to me the noblest work of God. It appeared to pierce the skies. It was nearly three hundred feet high. In those days I pondered the subject much, but I never could understand why it did not swathe its summit with never-failing clouds and crown its majestic brow with everlasting snows. I had heard that such was the custom of great mountains in other parts of the world. I remembered how I worked with another boy, at odd afternoons stolen from study and paid for with stripes, to undermine and start from its bed an immense boulder that rested upon the edge of that hilltop; I remembered how, one Saturday afternoon, we gave three hours of honest effort to the task, and saw at last that our reward was at hand; I remembered how we sat down then and wiped the perspiration away, and waited to let a picnic party get out of the way in the road below—and then we started the boulder. It was splendid. It went crashing down the hillside, tearing up saplings, mowing bushes down like grass, ripping and crushing and smashing everything in its path—eternally splintered and scattered a woodpile at the foot of the hill, and then sprang from the high bank clear over a dray in the road—the Negro glanced up once and dodged—and the next second it made infinitesimal mincemeat of a frame cooper shop, and the coopers swarmed out like bees. Then we said it was perfectly magnificent and left. Because the coopers were starting up the hill to inquire.

Still, that mountain, prodigious as it was, was nothing to the pyramid of Cheops. I could conjure up no comparison that would convey to my mind a satisfactory comprehension of the magnitude of a pile of monstrous stones that covered thirteen acres of ground and stretched upward four hundred and eighty tiresome feet, and so I gave it up and walked down to the sphinx.

After years of waiting it was before me at last. The great face was so sad, so earnest, so longing, so patient. There was a dignity not of earth in its mien, and in its countenance a benignity such as never anything human wore. It was stone, but it seemed sentient. If ever image of stone thought, it was thinking. It was looking toward the verge of the landscape, yet looking *at* nothing—nothing but distance and vacancy. It was looking over and beyond everything of the present and far into the past. It was gazing out over the ocean of Time—over lines of century waves which, further and further receding, closed nearer and nearer together, and blended at last into one unbroken tide, away toward the horizon of remote antiquity. It was thinking of the wars of departed ages; of the empires it had seen created and destroyed; of the nations whose birth it had witnessed, whose progress it had watched, whose annihilation it had noted; of the joy and sorrow, the life and death, the grandeur and decay, of five thousand slow revolving years. It was the type of an attribute of man—of a faculty of his heart and brain. It was MEMORY—RETROSPECTION—wrought into visible, tangible form. All who know what pathos there is in memories of days that are accomplished and faces that have vanished—albeit only a trifling score of years gone by—will have some appreciation of the pathos that dwells in these grave eyes that look so steadfastly back upon the things they knew before History was born—before Tradition had being—things that were and forms that moved in a vague era which even Poetry and Romance scarce know of—and passed one by one away and left the stony dreamer solitary in the midst of a strange new age and uncomprehended scenes.

The sphinx is grand in its loneliness; it is imposing in its magnitude; it is impressive in the mystery that hangs over its story. And there is that in the overshadowing majesty of this eternal figure of stone, with its accusing memory of the deeds of all ages, which reveals to one something of what he shall feel when he shall stand at last in the awful presence of God.

There are some things which, for the credit of America, should be left unsaid perhaps; but these very things happen sometimes to be the very things which, for the real benefit of Americans, ought to have prominent notice. While we stood looking, a wart or an excrescence of some kind appeared on the jaw of the sphinx. We heard the familiar clink of a hammer and understood the case at once. One of our well-meaning reptiles—I mean relic-hunters—had crawled up there and was trying to break a "specimen" from the face of this the most majestic creation the hand of man has wrought. But the great image contemplated the dead ages as calmly as ever, unconscious of the small insect that was fretting at its jaw. Egyptian granite that has defied the storms and earthquakes of all time has nothing to fear from the tack hammers of ignorant excursionists—highwaymen—like this specimen. He failed in his enterprise. We sent a sheikh to arrest him if he had the authority, or to warn him, if he had not, that by the laws of Egypt the crime he was attempting to commit was punishable with imprisonment or the bastinado. Then he desisted and went away.

The sphinx: a hundred and twenty-five feet long, sixty feet high, and a hundred and two feet around the head, if I remember rightly—carved out of one solid block of stone harder than any iron. The block must have been as large as the Fifth Avenue Hotel before the usual waste (by the necessities of sculpture) of a fourth or a half of the original mass was begun. I only set down these figures and these remarks to suggest the prodigious labor the carving of it so elegantly, so symmetrically, so faultlessly, must have cost. This species of stone is so hard that figures cut in it remain sharp and unmarred after exposure to the weather for two or three thousand years. Now, did it take a hundred years of patient toil to carve the sphinx? It seems probable.

Something interfered, and we did not visit the Red Sea and walk upon the sands of Arabia. I shall not describe the great mosque of Mehemet Ali, whose entire inner walls are built of polished and glistening alabaster; I shall not tell how the little birds have built their nests in the globes of the great chandeliers that hang in the mosque, and how they fill the whole place with their music and are not afraid of anybody because their audacity is pardoned, their rights are respected, and nobody is allowed to interfere with them, even though the mosque be thus doomed to go unlighted; I certainly shall not tell the hackneyed story of the massacre of the Mamluks, because I am glad the lawless rascals were massacred, and I do not wish to get up any sympathy in their behalf; I shall not tell how that one solitary Mamluk jumped his horse a hundred feet down from the battlements of the citadel and escaped, because I do not think much of that—I could have done it myself; I shall not tell of Joseph's well, which he dug in the solid rock of the citadel hill and which is still as good as new, nor how the same mules he bought to draw up the water (with an endless chain) are still at it yet and are getting tired of it, too; I shall not tell about Joseph's granaries, which he built to store the grain in what time the Egyptian brokers were "selling short," unwitting that there would be no corn in all the land when it should be time for them to deliver; I shall not tell anything about the strange, strange city of Cairo, because it is only a repetition, a good deal intensified and exaggerated, of the Oriental cities I have already spoken of; I shall not tell of the Great Caravan which leaves for Mecca every year, for I did not see it; nor of the fashion the people have of prostrating themselves and so forming a long human pavement to be ridden over by the chief of the expedition on its return, to the end that their salvation may be thus secured, for I did not see that, either; I shall not speak of the railway, for it is like any other railway—I shall only say that the fuel they use for the locomotive is composed of mummies three thousand years old, purchased by the ton or by the graveyard for that purpose, and that sometimes one hears the profane engineer call out pettishly, "D—n these plebeians, they don't burn worth a cent—pass out a king"; * I shall not tell of the groups of mud cones stuck like wasps' nests upon a thousand mounds above high-water mark the length and breadth of Egypt—villages of the lower classes; I shall not speak of the boundless sweep of level plain, green with luxuriant grain, that gladdens the eye as far as it can pierce through the soft, rich atmosphere

---

* Stated to me for a fact. I only tell it as I got it. I am willing to believe it. I can believe anything.

of Egypt; I shall not speak of the vision of the pyramids
seen at a distance of five-and-twenty miles, for the picture is
too ethereal to be limned by an uninspired pen; I shall not
tell of the crowds of dusky women who flocked to the cars
when they stopped a moment at a station, to sell us a drink
of water or a ruddy, juicy pomegranate; I shall not tell of
the motley multitudes and wild costumes that graced a fair
we found in full blast at another barbarous station; I shall
not tell how we feasted on fresh dates and enjoyed the
pleasant landscape all through the flying journey; nor how
we thundered into Alexandria, at last, swarmed out of the
cars, rowed aboard the ship, left a comrade behind (who
was to return to Europe, thence home), raised the anchor,
and turned our bows homeward finally and forever from
the long voyage; nor how, as the mellow sun went down upon
the oldest land on earth, Jack and Moult assembled in
solemn state in the smoking room and mourned over the lost
comrade the whole night long, and would not be comforted.
I shall not speak a word of any of these things or write a
line. They shall be as a sealed book. I do not know what a
sealed book is, because I never saw one, but a sealed book is
the expression to use in this connection, because it is popular.

We were glad to have seen the land which was the mother
of civilization—which taught Greece her letters, and through
Greece Rome, and through Rome the world; the land which
could have humanized and civilized the hapless children of
Israel, but allowed them to depart out of her borders little
better than savages. We were glad to have seen that land
which had an enlightened religion with future eternal re-
wards and punishment in it, while even Israel's religion
contained no promise of a hereafter. We were glad to have
seen that land which had glass three thousand years before
England had it, and could paint upon it as none of us can
paint now; that land which knew, three thousand years ago,
well-nigh all of medicine and surgery which science has *discovered* lately; which had all those curious surgical instruments which science has *invented* recently; which had in
high excellence a thousand luxuries and necessities of an
advanced civilization which we have gradually contrived and
accumulated in modern times and claimed as things that
were new under the sun; that had paper untold centuries
before we dreamt of it—and waterfalls before our women
thought of them; that had a perfect system of common

schools so long before we boasted of our achievements in
that direction that it seems forever and forever ago; that so
embalmed the dead that flesh was made almost immortal—
which we cannot do; that built temples which mock at
destroying time and smile grimly upon our lauded little prod-
igies of architecture; that old land that knew all which we
know now, perchance, and more; that walked in the broad
highway of civilization in the gray dawn of creation, ages
and ages before we were born; that left the impress of
exalted, cultivated Mind upon the eternal front of the sphinx
to confound all scoffers who, when all her other proofs had
passed away, might seek to persuade the world that imperial Egypt, in the days of her high renown, had groped in
darkness.

59

We were at sea now, for a very long voyage—we were to
pass through the entire length of the Levant, through the
entire length of the Mediterranean proper also, and then
cross the full width of the Atlantic—a voyage of several
weeks. We naturally settled down into a very slow, stay-at-
home manner of life, and resolved to be quiet, examplary
people, and roam no more for twenty or thirty days. No
more, at least, than from stem to stern of the ship. It was
a very comfortable prospect, though, for we were tired and
needed a long rest.

We were all lazy and satisfied now, as the meager entries
in my notebook (that sure index, to me, of my condition)
prove. What a stupid thing a notebook gets to be at sea anyway. Please observe the style:

Sunday—Services, as usual, at four bells. Services at night
also. No cards.

Monday—Beautiful day, but rained hard. The cattle purchased at Alexandria for beef ought to be shingled. Or else
fattened. The water stands in deep puddles in the depres-

sions forward of their aftershoulders. Also here and there all over their backs. It is well they are not cows—it would soak in and ruin the milk. The poor devil eagle * from Syria looks miserable and droopy in the rain, perched on the forward capstan. He appears to have his own opinion of a sea voyage, and if it were put into language and the language solidified, it would probably essentially dam the widest river in the world.

Tuesday—Somewhere in the neighborhood of the island of Malta. Cannot stop there. Cholera. Weather very stormy. Many passengers seasick and invisible.

Wednesday—Weather still very savage. Storm blew two land birds to sea, and they came on board. A hawk was blown off also. He circled round and round the ship, wanting to light, but afraid of the people. He was so tired, though, that he had to light, at last, or perish. He stopped in the foretop repeatedly, and was as often blown away by the wind. At last Harry caught him. Sea full of flying fish. They rise in flocks of three hundred and flash along above the tops of the waves a distance of two or three hundred feet, then fall and disappear.

Thursday—Anchored off Algiers, Africa. Beautiful city, beautiful green hilly landscape behind it. Stayed half a day and left. Not permitted to land, though we showed a clean bill of health. They were afraid of Egyptian plague and cholera.

Friday—Morning, dominoes. Afternoon, dominoes. Evening, promenading the deck. Afterwards, charades.

Saturday—Morning, dominoes. Afternoon, dominoes. Evening, promenading the decks. Afterwards, dominoes.

Sunday—Morning service, four bells. Evening service, eight bells. Monotony till midnight. Whereupon, dominoes.

Monday—Morning, dominoes. Afternoon, dominoes. Evening, promenading the decks. Afterward, charades and a lecture from Dr. C. Dominoes.

No date—Anchored off the picturesque city of Cagliari, Sardinia. Stayed till midnight, but not permitted to land by these infamous foreigners. They smell inodorously—they do not wash—they dare not risk cholera.

Thursday—Anchored off the beautiful cathedral city of Málaga, Spain. Went ashore in the captain's boat—not ashore, either, for they would not let us land. Quarantine. Shipped my newspaper correspondence, which they took with tongs, dipped it in seawater, clipped it full of holes, and then fumigated it with villainous vapors till it smelled like a Spaniard. Inquired about chances to run the blockade and visit

---

* Afterwards presented to the Central Park.

the Alhambra at Granada. Too risky—they might hang a
body. Set sail—middle of afternoon.

And so on, and so on, and so forth, for several days. Finally, anchored off Gibraltar, which looks familiar and homelike.

It reminds me of the journal I opened with the New Year
once, when I was a boy and a confiding and a willing prey
to those impossible schemes of reform which well-meaning
old maids and grandmothers set for the feet of unwary
youths at that season of the year—setting oversized tasks for
them, which, necessarily failing, as infallibly weaken the
boy's strength of will, diminish his confidence in himself, and
injure his chances of success in life. Please accept of an extract:

Monday—Got up, washed, went to bed.
Tuesday—Got up, washed, went to bed.
Wednesday—Got up, washed, went to bed.
Thursday—Got up, washed, went to bed.
Friday—Got up, washed, went to bed.
Next Friday—Got up, washed, went to bed.
Friday fortnight—Got up, washed, went to bed.
Following month—Got up, washed, went to bed.

I stopped then, discouraged. Startling events appeared to
be too rare in my career to render a diary necessary. I still
reflect with pride, however, that even at that early age I
washed when I got up. That journal finished me. I never have
had the nerve to keep one since. My loss of confidence in
myself in that line was permanent.

The ship had to stay a week or more at Gibraltar to take in
coal for the home voyage.

It would be very tiresome staying here, and so four of us
ran the quarantine blockade and spent seven delightful days
in Seville, Córdoba, Cadiz, and wandering through the
pleasant rural scenery of Andalusia, the garden of Old Spain.
The experiences of that cheery week were too varied and
numerous for a short chapter and I have not room for a long
one. Therefore I shall leave them all out.

60

Ten or eleven o'clock found us coming down to breakfast one morning in Cadiz. They told us the ship had been lying at anchor in the harbor two or three hours. It was time for us to bestir ourselves. The ship could wait only a little while because of the quarantine. We were soon on board, and within the hour the white city and the pleasant shores of Spain sank down behind the waves and passed out of sight. We had seen no land fade from view so regretfully.

It had long ago been decided in a noisy public meeting in the main cabin that we could not go to Lisbon, because we must surely be quarantined there. We did everything by mass meeting, in the good old national way, from swapping off one empire for another on the program of the voyage down to complaining of the cookery and the scarcity of napkins. I am reminded now of one of these complaints of the cookery made by a passenger. The coffee had been steadily growing more and more execrable for the space of three weeks, till at last it had ceased to be coffee altogether and had assumed the nature of mere discolored water—so this person said. He said it was so weak that it was transparent an inch in depth around the edge of the cup. As he approached the table one morning he saw the transparent edge—by means of his extraordinary vision—long before he got to his seat. He went back and complained in a high-handed way to Captain Duncan. He said the coffee was disgraceful. The captain showed his. It seemed tolerably good. The incipient mutineer was more outraged than ever then at what he denounced as the partiality shown the captain's table over the other tables in the ship. He flourished back and got his cup and set it down triumphantly and said:

"Just try that mixture once, Captain Duncan."

He smelled it—tasted it—smiled benignantly—then said:

"It *is* inferior—for *coffee*—but it is pretty fair *tea*."

The humbled mutineer smelled it, tasted it, and returned

to his seat. He had made an egregious ass of himself before the whole ship. He did it no more. After that he took things as they came. That was me.

The old-fashioned ship life had returned, now that we were no longer in sight of land. For days and days it continued just the same, one day being exactly like another and, to me, every one of them pleasant. At last we anchored in the open roadstead of Funchal, in the beautiful islands we call the Madeiras.

The mountains looked surpassingly lovely, clad as they were in living green; ribbed with lava ridges; flecked with white cottages; riven by deep chasms purple with shade; the great slopes dashed with sunshine and mottled with shadows flung from the drifting squadrons of the sky, and the superb picture fitly crowned by towering peaks whose fronts were swept by the trailing fringes of the clouds.

But we could not land. We stayed all day and looked, we abused the man who invented quarantine, we held half a dozen mass meetings and crammed them full of interrupted speeches, motions that fell stillborn, amendments that came to naught, and resolutions that died from sheer exhaustion in trying to get before the house. At night we set sail.

We averaged four mass meetings a week for the voyage —we seemed always in labor in this way, and yet so often fallaciously that whenever at long intervals we were safely delivered of a resolution, it was cause for public rejoicing, and we hoisted the flag and fired a salute.

Days passed—and nights; and then the beautiful Bermudas rose out of the sea, we entered the tortuous channel, steamed hither and thither among the bright summer islands, and rested at last under the flag of England and were welcome. We were not a nightmare here, where were civilization and intelligence in place of Spanish and Italian superstition, dirt, and dread of cholera. A few days among the breezy groves, the flower gardens, the coral caves, and the lovely vistas of blue water that went curving in and out, disappearing and anon again appearing through jungle walls of brilliant foliage, restored the energies dulled by long drowsing on the ocean and fitted us for our final cruise—our little run of a thousand miles to New York—America—HOME.

We bade good-bye to "our friends the Bermudians," as our program hath it—the majority of those we were most intimate with were Negroes—and courted the great deep

again. I said the majority. We knew more Negroes than
white people because we had a deal of washing to be done,
but we made some most excellent friends among the whites,
whom it will be a pleasant duty to hold long in grateful remembrance.

We sailed, and from that hour all idling ceased. Such
another system of overhauling, general littering of cabins
and packing of trunks we had not seen since we let go
the anchor in the harbor of Beirut. Everybody was busy.
Lists of all purchases had to be made out, and values attached, to facilitate matters at the customhouse. Purchases
bought by bulk in partnership had to be equitably divided,
outstanding debts canceled, accounts compared, and trunks,
boxes, and packages labeled. All day long the bustle and
confusion continued.

And now came our first accident. A passenger was running
through a gangway, between decks, one stormy night, when
he caught his foot in the iron staple of a door that had been
heedlessly left off a hatchway, and the bones of his leg broke
at the ankle. It was our first serious misfortune. We had
traveled much more than twenty thousand miles, by land
and sea, in many trying climates, without a single hurt, without a serious case of sickness, and without a death among
five-and-sixty passengers. Our good fortune had been wonderful. A sailor had jumped overboard at Constantinople one
night, and was seen no more, but it was suspected that his
object was to desert, and there was a slim chance at least that
he reached the shore. But the passenger list was complete.
There was no name missing from the register.

At last, one pleasant morning, we steamed up the harbor
of New York, all on deck, all dressed in Christian garb—by
special order, for there was a latent disposition in some
quarters to come out as Turks—and amid a waving of handkerchiefs from welcoming friends, the glad pilgrims noted
the shiver of the decks that told that ship and pier had
joined hands again and the long, strange cruise was over.
Amen.

61

In this place I will print an article which I wrote for the
New York *Herald* the night we arrived. I do it partly because my contract with my publishers makes it compulsory;
partly because it is a proper, tolerably accurate, and ex-
haustive summing up of the cruise of the ship and the
performances of the pilgrims in foreign lands; and partly
because some of the passengers have abused me for writing
it, and I wish the public to see how thankless a task it is to
put oneself to trouble to glorify unappreciative people. I
was charged with "rushing into print" with these compliments.
I did not rush. I had written newsletters to the *Herald*
sometimes, but yet when I visited the office that day I did
not say anything about writing a valedictory. I did go to
the *Tribune* office to see if such an article was wanted, because I belonged on the regular staff of that paper and it
was simply a duty to do it. The managing editor was absent, and so I thought no more about it. At night, when the
Herald's request came for an article, I did not "rush." In
fact, I demurred for a while, because I did not feel like
writing compliments then, and therefore was afraid to speak
of the cruise lest I might be betrayed into using other than
complimentary language. However, I reflected that it would
be a just and righteous thing to go down and write a kind
word for the hadjis—hadjis are people who have made the
pilgrimage—because parties not interested could not do it
so feelingly as I, a fellow hadji, and so I penned the valedictory. I have read it, and read it again; and if there is a
sentence in it that is not fulsomely complimentary to captain, ship, and passengers, *I* cannot find it. If it is not a
chapter that any company might be proud to have a body
write about them, my judgment is fit for nothing. With these
remarks I confidently submit it to the unprejudiced judgment of the reader:

RETURN OF THE HOLY LAND EXCURSIONISTS—THE STORY OF
THE CRUISE

To THE EDITOR OF THE *Herald*:

The steamer *Quaker City* has accomplished at last her extraordinary voyage and returned to her old pier at the foot of Wall Street. The expedition was a success in some respects, in some it was not. Originally it was advertised as a "pleasure excursion." Well, perhaps it was a pleasure excursion, but certainly it did not look like one; certainly it did not act like one. Anybody's and everybody's notion of a pleasure excursion is that the parties to it will of a necessity be young and giddy and somewhat boisterous. They will dance a good deal, sing a good deal, make love, but sermonize very little. Anybody's and everybody's notion of a well-conducted funeral is that there must be a hearse and a corpse, and chief mourners and mourners by courtesy, many old people, much solemnity, no levity, and a prayer and a sermon withal. Three-fourths of the *Quaker City's* passengers were between forty and seventy years of age! There was a picnic crowd for you! It may be supposed that the other fourth was composed of young girls. But it was not. It was chiefly composed of rusty old bachelors and a child of six years. Let us average the ages of the *Quaker City's* pilgrims and set the figure down as fifty years. Is any man insane enough to imagine that this picnic of patriarchs sang, made love, danced, laughed, told anecdotes, dealt in ungodly levity? In my experience they sinned little in these matters. No doubt it was presumed here at home that these frolicsome veterans laughed and sang and romped all day, and day after day, and kept up a noisy excitement from one end of the ship to the other; and that they played blindman's buff or danced quadrilles and waltzes on moonlight evenings on the quarterdeck; and that at odd moments of unoccupied time they jotted a laconic item or two in the journals they opened on such an elaborate plan when they left home, and then skurried off to their whist and euchre labors under the cabin lamps. If these things were presumed, the presumption was at fault. The venerable excursionists were not gay and frisky. They played no blindman's buff; they dealt not in whist; they shirked not the irksome journal, for alas! most of them were even writing books. They never romped, they talked but little, they never sang save in the nightly prayer meeting. The pleasure ship was a synagogue, and the pleasure trip was a funeral excursion without a corpse. (There is nothing exhilarating about a funeral excursion without a corpse.) A free, hearty laugh was a sound that was not heard oftener than once in seven days about those decks or in those cabins, and when it was heard it met with precious little sympathy. The excursionists danced, on three separate evenings, long, long ago (it seems an age), quadrilles, of a single set, made up of three ladies and five gentlemen (the latter with handkerchiefs around their arms to signify their sex), who timed their feet to the solemn wheezing of a melodeon; but even this melancholy orgy was voted to be sinful, and dancing was discontinued.

The pilgrims played dominoes when too much Josephus or Robinson's *Holy Land Researches* or book-writing made recreation necessary—for dominoes is about as mild and sinless a game as any in the world, perhaps, excepting always the ineffably insipid diversion they call croquet, which is a game where you don't pocket any balls and don't carom on anything of any consequence, and when you are done nobody has to pay, and there are no refreshments to saw off, and consequently there isn't any satisfaction whatever about it—they played dominoes till they were rested, and then they blackguarded each other privately till prayer time. When they were not seasick they were uncommonly prompt when the dinner gong sounded. Such was our daily life on board the ship—solemnity, decorum, dinner, dominoes, devotions, slander. It was not lively enough for a pleasure trip; but if we had only had a corpse it would have made a noble funeral excursion. It is all over now; but when I look back, the idea of these venerable fossils skipping forth on a six months' picnic seems exquisitely refreshing. The advertised title of the expedition—"The Grand Holy Land Pleasure Excursion"—was a misnomer. "The Grand Holy Land Funeral Procession" would have been better—much better.

Wherever we went, in Europe, Asia, or Africa, we made a sensation and, I suppose I may add, created a famine. None of us had ever been anywhere before; we all hailed from the interior; travel was a wild novelty to us, and we conducted ourselves in accordance with the natural instincts that were in us, and trammeled ourselves with no ceremonies, no conventionalities. We always took care to make it understood that we were Americans—Americans! When we found that a good many foreigners had hardly ever heard of America, and that a good many more knew it only as a barbarous province away off somewhere, that had lately been at war with somebody, we pitied the ignorance of the Old World, but abated no jot of our importance. Many and many a simple community in the Eastern Hemisphere will remember for years the incursion of the strange horde in the year of our Lord 1867 that called themselves Americans and seemed to imagine in some unaccountable way that they had a right to be proud of it. We generally created a famine, partly because the coffee on the *Quaker City* was unendurable, and sometimes the more substantial fare was not strictly first class; and partly because one naturally tires of sitting long at the same board and eating from the same dishes.

The people of those foreign countries are very, very ignorant. They looked curiously at the costumes we had brought from the wilds of America. They observed that we talked loudly at table sometimes. They noticed that we looked out for expenses and got what we conveniently could out of a franc, and wondered where in the mischief we came from. In Paris they just simply opened their eyes and stared when we spoke to them in French! We never did succeed in making those idiots understand their own language. One of our passengers said to a shopkeeper, in reference to a proposed return to buy a pair of gloves, *"Allong restay trankeel—maybe ve coom Moonday";* and would you believe it, that shopkeeper, a born Frenchman, had to ask what it was that had been said. Sometimes it seems to me, somehow, that there must be a difference between Parisian French and *Quaker City* French.

The people stared at us everywhere, and we stared at them. We generally made them feel rather small, too, before we got done with them, because we bore down on them with America's greatness until we crushed them. And yet we took kindly to the manners and customs, and especially to the fashions of the various people we visited. When we left the Azores, we wore awful capotes and used fine-tooth combs—successfully. When we came back from Tangier, in Africa, we were topped with fezzes of the bloodiest hue, hung with tassels like an Indian's scalplock. In France and Spain we attracted some attention in these costumes. In Italy they naturally took us for distempered Garibaldians, and set a gunboat to look for anything significant in our changes of uniform. We made Rome howl. We could have made any place howl when we had all our clothes on. We got no fresh raiment in Greece— they had but little there of any kind. But at Constantinople, how we turned out! Turbans, scimitars, fezzes, horse pistols, tunics, sashes, baggy trousers, yellow slippers—oh, we were gorgeous! The illustrious dogs of Constantinople barked their underjaws off, and even then failed to do us justice. They are all dead by this time. They could not go through such a run of business as we gave them and survive.

And then we went to see the Emperor of Russia. We just called on him as comfortably as if we had known him a century or so, and when we had finished our visit we variegated ourselves with selections from Russian costumes and sailed away again more picturesque than ever. In Smyrna we picked up camel's hair shawls and other dressy things from Persia; but in Palestine—ah, in Palestine—our splendid career ended. They didn't wear any clothes there to speak of. We were satisfied, and stopped. We made no experiments. We did not try their costume. But we astonished the natives of that country. We astonished them with such eccentricities of dress as we could muster. We prowled through the Holy Land, from Caesarea Philippi to Jerusalem and the Dead Sea, a weird procession of pilgrims, gotten up regardless of expense, solemn, gorgeous, green-spectacled, drowsing under blue umbrellas, and astride of a sorrier lot of horses, camels, and asses than those that came out of Noah's Ark after eleven months of seasickness and short rations. If ever those children of Israel in Palestine forget when Gideon's Band went through there from America, they ought to be cursed once more and finished. It was the rarest spectacle that ever astounded mortal eyes perhaps.

Well, we were at home in Palestine. It was easy to see that that was the grand feature of the expedition. We had cared nothing much about Europe. We galloped through the Louvre, the Pitti, the Uffizi, the Vatican—all the galleries— and through the pictured and frescoed churches of Venice, Naples, and the cathedrals of Spain; some of us said that certain of the great works of the old masters were glorious creations of genius (we found it out in the guidebook, though we got hold of the wrong picture sometimes), and the others said they were disgraceful old daubs. We examined modern and ancient statuary with a critical eye in Florence, Rome, or anywhere we found it, and praised it if we saw fit, and if we didn't we said we preferred the wooden Indians in front of the cigar stores of America. But the Holy Land brought out all our enthusiasm. We fell into raptures by the barren shores of Galilee; we pondered at Tabor and at Nazareth; we exploded into poetry over the questionable loveliness of Esdraelon; we meditated at Jezreel and Samaria over the missionary zeal of Jehu: we rioted—fairly rioted—among the holy places of Jerusalem; we bathed in Jordan and the Dead Sea, reckless whether our accident-insurance policies were extrahazardous or not, and brought away so many jugs of precious water from both places that all the country from Jericho to the mountains of Moab will suffer from drouth this year, I think. Yet, the pilgrimage part of the excursion was its pet feature—there is no question about that. After dismal, smileless Palestine, beautiful Egypt had few charms for us. We merely glanced at it and were ready for home.

They wouldn't let us land at Malta—quarantine; they would not let us land in Sardinia; nor at Algiers, Africa; nor at Málaga, Spain, nor Cadiz, nor at the Madeira Islands. So we got offended at all foreigners and turned our backs upon them and came home. I suppose we only stopped at the Bermudas because they were in the program. We did not care anything about any place at all. We wanted to go home. Homesickness was abroad in the ship—it was epidemic. If the authorities of New York had known how badly we had it, they would have quarantined us here.

The grand pilgrimage is over. Good-bye to it, and a pleasant memory to it, I am able to say in all kindness. I bear no malice, no ill will toward any individual that was connected

with it, either as passenger or officer. Things I did not like
at all yesterday I like very well today, now that I am at
home, and always hereafter I shall be able to poke fun at
the whole gang if the spirit so moves me to do, without ever
saying a malicious word. The expedition accomplished all that
its program promised that it should accomplish, and we ought
all to be satisfied with the management of the matter certainly. Bye-bye!

MARK TWAIN

I call that complimentary. It *is* complimentary; and yet I
never have received a word of thanks for it from the hadjis;
on the contrary I speak nothing but the serious truth when
I say that many of them even took exceptions to the article.
In endeavoring to please them I slaved over that sketch for
two hours, and had my labor for my pains. I never will do
a generous deed again.

CONCLUSION

Nearly one year has flown since this notable pilgrimage was ended; and as I sit here at home in San Francisco thinking, I am moved to confess that day by day the mass of my memories of the excursion have grown more and more pleasant as the disagreeable incidents of travel which encumbered them flitted one by one out of my mind—and now, if the *Quaker City* were weighing her anchor to sail away on the very same cruise again, nothing could gratify me more than to be a passenger. With the same captain and even the same pilgrims, the same sinners. I was on excellent terms with eight or nine of the excursionists (they are my staunch friends yet) and was even on speaking terms with the rest of the sixty-five. I have been at sea quite enough to know that that was a very good average. Because a long sea voyage not only brings out all the mean traits one has and exaggerates them, but raises up others which he never suspected he possessed, and even creates new ones. A twelve months' voyage at sea would make of an ordinary man a very miracle of meanness. On the other hand, if a man has good qualities, the spirit seldom moves him to exhibit them on shipboard, at least with any sort of emphasis. Now I am satisfied that our pilgrims are pleasant old people onshore; I am also satisfied that at sea on a second voyage they would be pleasanter, somewhat, than they were on our grand excursion, and so I say without hesitation that I would be glad enough to sail with them again. I could at least enjoy life with my handful of old friends. They could enjoy life with *their* cliques as well—passengers invariably divide up into cliques, on *all* ships.

And I will say here that I would rather travel with an excursion party of Methuselahs than have to be changing ships and comrades constantly, as people do who travel in the ordinary way. Those latter are always grieving over some

473

other ship they have known and lost, and over *other* comrades whom diverging routes have separated from them. They learn to love a ship just in time to change it for another, and they become attached to a pleasant traveling companion only to lose him. They have that most dismal experience of being in a strange vessel, among strange people who care nothing about them, and of undergoing the customary bullying by strange officers and the insolence of strange servants, repeated over and over again within the compass of every month. They have also that other misery of packing and unpacking trunks—of running the distressing gauntlet of customhouses—of the anxieties attendant upon getting a mass of baggage from point to point on land in safety. I had rather sail with a whole brigade of patriarchs than suffer so. We never packed our trunks but twice—when we sailed from New York and when we returned to it. Whenever we made a land journey, we estimated how many days we should be gone and what amount of clothing we should need, figured it down to a mathematical nicety, packed a valise or two accordingly, and left the trunks on board. We chose our comrades from among our old, tried friends and started. We were never dependent upon strangers for companionship. We often had occasion to pity Americans whom we found traveling drearily among strangers with no friends to exchange pains and pleasures with. Whenever we were coming back from a land journey, our eyes sought one thing in the distance first—the ship—and when we saw it riding at anchor with the flag apeak, we felt as a returning wanderer feels when he sees his home. When we stepped on board, our cares vanished, our troubles were at an end— for the ship was home to us. We always had the same familiar old stateroom to go to, and feel safe and at peace and comfortable again.

I have no fault to find with the manner in which our excursion was conducted. Its program was faithfully carried out—a thing which surprised me, for great enterprises usually promise vastly more than they perform. It would be well if such an excursion could be gotten up every year and the system regularly inaugurated. Travel is fatal to prejudice, bigotry, and narrow-mindedness, and many of our people need it sorely on these accounts. Broad, wholesome, charitable views of men and things cannot be acquired by vegetating in one little corner of the earth all one's lifetime.

The excursion is ended, and has passed to its place among the things that were. But its varied scenes and its manifold incidents will linger pleasantly in our memories for many a year to come. Always on the wing, as we were, and merely pausing a moment to catch fitful glimpses of the wonders of half a world, we could not hope to receive or retain vivid impressions of all it was our fortune to see. Yet our holiday flight has not been in vain—for above the confusion of vague recollections, certain of its best prized pictures lift themselves and will still continue perfect in tint and outline after their surroundings shall have faded away.

We shall remember something of pleasant France; and something also of Paris, though it flashed upon us a splendid meteor, and was gone again, we hardly knew how or where. We shall remember always how we saw majestic Gibraltar glorified with the rich coloring of a Spanish sunset and swimming in a sea of rainbows. In fancy we shall see Milan again, and her stately cathedral with its marble wilderness of graceful spires. And Padua—Verona—Como, jeweled with stars; and patrician Venice, afloat on her stagnant flood —silent, desolate, haughty—scornful of her humbled state —wrapping herself in memories of her lost fleets, of battle and triumph, and all the pageantry of a glory that is departed.

We cannot forget Florence—Naples—nor the foretaste of heaven that is in the delicious atmosphere of Greece—and surely not Athens and the broken temples of the Acropolis. Surely not venerable Rome—nor the green plain that compasses her round about, contrasting its brightness with her gray decay—nor the ruined arches that stand apart in the plain and clothe their looped and windowed raggedness with vines. We shall remember St. Peter's—not as one sees it when he walks the streets of Rome and fancies all her domes are just alike, but as he sees it leagues away, when every meaner edifice has faded out of sight and that one dome looms superbly up in the flush of sunset, full of dignity and grace, strongly outlined as a mountain.

We shall remember Constantinople and the Bosporus— the colossal magnificence of Baalbek—the pyramids of Egypt —the prodigious form, the benignant countenance of the sphinx—Oriental Smyrna—sacred Jerusalem—Damascus, the "Pearl of the East," the pride of Syria, the fabled Garden of Eden, the home of princes and genii of *The Arabian*

Nights, the oldest metropolis on earth, the one city in all the world that has kept its name and held its place and looked serenely on while the kingdoms and empires of four thousand years have risen to life, enjoyed their little season of pride and pomp, and then vanished and been forgotten!

AFTERWORD

It is now nearly a hundred years since Mark Twain embarked on "the first organized pleasure party ever assembled for a transatlantic voyage," and began making the notes which were to become that occasionally mad, often tedious, but somehow eminently satisfactory travel book, *The Innocents Abroad or the New Pilgrim's Progress: Being Some Account of the Steamship QUAKER CITY'S Pleasure Excursion to Europe and the Holy Land*. A century later, we find it perfectly natural that Twain should have been present as a kind of laureate-*ex-officio* to the initiation of mass tourism in the United States—his way, to the tune of $1250, paid by a California newspaper, for we know now that with the publication of his "New Pilgrim's Progress," he was launching a literary career marked by an almost obsessive concern with Europe and the quest for American identity.

No one, however, had any sense of this on June 8, 1867, when the *Quaker City* sailed, since—though Twain had already done some newspaper pieces about a voyage to Hawaii —his sole published volume, *The Celebrated Jumping Frog and Other Sketches*, suggested an exclusive concern with quite other, much more parochial, material. Yet, over and over, he was to return to the themes of *The Innocents Abroad*: not only in other self-declared travel books like *A Tramp Abroad* or *Following the Equator*, but in such fictions as *The Prince and the Pauper*, *A Connecticut Yankee in King Arthur's Court*, *Personal Recollections of Joan of Arc*, *Tom Sawyer Abroad*, *The Mysterious Stranger*. Even in his greatest work, *Huckleberry Finn*, the encounter with Europe is represented, despite the exclusively American scene, in the ill-fated meeting between Jim and Huck, on the one hand, and the Duke and the Dauphin, on the other. To be sure, those two self-styled Europeans are arrant frauds; but precisely insofar as they are fraudulent, they embody what

477

Twain took to be the essential nature of Old World aristocracy.

At any rate, Twain's participation in the excursion seems
to have been more suffered than welcomed, the representatives of the Plymouth Church (apparently the moving spirit
behind the whole enterprise) preferring to advertise such
better-known prospective passengers as Henry Ward Beecher
and General Sherman, neither of whom finally went along.
Mark Twain, however, was there on schedule, along with
"three ministers of the gospel, eight doctors, sixteen or
eighteen ladies, several military and naval chieftains," and
other similarly undistinguished but pious fellow-adventurers.
"The whole affair," Bret Harte was acute enough to point
out in 1870, "was a huge practical joke, of which not the
least amusing feature was the fact that 'Mark Twain' had
embarked on it." Yet that joke eventuated in a classic work
which, without ceasing to be amusing, marks a critical
point in the development of our literature, and especially
in our attempt through literature to find out who we Americans are.

We have always been aware that ours is a country which
has had to be invented as well as discovered: invented even
before its discovery (as Atlantis, Ultima Thule, a Western
World beyond the waves), and re-invented again and again
both by the European imagination—from, say, Chateaubriand
to D. H. Lawrence or Graham Greene—and by the deep
fantasy of its own people, once these existed in fact. Europeans, however, begin always with their own world, the
Old World, as *given*; and define the New World in contrast to
it, as nature versus culture, the naive versus the sophisticated,
the primitive versus the artificial. We Americans, on the
other hand, are plagued by the need to invent a mythological
version of Europe first, something against which we can
then define ourselves; since for us neither the Old nor
the New World seems ever given, and we tend to see ourselves not directly but reflexively: as the Other's Other. Only
when the two worlds become one, as they seem now on the
verge of doing, will Europeans and Americans alike be delivered from the obligation of writing "travel books" about
each other, *i.e.*, books whose chief point is to define our
archetypal differences and prepare for our historical assimi-
lation.

In the past, certainly, most American writers have, either
in avowed fictions or presumed factual accounts, created

myths of the two worlds and their relationship; from Washington Irving and James Fenimore Cooper, through Poe and Hawthorne and Melville, to James and Hemingway, Eliot and Pound, scarcely any of our major authors has failed to face up to this task. Those few who have rejected it—Thoreau and Whitman come first to mind—have felt their refusal in itself as somehow heroic, and if not quite a sufficient *raison d'être*, at least a satisfactory *raison d'écrire*. For a long time, however, the general American obligation to accommodate to each other the myths of Europeans and ex-Europeans was oddly parochialized by being entrusted to the small group of highly educated White Anglo-Saxon Protestants from a few Atlantic seaboard cities, who remained for decades the sole public spokesmen of the United States.

It was that group, in any case, which first undertook the archetypal voyage to Europe (Dr. Franklin, in his disguise as a good, gray Quaker, being the mythological forerunner of them all), defining it in letters, articles, and books as simultaneously a Descent into Hell and an Ascent to Olympus. The Inferno into which the earlier travelers thought of themselves as descending was the Hell of surviving medievalism, which is to say, of oppression, class distinction, "immorality" (belated vestiges of Courtly Love), and, especially, Roman Catholicism; while the Olympian heights they fancied themselves as scaling were represented by the preserved monuments of antiquity, the reconstructed cathedrals of the Middle Ages, and the artistic achievements of the Renaissance as displayed in museums. Unfortunately for their peace of mind, the works of art which such WASP travelers admired to the point almost of worship were hopelessly involved with the values, religious and political, which such travelers most despised. The benign culture-religion into which the faith of their mothers was, by slow and imperceptible degrees, lapsing came into inescapable conflict with the violent anti-Catholicism to which the fiercer faith of their fathers had, just as gradually, shrunk. And though they did not often confess the dis-ease bred by that conflict, they were surely troubled by it.

A little later, their direct descendants, Henry James and Henry Adams, were to suggest a solution, fully achieved only later still by their remoter heirs, T. S. Eliot and Ezra Pound (in whom anti-Semitism tended anyhow to replace anti-Catholicism): the total abandonment of the negative vestiges of Protestantism in favor of the culture-religion and whatever fashionable cults were best adapted to it. But so drastic an accommodation was achieved only at the risk of expatriation and apostasy, which is to say, the surrender of essential "Americanism," as defined in the WASP tradition. How different the Old World was to look to such recusant Puritans, only the twentieth century was able to reveal; yet that century revealed, too, how like one half of the older view, at least, their revision of it remained.

One need only contrast their point of view with the versions of Europe and Americans in Europe produced by the quite different kinds of writers to whom the task of re-inventing the two worlds was transferred in the new century: with those birthright Roman Catholics, for instance, like F. Scott Fitzgerald in *Tender Is the Night*; or with those post-Jamesian urban Jews, like H. J. Kaplan in *The Plenipotentiaries*, or Bernard Malamud in his Italian stories. The ultimate contrast, however, is with myths of Americans abroad imagined by those absolutely non-European Americans, the Negroes, best represented perhaps by James Baldwin in his novel *Giovanni's Room* or his pioneering essay, "A Stranger in the Village." We have had to travel far, indeed, on a journey for which the only maps are precisely the books we have been discussing, to get from the Old World of Irving or Longfellow or Hawthorne or Melville, even of James or Eliot, to stand in the Europe Baldwin experiences and overhear his musing, as he watches a group of Swiss villagers: "the most illiterate among them is related in a way I am not to Dante, Shakespeare, Michelangelo . . . the Cathedral of Chartres says to them what it cannot say to me. . . ."

But this is also true of the most illiterate among the Western Americans of the mid-nineteenth century, in whose name Mark Twain pretended to speak; for Twain represents merely the other side of the old WASP ambivalence, its secular Puritanism, that fear of High Art and High Church worship which the followers of Henry Adams had rejected in favor of the religion of Art. Twain may refuse the Virgin and choose the Dynamo, but he remains immeasureably closer to the first American travelers in Europe than any latter-day American Catholic or Negro or Jew. Whatever sense of alienation he may feel from Dante, Shakespeare, and Michelangelo, to Shakespeare at least he is bound by a kinship of blood and tradition he can never quite disavow. To be sure, his relationship to Michelangelo is more than a little ambivalent, for Michelangelo was a Mediterranean and a lackey of cardinals and popes. "I used to worship the great genius of Michael Angelo," he tells us, ". . . but I do not want Michael Angelo for breakfast—for luncheon—for dinner—for tea. . . . I never felt so fervently thankful, so soothed, so tranquil, so filled with a blessed peace, as I did yesterday when I learned that Michael Angelo was dead."

Yet even here, Twain's is no more the utterly alienated view of a James Baldwin than it is, say, the tormentedly involved response of a second-generation Italo-American, the son of an illiterate peasant from the Abruzzi who has grown rich and returns to confront the world his father had fled. Twain stands on precisely the Protestant Anglo-Saxon middle ground, from which Mediterranean Europe was being surveyed in his time by such more genteel exploiters of experience abroad as William Dean Howells and Bayard Taylor. As a matter of fact, by the time Twain was beginning to write, Taylor himself had decided that Europe was pretty well used up as a literary subject; and in *By-Ways of Europe* (a book about spots off the main lines of travel, published in the same year as *The Innocents Abroad*), had vowed that he would produce no more such essays. Twain, however, being the spokesman for the lowbrow tourism which succeeded the upper-middle-brow variety in whose name Taylor had written, follows the old routes with no sense that they have suffered from literary overexposure, or that, indeed, there are any others.

He was, to be sure, the prisoner of a tour plan laid out by organizers for whom the world worth seeing had been defined once and for all by the genteel essayists of the generations before, and the writers of guidebooks, who were their degenerate heirs; but he, who protested against so much else, does not protest against the limits thus imposed on him. Bret Harte, in his otherwise extremely laudatory review, complains of precisely this: "Yet, with all his independence, 'Mark Twain' seems to have followed his guide and guidebooks with a simple, unconscious fidelity. He was quite content to see only that which everybody else sees, even if he was not content to see it with the same eyes. . . ." In one sense, the case can be made even stronger; for more often than anyone seems ever quite to remember Twain saw those "same sights" with exactly the "same eyes" as those who had gone the same route before him.

He shares especially the bad taste of his generation and its immediate predecessors: admiring extravagantly, for instance, the mediocre Cathedral of Milan ("a poem in marble"), the gross funeral statuary in the cemetery of Genoa, the inferior sculptures exhumed at Pompeii, and even—despite his general contempt for "old paintings"—the Guido Reni "Saint Michael Conquering the Dragon," which the pale heroine of Hawthorne's *The Marble Faun* had also overesteemed. But he shares also their sentimental-hypocritical politics and morality: combining a theoretical hatred of royalty, for instance, with an actual willingness to submit to the charms of emperors, if they are efficient (like Louis Napoleon) or kind to their pretty young daughters (like the czar of all the Russias); and complementing a theoretical abhorrence for European frankness about sex with an actual eagerness for seeking out occasions to put that abhorrence to work.

Like many of the contemporaries he affected to despise, he wants to have it both ways—to attend unashamedly a performance of the cancan ("I placed my hands before my face for very shame. But I looked through my fingers"), but to be morally offended at the presence beside him of "staid, respectable, aged people." ("There were a good many such people present. I suppose French morality is not of that strait-laced description which is shocked at trifles.") As long as it is understood that sex is for the consumption of men only, and especially of young bachelors, Twain is not morally troubled. He even manages to admire certain pictures "which no pen could have the hardihood to describe," drawn on the walls of what he calls delicately "the only building in Pompeii which no woman is allowed to enter"; and barely manages to work up, in a dutiful climax, a vision of the wrath of Heaven being visited upon its long-dead clients.

Only when sex threatens the purity of women, or, more precisely, I suppose, of ladies, is his Puritan indignation genuinely stirred; and that indignation is doubled, of course, when a Churchman is involved in the dubious proceedings. Surely, one of the most extraordinary passages in *The Innocents Abroad* (the feeling invoked absurdly out of proportion with the declared occasion) is the long digression on the seduction of Héloïse by Abelard and the consequent decline of Abelard's fortunes. With what prurient relish Twain recounts the disasters which overwhelmed "the dastardly Abelard," summing up his downfall finally with that Protestant, bourgeois, American phrase of utter contempt: "He died a nobody . . ." But on the way to that climax, he pauses to linger with especial pleasure over Abelard's castration, which he does not name, falling back on a quotation from an anonymous "historian" to hint at it: " 'Ruffians, hired by Fulbert, fell upon Abelard by night, and inflicted upon him a terrible and nameless mutilation.' " To which Twain adds: "I am seeking the last resting-place of those 'ruffians.' When I find it I shall shed some tears on it . . . and cart away from it some gravel whereby to remember that howsoever besotted by crime their lives may have been, those ruffians did one just deed. . . ."

The notion of an adulterous passion committed and generous enough to be redemptive, seems to Twain only "nauseous sentimentality"; for he is as immune to the continental tradition of Courtly Love as any Anglo-American lady novelist. Even in its most attenuated and spiritualized form, as celebrated for instance in the poems of Petrarch to Laura, the medieval love-code finds no sympathetic response in Twain, who only cries by way of protest, "Who glorifies poor Mr. Laura?" Not that he ever blames the young ladies involved, considering them by definition innocent victims. "I have not a word to say against the misused, faithful girl," he comments of Héloïse herself, taking her side as instinctively as Harriet Beecher Stowe had taken that of Mrs. Byron, in an article printed in the very issue of *The Atlantic Monthly* in which Howells had reviewed Twain's travel book; for, like Mrs. Stowe, Mark Twain believed that a "reverence for pure womanhood is . . . a national characteristic of the American. . . ."

Certainly, it was a characteristic of those genteel vestigial Puritans to whose company Twain aspired; and whenever he found a living example of that "pure womanhood" ready to hand—as he did in Mary Mason Fairbanks aboard the *Quaker City,* he submitted to her censorship in an act of guilt-ridden hypocrisy, which he apparently took for virtue. "I was never what she thought me," he wrote on the occasion of "Mother" Fairbanks' death in 1899, "but I was glad to seem to her to be it." Such submission to conscience as embodied in a surrogate mamma of genteel taste and sentimental Christian principles appeared to Twain, at any rate, a way into the cultured WASP world; and this conviction seemed to him justified when the book which had taken final shape under Mrs. Fairbanks' supervision was hailed by William Dean Howells, spokesman-in-chief for that world.

His spontaneous expression of pleasure at that review is, however, a give-away, not only in its unguarded vulgarity, but in the implications of its metaphor. He had felt reading it, Twain said, like the woman whose baby had come white; and, indeed, with the acceptance of *The Innocents Abroad*, he had been accepted as fully "white," in the sense that the Anglo-Saxon first settlers of America had given that mythological adjective.

But he was not, finally, quite one of them, as was to become embarrassingly evident to his genteel defenders at the infamous Whittier Birthday Dinner, a decade or so after his voyage on the *Quaker City*. Confronting what Stuart P. Sherman would still be able to call as late as 1910, "the leading geniuses of New England," *i.e.*, the most proper literary Bostonians, Twain told into the "black frost" of their disapproval an utterly irreverent, pseudo-Western yarn involving "Mr. Longfellow, Mr. Emerson, Mr. Oliver Wendell Holmes—confound the lot. . . ." Twain was never able really to understand why his homely anecdote had failed to tickle his auditors; but Mr. Sherman, last apologist for the values he had unwittingly challenged, is in no doubt. "I know very well," he asserts, "that Congreve or Addison or George Meredith would have agreed . . . that Mark Twain's reminiscence was a piece of crude, heavy intellectual horseplay— an impudent affront offered to Puritan aristocracy by a rough-handed plebeian jester from Missouri."

But why, Twain must have wondered, was his Whittier's Birthday speech rejected by the sort of men who had accepted his European travel book, much of which was precisely the same sort of "crude, heavy, intellectual horseplay," presented through exactly the same sort of *persona*, "a rough-handed plebeian jester from Missouri." Stuart Sherman himself, as a matter of fact, is quite as ready to condemn the book as the speech, and on similar grounds: "The Mississippi pilot, homely, naive, arrogantly conceited . . . turns the Old World into a laughing stock by shearing it of its humanity—simply because there is nothing in him to respond to the glory that was Greece, to the grandeur that was Rome—simply because nothing is holier to him than a joke." William Dean Howells, however, had not been nearly so severe in his review of the book by the man he kept referring to as "Mr. Clements"—only a little condescending, perhaps: "It is no business of ours to fix his rank among the humorists California has given us, but we think he is in an entirely different way from all the others, quite worthy of the company of the best."

Finally, however, Howells is willing to exempt the "California humorist" from charges of *lèse-majesté* in the realm of culture: ". . . it is always good-humored humor, too, that he lavishes on his reader, and even its impudence is charming; we do not remember where . . . it is insolent, with all its sauciness and irreverence." Even here the descriptive phrases remain condescending, though they are apt enough, after all, in defining a writer who composed his book to shock (a little) and mollify (a lot) the woman whom he had appointed his shipboard "mother." "Charming . . . impudence," "insolent," "sauciness"—these are terms suitable not so much to a man as to a boy, one of those naughty boys who is not in the final analysis downright "bad." And, indeed, Twain himself uses the word "boys" constantly to describe his closest associates among the pilgrims, the lively few who, with him, constantly sought to flee the more aged and grim members of what he likes to call the "synagogue." Already at the very beginning of his career, he is beginning to trade on that "boyishness" which he never willingly surrendered, in order to get away with what would have been counted sacrilege in a full-fledged man. And a sufficiently perspicacious critic might well have predicted at that point that the hero in whom Twain was to embody his most mature definition of the American character would necessarily be a juvenile, just one more boy in a cast of boys.

But the "Mark Twain" of *The Innocents Abroad* is a bigger boy than Huck Finn: a boy full-grown enough to regret that his fellow-voyagers scanted whist and dancing and love-making in favor of prayers and the singing of hymns, and to wander the streets of Europe in search of good cigars, a decent shave, and an authentic pool table—yet one not too mature to steal bunches of grapes on his way down from the Acropolis, and to torment his guides with childish horseplay. The "Mark Twain" of 1867 was, in short, the kind of boy-man we think of referring to as a "Westerner," one in whom the power of adulthood and the irresponsibility of childhood ideally combine. Twain, however, did not consider himself quite such a "Westerner" as he was later to describe in *Roughing It,* "stalwart, muscular, dauntless, young braves . . . erect, bright-eyed, quick-moving, strong-handed young giants . . ."; for these exist only as legend, *i.e.,* as someone else.

The character called "Mark Twain" in *The Innocents Abroad* is a comic version of these heroic types, a *schlemiel-* or clown-Westerner, a wandering jester who has learned among the "young braves" (to whom, of course, he had always been a butt) to hate cant, despise sentimentality, distrust sophistication; and who has picked up from them a new vocabulary—a native American diction—in which that hatred, despite, and distrust can become a kind of humor acceptable to the New England Brahmins themselves: a way of discharging in laughter the nagging doubts about high art and European civilization that troubled their social inferiors if not them. Moreover, "Mark Twain" had lived in a landscape so terrifyingly beautiful in its aloofness from man's small necessities, so awesomely magnificent in its anti-human scale, that beside it the scenery of the Old World was bound to seem pallid, domesticated, dwarfed.

"Como? Pshaw! See Lake Tahoe," one of his chapter headings reads; and in a footnote to another, this time concerned with the Sea of Galilee, Twain notes: "I measure all lakes by Tahoe, partly because I am far more familiar with it than with any other, and partly because I have such a high admiration for it. . . ." Yet each time he begins by evoking the peaceful splendor of that Western lake, he ends in rage— rage at the rest of the world, which he considers somehow betrays its mythical splendor. On the shores of the Sea of Galilee, for instance, he remembers dreamily how on Tahoe "the tranquil interest that was born with the morning deepens and deepens, by sure degrees, till it culminates at last in resistless fascination!" But an instant later he is near hysteria, scolding the Palestinian landscape, as it were, for failing him and his memories: "these unpeopled deserts, these rusty mounds of barrenness . . . that melancholy ruin of Capernaum; this stupid village of Tiberias . . . yonder desolate declivity where the swine of the miracle ran down into the sea, and doubtless thought it was better to swallow a devil or two and get drowned into the bargain than have to live longer in such a place. . . ."

Earlier, taking off from a comparison with Lake Como, he had been even more extravagant in his praise of Tahoe: "a sea whose every aspect is impressive, whose belongings are all beautiful, whose lonely majesty types the Deity!" But he subsides quickly from the high-level banality of such school-room English prose, into pure barroom American and once more into the rage, which seems as appropriate to the latter, as platitudes to the former style. This time, however, his rage is directed, quite unexpectedly, against the American Indians.

> Tahoe means grasshoppers. It means grasshopper soup. It is Indian, and suggestive of Indians. . . . People say that Tahoe means "Silver Lake"—"Limpid Water"—"Falling Leaf." Bosh! It means grasshopper soup, the favorite dish of the Digger tribe. . . . It isn't worthwhile, in these prac-tical times, for people to talk about Indian poetry—there never was any in them—except in the Fenimore Cooper Indians. But *they* are an extinct tribe that never existed. I know the Noble Red Man. I have camped with the In-dians; I have been on the warpath with them, taken part in the chase with them—for grasshoppers; helped them steal cattle; I have roamed with them, scalped them, had them for breakfast. I would gladly eat the whole race if I had a chance.

It is an astonishing performance, which begins by puzzling us, ends by sending us back to a novel published more than a decade before—to Melville's *The Confidence Man,* a book which Mark Twain doubtless never read, but one whose twenty-sixth chapter, "Containing the Metaphysics of In-dian-Hating, according to the views of one evidently not so prepossessed as Rousseau in Favor of Savages," serves as a gloss to his meditations beside Como.

Attempting to answer, via a series of shadowy spokesman characters, the question: "why the backwoodsman still re-gards the red man in much the same spirit that a jury does a murderer, or a trapper a wild cat," Melville finds himself impelled to define the essential nature of the "backwoods-man," which is to say, precisely the kind of man through whose mask Twain has chosen to comment on Europe in *The Innocents Abroad.* "Though held in a sort a barbarian,"

Melville tells us, "the backwoodsman would seem to Americans what Alexander was to Asia—captain in the vanguard of a conquering civilization. . . . The tide of emigration, let it roll as it will, never overwhelms the backwoodsman into itself; he rides upon the advance, as the Polynesian upon the comb of the surf. Thus though he keep moving on through life, he maintains with respect to nature much the same unaltered relation throughout; with her creatures, too, including panthers and Indians." And more generally, Melville observes, "The backwoodsman is a lonely man. . . . Impulsive, he is what some might call unprincipled. At any rate, he is self-willed; being one who less hearkens to what others may say about things, than looks for himself, to see what are things themselves."

But what does the backwoodsman see, when he "looks for himself, to see what are things themselves" in respect to culture rather than nature, Europe rather than the wilderness, when he becomes an "innocent abroad"? The Westerner's bleak vision of the Old World was recorded much later by Ezra Pound—who was born properly enough in Hailey, Idaho—rendered in verse at the moment of America's entry into World War I, itself, in a sense, the continuation of tourism by other means.

> There died a myriad,
> And of the best, among them,
> For an old bitch gone in the teeth,
> For a botched civilization,
>
> Charm, smiling at the good mouth,
> Quick eyes gone under the earth's lid,
>
> For two gross of broken statues,
> For a few thousand battered books.

Two major American talents had begun to wrestle with the problem, however, long before the nineteenth century was over: the two writers of their generation by whom Europe was most obsessively felt as an enigma to be endlessly attacked, precisely because it could never be entirely solved —Samuel Clemens and Henry James. Both, at any rate, were the authors of novels in which a Western American, defined as pristine Protestant and incorruptible democrat, tries to come to terms with a Europe seen as essentially aristocratic and Roman Catholic.

James's *The American* was not published until 1877, eight years after the appearance of Twain's *The Innocents Abroad*, but in terms of fictional time, their protagonists missed meeting each other in the museums of France by less than a year; for it was, James tells us, "On a brilliant day in May, in the year 1868" that *his* gentleman from San Francisco—called with obvious symbolic intent Christopher Newman—was lounging in the Louvre. Like that other San Franciscan, "Mark Twain," Newman, we learn, was suffering from an "aesthetic headache" in the presence of all those masterpieces; and like his improbable opposite number, he was convinced from the start that the fresh copies of the Old Masters being made by various young ladies right before his eyes were superior to the dim and dusty originals.

It is easy enough to surmise what Newman is supposed to represent, but a certain Mrs. Tristram (who most nearly speaks for James in the book) makes Newman's meaning explicit, by explaining to him, "You are the great Western Barbarian stepping forth in his innocence and might, gazing a while at this poor effete Old World, and then swooping down on it." At that point, however, the "great Western Barbarian"—whom James never quite understood, in fact—demurs, crying out, "I am a highly civilized man"; and spends the rest of the novel trying to prove it, at considerable cost not only to himself but to his author, who loses thereafter the comic tone on which he has opened in melancholy and melodrama. But if one chronicler of the New Barbarian in the Old World failed because of his distance from the character he was attempting to portray, the other continually risks disaster because of his uncomfortable closeness to the *persona* he has assumed.

Neither the reader nor the author of *The Innocents Abroad* is ever quite sure where Samuel Clemens stops and "Mark Twain" begins, how far Clemens is in fact what Stuart Sherman described as "the kind of travelling companion that makes you wonder why you went abroad" (in more contemporary terms, the kind of American consumer for whom Europe is just one more item on the menu of mass culture), and how far he is the satirist of that kind of traveler. There is no doubt, in any case, that his book is primarily about such travelers rather than about the Old World itself; that it is consequently not a "travel book" at all in the traditional sense, but a chronicle of tourism at the precise point when the Puritan aristocrat abroad is giving way to the Puritan plebeian on tour.

What that plebeian—that unforeseen new man—finds wrong with the Old World, the Old Masters, the land of the Old Testament is precisely that they are all *old, i.e.,* worn out, shabby, dirty, decaying, down at the heels. This abject prejudice against seediness, however ennobled by time, both Clemens and "Twain" share with their fellow-travelers. To be sure, there is ambivalence aplenty in *The Innocents Abroad,* most spectacularly exemplified in the chapters on Venice, where the wary Westerner, the man resolved at all costs not to be had, begins by asserting pointblank, "This famed gondola and this gorgeous gondolier!—the one an inky, rusty old canoe with a sable hearse body clapped onto the middle of it, and the other a mangy, barefooted guttersnipe with a portion of his raiment on exhibition which should have been sacred from public scrutiny." But a few pages later, he has apparently changed his mind, observing in conventional panegyric tones, "The Venetian gondola is as free and graceful in its gliding movement as a serpent. . . . The gondolier *is* a picturesque rascal for all he wears no satin harness, no plumed bonnet, no silken tights."

This doubleness of vision, however, this alternation between daytime debunking and nighttime subscription to a dream ("In the glare of day there is little poetry about Venice, but under the charitable moon her stained palaces are white again . . .") does not arise out of the dialogue between Clemens the artist and "Twain" the comic innocent; it has lain deep in the heart of every run-of-the-mill tourist ever since that memorable year of 1867, when, for the first time on record at least, "Everybody was going to Europe. . . ." Occasionally, of course, Twain moves from echoing the Americans abroad to mocking them, but never for their vulgarity, their grossness of perception, their smug contempt for culture. What stirs his satirical impulse is rather their pretentiousness, their pitiful attempts at culture climbing: their signing hotel registers in French, or claiming loudly never to have eaten a meal without the proper wine— or, especially, their mouthing of high-flown phrases out of guidebooks in the presence of works of art they do not really understand.

When he is recounting the playful desecration of revered

cultural sites, his tone is bafflingly equivocal—as in the episode in the crater of Mount Vesuvius which so infuriated Stuart Sherman. "Some of the boys thrust long slips of paper down into holes and set them on fire, and so achieved the glory of lighting their cigars by the flames of Vesuvius, and others cooked eggs over fissures in the rocks and were happy." Surely, there is a note of friendly mockery here, but none of that cold fury with which Twain reports, say, the credulity of Europeans in the face of holy "relics" and "miracles," or the gushing response of some of his fellow-Americans to such utterly ruined pictures as Da Vinci's *Last Supper* ("Maybe the originals were handsome when they were new, but they are not now.").

Only at the climax of the book, when the author-protagonist stands face to face with the oldest monument he has encountered, with, that is to say, an ultimate incarnation of the persistence of the past, toward which he has been as ambivalent as any other ignorant American, are his last scruples overcome, his final equivocation resolved. It is the Sphinx that conquers him: "After years of waiting, it was before me at last. . . . There was a dignity not of earth in its mien. . . . It was gazing out over the ocean of Time. . . . It was MEMORY—RETROSPECTION—wrought into visible, tangible form. . . . And there is that in the overshadowing majesty of this eternal figure of stone . . . which reveals to one something of what he shall feel when he shall stand at last in the awful presence of God." But at this point, when he has been converted however temporarily to the religion of culture, Twain looks up and sees on the jaw of the Sphinx "a wart, or an excrescence of some kind," which turns out to be, of course, a fellow American, a companion on the tour—in search of a souvenir.

"We heard," Twain tells us, abandoning himself finally to total rage against just such an "innocent" as he had all along pretended to be, "the familiar clink of a hammer and understood the case at once. One of our well-meaning reptiles—I mean relic-hunters—had crawled up there and was trying to break a 'specimen' from the face of this the most majestic creation the hand of man has wrought." Confronted with such absolute sacrilege, however, all Twain can conceive of doing is to call a cop, *i.e.*, a sheikh, whom he urges to warn the intruder that his offense is "punishable with imprisonment or the bastinado." A hundred years later, it has become clear just how ineffectual such sanctions are against the American tourist's irrepressible need to chip away piece by piece the Old World he does not quite dare confess bores him; but what else was there then for Twain to do in response—except, of course, to write a book.

Leslie A. Fiedler

SELECTED BIBLIOGRAPHY

OTHER WORKS BY MARK TWAIN

The Celebrated Jumping Frog of Calaveras County, 1865
   Story (Signet CP389)
Roughing It, 1872   Travel (Signet CT143)
The Gilded Age: A Tale of Today, 1873   Novel (in collaboration with Charles Dudley Warner) (Signet CY459)
The Adventures of Tom Sawyer, 1876   Novel (Signet CD2)
The Facts Concerning the Recent Carnival of Crime in Connecticut, 1876   Story (Signet CP389)
A Tramp Abroad, 1880   Travel
The Prince and the Pauper, 1882   Novel (Signet CD230)
The Stolen White Elephant, 1882   Story (Signet CP389)
Life on the Mississippi, 1883   Travel (Signet CP436)
The Adventures of Huckleberry Finn, 1884   Novel (Signet CD5)
A Connecticut Yankee in King Arthur's Court, 1889
   Novel (Signet CP315)
Luck, 1891   Story (Signet CP389)
The American Claimant, 1892   Novel
The £1,000,000 Bank-Note, 1893   Story (Signet CP389)
Those Extraordinary Twins, 1894   Story
Pudd'nhead Wilson, 1894   Novel (Signet CD184)
In Defense of Harriet Shelley and Other Essays, 1894
Tom Sawyer Abroad, 1894   Novel
Personal Recollections of Joan of Arc, 1896   Novel
Tom Sawyer: Detective, 1896   Novel

How to Tell a Story and Other Essays, 1897

Following the Equator, 1897   Travel

The Man that Corrupted Hadleyburg, 1899   Story (Signet CP389)

The Five Boons of Life, 1902   Story (Signet CP389)

Was It Heaven? Or Hell? 1902   Story (Signet CP389)

Extract from Captain Stormfield's Visit to Heaven, 1909 Story

Mark Twain's Speeches, 1910

The Mysterious Stranger, 1916   Short Novel (Signet CP389)

Mark Twain's Letters, 1917

BIOGRAPHY AND CRITICISM

Benson, Ivan. *Mark Twain's Western Years.* Palo Alto, California: Stanford University Press; London: Oxford University Press, 1938.

Blair, Walter. *Mark Twain and Huck Finn.* Berkeley, California: University of California Press, 1960.

Brashear, Minnie M. *Mark Twain: Son of Missouri.* Chapel Hill, N.C.: University of North Carolina Press; London: Oxford University Press, 1934.

Brooks, Van Wyck. *The Ordeal of Mark Twain.* Rev. ed. New York: E. P. Dutton and Company, Inc., 1933; London: J. M. Dent and Sons, Ltd., 1934.

De Voto, Bernard. *Mark Twain's America.* Boston: Little, Brown and Company, 1935.

———. *Mark Twain at Work.* Cambridge: Harvard University Press, 1942.

Ferguson, John DeLancey. *Mark Twain: Man and Legend.* Indianapolis: Bobbs-Merrill Company, 1943.

Gabrilówitsch, Clara (Clemens). *My Father, Mark Twain.* New York: Harper and Brothers, 1931.

Howells, William Dean. *My Mark Twain: Reminiscences and Criticisms.* New York: Harper and Brothers, 1910. (Reprinted in *Selected Writings.* New York: Random House, Inc., 1950.)

Leacock, Stephen. *Mark Twain*. New York: D. Appleton-Century Company, 1933.

Lynn, Kenneth S. *Mark Twain and Southwestern Humor*. Boston: Little, Brown and Company, 1959.

Paine, Albert Bigelow. *Mark Twain, A Biography*. Rev. ed. New York: Harper and Brothers, 1935. 2 vols.

Scott, Arthur L. (ed.). *Mark Twain: Selected Criticism*. Dallas, Texas: Southern Methodist University Press, 1955.

Smith, Henry Nash (ed.). *Mark Twain*. Englewood Cliffs, New Jersey: Prentice-Hall, Inc., 1963.

Wagenknecht, Edward. *Mark Twain: The Man and His Work*. New Haven: Yale University Press; London: Oxford University Press, 1935.

Wecter, Dixon. *Sam Clemens of Hannibal*. Boston: Houghton Mifflin Company, 1952.

A NOTE ON THE TEXT

The Signet Classic text of *The Innocents Abroad* is reprinted from the first edition, which was published in 1869 by the American Publishing Company, Hartford, Conn. Spelling and punctuation have been brought into conformity with current American usage.